THE STRUGGLE FOR THE SOUL OF JOURNALISM

THE STRUGGLE FOR THE SOUL OF JOURNALISM

The Pulpit versus the Press 1833–1923

RONALD R. RODGERS

UNIVERSITY OF MISSOURI PRESS
Columbia

The volumes of this series are published through the generous support of the University of Missouri School of Journalism.

University of Missouri Press, Columbia, Missouri 65211
Printed and bound in the United States of America

Library of Congress Cataloging-in-Publication Data

Names: Rodgers, Ronald R.
Title: The struggle for the soul of journalism : the pulpit versus the press, 1833-1923 / by Ronald R. Rodgers.
Description: Columbia : University of Missouri Press, 2018. | Series: Art of the journalism in perspective: continuities and disruptions | Includes bibliographical references. |
Identifiers: LCCN 2017050789 (print) | LCCN 2018001364 (ebook) | ISBN 9780826274076 (e-book) | ISBN 9780826221582 (hardcover : alk. paper)
Subjects: LCSH: Religion and the press--United States--History--19th century. | Religion and the press--United States--History--20th century. | Journalism, Religious--United States--History--19th century. | Journalism, Religious--United States--History--20th century. | Journalistic ethics--United States--19th century. | Journalistic ethics--United States--20th century.
Classification: LCC PN4888.R4 (ebook) | LCC PN4888.R4 R48 2018 (print) | DDC 070.44920097309/034--dc23
LC record available at https://lccn.loc.gov/2017050789

™ This paper meets the requirements of the American National Standard for Permanence of Paper for Printed Library Materials, Z39.48, 1984.

Typefaces: Grotesk and Minion

Journalism in Perspective: Continuities and Disruptions

Tim P. Vos, Series Editor

Journalism is a central institution in the social, cultural, and political life of communities, nations, and the world. Citizens and leaders rely on the news, information, and analysis that journalists produce, curate, and distribute each day. Their work must be understood in the context of journalism's institutional features, including its roles, ethics, operations, and boundaries. These features are themselves the product of a history emerging through periods of stability and change. The volumes in this series span the history of journalism, and advance thoughtful and theoretically-driven arguments for how journalism can best negotiate the currents of change.

This book is dedicated to the reasoned and constructive critics of journalism.

Contents

Preface

> **I take it that one of the greatest services which can be rendered to the age in which we live—yes, and to the ages that will come after us—is to promote a truer conception, a deeper appreciation of the ethical obligations, the moral mission, of journalism.**
>
> —William Samuel Lilly, *On Shibboleths*

THIS STUDY'S TERRAIN OF ANALYSIS is the decades of pastoral press criticism that arose around the rise of journalism as a force that helped to upend and reconstitute society and that shouldered aside religion and long-held traditions in the late nineteenth and early twentieth centuries. It seeks to trace religion's struggle to hinge the notion of social responsibility and all that entailed to the news ethic of daily journalism. Within the ambit of that criticism was censure, but also discussion, analysis, judgment, proffered solutions, and even approbation. This historical analysis attempts to isolate as much as is possible one stream of influential discourse in the late nineteenth and early twentieth centuries. It does so by thematically analyzing hundreds of intellectual discussions and debates that appeared in books, the newspaper trade journals, religious and popular periodicals, sermons, speeches, tracts, secular and religious press accounts, autobiographies and memoirs, and reports of religious associations. All of these media were the source of considerable critical discourse about the newspaper, which in their totality foster an ethos of proper journalistic conduct.[1]

The year 1923 is roughly the end point of the time frame of this book. It is that year the American Society of Newspaper Editors adopted the Canons of Journalism,[2] the first nationwide code of ethics for the profession and the first formal call for press responsibility in the United States long before the Hutchins Commission report in 1947.[3] While it is difficult to signpost any particular year, given the slow and haphazard pace of change, this book begins with the antebellum rise of the penny press in 1833 and accounts for the influence on the pulpit and the press of the postbellum rise of modernity, the growth of Gilded Age industrialism and powerful corporations, the political and corporate corruption of the age, the changing face of the United States with hundreds of thousands of immigrants arriving to feed the industrial machine, the population shift from rural to urban areas, and the subsequent surge of the reactionary agrarian Populist and, later, more middle-class Progressive movement, which was entwined with the religiously oriented and influential Social Gospel movement—each of which were voluminous in their critique of the daily press. Enmeshed in all this change and reaction was the growing and transforming newspaper, which, at its core, had substituted "the market for the mission," as one scholar has asserted.[4] Indeed, the long conversation about the newspaper's mission in society correlated with the growth of newspapers. And it was this conversation, I have argued elsewhere, that informed an ethos that helped codify journalistic norms for the twentieth century—seen at its earliest and most pronounced in the Canons of Journalism.[5]

So often the substrate of any conversation about calls for change is memory recalled through lived or mediated experience. That is especially true when an influential institution with deep roots in society's past such as the newspaper is under consideration. And that is especially true during the time frame of this study when the imperative function of that radically changing institution was a constant topic of debate and discussion from all quarters. For instance, in 1880, one observer pointed to the growth and the far-reaching transformation of the newspaper that had already entwined itself into every endeavor of society. Thus, the "mission of the newspaper of to-day" was not what it was a century ago, the writer contended. Which is why "the origin, mission and results of the American newspaper form a profitable theme for contemplation."[6] The next year, the Reverend Simeon Gilbert, editor of the *Advance*, a Congregational weekly, observed that the newspaper had begun in earnest only a century and a half before and had greatly affected the "older agencies of civilization and of evangelization"—the pulpit, the school, the legislature, and the judiciary. The newspaper may have not exceeded these agencies in power, but it was "coordinate with them, and persistently, inevitably, encroaching upon their domains."[7] This conversation continued nearly a decade later with the renowned journalist and editor Noah Brooks's lamenting that "the original functions of a daily newspaper appear to have been forgotten." Brooks then reached into the past to counterpoise the present. He observed that in its earliest manifestation, the very name *newspaper* designated "its single function and mission in the world"—as newsletters read and passed from one reader to another. It was only later that editors began adding commentary that then became the editorial or leading article. Around that same time, he observed, some alert tradesmen recognized "the value of this new channel of communication" to advertise their wares to consumers. And there—driven by the demands of the market—began what the "magazinists" of his time criticized as the increasing "faultiness of the newspaper press," to include "its looseness of statement, its disregard of truth, and its often willful perversion of facts." Thus, when thinking of the newspaper of the future, Brooks advised, one must hark back to the "original idea of the newspaper," which was to furnish the news. "When we return to that idea, the advertiser will be relegated to his proper subordinate place."[8]

The implication here in Brooks's analysis is of unalloyed news in which the constraints of the market play no part in either the conduct of journalists or the content and product of their labors. For many observers, this was a vital ideal because journalism—the product of newspapers—is not a self-governing social force but is enmeshed in the power centers and institutions of society. Of course, since politically partisan support was no longer a source of sustenance for most papers, advertising was not going to go away if newspapers were to survive. In fact, by 1900 advertising was bringing in more money than sales of newspapers.[9] It was advertising money that redefined news as a "commodity, as a commercial product to be shaped, packaged and marketed with a constant eye to profit," observed Gerald Baldasty. It also transformed the notion of a newspaper reader as a voter to a reader as a consumer,[10] thus uprooting a news ethic based in a political partisanship that comported with the values and perspective of the reader. As a consequence, the newspaper had lost its ethical footing. And some of the symptoms of maladjustment in an age in which journalists had yet to define a news ethic under a commercial paradigm included salacious sensationalism, invasions of privacy, graphic reporting of suicides and crime, and checkbook journalism—all driven by the increasingly commercial side of the newspaper seeking the most circulation. But also, out of that transformation, two primary questions arose. At a commercialized newspaper, whom did journalists now serve? And what was the place of comment, opinion, and interpretation, so long the backbone of the partisan newspaper? Attempts to answer those questions were part and parcel of both the pastoral and secular critiques of the newspaper and the numerous state newspaper ethics codes that arose over the years.[11]

One argument I make in this study is that today, many journalists—whether at newspapers or at the panoply of digital venues captured under the rubric of "news media"—are as equally unmoored as their brethren decades ago. The advertising budgets of newspapers have been gutted. The Internet, social platforms, and mobile devices have transformed how news is consumed and shared. The industry is struggling to find new ways of supporting journalism. And in the process, journalists are struggling to keep their footing as they attempt to redefine their news ethic for a new era. This, then, is a struggle to define the mission of journalism not unlike that of the past. But one thing the journalists of the past had that those of the present do not is a recent history from which they could draw to redefine that news ethic—the exemplars of an old ideal of newspapering from an era that one writer has described as the "Golden Age of the Newspaper," when "editors and reporters labored to make newspapers for sensible people, never for fools."[12] These editors include several "figures of a great past,"[13] such as poet William Cullen Bryant (1794–1878) of the *New York Evening Post*; Horace Greeley (1811–72) and Charles A. Dana (1819–97), both of the *New-York Tribune*; and Henry J. Raymond (1820–69), founder of the *New York Times*.

Part of a "group of journalists who are constantly referred to as the greatest editors of our newspaper history," each of these men's work as editors was often pointed to as a fairly recent model for defining the mission of the newly commercialized newspaper.[14] For instance, in 1894 Charles R. Williams, the editor of the *Indianapolis News*, extolled the virtues of these and other such editors of the era for regarding "their work more as a profession than as a business—more as an opportunity to make ideas prevail than as a chance to win money. The old puritan sense of duty and obligation and responsibility, has been upon them. They have mixed their ink with conviction; they have run their presses with conscience." And newspaper and magazine publisher Frank Munsey noted in 1898 that "counting-room journalism" was unknown to each of these editors. In fact, he pointed out, Greeley "gave no thought to that side of journalism. He studied the people; he studied principles, and, according to the light he had, he aimed, through his journal, to lead his fellowmen to a higher and better plane of life." Munsey wrote that Dana had been the last of this line of editors "whose policy was independent of counting-room influences."[15] When he began the *New-York Tribune*, he rejected both the "servile partisanship" of the politically enthralled papers of the time and the "gagged, mincing neutrality" of the penny press. Instead, he sought a middle way in "which a journalist might openly and heartily advocate the principles and commend the measures of that party to which his convictions allied him, yet dissent frankly from its course on a particular question, and even denounce its candidates, if they were shown to be deficient in capacity or (far worse,) in integrity."[16]

Today, our recent history is not that of another paradigm but solely that of a century of the commercialized newspaper in which the editors of the distant nineteenth century have "been superseded by the astute business manager."[17] We can see a recognition of that displacement in an editorial in the *Nation* in 1918 that declared in an encomium to the renowned old-time editor Henry Watterson that "the commercializing of our press, or its changed ideals, has brought to an end the day of great editors." In the past century, little formal and rigorous thought has been given to the mission of journalism except for the Hutchins Commission report. Thus, we need to look to the past of a century and more ago in order to reconsider the arguments of the past and draw on them as originalist thought as we attempt to redefine that mission in a new age. As contemporary writer Walt Harrington so cogently contended, "The kind of journalism we end up doing is shaped by the way we think about our mission."[18]

Some Terms Defined

To help the reader better understand the context of the times and my argument, it is important to define some of the terms used in this study.

Religion

While I do cite a handful of representatives of other religions, the bulk of this press criticism comes from the Protestant religion, those major non-pastoral voices and influential journalists and academics whose worldviews were greatly influenced by the religion and representatives of the influential Social Gospel movement, which was, essentially, a radical reformation of Protestantism entwined to a degree with the sentiments of the era's Progressive movement.[19] This book draws on the criticism of the Protestant religion because it was *the* powerful force in society that had held an enormous influence over public opinion for many decades. Indeed, the crux of this book is the response of Protestants to the slow reveal of the diminution of that religion's power in the face of modernity, driven by such things as the industrialization of society, urbanization, the influx of hundreds of thousands of people of other religions or no religion at all, and the subsequent growing power of the market-driven newspaper in affecting public opinion. Thus, the dawning realization that the Protestant religion no longer influenced public opinion as it once did became the impulse for much of the seemingly endless discussions about the newspaper's proper mission in society.

The Soul of Journalism

"As the human soul is greater than the body and its skill, is not the spirit of a newspaper of more importance than its physical plant and its routine methods?" writer and press critic Charles Grant Miller asked. A former managing editor of the *Christian Herald*, Miller's question came in a profile in *Editor & Publisher* of the Progressive and reform-minded *Brooklyn Eagle*. About that newspaper, he asserted, "shines steadily the light of a great soul." But the ineffable notion of the soul of a newspaper was difficult to define in specific terms, he wrote. He would have to unearth its expression in the "manifestations" of the public-service mission at the core of the *Brooklyn Eagle*. The soul, then, is part and parcel of a moral argument about journalism and service to society. As renowned muckraking editor Norman Hapgood declared, what interested him most about any publication was "its soul—the thing it is undertaking to accomplish in the far-reaching struggles of the day." Such publications, he said, must represent "moral freedom, disinterested thought, genuine enthusiasm for progress and for principles."[20]

The soul of journalism was a conceit imbued with a religious sensibility voiced by pastors, politicians, the pew, the public, and even poets.[21] And a common indictment of the age was that corporations—often the overseers of newspapers—were a soulless "Frankenstein" that had become "the nightmare of this age."[22] For instance, the Reverend Washington Gladden, one of the founders of the powerful Social Gospel movement of the late nineteenth and early twentieth centuries and a renowned preacher with a "long and intimate association with the press," agreed that the corporation lacked a soul.[23] In an essay titled "The Relation of Corporations to Public Morals" (1895), he held that without a soul, it also lacked a conscience, which meant that whenever the corporation did anything wrong, there was no one to hold responsible. "But a great many corporations have accepted the theory of their own soullessness, and live up to it as well as they can," Gladden lamented. "Their power is used in a perfectly conscienceless manner for the spoliation of the community and for their own enrichment."[24]

Objectivity

The enigmatic notion of journalistic objectivity—"the great virtue of the American press"[25]—has been ill-defined in its application over the past century. As Shailer Mathews, dean of the Divinity School at the University of Chicago, observed in 1922, "We cannot expect the public press to be impartial, even if such a miracle were desirable." Because this book brushes up against the notion of journalistic objectivity, some words are needed here about this abstract term and the various meanings attributed to it. Michael Schudson, who has written some of the most substantive inquiries into the meaning and origin of objectivity, has observed that what he calls the "objectivity norm . . . was not always a norm in American journalism. It has a history. It has a point of origin. Specifying that point of origin, identifying its sources, and locating it in particular journalists or news organizations is not easy."[26]

In my own experience as both a reporter and an editor, I found that for most readers who use the term when criticizing some perceived journalistic slight, the concept boils down to neutrality: fairness, detachment, and impartiality. This theory of objectivity is best represented by a he-said, she-said form of reporting that fairly represents both sides of a story—as if there were ever just two sides—and then allows the reader, like the commoner in Akira Kurosawa's *Rashomon*, to interpret the testimony of sources and determine the supposed truth. One prominent example of this approach to journalism is the nightly news broadcast *PBS NewsHour*, whose mission has been described as "civility, objectivity and thoughtful reporting and analysis."[27] Certainly, this decades-old nightly broadcast is much to be admired when compared to the substance—or lack of substance—of many local and national news broadcasts. Still, it can be frustrating to some viewers when *NewsHour* journalists allow unevidenced assertions to pass without questioning their veracity out of a commitment to their mission of civility and objectivity. Still, this theory of neutral journalism in which dabs of facticity and testimony are offered without context and interpretation lies at the core of a notion of objectivity going back decades. And relatedly, the naive conceit of the news as a simple mirror of society was often used to describe the newspaper's mission.[28]

Many observers have noted that the word *objectivity* was never even used by journalists to describe their work until the 1920s. Schudson observed that it was not until after World War I that "serious professional discussion about 'objectivity'" began to be heard. Indeed, Richard Streckfuss, who researched the origins of the term, found that the American Society of Newspaper Editors in its annual conference sessions that dealt with fairness, balance, and like variants never used the word *objectivity* until its sixth annual conference in 1928. Instead, he observed, from the 1890s into the twentieth century, *unbiased* and *uncolored* were used to describe impartial reports of news events.[29]

Still, this distinction between "unbiased" and "uncolored" and "objective" news was not all that clear-cut. For instance, in 1908 William Jennings Bryan, in a speech to a joint banquet of the Associated Press and the American Newspaper Publishers Association, advised that "unbiased, uncolored truths" in the news required "absolute impartiality" in which reporters did not "inject their own opinions." That is not a far walk from the common notion of journalistic objectivity. And then in 1911 in a book on newswriting and editing, Charles G. Ross, who won the Pulitzer Prize in 1932, cited an editorial in the *St. Louis Republic* that described the term *objective*. The editorial declared that "the three notes of modern reporting are clarity, terseness, objectivity" and that the latter meant the journalist must "keep himself, his prejudices, preferences, opinions, out of the story altogether." Ross went on to emphasize that the reporter must have a "mind open to the facts and he must record the facts unvarnished by his own preferences and opinions."[30] Here, again, it is difficult to imagine a large distinction between this notion of "objective" and "uncolored" or "unbiased" in which news is, essentially, bereft of reportorial values of any sort.

Certainly, by the 1920s this distinction became somewhat clearer when journalism became yoked to the techniques of the social sciences, which held that knowledge was valid only if it was acquired through objective scientific inquiry.[31] Thus, Streckfuss observed, "In its original sense, objectivity meant finding truth through the rigorous methodology of the scientist."[32] The impulse for this shift in thought stemmed from the growing postwar recognition of how the irrationality of citizens could threaten democracy as power groups used facts to create illusions and distort truth.[33] However, Streckfuss noted, over the years as objectivity became part of the vocabulary of journalism, the "rigorous and difficult" methodology of scientific naturalism became attenuated. Instead, the ethos of journalism called for reporters to write objectively by keeping "themselves and their opinions out of their stories"—essentially the news ethic of fairness, detachment, and impartiality of my own experience. The height of workmanlike professional journalism to which the word *objectivity* could be applied became publishing unvarnished, unbiased, nonpartisan stories. "The ideology of objective reporting emerged," media ethics scholar Clifford Christians noted, "with the press declaring as virtuous the impartial transmission of pure information." Essentially, Schudson argues, objectivity became a "faith in 'facts,' a distrust of 'values,' and a commitment to their segregation."[34] This meant a separation of facts from values in news stories that gradually took hold from about 1870 to World War I.[35] And along with the general "faultiness of the newspaper press," this separation of facts from values was a large part of the impulse for religion's criticism of the newspaper.[36]

The New Journalism versus a Journalism of Discernment

A key concept indelibly linked to the notion of objectivity and as relevant to a century ago as it is to today is the model of "new journalism." This is another term with several alternative meanings that has been hauled out to describe various forms of journalistic endeavor. The preferred meaning is at the core of much of religion's press criticism. I use the term not as a pejorative to describe the yellow press or news "written in sketchy primer style, calculated to entertain the reader with the least possible expenditure of mental effort."[37] Neither do I use it in the modern sense of reporting through immersion and the techniques of fiction. Instead, I hold with the original definition of the term as it was coined in 1886 by radical reform journalist William T. Stead to distinguish between contemporary forms of journalism of his time.[38] A year later, Matthew Arnold made the term famous—or rather infamous—by disparaging it as a "feather-brained" mode of journalism that "throws out assertions at a venture because it wishes them true; does not correct either them or itself, if they are false; and to get at the state of things as they truly are seems to feel no concern whatever."[39] Arnold's accusations were a manifestation of the slow reveal of a critical juncture between an increasingly popular new journalism of the "short, snappy style"[40] and the "taboos and restraints"[41] of a genteel journalism, which for so long had held primacy in publications with its opinion-forming news leaders and an emphasis on belles lettres. Instead, as Patrick Collier observes, "Shorter leaders meant less newspaper content sought to influence readers directly, while miscellaneous content—advertisements, reviews, police reporting, fiction, gossip, etc.—took on the more subtle, elusive role of interpellating readers as consumers, conversationalists, and moral and ethical agents."[42]

Arnold's dislike of this new journalism sounds not unlike some of the complaints about certain modes of contemporary journalism, especially emanating from online news media, that "frequently promote misinformation in an attempt to drive traffic and social engagement," as one indictment put it.[43] But setting aside Arnold's criticism and the many subsequent complaints about sensationalism that coalesced around the term *new journalism*, what interests me here is the kind of journalism the press critics demanded, what Stead described as "the true journalism of the governing and guiding order, as distinguished from journalism of the mere critical and paragraph-quilting species." Stead called for what I describe as a "journalism of discernment" in which journalists as free moral agents strive to get to the bottom of things—unhindered by ideological or market constraints—by moving from the center to the periphery and expanding the range of their sources to every rung of society. By doing so, Stead argued, the press would act as "an engine of social reform."[44]

There can be little argument that although Stead never uses the term, he is speaking to the limitations of the modern notion of journalistic objectivity, which, Carey observed, the Hutchins Commission report in 1947 designated as a "menace to understanding." One contemporary theory about journalistic objectivity that extends Stead's ideal is "standpoint epistemology," which Ryan Michael describes as a product of feminist critique of objective scientific inquiry and "a counterhegemonic discourse that destabilizes hegemonic discourse." That is, the reporting of a story should begin from the "perspective of the marginalized groups that are affected by events and issues so that the unrecognized weight of the socially dominant 'insider' positions would be counterbalanced." One early expression of this inclusive way of revealing the world comes from Jane Addams, the first woman "public philosopher" in America, who was renowned for her work with and writings about the social settlement movement a century ago. In *Democracy and Social Ethics* (1907), she wrote, "We have learned as common knowledge that much of the insensibility and hardness of the world is due to the lack of imagination which prevents a realization of the experiences of other people." The truth, she argued, could be discovered only "by a rational and democratic interest in life." In other words, if true understanding is the goal of a newspaper, its news must be informed by a wide-spectrum view of life to the furthest margins of society. "Thus," Addams insisted, "the identification with the common lot which is the essential idea of Democracy becomes the source and expression of social ethics."[45]

Such a stance did not rise from a vacuum. Its impulse can be found in the context of the times when several factors were coming together. One was the incremental sloughing off of political partisanship as a newspaper business model that was being replaced by a commercial model. And commercialism was a product of postbellum industrialization whose often untoward effects on society prompted the agrarian Populist movement and, later, Progressive reform. The industrialization of America along with the growing commercial arena and slow diminishment of the partisan press had far-reaching effects on the conduct of journalists who were trying to find their way in this new, commercialized newspaper model. For example, even by the early twentieth century, Will Irwin, one of the best-known reporters and press critics of the century, recalled that he "had no precedents to go by" as a journalist because "journalism was still finding itself."[46]

A Method in Search of the Meaning of Mission

My research, which took place over the last decade and a half, involved searching for references to variant descriptions of the press and pulpit and to the key religious and secular figures of the time. I searched the relevant dates in the *Readers' Guide to Periodical Literature*; the American Periodical Series Online, 1741–1900; Access NewspaperARCHIVE, which contains tens of millions of newspaper pages dating back to the 1700s; ProQuest Historical Newspapers; Google Book Search; the Internet Archive's Text Archive; and every available issue of the newspaper trade journal *Editor & Publisher* within the time frame. Indeed, *Editor & Publisher* held to the American newspaper's tradition of clipping items and running them verbatim or in a summary. In doing so, the trade journal acted as a public sphere for issues of journalism, with portals to venues across the country. Its pages offered criticisms, laudations, and discussions by politicians, government officials, divines, social scientists, reformers, academics, readers, editors, publishers, and even journalists working in the trenches, much of which would have undoubtedly been lost to history.[47]

Relevance and Resonance

Given the near-endless reams of such criticism available for review and analysis, I was left in a similar quandary to the one Henry James described in an essay about his visit to Florida. He complained that it is "the penalty of receiving too many impressions of too many things that when the question arises of giving some account of these a small sharp anguish attends the act of selection and the necessity of omission."[48] Even so, in order for this study to proceed, it was necessary to focus on the standard markers of this critique and identify the themes and patterns of the many voices offering counsel to the press. That is because this is not a study solely about the pulpit's criticism of the press leading to some sort of attenuated notion of press accountability. I am much more interested in identifying places of agreement about the mission of journalism that lie embedded in that powerful and influential critique. This study seeks to arrive at—shall I call it?—an originalist understanding of journalism's mission. It seeks the semblance of an ideal, possibly unattained or unattainable, beyond which there is little room left for discussion, the pure aerie in which the product of journalism—the news—is uninfluenced by market constraints.

English writer on law Frederic W. Maitland remarked, "The essential matter of history is not what happened but what people thought or said about it." From this long conversation of criticism, approbation, and prescription over the decades, we can begin to dislodge the notions defining the mission of the newspaper. As Emerson observed, "The ancestor of every action is a thought,"[49] and as Richard Hofstadter declared in his study of the age of reform, "Before there could be action, there must be information and exhortation." I hold with contemporary historian and economist Deirdre McCloskey, who discounts Tocqueville's assertion that the "habits of the heart" and the "habits of the mind" are "the whole moral and intellectual state of a people." Rather, McCloskey argues, it is "the habits of the lip that shape the habits of the mind and heart." Consequently, she contends, rhetoric is key, and "we can know the rhetoric of an age, the habits of the lip, by reading its literary and other written products. We can from this infer the habits of the corresponding minds much more directly than can any brain scientist of the new phrenology."[50]

This study also takes as a guide media historian Hazel Dicken-Garcia, who noted that criticism of the press lies at the "intersection between society and journalism" and that from that we can identify the values that inform "journalistic conduct" and, I would add, journalistic content. Such criticism in its many forms can be explored to tease out the "essential functions" of journalism—both for sustaining itself and for identifying its role and responsibility to the society in which it exists. Whether implicit or explicit, assertions about journalism's mission as aspirational and transformational visions grounded in a moral center were part and parcel of much of the pulpit's critique. The Reverend George T. Rider alluded to just that when he charged, "There is a deep and growing belief . . . that there are fundamental failures in journalism, that there are portentous and perilous abuses of function and misconception of duty, that there are infringements and intrusions, both insolent and incendiary, together with pretensions that threaten private right and public well-being."[51] Rider was speaking about the newspaper's mission to society sixty-five years before that cornerstone of modern journalism, the Hutchins Commission report.

The problem with identifying the mission of the newspaper is not unlike writer David A. Curtis's problem with defining the word *press*, because it carries the burden of so many meanings. The press in America, he lamented in 1895, "is a nebulous mass of heterogeneous atoms which is not properly to be considered as an entity, or to be referred to even collectively." When Curtis considered the methods of publication at the time, he was as puzzled as contemporary scholars, courts, and news media professionals in their efforts to define who is a journalist in this digital age. "In these days of cheap printing," he wrote, "almost anybody can prepare and offer for sale any collection of words he may choose" and then call it a newspaper. However, Curtis declared, "No criticism directed at 'the press' can have any effect, since there is no guild, no organization, no professional limitation, no community of interest, of principle, or of thought to appeal to. There is not even a system of newspaper ethics to cite."[52]

Still, that lack of a substantive entity to speak to did little to limit the outpouring of just such criticism of the newspaper. Indeed, that deficiency may even have contributed to the reams of criticism published during that decades-long conversation about the function of the newspaper. And, I would argue, the hundreds of examples of that criticism analyzed for this study offer us a resource to better understand journalism's role in society today. The goal of this study is to discern from the criticism of the past—at a moment when the news media began to arise as a modern institution—what those critics meant by the mission of journalism. Getting a better handle on the meaning of the mission would allow us to better weather contemporary intrusions into the ethics of news by the "assumptions of the market," which Carey warned "have so invaded and transformed all human activity and relations that little remains outside the imaginative orbit of the market." This study's impulse, then, derives from much the same cause as Noah Brooks's lament that the "original functions" of the newspaper had been forgotten.[53] Brooks used the word *function*, while others employed such terms as *purpose* or *role*. All are attenuated synonyms for the oft-employed word *mission*, imbued with all its religious connotations. That is, many observers held that the newspaper was both a moral agent and a species of ministry in that the newspaper's mission is to serve its readers—and, in turn, society.

This is apparent, for instance, in the words of a Tennessee editor who told a meeting of his peers in 1906:

> The first question with regard to a newspaper is its purpose. Is it published to promote some single cause, good or bad? Is it published to foster the ambition of some man or set of men? Or is it, in the words of Joseph Pulitzer, "both a daily schoolhouse and a daily forum, both a daily teacher and a daily tribune, an instrument of justice, a terror to crime"—forever unsatisfied with merely printing the news—forever fighting every form of wrong—forever independent—forever advancing in enlightenment and progress—forever wedded to truly democratic ideas—forever aspiring to be a moral force—forever rising to a higher plane of perfection as a public institution.[54]

That quote about the motives and purposes of Pulitzer's *New York World* arrived as part of a cablegram from Pulitzer in 1889 at the dedication of the paper's new building and was enshrined in the cornerstone. Schudson noted that in the late nineteenth century, as Pulitzer created the first modern mass-circulation daily newspaper, he did so "as the last of the old-fashioned editors." The quotation from Pulitzer encapsulates the tension between the mission and the market arising with the era of the commercialized daily press. As Schudson observed, "Most leading newspaper proprietors of the late nineteenth century were businessmen rather than political thinkers, managers more than essayists or activists."[55]

My interest in defining journalism's mission is partly driven by my own sometimes disheartening—and enlightening—involvement as both a reporter and an editor. I spent more than twenty years in newspapers. I worked on an English-language daily in South Korea, where I saw up close the overt and often harsh hand of propaganda and press censorship in an authoritarian state where I saw bludgeoned and bloodied reporters and photographers return to the newsroom from covering student protests. Later I worked in the United States, where I saw the more covert and nuanced influences on news driven by the market and ideology, which was so often linked to market forces. I would venture to say it comes as no surprise for most US journalists when they observe the restrictions on reporting the news by their compatriots working under a totalitarian regime in countries with little or no tradition of a free press. Indeed, in the oppression of the press, we can divine from the negative the essential role and function of journalism in society.[56] It is when journalists return to a country with a purported free-press tradition or enter the business from a university where they have been inculcated in the notions of free expression in the works of Milton, Locke, Mill, and Holmes that a revelation about the realities of the news business can leave them with a choice between a career change or a soul-crushing compromise. As the Reverend Edwin A. Rumball contended in a sermon more than a century ago, "Editors and journalists tell us that newspapers are run for dividends and not for ideas." Thus, he continued, "Many a young journalist is asked to step on his conscience, and when bread and butter are the price he does not always find it easy to decide."[57]

The goal of this book is simply this: before we continue to transform our present news ethic, we need to understand the past in order to discern and save what is fundamental about the mission of journalism. That is because those past conversations about the newspaper's mission have resonance in this present conversation aimed at identifying an accepted news ethic of contemporary journalism. This current conversation is not unlike that which arose a century and more ago during an era of similar disruption as newspapers shifted from a partisan to a commercial business model. Flash forward from that time to the rise of digital outlets that have drastically cut into the news media's—and especially the newspaper's—advertising revenue stream. This upheaval has prompted an often frantic search for new ways of generating income and new ways of leveraging the digital arena for profit—many of which have intruded into traditional ethical norms.

This intrusion is evident in the demand for new books about ethics in the digital age, such as Stephen J. A. Ward's *Radical Media Ethics: A Global Approach* (2015). Ward calls for a radical rethinking of media ethics. The minor tweaks and changes to existing ethics codes are insufficient within the new digital paradigm, he writes. Such changes do not, he argues, "address the larger conceptual swamp in which we find media ethics." One manifestation of this clash between journalistic fundamentals and market demands took place in late 2015 at that bastion of traditional journalism the BBC, when journalists there were told to begin emulating the sixty- to ninety-second "dynamic" and "informal" videos of such youth-oriented sites as *Buzzfeed* and *Vice*. That directive, according to the *Independent*, "angered traditionalists in the BBC newsroom who feel the organisation's journalistic values are being compromised by a desire to go after 'clickbait' content in order to drive up online traffic numbers." This kerfuffle is not unlike the uproar in some newsrooms not so many years ago about requiring reporters to carry cameras and shoot photos while out on assignment. Today, that is a standard expectation. The dispute at the BBC will eventually resolve itself, and out of the settlement will arise a new news ethic about conduct and content. It will certainly end up being a settlement few are entirely pleased with. And many will still say it jeopardizes the mission of journalism. But as a writer in an essay titled "Newspapers" in 1841 lamented, "The perfection of Journalism, in sad truth, is something to be talked of and desired rather than be often seen."[58]

Acknowledgments

A NUMBER OF INSTITUTIONS AND people are in need of thanks for their counsel and support over the past decade and a half of research and writing.

I would first like to thank the Scripps Howard Foundation for their fellowship in journalism that allowed me to bring to a close my more than twenty-year career in newspapers and to enter the doctoral program at Ohio University. I also offer thanks to current and former professors at that institution to include Patrick Washburn, whose abilities at writing, editing, and history honed my own craft; Joseph Bernt, for his guidance on doing historical research; and Katherine Jellison, for both her knowledge of history and her advice about how to make what I research and write relevant to current times. I need to also thank my patient editor at the University of Missouri Press, Gary Kass, and copy editor Annette Wenda, who have both helped me hone the rough edges of this endeavor.

I would also like to acknowledge my current institution, the University of Florida College of Journalism and Communications, Dean Diane McFarlin, Journalism Department chair Ted Spiker, and the members of the Sabbatical Committee who all played a part in allowing me to sequester myself in my study for a year to complete the research and writing of this book.

Grateful acknowledgment is also made to the following publications of earlier work in which some parts of this book are derived, though in most cases here earlier work has been substantially revised, rearranged, and considerably enlarged through further research. These publications include “‘One of the Most Crying Needs of the Present Time’: The Call for a Christian Daily Newspaper,” *American Journalism* 30, no. 3 (2013): 393–413, http://www.tandfonline.com/doi/abs/10.1080/08821127.2013.816899; “The Social Gospel and the News,” *Journalism & Communication Monographs* 13, no. 2 (2011): 69–134, https://doi.org/10.1177/152263791101300202; “The Press, Pulpit and Public Opinion: The Clergy’s Conferral of Power and the Concomitant Call for a Journalism of Advocacy in an Age of Reform," *Journal of Media and Religion* 9, no. 1 (2010): 1–18, http://dx.doi.org/10.1080/15348420903536307; and "'Goodness Isn't News': The Sheldon Edition and the National Conversation Defining Journalism's Responsibility to Society," *Journalism History* 34, no. 4 (2009): 204.

Finally, I would like to thank the love of my life, my wife, Joy, for her support and encouragement over the past many years. It goes without saying, but I will say it anyway: I could not have done this without her.

THE STRUGGLE FOR THE SOUL OF JOURNALISM

INTRODUCTION

The Tangled Web of the Press and the Pulpit

> **The first, greatest and perhaps only evil of the press is the power and tyranny of commercialism.**
>
> —The Reverend Edwin A. Rumball, "Sermon on Newspapers: New York State Minister Appeals for Freedom of the Press"

IN THE TRANSFORMATION OF THE newspaper, many critics recognized the vulnerability of this increasingly powerful institution. The shift from a partisan to a market-oriented and mass-appeal model of journalism, as the press became a modern commercial enterprise with a growing influence on society, prompted these critics to urge a redefinition of press responsibility. Their goal was to protect what was variously defined as the mission of journalism from the toxic influence of market and ideological constraints on journalistic conduct and content—the news. The critics demanded as compensation a moral bulwark—a news ethic that set forth the true mission of the newspaper to guide it. One such critic was the "dean of American correspondents," George W. Smalley, who observed that if the newspaper's role was "doubtful, or the rules which govern its conduct less definite than those which prevail elsewhere, the more reason for trying to ascertain its true relation to social and political life, and the right methods to be followed in its pursuit."[1]

As with so many such notions, a mutual understanding of the meaning of mission becomes lost in the scattered and historically dispersed criticism originating from a diffuse community of critics who came to the issue with their own agendas and views of the world. Indeed, Charles Dudley Warner observed in 1890, "Criticism of our newspaper press is pretty nearly universal." By 1912 Roy W. Howard, chairman of the board of United Press, declared that the "vivisection of American journalism has become a great national pastime." And reformer Roger William Riss observed that much of this discussion about newspapers was about "whether or not they are performing the service expected of them."[2] The impulse for much of this criticism stemmed from the recognition that as a pervasive institution, the newspaper had the ability to do enormous good but also to do enormous harm—especially when the news was tainted by market and ideological forces—a fairly common talking point used in critical discussions about the newspaper.[3] Thus, the newspaper and its journalists became the focus of much of the Progressive Era's tendencies to offer corrective criticism and call for change—in this case change in journalistic conduct and content. Richard Hofstadter has noted that after 1900, this kind of remedial criticism was "everywhere so conspicuous" and an extension of the earlier "agrarian discontent" that was picked up by "the growing enthusiasm of middle-class people for social and economic reform."[4] The impulse for this ethos of reform could be found in such things as the growing complexity of modern life, the demographic shift to urban centers sustained by industrial forces, the reckless behavior of impersonal corporations, and the rise of Gilded Age inequities and political corruption.

Thus, in contrast to the present, one subtext of much of this criticism was a nostalgic harking back to the economic independence and democratic institutions of the past. It reflected nostalgia for a kind of American pastoral. Progressives believed that this restoration of an older order would "bring back a kind of morality and civic purity" to daily life.[5] To that point Josiah Strong, a renowned Protestant clergyman and an analyst of the age, looked back in 1902 at the changes in America over the previous century and noted how much more complex life had become and how in the past, "the great problems were those of the individual; in the new, they are those of society." He also identified the results of the increase in wealth and knowledge that had led to a rise in the standard of living. While seemingly a good thing, he warned, wealth had "been multiplied and centralized," thus the "popular discontent" of the age.[6] That dissatisfaction was aimed at the many institutions that influenced life—including the newspaper. Indeed, in 1913 John McNaught, an editorial writer for the *New York World*, surveyed the present and peered into the past and declared that "our fathers through the Revolutionary War and other wars worked out the ideas of political freedom, an independent judiciary, and representative government as the bulwarks of liberty for the people. With all of these institutions, including the free press, the people are growing discontented."[7]

Religion and the Ethics of News

That discontent provoked criticism of those institutions. And no better representation of the dialectic of the mission versus the market can be found in religion's criticism of newspapers. Such critiques of the press were numerous and spanned many decades, for as the Reverend Lyman Abbott, one of the elders of social Christianity in America, noted in 1901, "It is as customary for ministers and platform orators to jeer at newspapers as it is for newspapers to jeer at ministers and platform orators." One early representative example of these critiques grounded in the ethics of news emanated from the American Congress of Churches in May 1885 at an ecumenical gathering intended to promote discussion of "the great religious, moral, and social questions of the time." The topic of the Tuesday evening session was "The Attitude of the Secular Press in America toward Religion," in which an "immense assemblage" gathered to hear the speakers.[8] They included the Reverend Julius H. Ward of Boston and Senator Joseph Hawley of Connecticut, a lifelong editor.[9] But the most prominent of the speakers was the Reverend Washington Gladden, who attracted a "great audience" to listen to him speak. Indeed, the *Christian Union* observed, Gladden was a renowned preacher with "long and intimate association with the press," which "made him an intelligent interpreter of editorial opinion."[10]

The *New York Times* described Gladden's paper as "a close, careful review of the attitude of the press generally, criticizing it sharply at times." Gladden sent a ripple of laughter through the crowd with his opening statement when he observed that the average editor's stance toward religion was from a place of superiority. "He has no more doubt of what should be said about the views of great divines" than what should be said about the politicians of the day, "and in short he has no more respect for ecclesiastical than political celebrities."[11] Gladden later recalled that he joined in the chorus of praise for the press, citing religion's indebtedness to newspapers for their aid. But, too, his remarks diverted from those of the other speakers in being critical of the press. And it was that criticism, he noted, that had sparked some editorializing in publications across the country that ranged from dissent and resentment to outright contempt. Only "one or two papers" actually admitted some truth to his criticism. "This fact is itself significant. Is the secular press, then, infallible, or does it think itself infallible?" he asked.

His critical remarks involved two topics. One was the often ill-informed discussion in the newspapers about matters of religion. But his other target of criticism "touched a much more sensitive spot." It included disapproval of "the domination of the counting-room over the sanctum" and "the subjection of the teaching function to the business of money-making." Both topics seemed to Gladden statements of common knowledge hardly worth all the editorial clamor they had engendered. In fact, he pointed out, many of the leading papers in the country were owned by corporations or stock companies that did so for a profit. "The doctrines, political or moral or religious, taught by their journal concern them less than the annual balance sheet. . . . That is the paramount consideration. The newspaper business is, primarily, business."[12] Here Gladden is rejecting the then extant notion that economic issues had no connection to morality and that one should not consider Christian principles when contemplating economic issues. Essentially, Gladden was condemning classical economics and unregulated competition—a constant theme of social Christianity[13] and the era's Populist and later Progressive movements.

For a pastor of any distinction to criticize the detrimental influence the secular press had on society was certainly a commonplace. But Gladden's views are especially revealing for two reasons. First, he was one of the key founders and a "tireless tractarian"[14] of the reform-minded and influential Social Gospel movement. The movement revamped Protestantism while confronting modernity, capitalism, and the growing industrialization most explicitly represented by large-circulation and mass-appeal newspapers. (A later chapter will more fully explore this movement and its efforts to influence journalism.) The second reason was his pronounced view that newspapers had a "teaching function" as a tool of reform in an age of reform. The latter was a stance about the role and responsibility of journalism that called for an activist and advocatory journalism that emphasized news that interpreted events. That was because, as Gladden argued, all businesspeople, including the managers of newspapers, were each "God's servant, whether he will or no."[15] An early sounding of this view long before the rise of social Christianity appeared in an ephemeral labor publication from 1874. It declared that "the press ought to be the right arm of the Labor Reform movement" and that it planned to offer a thorough discussion about the problems of labor through the lens of Christianity.[16] Here is evidence of an early inclination of religion to view the press as a tool of reform. Charles Howard Hopkins showed through his history of the Social Gospel movement that the pastorate saw the advantages of using the press as viaducts for propaganda. Hopkins described the 1890s as the "great flowering period" of social Christianity when it "often marched hand in hand with the muckrakers of the period." Indeed, Hopkins noted, arising with the Social Gospel movement was a "vast literature of analysis, prescription, and challenge."[17]

Understanding the context of the times helps us understand the prompts for that literature. In 1912 German theologian Ernst Troeltsch succinctly described "the modern social problem" that was "vast and complicated." It included the problems created by capitalism and industrial forces, the rise of large "militaristic and bureaucratic" states, an increasing population, and the spreading use of efficient machinery that produced massive numbers of consumer goods that mobilize "the whole world for purposes of trade, but which also treats men and labour like machines." These were new problems the church had never faced before. But the church, in order to remain relevant, needed to address them. As contemporary scholar Gary J. Dorrien has observed, religion "embraced a new understanding of its social mission" during this rise of modernity, reflected in this new "social order created by Enlightenment criticism, modern society and technology, and capitalist economics."[18]

Here was the problem, however. Religion no longer held the keys to public opinion, that great force for societal reform. That is one reason the nation's pastorate concerned itself with the conduct of the emerging newspaper press. Indeed, most observers agreed that the press's modern ability to define and influence public opinion meant the newspaper had grown "mightier than the pulpit."[19] That was an axiom expressed in various ways by many before and after the turn of the last century.[20] Even as early as 1851, a writer for a Presbyterian weekly newspaper declared that "the newspaper is both Bible, church and priest. All the forms of venerable authority have been superseded by the journal; and much of the power once claimed and wielded by the confessional and pulpit, has been silently given over to this priesthood of letters." Similarly, just after the turn of the century, Josiah Strong wrote, "The press is producing a climate of opinion which is becoming ever wider and is destined to be universal. Millions now read the same printed page and think the same thoughts." Yes, agreed the Reverend Charles Stelzle, a writer and an expert in church publicity. In 1903 he bemoaned the fact that "the accursed daily newspaper" was replacing the church.[21] Stelzle's own later study of how workingmen spent their spare hours found newspaper reading occupied more of their time than any other interest.[22] And by 1910 the Reverend Reynold E. Blight conceded that the newspaper superseded "the pulpit, the school, the forum" in its power over public opinion as the primary information source and guide to life in the modern world.[23]

But the press's power over public opinion was a sword of two edges that the many pastoral critics acknowledged and warned of. This is well summarized in an editorial titled "The Church and the Newspaper" (1901) in the *Christian Advocate*. It contended that "the Church in its highest work often finds the newspaper helping it much with one hand, and holding back or crowding it aside even more greatly with the other." To that point, Shailer Mathews, the dean of the Divinity School at the University of Chicago, argued that while the "agents of public opinion" needed to be free to allow the unhobbled discussion at the core of democracy, "We ought, however, to be protected against the manipulation of facts by those who have ulterior motives for such manipulation." That is why the Reverend Blight called for an ethos in which newspapers acted with conscience. A newspaper conducted without conscience but only to make money "will pander to the prejudices and the passions of the ignorant masses," he argued. When the business side of a newspaper determines what is published as news, "vicious ideals and cynical sophistry prevail."[24] Here in Blight's indictment is an echo of Gladden's warning from a quarter century before about the market's incursions on the mission of newspapers.

"An Era of Paper, and the Age of Print"

These warnings about the intrusion of the market on religious life and the consequent calls for newspapers to act with conscience or variants of that ideal involving righteous conduct or the newspaper as a moral force were fueled by the rising popularity of print over many decades. This is apparent in a representative instance of the perceived need for harnessing newspapers for social good in an 1866 essay in the *New York Times* about how the "enormous circulation" attained by the newspaper and the novel was affecting society. The writer noted that this "greatly troubled" both moralists and philosophers, which prompted the occasional calls for adding a "religious character" to the novel and newspaper.[25]

Indeed, not long after printers began turning out newspapers in America, the religious societies responded and followed suit. By the beginning of the nineteenth century, religious newspapers that did not look unlike secular newspapers began to appear.[26] These papers published secular news and much about religion and individual denominations. By the early 1830s, there were about 100 of these newspapers—all weeklies—across the

United States.[27] Another estimate put the number of religious periodicals at 188—which, between 1820 and 1852, made up 39 percent of the periodicals published during that period.[28] The vast quantities of religious publications in the early nineteenth century were riding what poet Grenville Mellen described in 1830 as "an Era of Paper, and the Age of Print." David Paul Nord has suggested, "Perhaps, more than anything else, the missionary impulse—first in purely religious crusades and then in more secular reform movements—lay at the foundation of the popularization of print in the nineteenth century." Indeed, another scholar has argued that just as the eighteenth century's Great Awakening helped alter oratory, the Second Great Awakening that began to gain momentum around 1800 contributed to the rise in print consumption in the nineteenth century.[29]

The recollections of Samuel Griswold Goodrich, a writer, bookseller, and publisher in Boston, gives some perspective to this rise in the popularity and importance of print. In a memoir published in 1857 near the end of his life, Goodrich looked back over the decades of change in communications in America, a change that historian Nathan O. Hatch has argued launched "an age of mass communication," in which religious institutions held point.[30] Goodrich recalled:

> Books and newspapers—which are now diffused even among the country towns, so as to be in the hands of all, young and old—were then scarce, and were read respectfully, and as if they were grave matters, demanding thought and attention. They were not toys and pastimes, taken up every day, and by everybody, in the short intervals of labor, and then hastily dismissed, like waste paper. The aged sat down when they read, and drew forth their spectacles, and put them deliberately and reverently upon the nose. These instruments were not as now, little tortoise-shell hooks, attached to a ribbon, and put off and on with a jerk; but they were of silver or steel, substantially made, and calculated to hold on with a firm and steady grasp, showing the gravity of the uses to which they were devoted. Even the young approached a book with reverence, and a newspaper with awe. How the world has changed![31]

In early-nineteenth-century religious circles, societal reform was hinged to religious conversion through the power of the preaching of the Gospel. But such change would not happen by itself. It required Christian agents of change that would promote the word of God. Thus, Nord suggests, religious social reformers "idealized the power of print" and made such things as Bibles, tracts, periodicals, and newspapers fundamental communicative tools of the associations that had sprung up across the nation. And it was quickly realized that one of the primary instruments of communication was the newspaper, because, as Alexis de Tocqueville observed during his tour of America in the early nineteenth century, "only a newspaper can deposit the same thought in a thousand minds at once."[32]

The recognition of that power of the newspaper was behind the founding of what has been called the first religious newspaper in the United States, the *Herald of Gospel Liberty*, in 1808, by Elias Smith, a preacher, physician, journalist, and clergyman.[33] And by 1823, the *Christian Herald* extolled the evangelical efficacy of "the divine art of printing" as a "common blessing through the civilized world." Smith, in a message to readers in that first issue of the weekly, held, "A religious News-paper, is almost a new thing under the sun. I know not but this is the first ever published to the world." Of course, as John Pressley Barrett noted in 1908 in *The Centennial of Religious Journalism*, there had been religious newspapers in Europe before that date. And while three other American religious papers had claimed being the first, the facts disputed their assertions of primacy. According to Barrett's own research, the *Religious Observer* of Philadelphia, which had changed its name to the *Christian Observer*, began in 1813. The *Weekly Recorder* of Philadelphia was first published in 1814. And the *Boston Recorder*, which changed its name to the *Congregationalist*, began life in 1816. Media historian Frank Luther Mott also noted that by 1824 there were many weekly religious newspapers that covered both secular and sectarian news, but the first of these was the *Herald of Gospel Liberty*. While the debate over primacy need not detain us too long, it should be noted that other historians have claimed that the world's first such paper was the weekly *Christian History*, which began in 1743 in Boston.[34]

Smith drew his template for the *Herald* from secular newspapers. In that message to his readers, Smith declared, "The utility of such a paper has been suggested to me, from the great use other papers are to the community at large. In this way almost the whole state of the world is presented to us at once. In a short and cheap way, a general knowledge of our affairs is diffused through the whole. . . . If we are profited in political affairs in this way, I do not see why the knowledge of the Redeemer's kingdom may not be promoted or increased in the same way."[35]

But there was certainly a difference between the kinds of publications. For example, one scholar has noted that secular papers were more temporal—in the sense of both being more worldly and keying news to recent events—while religious newspapers were more spiritual in the presentation of their news. And the religious papers' "selection and placement of useful texts" separated into departments formed a "curriculum essential to the well-informed Christian family."[36] Horace Bushnell, a renowned American Congregational clergyman and theologian, recognized the power of the press as an instrument of evangelization—but he also offered up a caveat. Writing in 1847, he argued, "There is no instrument of power, in this age, as we are just beginning to discover, that can be compared with a newspaper." Yet Bushnell cautioned those who proclaimed the power of the press, "as if types of lead and sheets of paper may be the light of the world." To believe that the press was "a substitute for piety, or a piety-saving machine, is an egregious delusion," he warned.[37]

Still, by 1850, the American Tract Society, an organization founded with the goal of publishing and disseminating Christian literature, described the scientific progress behind the improving communication technologies and transportation networks as "providential facilities" for rapidly disseminating the Gospel by "annihilating space, and bringing the extremes of a continent into fraternal neighborhood." The society went on to contrast the small-circulation newspaper and its limited news hole of a century and a half before with the "enterprise and wide-reaching influence of a daily journal of our own times." Thus, it argued, these new tools and facilities must become the instruments of modern evangelization. And in that argument, too, is an early critique of the secular press driven by partisan politics and commercial success: "Shall we content ourselves with the post-coach speed of the eighteenth century, in schemes for evangelization, while all worldly schemes are propelled with the locomotive speed of the nineteenth century? Shall we creep along the beaten path our fathers trod, and because they trod it, eschewing or neglecting all the increased facilities Providence has given us for publishing the great salvation, while steam, and electricity, and the printing-press are left to be the agents of ambition, avarice and revolution?"[38]

Growth of the Newspaper as a Social Force

An early example of the criticism of the American newspaper's conduct and content is evident in one of the earliest successful colonial newspapers, Boston's *New-England Courant*, the "first overtly heretical newspaper" in America.[39] Encouraged by Anglicans in Boston who sought to "challenge the preeminence of Cotton Mather and the Puritan establishment," James Franklin—elder brother of Benjamin—began publishing the *Courant* on August 7, 1721. And it was not long before it garnered a hellfire-and-brimstone round of criticism from the Reverend Increase Mather, who published a letter in the *Boston Gazette* castigating the *Courant* after it listed him as one of the paper's supporters.[40] The letter read, in part, "I that have known what New-England was from the Beginning, cannot but be troubled to the Degeneracy of this place. I can well remember when the Civil Government could have taken an effectual Course to suppress such a Cursed Libel which if it be not done I am afraid that some Awful Judgment will come upon this Land, and that the Wrath of GOD will arise, and there will be no Remedy."[41]

In the following years since those "humblest of beginnings" with colonial broadsheets, one writer observed in 1902 that the evolution of the newspaper had proceeded to the point that it had "reached the foremost rank among social and political forces. It has grown from the old hand-set, handpressed four-page weekly, printed at the rate of 150 an hour, which our fathers read, to the modern linotyped, stereotyped, 24 page 7 edition daily run off on an octuple cylinder steam press at the rate of 25,000 an hour." Similarly, George Perry Morris, the associate editor of the *Congregationalist and Christian World*, observed in 1905 that the impulse for the "marked changes" in journalism in the late nineteenth century included the following: "multiple telegraphy, the telephone, the Hoe press, express locomotives, and a systematized collection of news and dispersion of the printed page, together with the organization of newspaper properties in stock companies with diffusion of ownership, all these contributing to make the creating and the selling of newspapers and periodicals an industry of such proportions as Franklin or Greeley never dreamed of."[42]

Consequently, along with increased urbanization and a rising populace, the newspaper grew and transformed in substantive terms. For instance, in 1890 there were fewer than 1,000 dailies in the United States. By 1910 more daily papers were being published in the United States than ever before—or since—when the number of dailies peaked at 2,600.[43] And as a consequence of growing circulation and wider distribution networks, the newspaper's need for a reliable revenue source from advertising increased exponentially. Indeed, by 1909, Milton A. McRae of the Scripps-McRae League of Newspapers and one of the founders of the American Newspaper Publishers Association, noted, "Printing and publishing now constitute the seventh largest industry in the United States. The growth in 20 years has excelled all else, except perhaps the business use of the telephone. The cost of producing a newspaper has doubled in a decade."[44]

Walter Lippmann, writing in the *Yale Review* in 1931 and looking back at the history of the newspaper in America, observed that it had gone through three phases during its life and was then on the border of entering its fourth. Those phases began with publication as a "monopoly of the government," followed by the partisan press, and then the newspapers independent of political party and government control through the aegis of "the commercially profitable support of a large body of readers." Of course, with such bright-line demarcations of history, there are always encroachments in time. For instance, even during the dominance of the partisan-subsidized press and long before the rise of the market-driven and mass-appeal sensationalist newspapers of the late nineteenth century, the penny newspaper began and became a force in society. In 1837 author and editor Asa Greene declared that "the introduction of the penny press, in this country—in which New York took the lead—deserves to be recorded as an important era in the history of our newspapers." It was important, he held, because "many thousand persons are provided with information, instruction and amusement, where there was none of a similar kind before. Not only is the mind greatly enlarged and improved, but the morals are amended—as they always are, where the mind is enlightened."[45]

The penny press was a harbinger of the future and the wedge at the center of the rupture of the old ways of doing journalism. Rather than the sixpenny journals that few people could afford, the penny papers were open to nearly all. And their very popularity swelled the demand for news. For example, circulation of New York City's eleven daily newspapers before Benjamin H. Day founded the *New York Sun* in 1833 was 25,500 total. But by January of the next year, the *Sun* had a circulation of 5,000 a day, two years later 15,000, and by 1836 it had 20,000 readers—becoming by 1860 the world's biggest newspaper, with a circulation of 77,000.[46] And Day's success with the *Sun* in the early 1830s spawned many other penny papers in New York and across the country, "which sprang up at the rate of a dozen a year."[47] More than one writer has noted that the commercial press had its start with the penny papers in the 1830s.[48] Helen MacGill Hughes observed that the penny press challenged the "professional attitude" of the older papers and their editors, though it continued until after the Civil War. And even in the late twentieth century, there were "still editors and readers who, as Lippmann put it, think of the newspaper 'as if it were a church or a school,'" Hughes wrote. "But the commercial penny press substituted the market for the mission." And for the penny press, the commodity it had for sale was the news, not the influence of the editors and their interpretation of the news.[49]

In addition, the penny papers, in attracting a wider audience, also redefined the scope of news by focusing on such things as court proceedings, police news, human-interest stories, and scandals, while also criticizing institutions and taking stands on issues facing society. One of the founders of the first penny papers, James Gordon Bennett of the *New York Morning Herald*, which began in 1835 and published stories about private scandals, vice, crimes, and salacious murder cases, was the subject of much of the sort of criticism ladled upon newspapers of the—as historian Willard Bleyer termed it—"lively, saucy, and spicy" genre that "published much material of a highly objectionable kind." For example, the *New York Journal of Commerce* described the *Herald* as a "dirty little penny paper . . . whose Editor, if he got his deserts, would be horsewhipped every day." In fact, the distasteful character of the *Herald* prompted several New York papers and some in other cities to launch a "Moral War" against Bennett and the *Herald*. Those papers charged Bennett with indecency, blasphemy, blackmail, lying, and libel. "The *Herald* was declared unfit to be read by self-respecting men and women," Bleyer recounted. "Advertisers and subscribers were urged to withdraw their support. Hotels, clubs, and reading rooms were requested to exclude the paper."[50]

And finally, it was the commercial aspect at the heart of the penny papers that sloughed off the need for support from partisan interests as they began to emphasize profit as the principal purpose of the press rather than, as the *New York Daily Times* once put it, acting as "a small hollow tube for politicians to speak through." A marked example of the political-party press in the early nineteenth century was the *New-York Evening Post*. It was founded in November 1801 by Federalists who felt the need for such an organ in the wake of their defeat in the national and New York elections. The *Post* followed the pattern of other such newspapers by nearly subordinating the news to political discussion through letters and editorials. The only news a reader was sure to find in the *Post* was such commercial information as the arrival and departure of ships, speeches, and reports on Congress. The *Post* and other political-party newspapers had no organized system for sending out reporters to collect the news of the day locally, nationally, or internationally. Editors would occasionally clip and run items from foreign newspapers and publish private letters given to them by merchants and others.

"No attempt," Bleyer noted, "was made to appeal to the great bulk of the population by presenting news attractively."[51]

As with so much involving change, the end of the partisan press and the triumph of the commercial newspaper involved a slow reveal over many years. For instance, early on the founder of the *New York Times*, Henry J. Raymond, "stood for a strangely objective non-partisanship in his paper," even though he was a national political figure.[52] In 1857 the *Times* reacted to the commentary "from its brethren" after it declared its news was "entirely independent of Political Parties—judging all men upon their merits, and giving praise and censure, support and opposition, where either may be deserved by a strict and impartial regard to the public welfare." And in its defense of its news policy, the *Times* asked, "A newspaper is designed to accompany its reports of fact with comments and explanations:—why should it make these comments in the interest of a party rather than of the public at large?"[53]

Nearly a half century later, an editorial in *Editor & Publisher* suggested that no change in modern newspapers when compared to those of the past was more noticeable than "their tendency to break away from party domination and preserve their own independence of opinion." In the past, a partisan newspaper had to promote the chosen candidate of its party. "If he was a numskull it was the editor's business to make him a little god." But all this had changed by 1903, the editorial writer noted, with most newspapers taking up the "cudgels for the best man, irrespective of party." And there were two reasons for this independence—the newspaper had become more profitable through the aegis of advertising, and news had become more valued than comment. That meant a newspaper could no longer exclude certain types of news, as partisan publications must.[54] Two years later, the trade journal ran a series of quotations from newspaper commentaries that "show the trend away from the partisan journal idea to one of broad independence." Each reiterated the words of the *Nashville American*, which held that recent history had seen a marked change in newspaper policy regarding partisan politics. "The modern newspaper is an entity and speaks as a public journal, not as the vehicle or personal mouthpiece of an individual and special pleader. Newspapers have not only vastly improved as purveyors of impartial news, but they have improved in the fairness and impartiality of their editorial pages."[55]

Still, the commercial paper had its own dynamic that was the impulse for much of the criticism aimed at it. For instance, in a speech in 1911, Livy S. Richard, the editor of the *Boston Common*, a press critic and a Progressive figure of some note, offered several anecdotes as evidence that the nation's commercial newspaper press had sold "their independence to business interests." That fact was inevitable, he warned, as long as "newspaper readers let big advertisers carry three-fourths of the burden of supporting the newspapers while they themselves carry only one-fourth. . . . So as we pay only a penny a day for our news and thus acquiesce in the arrangement which forces the publisher to live by the advertiser's favor; so long as we take no concerted steps to show that we are displeased with newspapers notoriously subsidized or with biased news reporting, there will be no great improvement in newspaper service of the people."[56]

Yet questions remained: Whom do newspapers serve, and what, exactly, was their role in society? In 1910 an editorial in *Current Literature* discounted the ongoing talk about how the changing landscape had led to "the waning power of the press." Newspapers were more popular than ever, the editorial contended, and they were improving in quality and not deteriorating. "What seems to be happening is that the press is undergoing fundamental change, to meet new and changed conditions. This change may be regarded as desirable or undesirable, according to the point of view." To put this "fundamental change" in its simplest terms, the longtime guiding star of journalistic conduct and content—partisanship—was fading. For instance, in 1914 the Reverend Frank Crane recalled that it had not been that long before that "almost all newspapers were political organs. It was considered a disgrace not to be. Most of the great newspapers of the United States today have gotten out of this wallow." But that change had an effect on the work of those who reported and edited the news. On partisan newspapers, journalists fundamentally understood what their roles and responsibilities were and whom they served. However, at a commercially driven mass-appeal publication largely sustained by advertising and unhinged from politics, politicians, and political parties, whom did journalists serve? That was the question many in the newspaper industry struggled to answer. As writer Charles Dudley Warner observed in 1897, the modern newspaper had "hardly yet got itself adjusted to its sudden accession of enormous influence." And a year later, *Current Literature* observed, "The newspaper has brought into the world a new code of morals."[57]

This shift in how the newspapers were sustained led to a moral vacuum—many critics believed—grounded in the pecuniary interests of those who controlled the editorial policy of newspapers. One of the more renowned of those critics, Samuel Bowles, editor of the *Springfield (MA) Republican*, observed that while the party organ of the past could no longer survive, "the political thralldom of the press has been succeeded by a commercial thralldom more insidious and more dangerous to the welfare of society." Oswald Garrison Villard, editor of the *New York Post*, in a speech titled "Ethics of Journalism" (1910), similarly reproved this shift from obeying the commands of politicians to "toadying to the advertiser," which fundamentally threatened the "integrity of the press."[58] In response, over the years the newspaper-industry trade journal *Editor & Publisher*, which was read by editors, reporters, advertising executives, and publishers alike, began to issue a stream of criticism[59] and call in 1906 for a professionalization of the ranks.[60] And then in 1909, Hamilton Holt, the progressive editor of the *Independent*, published a book-length critique of newspapers starkly titled *Commercialism and Journalism*. Thus, in the late nineteenth and early twentieth centuries, there was a window of time that spanned many years during the incremental evolution from partisan responsibility to a yet undefined public responsibility within the confines of a commercialized newspaper. In 1910 *Editor & Publisher* described this era as a time "when the newspaper, as an institution, is undergoing a searching investigation and analysis."[61]

It was during this window of time that both pastoral and secular critics began to discern a wedge into which they could offer countless guidance about the mission of journalism. From the pastoral perspective, Josiah Strong saw this as early as 1893. Strong, one of the great publicists of social Christianity, recognized that in the last decade of the nineteenth century, the pulpit suddenly had access to unprecedented "organization and facilities for communication" with the masses—to include the daily newspaper. "We have seen the significance of popular discontent; we are evidently in a transition state; our social institutions are in flux; in due time they will recrystallize. This is such an opportunity to give them Christian form as may not come again for ages." Three years before Strong's recognition of this transition state, the Reverend W. N. M'Elroy observed that discussion about the press's role and responsibility to society was sorely needed, especially given the upheavals by the forces of modernity and industrialization. He argued that society, the world of business, and journalism were groping for a proper mode of conduct to inform a social ethic. That was because the modern world contained many things the ethics of which had not been predetermined. Instead, they required analysis and decision in the context of current times. Modern journalism was one notable example, wrote

M'Elroy, who went on to analogize it to the power and proclivities of the modern corporate world. "No moral philosopher, heathen or Christian, has taught us anything concerning the ethics of the press. The press as we now have it is a comparatively modern thing, and in some of its phases entirely new. Like trusts and combines in the commercial world, its ethical qualities are largely undefined, and are therefore subjects of diverse and conflicting views and opinions."[62]

Newspaper as Public Utility

Ultimately, a consensus among many critics was that the newspaper—whether privately owned by corporations or individuals—served the public. That is, the newspaper press is "a privately owned public function," University of Minnesota president George E. Vincent told the National Newspaper Conference in 1912.[63] The conference, billed as the first nationwide gathering of journalists to discuss the newspaper business,[64] was partly prompted by several investigations of the press over the previous years. The most notable of these was Will Irwin's now classic fifteen-part dissection of the newspapers in America that ran in the renowned muckraking magazine *Collier's* over fifteen weeks in 1911.[65] The conference was essentially about defining the mission of journalism in its confrontation with market constraints. Sociologist Edward Alsworth Ross described it as a gathering of journalists "assembled for the sole purpose of considering whether or not they are doing their full duty by the public." And in commentary on the conference, the left-leaning *La Follette's Weekly Magazine* crowed, "More and more the attention of the public is being directed toward this important subject of a shackled press."[66]

By training Vincent was a sociologist and not a lawyer, and his speech, "The People and the Press," was not about the law but about the newspaper's responsibility to society. That is, as he put it, "If the press be a corporation, it is a public service corporation with all of the social responsibility that this implies." On the face of it, his assertion that a privately owned commercial entity such as a newspaper served a public function that encroached on the rights of property seems a dissident notion. However, we need only flash forward thirty-four years to the US Supreme Court decision in *Marsh v. Alabama* that applied the "public function doctrine" to privately held entities. The court ruled that residents of a town owned by a private company were still constitutionally protected from the company abridging their freedom of speech, right to assemble, and freedom of religion. In the majority decision, Justice Hugo Black wrote that since the town's "facilities are built and operated primarily to benefit the public, and since their operation is essentially a public function," the private corporate owner's rights "become circumscribed by the statutory and constitutional rights" of the public that uses those facilities.[67]

So it appears that Vincent was onto something here. However, his declaration that a privately owned newspaper served a public function beyond profit did not proceed from a vacuum. That the newspaper, a privately held corporate institution, should recognize its "quasi-public function"[68] and was therefore accountable to the public good was a view of journalism's "peculiar responsibility"[69] as a public utility—and public servant—that had long adhered to it. It was, University of Kansas journalism professor Leon Nelson Flint observed, "a suggestion that gave rise to much profitable discussion."[70] For instance, Albert J. Beveridge, a historian, senator from Indiana, and intellectual leader of the Progressive Era, declared, "A newspaper man ought to be a servant of the people quite as much as the man whom the people elect to public office. If anything, the newspaper man ought to be more careful in the discharge of public duty than the office-holder, for the newspaper man daily gives to the people that information and counsel upon which the people form their judgment of men and measures." This was a view also well illustrated by the editor of the *Toledo (OH) News-Bee* Negley Cochran: "In my opinion a Scripps editor should consider himself a servant of the people, every bit as much as though he had been elected editor by the people." That was a view certainly agreeable to Theodore Roosevelt, who once said, "I feel that a man who writes for the public press is just as emphatically a public servant as the man who holds public office."[71]

Excellent thought, but we need to keep in mind that Roosevelt was speaking from a point of view as a politician—especially one running for president—who well knew how to manipulate the press to his own ends.[72] Arguably more reliable was the counsel of two renowned educators at the dawn of the journalism school movement when the faculty was still determining what to teach aspiring journalists. Willard Grosvenor Bleyer, the founder of the University of Wisconsin–Madison's journalism school, told students in a speech called "The Function of the Newspaper" (1913), "Like common carriers, such as railroads, the newspapers have a public function as well as the private need of making money, and that public function is to furnish the news commodity in which they deal in complete and accurate form." Similarly, Walter Williams, the founding dean of the School of

Journalism at the University of Missouri, argued that aside from instruction in the basics of journalism, schools should also teach students about the responsibility of journalists and that journalism is a public service. "The schools will teach that there is more in journalism than bread and butter—necessary as that is—or than dividends upon shares of stock." The newspaper, Williams argued, was "the greatest public utility institution. While all other public utility institutions have been regulated by law, the newspaper is, in a special sense, its own regulator.... Peculiar responsibility, therefore, rests upon journalism to recognize its mission as a public servant." Essentially, that was the policy of the much-admired and oft-quoted editor of the *Springfield (MA) Republican*, Samuel Bowles, who held that a newspaper's devotion was to the whole community and nothing else, as it avoided all entanglements that might shunt it from that goal. These and iterations of similar conversations about the newspaper's role in society informed the American Society of Newspaper Editors' adoption of the Canons of Journalism in 1923. At that organization's first meeting, the society's founder, Casper Yost, declared to those in attendance and to a national audience, "Journalism is predominantly an instrument of public service."[73]

One of the more substantive considerations of the newspaper as public utility was Flint's contention that the best newspapers were, in fact, a space where journalists "work out their professional responsibilities to the public." But, Flint argued, any such discussion had to be grounded in acknowledging that like the utilities owned by the public that supply the people with the necessities of life such as light, water, and transportation, "the newspaper supplies them with a no less essential 'commodity,' news." To understand the importance of this "raw material of public opinion," Flint proposed trying to imagine what the world would be like if newspapers did not exist.[74] Extending the public utility metaphor a bit further, the Reverend D. M. Fisk held that the newspaper's influence was, at its core, moral, and, given that, the newspaper was in many ways a kind of "social service." The press, he argued, was not unlike other professions that were in reality "social workers." Take, for example, the judge, who is expected to resist bribes and threats of harm in acting fairly. The same applied to the doctor who could make money by "abetting crime" rather than following the ethics of the medical profession. "Why the doctor and not his neighbor, the editor?" the reverend asked. Fisk, pastor of the First Congregational Church in Topeka, Kansas, offered his counsel on newspapers in a sermon on the Sunday before the beginning of the Reverend Charles Sheldon's internationally publicized week editing the *Topeka Daily Capital* as Jesus would. (Chapter 5 relates this event in full.) Fisk told his parishioners that all dealings among people "ought to contribute to the completion of society."

So how does this apply to newspapers? It does because newspapers were "a highly human, ethical and personal form of social service," as Fisk intoned. That is, there were men and women—"a deciding brain"—behind all the mechanical apparatus of a newspaper. They were not extensions of those machines, "but human wills, facing choices, weighing reasons, deciding for men and sending out their work to mould men. Now such work is necessarily moral. It either helps men or it works men for the money there is in them." And this ethical responsibility traversed from the highest office of a newspaper to the lowest editor and reporter, the reverend contended. That was because everything a newspaper published down to the smallest headline written to draw in readers was as much a "moral interpretation" as the news itself.[75]

The origins of this notion of service yoked to the newspaper included an immigrant-driven shift in demographics subsuming a Protestant nation in which the once monolithic church was losing its sway over public opinion. It also involved the growing awareness that the "complex civilization of the age"[76] and the "complex problems"[77] of modern life required a newspaper that rejected the constraints of the market. Instead, it must act as a "moral and religious teacher"—as a prophet with a "supreme allegiance to truth," declared the Reverend Gladden. That was because, Gladden contended elsewhere, "the press has come to be the principal agency for the creation of public opinion." Additionally, the much-pilloried excesses of the Gilded Age industrialists were part and parcel of this notion of service. In 1912 Livy S. Richard, editor of the progressive *Boston Common* newspaper, in discussing the role of newspapers cited the "contemporary recoil from business for profit to business for service," brought on by the general reaction to the perceived venality of the times.[78] He observed that Americans had been told for years that they were living in a new era of service as "the mainspring of constructive activities" in the modern world. It was, philosopher Clifford L. Barrett wrote, a "New Era of Intercession and Communion, and this must have as one of its foundations, a deeper consciousness of the world's need and hope."[79]

This notion of the moral incumbency of service to society dovetailed with the demands for an untainted news as a service to society voiced by the social Christianity and Progressive movements. And it still reverberates in our present age in such things as the net-neutrality debate in which the Internet is described as a public utility vital as a service to society and democracy that the market must not hobble. Indeed, the market's influence on not just the news but also society in general has long been a point of consternation. As early as 1836—coincidentally around the rise of the penny press, the first inkling of a commercialized and mass-appeal news media—Ralph Waldo Emerson warned, "This age will be characterized as the era of Trade, for every thing is made subservient to that agency."[80]

Still, even among the press's critics, there were differences of opinion about the "quasi-public function of the newspaper," as Nelson Antrim Crawford observed in his often-cited *The Ethics of Journalism* (1924). His book reveals much about those differences just in the diversity of opinions reflected in many of the early ethics codes Crawford published. Crawford noted, however, that this notion of public utility was often defined by perspective. There were those, he observed, who were of a political mind and thus believed newspapers should be "run in the interest of their particular political interests." Likewise, there were clergy who felt that newspapers should be published primarily to maintain "morality or some other abstraction."[81]

To that latter point, in 1910 at its seventh annual convention in Nashville, Tennessee, the Religious Education Association adopted "A Declaration of Principles." The declaration noted its one main goal was to "inspire educational institutions and forces of our country with the religious ideal, and to inspire the religious institutions and forces of our country with the educational ideal." And it held that the power of the press should be better used to further moral and religious education. "In the press of today, there is offered to church and school an unrealized opportunity for spreading ideals through the nation and educating men and women to deeper conceptions of duty, character and public service."[82] This formal declaration was representative of many similar calls over the decades for a religiously oriented and value-based journalism. These sorts of pleas were first heard in earnest in the mid-nineteenth century. They began not long after journalistic innovators began to leverage improved printing technology and transportation infrastructure to establish the first successful—though still limited—secular and advertiser-driven mass-appeal penny newspapers in the 1830s. It is then that the pastorate began to react to the mass-appeal papers' deleterious effects on society and the loosening of religion's long-established hold on public opinion that it was ceding to the secular newspaper press.

* * * * *

That, then, is the core of the following chapters. One caveat, however. This is not a macrohistory of press criticism. Within the frames of several narratives, this study essentially isolates as much as is possible one major stream of criticism from a powerful and influential institution related to early notions of the press's responsibility to and role in society under the rubric of its mission. This critique took many forms from many starting points and ranged over time from outright castigation and rejection of the secular newspaper to the pulpit's acquiescence to a new reality—that in the face of modernity in a growing industrializing and increasingly diverse nation, it no longer held the reins of power over public opinion. But this acceptance came with the effort by the pulpit in alliance with politicians, social scientists, educators, members of the Progressive movement, and journalists themselves to influence newspaper conduct and content—the very epistemology of news. And that concentration of criticism buttressed by the constant dialectic of the market versus the mission over many years as newspapers redefined their role as commercial enterprises offers a "concrete condensation" from which we can draw an argument for the foundational precepts of the mission of journalism.[83]

The question is, then, how did the still powerful and influential pulpit define those functions and duties in those early days? To answer that question, the following chapters explore the implications of several critical junctures between two powerful societal institutions—the increasingly market-oriented press and a church whose very foundation was at the same time shifting. These junctures manifest the larger overarching critical juncture between the market and the mission that journalism found itself in a century and more ago and finds itself in at present. Media scholar Robert W. McChesney describes a critical juncture as "a period in which the old institutions and mores are collapsing under long-run and powerful pressures," which helps "explain how social change works."[84] A similar juncture more than a century ago spawned both a critique and a defense of newspapers that contributed to shaping the ethical norms of journalistic conduct and content—much of which we still live with today. With journalism, critical junctures in which the objectives of opposing forces collide offer a space for exploring the buttressing or the transformation of a news ethic in which we can ask the question that Shakespeare asked: "How shall we find the concord of this discord?"[85] And out of this disputation we can draw some sense of the mission of journalism that we can hold fast to in the face of contemporary change and the demands of digitally driven market forces.

To introduce the major actors in the following narratives, chapter 1, "Six Apostles of the Reformation of Newspapers," offers some granularity to religion's view of the role and responsibility of journalism in society. This chapter briefly looks at the backgrounds, press criticism, and journalistic theories of six of the more influential voices of the era—economist Richard T. Ely and the Reverends Washington Gladden, Josiah Strong, Walter Rauschenbusch, Lyman Abbott, and Charles Sheldon. These men all had varying degrees of experience in journalism and were six of the primary diagnosticians and writers of the era whose work represented some of the most articulate and pointed criticisms of the secular press over many decades. The ideas and arguments of all of these men will be expanded upon in later chapters that individually examine several of the long-simmering narratives between the press and pulpit.

Chapter 2, "The Sunday Newspaper and the Modern World," examines the decades-long confrontation between the church and the commercially successful Sunday newspapers beginning in the nineteenth century and lasting well into the twentieth. Called by many critics a desecration of the Sabbath, the Sunday newspaper's growing success reveals the first rupture between the sacred and the secular worlds—one driven by the spiritual and the other by the market. The Sunday newspaper was, as the *Washington Post* put it in 1889, "an ineliminable feature of modern life." In a sense, in its mass appeal, its promotion of a consumer society through stories and advertising, its redefinition of news, and its expansion of topics covered about modern life, it was a medium of modernity.

Chapter 3, "The Press, the Pulpit, and Public Opinion," describes the pulpit's publicly stated conferral of its role of agent of education and moral uplift to the newspaper press as a moral agent for change in an age of reform and demographic upheaval. The pulpit's acknowledgment of the subsidence of the church's primacy in the area of public opinion and the enlargement of the perceived role of the press in society came with a call, however, for a journalism of interpretation and advocacy that urged a values-based mode of journalism in order to aid the struggle for reform and moral uplift.

Chapter 4, "The Call Goes Out for a Christian Daily Newspaper," examines the decades-long call for a Christian daily newspaper in the nineteenth and early twentieth centuries and the early failed attempts to create such a paper. There was a broadly felt desire for such a publication among the pastorate and many in the pews because of both the falloff of the popularity of once powerful religious weeklies and the perception of the pernicious effects on society by the modern mass-appeal newspaper. In exploring this desire, this chapter again unpacks the tension between the sacred and the secular found in the exigencies between creating a commercially profitable paper and still remaining true to Christian principles. Here will be discussed two themes that run throughout this book—the growing power of the press over public opinion and modern life and the resulting efforts of religion in various ways to confirm journalists as moral agents.

Chapter 5, "The Sheldon Edition and Journalism's Responsibility to Society," recounts the months-long widely publicized national conversation in 1900 about press responsibility that was sparked by the Reverend Charles Sheldon's serving a weeklong stint editing the *Topeka (KS) Daily Capital* as Jesus would. The experiment was an international sensation that offers a wealth of historical data and uncovers a vein of discourse about the pulpit's, the press's, and the public's notions of the responsibility of the press to society.

Chapter 6, "The Social Gospel and the Mission of Newspapers in the Modern World," considers the influential Social Gospel movement of the late nineteenth and early twentieth centuries. Besides a religious movement, the Social Gospel was a powerful intellectual movement intimately connected with the reform-minded Progressive movement of the era. A chapter is set aside for this movement because its advocates' belief in the immanence of God drew in all the markers of Gilded Age capitalism—including the press—holding that the mission of newspapers should not be replaced by the demands of the market. The advocates of the Social Gospel promoted the primacy of the common weal and rejected notions of extreme individualism.

The final chapter, "Conclusion: The Meanings of Mission," will articulate the meanings of the mission of journalism that stand out from the many decades of debate and discussion. It summarizes the findings and interpretations and discusses the pulpit's critique and its resonance in the twenty-first century—in other words, how much of that critique still acts as a foundation of our contemporary news ethic, and how much of that has been lost or is in danger of being lost in the new upheavals of the twenty-first century?

CHAPTER 1

Six Apostles of the Reformation of Newspapers

I wish we had some of those men who are prophets and apostles of the newspaper era to tell us what is the function of the daily press.

—William I. Fletcher, "Supplying of Current Daily Newspapers in Free Library Reading-Rooms"

MANY OF THE CHRISTIAN PUBLIC intellectuals of the age held a dim view of the newspaper's potential as a vehicle of social change as it then stood. It was, many pastoral critics declared, an institution in need of reform before it could be employed to bring about social change. They argued the newspaper's key mission was to influence social change by advancing public opinion and not merely reflecting it.[1] That was because influencing public opinion was the key to reform. For example, theologian Justin Wroe Nixon maintained that the failure of Prohibition clearly showed that reforms of any kind could not just be commanded but needed a "supporting 'ethos' in society at large."[2] Thus, inspiring the mass-appeal press to help create that ethos was the cornerstone of the criticism of many of those Christian public intellectuals' many sermons, essays, and influential books. And the most prominent of these were the Reverends Lyman Abbott, Washington Gladden, Josiah Strong, Charles Sheldon, and Walter Rauschenbusch and renowned economist Richard T. Ely, a founder and secretary of the Christian Social Union.

This chapter will briefly look at the backgrounds, press criticism, and journalistic theories of these six influential voices of the era. Most of these men had varying degrees of experience in journalism and were prolific writers and primary social diagnosticians of the era whose work represented some of the most articulate and influential criticisms of the secular press over many decades. And their work in journalism could not have helped but bring each of them closer to the struggles of daily life in a changing

America. As one historian has noted, normally a pastor was rarely "brought face to face with conditions in his own congregation which called upon him to consider seriously the problems of a changing society." It was therefore significant that many of the religious leaders of the era had worked as editors. Certainly, Gladden recalled that his own work on a country newspaper in the mid-nineteenth century brought him into close contact with all strata of society and gave him the opportunity to study human nature.[3]

Lyman Abbott

The Reverend Lyman Abbott rose to prominence during the Gilded Age as a well-known advocate of social Christianity and as editor of an influential weekly magazine. His Christian view of life melded—as it did with many reformers who came before and after him—with the grievous effects of the Industrial Revolution. Abbott recalled that his interest in studying the problems of labor in America over many decades grew out of two influences—his work as a reformer concerned with the welfare of his fellow Americans and his work as a journalist dealing with "the most important public question of the time." Abbott as a journalist saw the power of the press done correctly as an ablution for the age, which was, he wrote in his memoirs, a time

> of curious contrasts, of sordid selfishness and of impracticable idealism. Each, by reaction, intensified the other. The unconscious cruelty perpetrated by the current forms of industry made reformers too impatient to consider gradual remedies. The impracticability of their panaceas confirmed the practical business men in their conviction that the injustices of the prevailing industrial system were unavoidable, and the ministerial representatives of the capitalistic system were fond of quoting the text, "The poor ye have with you always," without remembering the addition, "and whensoever ye will ye may do them good."[4]

And as with Gladden, his fellow pastor and journalist, Abbott had much to say about the daily press and how journalism should be conducted. The newspaper, he wrote, had great power as an educator of the American people. And he believed that both the pulpit and the press could be powerful tools for reform and moral uplift, which, when they worked together, "can develop a better public conscience."[5]

Abbott was ordained a minister of the Congregational Church in 1860 but spent much of his career as a journalist. In a roundup of "religious journalism and journalists" in 1895, one writer observed, "The same qualities of mind and heart that have made him successful as a commentator and preacher have given him favor as an editor. He is catholic in spirit, open-minded to truth from any source, indifferent to the approval or disapproval of his fellow men providing his conscience approves, and peculiarly lucid in expressing his thought."[6] Early in his career, Abbott was the general secretary of the American Freedman's Union Commission, which was engaged in Reconstruction activities after the Civil War. Abbott also wrote for the society's monthly publication, the *American Freedman*. He also contributed to *Harper's* magazine, was the New York correspondent for the *Boston Congregationalist*, and wrote for both the *Independent* and the *Christian Union*, as well as other papers. Abbott's editorial career began with the *Independent*, a liberal Congregationalist paper founded in 1848. The *Independent* later cast off its connection to the denomination and became a popular and influential national publication that covered an array of religious, social, and cultural topics. In 1876, when he was forty-one years old, Abbott took over the editing reins of the *Christian Union*, which later changed its name to the *Outlook*. He remained the editor there until his death in 1922.

Abbott's interest in the problems of industrialization led to his joining the American Economic Association, founded in 1885 through the leadership of economist Richard T. Ely. Abbott—who influenced the economic thinking of his friend Walter Rauschenbusch, one of the leading lights of the Social Gospel movement[7]—was not alone in his membership. Washington Gladden and twenty-two other ministers helped to establish the association. The group, which reflected a "high degree of evangelical fervor," rejected classical economics and called for a more progressive policy. And as Ira Brown noted in his biography of Abbott, "They likewise declared their conviction that the government should fulfill an important ethical role." Brown also observed that while other religious leaders such as Gladden and Rauschenbusch were stronger adherents to the Social Gospel movement's call for social justice, "Abbott's position as a publicist enabled him to wield perhaps a broader influence," as his editorship of the *Christian Union*—and later the *Outlook*—played a major role in the movement. Abbott's newspaper was the first religious journal to include in its coverage news and discussion about the industrial strife then roiling the nation. Contemporary scholar Susan Curtis has observed that Abbott's leaving the church to join the *Christian Union* onward "gave him a chance to articulate the social gospel, which had important implications for American popular culture." That was a view espoused by the International Congregational Council in 1921, which lauded him as "a prophet who kept before the American people the thought of a new social order motived by Christian ideals" through both his pulpit and his work as a journalist.[8]

Abbott became an early practitioner of the social analytic "new journalism" of the late nineteenth century whose publications offered themselves as venues for discussing, debating, and analyzing the escalating social issues of the day. He once noted that this "new journalism" had its roots in the *Independent*, which "gave voice to the reforming spirit of the day"—most especially its support for the antislavery movement.[9] Renowned preacher Henry Ward Beecher became editor of that publication in 1861, and then after a fallout with management Beecher went on to found the *Christian Union*. Abbott later took over as editor and later renamed it the *Outlook*, which offered a snapshot of the opinions of contemporary religion about the issues and events of the day[10] and which Theodore Roosevelt once observed "desires in every way to represent, to guide aright, and to uphold the interests of those whom Abraham Lincoln called the plain people."[11]

Abbott had his own ideas about what the editorial policy of the *Christian Union* should be and began to gradually transform it from a weekly journal of "generally entertaining and instructive literature" to a weekly periodical that offered the "history and interpretation of current events." That was a change, magazine scholar Frank L. Mott observed, from "the moral and religious to the sociological and political."[12] Abbott began this by changing a regular feature that was essentially a "series of incidental editorial paragraphs into a systematic paragraph history of the week," titled "The Outlook."[13] In July 1893 that became the name of the magazine, indicating that it was changing its emphasis from "religious news and comment to the broader fields of public affairs and arts and letters."[14] The column also differed from other such features in that it was "prophetic rather than historical." That meant, Abbott said, narrating the week's events but also interpreting them in order "to turn the mind of the reader toward the future and help him to see in what direction current history was moving."[15]

By 1902 the *Outlook* reached a circulation of one hundred thousand and held above that for the next twenty years, garnering much influence and respect.[16] From the beginning, it was Abbott's goal to make the "paper Christian without making it either theological or ecclesiastical." In other words, "religious truth" would take on a cast other than discussions and sermonizing about religion, but by creating a paper people would like and "then express in it the truths and sentiments we wish them to imbibe." Abbott was attempting to bring the sacred and secular together and then ground his news ethic in Christian ethics. "Making books or publications too exclusively religious," he argued, "tends in some degree to dissociate religious sentiments and thoughts from the ordinary affairs and avocations of life, whereas it has always seemed to me desirable that the two sets of ideas and feelings should be indissolubly blended."[17]

Abbott held that while press censorship had been abolished in America, the secular newspaper's attendant responsibility to be truthful had yet to come fully to fruition.[18] Freedom of expression, he wrote, "gives us a journalism which does not distinguish between gossip and news" and that is more concerned with sensation than education. Even so, he insisted, the advantages of free expression to a community were worth much more than its disadvantages.[19] Still, more than once Abbott would discuss the malicious methods of journalism. For example, at one point rumor abounded that the *Outlook* was in the pocket of Standard Oil because a close associate of John D. Rockefeller owned stock in the *Outlook* company. Abbott noted, however, that 90 percent of the stock was owned by those who edited and published the publication. The effort by "journalistic prostitutes" to spin these facts into a lie was "an exasperating illustration of the vicious side of American newspaper publishing," he complained.[20]

Brown, the Abbott biographer, has also claimed that Abbott and the *Outlook* were disdainful of the muckrakers, describing muckraking and its literature of exposure as "a curious social and journalistic phenomenon." However, a closer look at what was said in the article titled "A Frenzied Financial Critic" that ran in the *Outlook* reveals a much too broad interpretation on Brown's part. Instead, a close reading of the article from which that quote was taken does reveal another analysis of the "vicious side" of journalism. Abbott was taking to task a series of articles in *Everybody's Magazine* called "Frenzied Finance" by controversial Boston stock promoter Thomas W. Lawson that purported to be an exposé of the workings of Wall Street. Abbott argued that Lawson's articles were "so violent, so sweeping, so undiscriminating, and so irresponsible, that he may justly be said to give his readers the impression that all great financiers and financial institutions are untrustworthy; and thus he fans the flame of class suspicion and hatred. This is why *The Outlook* believes the Lawson articles are unworthy of serious consideration except as a curious social and journalistic phenomenon." Abbott asserted that the series of muckraking articles stemmed from Lawson's love of notoriety and that Lawson—"the partner, agent, and tool of a small group of unscrupulous and vicious financiers"—was at odds with the group for some reason. Thus, Lawson's "craving for notoriety and a seeking for personal revenge are therefore the motives with which he writes, and not a public-spirited desire to serve the people as an unselfish adviser."[21]

This is not unlike the editorial position once taken by one of the most renowned muckraking editors of the early twentieth century, Norman Hapgood of *Collier's* magazine. Hapgood once had the opportunity to publish Upton Sinclair's book *The Jungle* as a serial. The magazine's owner, Robert Collier, wanted to run it, but Hapgood did not. As he explained to Collier, he worried that the book's very style conflicted with the principles and standards of truth that the magazine tried to uphold. He told Collier: "We have quickly made a great reputation for the weekly. In doing it we have used a method that is sensation, but it is our own special kind of sensation. It is the sensation of telling the exact truth about important things—as exact as science itself. Sinclair's sensationalism is of a more familiar type, the sensationalism of exaggeration, of piling on the colors, of saying, if there is blood on the floor of a slaughterhouse, that it is an inch thick, when it isn't." Here, Hapgood and Abbott are expressing the conscience-ridden ideals of a journalism that holds as close to the shore of truth as possible. Their views are not unlike those of William T. Stead whose "purpose was to give a 'soul' to sensational journalism."[22]

Such vicious journalism as Lawson's, Abbott wrote, reached its zenith with the assassination of President William McKinley in 1901 by anarchist Leon Czolgosz.[23] Indeed, journalist and editor Willis Abbot recalled that when he was editor in chief of the *New York Journal*, his paper was at the center of the controversy surrounding William Randolph Hearst's sensational journalism and the president's slaying. Abbot noted that the controversy began after William Goebel, a Democrat who had recently been elected governor of Kentucky, was shot, "and some imp of the perverse" prompted Hearst writer Ambrose Bierce to write the following quatrain:

> The bullet that pierced Goebel's breast
> Cannot be found in all the West.
> Good reason! It is speeding here
> To lay McKinley on his bier.

McKinley was shot a few days after the poem's publication, and "public sentiment raged over this 'incitement to assassination,'" as it became the topic of Sunday sermons and as societies passed critical resolutions and businessmen boycotted the *Journal*, Abbot recalled.[24]

But on a larger scale, Lyman Abbott argued, McKinley's death was more the product of a press-created ethos—of a pattern of "vehement rhetoric in vituperation of the chief magistrate of the nation" that had regularly been appearing in the nation's newspapers. He noted that the newspapers published such abusive accusations as part of a traditional partisan approach to journalism. But in an age when anarchists abounded in the nation, the scathing language of the newspapers' partisans and the "private teachings" of anarchists had congealed into a murderous compound. That is, the newspapers' accusation that McKinley was a tyrant combined with the anarchists' belief that all tyrants must die. Thus, Abbott argued, "The assassination of William McKinley was the ripened fruit of seed sown by lawless tongues in partisan invective which public opinion, regardless of party, should have sternly rebuked."[25]

Still, Abbott saw a place for the press in reform and moral uplift because he believed that as one of the permanent institutions of society, journalism's purpose was "to lift men up, not to drag men down." He believed that while the press certainly had its flaws, it furnished one vital service to reform by holding a "mirror up to American life." It was not always a true mirror but one sometimes out of proportion to reality, like a convex or concave carnival mirror in which the reflection is unrecognizable. Despite that, journalism's great power was to help awaken the public "to self-consciousness."[26] However, Abbott clung to the belief that people still needed to look to the ministry for "instruction in the moral principles of a true social order." Certainly, the editors of the daily press should be "public teachers, but with few exceptions they have abdicated." That abandonment of their mission, he charged, stemmed largely from the fact that money had become the measure of success. Newspapers with the largest circulations and the most advertising lines boasted about these achievements as proof of success, Abbott observed. "Whether it is promoting the moral and intellectual life of its subscribers, whether its advertisements are of things which aid or hinder that life, are questions scarcely considered." The newspapers' view of what constituted success was a metric of the old political economy, Abbott held, which clashed with the ideals of the new political economy. And economic reformers—including Ely—insisted that citizens were not simply cogs and consumers. Instead, the new economy's primary concerns were developing and maintaining society and that it "must deal with man as an intellectual and moral being,—must, in a word, be ethical." But in practice, Abbott wrote, life in America was more in accord with the old political economy, in which "he who has made a fortune we regard successful; he who has lost a fortune we say has failed." To illustrate, Abbott recalled a comment by the editor of a newspaper who asserted during a debate that "the daily paper was organized to make money, and that was what it ought to be organized for." Alas, Abbott lamented, if that was what editors believed, no newspaper could ever be a teacher.[27]

Washington Gladden

As early as 1882, "the father of the Social Gospel," Washington Gladden, pondered the Christianizing of journalism.[28] He observed that religion had yet to establish any influence over the conduct of the "vast enginery of the press," but one day it would do so.[29] Here, we have an early declaration that called for drafting the newspaper into the forces of religion to help in reform, social change, and moral uplift. And, as with Abbott, the economic considerations of newspapers prompted a similar criticism by Gladden. As noted earlier, he held that the drive for profit had led to the newspaper's "lack of prophetism," which was at its most basic a "supreme allegiance to truth." Gladden argued that the goal of a "moral and religious teacher" was not to make money. Once that was the case, the newspaper's true influence vanishes. "The prime condition of success in this calling is that the mercenary motive shall be consciously and manifestly subordinate." But the reality was, he charged, that any editor who would seek to tell the truth in order to make politics or public morals better faced the possibility that the publisher would kill the story. Anyone who knew anything about how newspapers worked knew that profit drove decisions about news content, what Gladden called the "paralysis of the counting-room."[30]

Gladden saw the press as an instrument of social change. Its primary reason for being was its "teaching function" as a tool of reform in an age of reform. Thus, he rejected the presumption that a newspaper was just like any other business—like a dry-goods store or livery stable—whose goals were to make money rather than promote righteousness. How could newspapers be guided by profit and also purport to be "guides of public opinion"? he wondered. "Is it difficult to see that this attempt to insert a teaching function into a business enterprise must somewhat weaken the teaching function?" Still, Gladden knew enough about the powerful political and commercial influences that constrained editors who sought to make their newspaper "an instrument of righteousness." One solution, he offered, required an ethos that readily accepted the power of newspapers as a service to society that would attract public-spirited publishers more concerned with prophetism than profits. "I see not how the newspaper can be a vigorous moral force unless the publisher has convictions," he wrote. He noted that some wealthy young men were becoming public servants as politicians out of a sense of patriotism. Thus, he wondered why some of these same men could not make a career in publishing newspapers that would be both readable and "serviceable to the highest ends."[31]

Gladden's view of the role of newspapers in society was informed by his role as a renowned religious reformer and by his own broad experience as a writer and later editor for numerous publications. In fact, Gladden refuted the allegation that he was just another pastor speaking out on a matter he knew nothing about. Not so, he pointed out. "I was brought up in a newspaper office, and have had, for thirty years, a pretty close connection, editorial or otherwise, with some newspaper or other; the inside history and operation of newspapers, big and little, is not unfamiliar to me; and the information vouchsafed by some of my brethren of the press as to the character and methods of modern journalism is really no news at all." Gladden noted in his memoirs that the many years he spent writing for various newspapers and magazines were in fact a large part of the work of his ministry. Indeed, he believed, the work of journalism rested on the same plane as the ministry, observing that the ministry of Apostles Matthew, John, and Paul was "mainly wrought with the pen."[32]

Gladden's career in journalism began in the mid-nineteenth century. When he was sixteen he worked at a small country weekly, setting type and writing a column of "local miscellany, news, anecdotes, jokes" that was headlined "Vital Statistics."[33] The paper was "the clearing-house of political and social gossip," where sundry kinds of people sought the paper's support for one cause or another.[34] This continued until he went off to college, where he became the senior-class editor of the *Quarterly* of Williams College and the college correspondent for the eminent *Springfield (MA) Republican*. And then during Gladden's first pastorate, the editor of the local newspaper offered him space for a local column.[35] Additionally, during his tenure as a pastor, he edited *Sunday Afternoon: A Magazine for the Household* (later renamed *Good Company*), a socially oriented monthly religious journal that began publication in January 1878. And during his time with that magazine, Gladden's dual role as both clergyman and journalist informed his thinking about journalistic content that would attract readers and at the same time educate them. First, much as Abbott changed the course of the *Christian Union*, Gladden's magazine would not be wholly a religious journal that was largely "devotional or meditative in character." Instead, questions about social problems and the well-being of the nation would be discussed, "but always in their relations to the Kingdom of God."[36]

In 1871 Gladden became religion editor of the *Independent*. He left his parish to go into journalism full-time because he believed working at the religiously oriented paper would give him more influence.[37] However, in his fourth year at the *Independent*, despite the good people he worked with, the highest pay he had ever received, and work that was "more congenial and inspiring" than anything he had ever done, Gladden decided he had to resign over an issue of ethics[38] that involved the publication's practice of running paid advertisements as editorial matter.[39] Such "skillfully disguised" advertisements as news were known in the trade as "reading notices." Gladden noted this was a fairly common practice and that the *Independent* was not, "in this matter, a sinner above all the weekly and daily journals of the period." Indeed, he wrote, "It was not uncommon to discover, in the editorial and news columns of some of these journals, matter which wore the garb of journalistic expression, but which the practiced eye discerned to be simply an advertisement." Still, he insisted, literary and editorial columns with which he worked were free of this kind of matter. In fact, only once during his time at the *Independent* did the business manager try to insert a reading notice in the editorial notes, "and the insurrection which that provoked brought a promise that it should never occur again." Finally, though, Gladden resigned his position and wrote a note to the publisher that began, "I cannot think as you do about those departments. They seem to me essentially evil, and a source of weakness to the paper. My scruple may be a foolish one, but I cannot overcome it. It is quite true that most of the other papers have something of the same sort, but if the thing is wrong, that is no excuse." Gladden recalled in his memoirs that it was his belief in the "sacredness of the newspaper as a public teacher, and of the grave immorality of perverting its function for hire," that prompted his resignation.[40]

That experience in itself shows us Gladden dealing early on with an issue he would raise as a theme of his later criticism of the secular press—the commercial priority of the modern newspaper intruding on the teaching function of a public servant. However, commercial reading notices bothered Gladden less than newspapers' efforts to mislead public opinion—the impulse for which rested in both market and partisan constraints. He recalled in 1909 that the use of reading notices had largely abated over the years. Yet he had still seen signs over the previous decade "of subterranean methods" in which the press was subsidized in order to mislead people. "Beyond a question large quantities of what purports to be reading-matter are supplied to the journals of the country by interested parties, and paid for by the line. Certain great corporations pay large sums of money for influencing, in this manner, public opinion." In comparison to the contemporary "vast schemes to deceive people," Gladden observed in 1909, "the disguised advertising of *The Independent* in the olden time was a venial offense."[41] The problem rested, Gladden observed, in the fact that newspapers spoke "in the interest of capital" in offering "one-sided and distorted representations" of labor's side of any issue.[42] That practice was especially grating, he wrote, because the press had become the key agent in creating public opinion, and the nation's well-being depended on an untainted public opinion. That role in telling the truth was sacred, he asserted. But when it becomes "an instrument for misleading the people, it becomes the worst of our public enemies."[43] Similarly, he became disenchanted with the "narrowly partisan" stance the *Independent* took during the election of 1872 in which the paper supported Ulysses S. Grant and often treated Horace Greeley unfairly. Gladden felt that those readers who depended on the paper to know about the policies and purposes of the other party were "seriously misled" by the paper. "That the religious influence of the paper must be impaired by such political methods, I could not help seeing." And while he protested to the powers that be, he had little influence on their policy.[44]

It is apparent in Gladden's writings why he believed in the instrumentality of the press in efforts at reform. It stemmed from seeking a remedy to the ill effects on society spawned by rampant industrialism. The remedy required not just a more enlightened government, which could not do everything, but more important "the application by individuals of Christian principles and methods to the solution of the social problem." However, Gladden recognized even as early as 1886 that while Christianity was often held up as a curative for society's ills, the fact was that a large swath of the population never attended church, and thus religion had no influence on their conduct. While this segment of the population was still a minority, he observed, it was a "minority large enough to cause us anxiety and to furnish us one of our hardest problems."[45] Thus, other means had to be found to reach these people. And, Gladden wrote, the principal means of doing so was to employ the secular press of America.

In an address to newspaper people in Kansas in 1914, Gladden entwined the newspaper industry of the day to religion's attempts to create what he called a "Republic of God" that is revealed by "those men and women who freely work together to make a better world of this." The principal factor that bound journalism to those efforts was "public opinion," Gladden asserted. And the responsibility for creating a "good, healthy public opinion" rested most strongly on the pulpit and the press—and probably more so on the press. However, Gladden offered a litany of complaints about the press, and the first of these were the "vice of extravagance, of exaggeration," and the widespread habit of overstating the facts. This was a grievance not unlike the positions Lyman Abbott and Norman Hapgood took on the distortion of reality by exaggeration. Such habits were detrimental to creating a reliable public opinion, Gladden warned. "We must learn, if we would prosper as a self-governing commonwealth, to see things as they are, and tell the truth about them." But, Gladden worried, he could not see how that would ever happen until the newsrooms of America adopted "a different code" of conduct in the reporting of the news.[46]

Josiah Strong

To understand the times in which the role of the newspaper was seen as central to the debate over reform, one needs to look no further than the Reverend Josiah Strong, a Protestant pastor, social reformer, editor, and influential sociological writer. He was once described as one of the "prophets of the new social message"[47] and included among his friends Washington Gladden, Walter Rauschenbusch, Rabbi Stephen Wise, Richard T. Ely, and Theodore Roosevelt. One scholar, in considering Strong's study of and writings about urban life in America, has described him as a "prophet of the twentieth-century city."[48] And one of the core themes of his book *The New Era; or, The Coming Kingdom* (1893) is the Social Gospel concern for what Walter Lippmann called the "acids of modernity"—especially industrialization, immigration, literacy, and urbanization—and their dissipation of the moral ground of America in which rapacious, unregulated capitalism had found root.[49]

From 1871 to 1873, Strong learned about the lower rungs of life while working as a missionary for the Congregational church in the Wyoming frontier town of Cheyenne. It was a place then called "Hell on Wheels," where "the scum of the earth followed the builders of the Pacific railway" and where the ratio of prostitutes to the population made it a "worse city than London, Paris or New York." Strong called his time there an "instructive experience"[50] that "convinced him of the need for a social gospel." That view was later accentuated by his work as a pastor in the industrial cities of Sandusky and Cincinnati, Ohio.[51] Thus, Strong echoed the Social Gospel critics of the ethos of the dominant old political economy. He described its laissez-faire approach as a "euphemism for Cain's famous, or rather infamous, answer, 'Am I my brother's keeper?'"[52] But it was this economically driven disconnectedness that confronted what Strong saw as the realities of life in American society. Instead, like his friend Ely and other progressives and advocates of the Social Gospel, he promoted the organic notion of the interdependence of society.[53] And that notion was a key fixture in his argument that the press assist in the informing of public opinion because the printing press had created an intellectual revolution by bringing "mind into contact with mind"—a media-driven notion of a community of people that runs through much of his work.[54]

Strong's faith in the truthful newspaper's role in reform echoes the Progressive Era's emphasis on science and facts. Indeed, one scholar has noted that other reformers and others in the Social Gospel movement cited Strong as among the first to promote "the social significance of statistics and factual information." For example, Strong once declared, "Facts are God's alphabet, from which we may decipher tendencies, and tendencies are prophetic."[55] He also argued that science's great facility was to expunge the "rubbish which lay in the path of progress. The scientific habit of mind is fatal to credulity and superstition; it rests not on opinions, but facts; it is loyal, not to authority, but truth."[56] After Strong's death in 1916, the Reverend Graham Taylor, a social reformer and founder of the Chicago Commons Settlement House, paid tribute to Strong as "a mediator of the new covenant between facts and faith."[57]

As early as 1885, Strong published a book titled *Our Country: Its Possible Future and Its Present Crisis*, which one scholar described as "the most spectacular avowedly social gospel book of the entire movement."[58] It went on to become one of the best nonfiction sellers of a decade that saw the publication of Edward Bellamy's *Looking Backward* and Henry George's *Progress and Poverty*.[59] In it he argued that civilization brought "men into closer contact" and that within the confines of the modern world, the press was one of three "great civilizing" agents of the age—the others being Christianity and steam. Each was purging society of diversity and creating in its stead a sense of oneness with the "bringing of men into closer and multiplied relations."

Thus, Christianity was slowly creating a brotherhood of men, aided by a press that had produced a worldwide "audience room" and the steam engine that had "annihilated . . . nine-tenths of space."[60]

A constant theme of Strong's that ran as a thread through many of his writings was his belief in progress and the power of public opinion as an armature of societal change—and especially reform and progress. For instance, he stressed in a book on the reform of the city (1911) that public opinion "creates and amends constitutions; it makes laws, and determines whether or not they shall be enforced; it shapes national policies, domestic and foreign."[61] In 1900 he argued that there then existed a new "world public opinion, which is the natural outgrowth of the daily newspaper." Looking back before the wide circulation of the press, Strong wrote, only a few people ever thought about the same things at the same time as the news crept "from mouth to ear" and from nation to nation. But by the turn of the century, hundreds of millions of people were "thinking at the same time of the same thing."[62] And then three years later, Strong observed that the press had grown so powerful that it was creating "a climate of opinion which is becoming ever wider." Echoing Alexis de Tocqueville's early-nineteenth-century observation that American newspapers deposited "the same thought in a thousand minds at once," Strong noted that now millions of people "read the same printed page and think the same thoughts." Thus, more and more Americans lived "in the same intellectual world."[63]

Strong once cited a passage from George Washington's Farewell Address in which the president observed, "In proportion as the structure of a government gives force to public opinion, it is essential that public opinion should be enlightened." Thus, Strong held, since public opinion was the superstructure of democratic government, "it is imperative that public opinion and the popular conscience be enlightened."[64] Strong believed that the primary social mission of the church was reform and that progress in that mission was not solely the pulpit's responsibility. It also required the cooperation of the press in educating public opinion. The pulpit needed that cooperation because in the modern age, the press had extended the definition of publicity, which, in turn, had increased its influence on society. In a bit of high-flown rhetoric not uncommon for the times that well illustrates his view of the power of public opinion and the moral suasive power of the press in collaboration with the pulpit, Strong declared, "When the popular conscience is properly educated, public opinion like the sun is found to have its rays of heat as well as of light. And when they are focalized by pulpit or press on some iniquity, and steadily held there as by a mighty burning-glass, that evil, no matter how deeply intrenched in human ignorance and prejudice and selfishness it may be, will at length scorch and writhe and smoke and blaze and consume away."[65]

But in addition to the problems of the industrial order, he held, the complexity of modern life was overwhelming. And the press only exacerbated this complexity, leaving the public perplexed by the many details of life it published. The newspaper, he observed, "distorts or destroys our perspective; it fixes attention on the happenings of the hour and passes before the mind a rapidly shifting panorama—a sort of continuous presentation of perpetually dissolving views, which to the average mind is a meaningless jumble of events."[66] These factors, Strong argued, were only exacerbated by the downturn in attendance in the nation's churches, where much of the population once received instruction. Strong argued that empty pews stemmed from the invasion of "Continental ideas of the Sabbath" and the hurried pace of life that left Sunday as a day of rest but not worship. All of this combined to diminish the pulpit's traditional sway over public opinion. "The pulpit once afforded the people most of their intellectual, as well as spiritual, stimulus." Now, he complained, it had to compete with books, periodicals, and newspapers, especially those published on Sunday morning. Given that falloff in the pulpit's influence, Strong echoed Gladden's call for a journalism of interpretation and advocacy not unlike the literature of exposure of the muckrakers' efforts. He argued that the "social wrongs, the industrial abuses, and the nameless evils which now thrive in secret" must somehow be revealed to those not cognizant but with the power to help right them. Such an education would undoubtedly prompt Christians to protest "until public sentiment was aroused; and in this country public sentiment is only less mighty than omnipotence."[67] But Strong was still concerned whether journalism was up to the task. For instance, just as his friend Gladden complained that the modern profit-driven newspaper lacked "prophetism," Strong asserted, "When the object in publishing a paper is to serve the public good, journalism is a profession, and the editor an educator. But when that object is simply to make money, journalism becomes a business, not a profession, and the editor a mere caterer, who aims to tickle the appetite of the public."[68]

Richard T. Ely

One of the key issues that religion in the late nineteenth and early twentieth centuries sought to address was the labor strife coeval with the era. And few focused more on the issue of labor than economist Richard T. Ely. He was, as one contemporary scholar has called him, the "lay spokesman for the Social Gospel."[69] Lyman Abbott observed that Ely was the first American "to treat economics as a human study; the first one to regard the industrial problem as one, not of labor and capital, but of laborers and capitalists; the first one to become personally acquainted with workingmen, to attend their meetings—I believe joining a labor union—to consider them not as machines supposedly governed solely by self-interest, but as men with wives and children, homes and aspirations, and, like other men, governed by a great variety of conflicting motives." Both progressives and the advocates of the Social Gospel viewed society as an organism, which lent credence to their emphasis on the interdependence of all people in that society. Ely described this notion as "social solidarity" and devoted an entire chapter of his book *The Social Law of Service* (1896) to the topic. And in a presentation to the World's Congress of Churches in 1893, he asserted that "Christianity means social solidarity or it means nothing." By social solidarity, he meant "the recognition of the identity of all human interests," in which each person acknowledged that they were part of an organic humanity. Ely believed that such things as art, music, literature, religion, and language were all "social products." And he held that literature—and we can assume he includes the newspaper under this term—"makes epochs when in a writer the national life pulsates and through him the nation speaks."[70]

Ely, who once taught Woodrow Wilson economics,[71] was the most well-known economist of the era and one of the founders of the American Economic Association. In 1892 Ely became director of the University of Wisconsin's new School of Economics, Political Science, and History, which eventually gained much renown as it became connected with the state's Progressive movement.[72] And he was one of the prime instigators of the nationwide Progressive movement because, one writer declared, Ely was the "first man to oppose in this country the old order of things—individualism, laissez faire, and all that."[73] Indeed, Ely believed that the economic situation of his time demanded a "wider diffusion of sound ethics." He rejected Herbert Spencer's ethical system of "laissez-faire politics" and "extreme individualism." Ely described this system as immoral because it promoted the notion that "we are not keepers of our brothers."[74]

In 1886 in *Report of the Organization of the American Economic Association*, Ely outlined his indictments of classical economics, which he called "palpably an unchristian science, for it has been avowedly organized selfishness. It is based on the assumption that the only motive for human action in trade and commerce worth considering is the motive of self-interest."

The old school, he insisted, was also unscientific. Its advocates and theorists failed to make an attempt to determine how people actually conduct themselves. Instead, the old school relied on philosophizing on the results as long as their actions comported with certain agreed-upon rules. On the other hand, the new school of political economy represented by the American Economic Association was scientific because it pursued knowledge through induction. It did so by gathering statistical and historical information and then "educing the laws of human action from a wide observation of phenomena, as the laws of nature have been educed since the days of Bacon."

Still, Ely wrote, the new political economy had yet to begin to influence public opinion as it should. One reason was that few prominent secular daily or weekly papers recognized "Christian principle or extended, pains-taking observation in the treatment of industrial and sociological questions."[75] Here, Ely offered a critique of the news ethic of secular journalistic conduct and content, which he found wholly inadequate to the demands of the times. In response, Ely was a great proponent of labor newspapers, and he believed if someone wanted to understand labor organizations, he should not rely on the "garbled newspaper accounts."[76] He cited the hostility of the daily press toward the labor movement. Instead, he believed that obstacles to improving conditions for workers could be overcome by increasing the number of workingmen's papers. Ely cautioned that by relying solely on the daily press to understand the labor situation and the plight of the worker, a reader would get only one side of the story. "Could you know both sides, your opinion would frequently be quite different about alleged misdoings of laborers. He who would follow both sides must take a labor paper." That was because, Ely complained, during controversies between employers and employees, the daily press would clearly give the side of employers but just the "garbled reports" of the employees that presented a seeming picture of journalistic impartiality and ended in readers damning "the laboring classes, and all their wicked organizations."[77]

The implication in this indictment was that the press had been corrupted by power. Indeed, more than once, Ely complained that the pages of the newspapers could be bought by the powerful to the detriment of the public. And thus, he held, the public had begun to have misgivings about the press because the interests of corporations and not the public interest dictated the news. The facts to show this were clear, he insisted. For instance, a newspaper controlled by corporations did not set the record straight but added to the confusion. It created "false issues," and it sullied the reputations of those "who are zealously endeavoring to promote the public weal."[78] For example, in the struggle over public and private utilities, if a private corporation supplied electricity to a community, that company's stock would be distributed "where it will do the most good"—to influential citizens, politicians, and the owners of newspapers.[79] Ely also indicted journalists who accepted railroad passes as an example of public corruption[80] because they were expected to later "render valuable services in editorial articles." At another point, he wrote, "Few, perhaps, realize how perfectly developed are the means which have been found to guard special and private interests when these are antagonistic to the public welfare." Railroad passes and paid advertisements were just two ways industry—in this case the railroads—induced "newspapers to twist and pervert public opinion for private interests."[81]

Ely also believed that newspapers that appealed "to the worst passions of the wealthy, teaching them to despise, distrust, and resist the humble social classes, are as dangerous as the incendiary sheets of the Anarchists, and should be unhesitatingly condemned and discountenanced by all who mean well."[82] And the harm from such depictions had ramifications beyond the moment but spread through society. Ely said the press, by failing to adequately give the full story from both sides, was creating "different psychical worlds" and a "clearly cut social cleavage." This was especially put into stark relief whenever there was a strike. He observed that those who read the daily newspapers had a worldview quite contrary from the view of those who read the labor press. That was because diametrically opposed viewpoints would appear in the daily press and in the labor papers, and "what appears black to the one is white to the other." Ely was willing to grant that different classes within a society could have good effects. The good came from diversity fostering the development of different gifts and talents, creating a "rich and diversified civilization." Still, they were inherently evil because their "natural tendency is, as they become sharply differentiated, to separate man from his fellows; and this is a bad thing."[83] Ely's concern here was that newspapers—enthralled to the constraints of the market—failed in their mission to help foster a Christianized, communitarian society. Thus, the press created disjuncture between classes and nurtured differentiation, a violation of the "permanent truths" of the Social Gospel—"social justice" and "the brotherhood of man."[84]

Charles M. Sheldon

One theme of much of the pastoral criticism of the press called not so much for a structural change in the newspaper but for newspaper editors and reporters to make moral decisions grounded in responsibility to society about what they reported and how they reported stories bound for the paper.[85] One such divine who was actually able to put his theories to the test was the Reverend Charles M. Sheldon, "one of the earliest and most consistent advocates of a better press."[86] A Congregationalist minister in Topeka, Kansas, Sheldon was well known nationally as a pastor and a writer of sermon novels and for his persistent call for establishing a Christian daily newspaper, which came to be known as the "Sheldon idea."[87] And in fact, he became famous worldwide by overseeing the *Topeka Capital* for a week in March 1900 as Jesus would have if he had been in the newspaper business. A later chapter will explore his stint at the *Capital* because it reveals much about the then contemporary criticism of the newspaper.

Sheldon was a graduate of Brown University and Andover Theological Seminary. During his time in the seminary, he wrote for the *Youth's Companion* and did such a fine job that Lyman Abbott offered him a department in the *Outlook* that he could make of what he wanted. But Sheldon turned down the job because he wanted to preach.[88] He began his ministry in Vermont as pastor of the Waterbury Congregational Church, and then three years later in 1889 he arrived as pastor of a Topeka Congregational church. He came to his new assignment having been much influenced by both the principles of the Social Gospel and his contact with the downtrodden of the industrial age. Before moving to Kansas, he worked in a settlement house in London, and then in Topeka he spent time with the city's working class, even to the point of wearing work clothes and looking for a job as a laborer. Both experiences affected him deeply and opened his eyes to the very uprootedness of a new age. In 1900 in an address to the Boston Congregational Club, Sheldon looked back fifty years at the world his father dealt with as a minister. It was a much simpler and less complex existence—both in society and at home. "It was not an age of organization," and aside from the slavery question, there were no outstanding social problems that would inform his preaching like there were in 1900.[89] But that simpler existence had certainly changed. Sheldon later recalled in his autobiography, "The thing lay on me like a monstrous burden that seemed more than I could bear. I believe that at that time in my experience I felt, as I have often wished I could feel again with the same intensity, the horrible blunder and stupidity of our whole industrial system. . . . I felt the isolation of the preacher and the minister from the great world of labor."[90]

From those experiences and the view that modern business methods driven solely by profit were largely unchristian, Sheldon drew several conclusions about the role of the newspaper in society. They included that while it was powerful, it was not Christian, and there were no Christian dailies in the United States, which sorely needed them; newspapers had no conception of what news was; there was too much written about too many things, and most of it was badly written; the newspaper played a larger role in the lives of people than the church; working people read newspapers, and those newspapers had a great influence on them; and, in addition, regular churchgoers spent more time reading newspapers than they did religious reading matter.[91]

The public was aware of Sheldon through his writings, lectures, and series of sermon novels, including the best seller *In His Steps: "What Would Jesus Do?"* One episode in the book involved an editor's attempt to publish a newspaper "as Jesus would do it." Through that editor Sheldon revealed his ideas about how to edit a newspaper by rejecting sensationalism and yellow journalism—which then was at its height—society news, sporting events (especially boxing), and advertising for any item (for example, liquor) that could injure a reader. In chapter 17 of *In His Steps*, the editor, Edward Norman, writes eleven rules of conduct to follow in running a newspaper as Jesus would. Given the fact that Sheldon wrote this as part of a story sermon delivered at church, one cannot divorce the author from his writing but assume this is a distillation of Sheldon's thoughts about newspapers, especially given his public and published statements about the press in America. The rules held that the guiding principle of the paper would "always be the establishment of the Kingdom of God in the world," and to do so they called for the paper to seek purity in every sentence and picture; to be nonpartisan and look at all political questions through the lens of the Kingdom of God and always considering "What is Right?"; to subscribe to a mission that would marginalize the seeking after profit and political influence, and instead act as a minister or missionary doing Christian work; to reject "questionable advertisements"; to "give large space to the work of the Christian world" and devote space to reform; "to fight the saloon as an enemy of the human race"; to not issue a Sunday edition; and to publish news "people ought to know" and to reject news of such things as "brutal prize-fights," long stories about crime, and the scandals of private families.[92] It was that novel and a speech Sheldon gave in 1899 expressing the need for a Christian daily newspaper that prompted the publisher of the *Daily Capital* in Topeka to invite him to edit his paper and make decisions about news and advertising grounded in that ideal.[93] The experiment drew much interest and became an international sensation.[94]

A constant theme of Sheldon's criticism during his career was that the newspaper owed "a debt to civilization which it ought to pay." For too long, he wrote, religion and individual citizens had borne the responsibility for "the regeneration of mankind." But that job was bigger than both, said Sheldon. Instead, he saw the press and its power over public opinion as an agency of moral uplift, but one that was constantly in arrears.[95] Similarly, during a symposium in 1915 in response to the question of whether a newspaper should surrender to commercial interests and give its readers what they wanted, he responded, "The daily paper, the magazine, and every other periodical, have just as much of a duty to give the people the thing they need instead of what they want, as the minister has to give his people what they need instead of what they want." He then went on to note his persistent theme about the daily press that "the printed page today is under the high command of God to help regenerate the world."[96]

Walter Rauschenbusch

A later light of the Social Gospel movement was "its greatest exponent," the Reverend Walter Rauschenbusch, a professor at the Rochester Theological Seminary from 1897 until his death in 1918.[97] Early on, his views of the problems of society derived from his work as a pastor in Kentucky and then from 1886 to 1897 in New York's Hell's Kitchen, where he saw the crowded, unsanitary living conditions of the poor and downtrodden as well as predatory, profit-driven capitalism's exploitation of labor—especially women and children. He was also influenced by such social theorists as Jacob Riis, George Herron, Henry George, and Richard T. Ely. Historian Charles Howard Hopkins describes Rauschenbusch as "the greatest prophet of the social gospel." And a later scholar has observed that in his twelve books, the Social Gospel as he saw it could be summarized in just eight words: "the righteous rule of God in human affairs."[98] But within many of his writings, a constant theme is a condemnation of the press influenced by the powerful industrial interests that he believed were the root cause of much of the ills of society.[99] He once observed that the commercialization of nearly every aspect of life had created "a fierce competitive thirst for wealth" that had focused "all minds on money, and accordingly all callings which serve the intellectual and spiritual life have dropped in the relative importance and honor assigned to them."[100] Rauschenbusch viewed modern society as organic, and he likened the daily press to the body's nervous system that "registers the facts, communicates them to the centers concerned, and spreads before the community the data on which public action must be based." But, he held, if the press intentionally made false statements or colored the truth at the behest of some controlling power, "then it breaks faith with the public and becomes a treacherous force to be watched." This organicism stems from Rauschenbusch's rejection of the notion of an individualistic society. Instead, he saw it becoming through the forces of modernity more interdependent—less like "a colony of mollusks" and more "like the body of a man." Thus, society's individuals must "live by faith in one another" because of all the modern complexities of life.[101]

Rauschenbusch defined sin as selfishness in that it had a "social dimension" entwined in the social institutions around us.[102] At one point, he lamented that the moral foundation of civilization was covetousness, whose effect on science led to new ways of killing, whose effect on finance led to new ways of stealing, and whose effect on newspapers led to learning "how to bear false witness artistically to a globeful of people daily."[103] That covetousness—what he called "the business point of view"—led to a "surrender of the human point of view, a relaxing of the sense of duty, and a willingness to betray the public if it pays."[104] In doing so—in stating falsehoods or coloring the truth and thus creating a tainted public opinion—the press violated the public's trust and "commits a crime against the common good."[105] Rauschenbusch's core belief was that "social ills are bred in the unchristianized areas of modern life, notably in the business world."[106] Indeed, Rauschenbusch saw newspapers as part of a cabal of raw capitalistic institutions wreaking ill upon society. He once cited a well-known Midwest editor who told the press association of his state, "There is not a man in the United States today who has tried honestly to do anything to change the fundamental conditions that make for poverty, disease, vice, and crime in our great cities, in our courts and in our legislatures, who, at the very time at which his efforts seemed most likely to succeed, has not been suddenly turned upon and rent by the great newspaper publications."[107]

In *Christianity and the Social Crisis* (1907)—which Justin Wroe Nixon, a theologian and a former student and colleague of Rauschenbusch, described as "perhaps the most influential of all the books of the social-gospel movement"—Rauschenbusch weaves a constant indictment of the press in America and its ill effects on society.[108] In it he echoes Gladden's earlier contention that "some newspapers are directly in the pay of certain interests and are their active champions." That was because the policies of the counting room influenced the newspapers' editorial policy, which meant that advertisers could "muzzle most papers," he charged. Rauschenbusch then offered a litany of examples. For instance, after an election in Chicago in 1902 when "an astonishing majority" of voters passed a referendum requiring municipal ownership of street railways and the gas and electric utilities, both the Associated Press and the New York dailies printed hardly a word about a significant vote representing public opinion about the issue of public ownership. He also noted that after the presidential election of 1892 when the Populist Party was a major factor, he scanned the New York dailies but could find no mention about the votes the party received. And after the presidential election of 1904 in which the Socialist Party "vote took its first large leap forward," he journeyed across several states but could not find one newspaper that informed its readers of the statistics of the party's vote.

But aside from politics, Rauschenbusch pointed to an example dealing with the power of commercial interests over the press. He noted one anecdote related to the New York Legislature's consideration of a mercantile inspection bill, which, among other things, called for the state labor department to be given the power to enforce the child labor law in department stores in major cities. While the bill was before the legislature, one of the major newspapers often published articles and interviews opposing the bill from the department stores' point of view. A friend of Rauschenbusch's who supported the proposed law asked a friend on the staff of the paper if his publication, out of fairness, could not print an interview on the other side. "The man replied, 'Certainly, that is only fair, I will go and arrange for it.'" But instead, the friend was told that "the counting-room" had ordered that nothing favorable about the bill be printed. "Now," Rauschenbusch wrote, "the justice and efficiency of democratic government depend on the intelligence and information of the citizens." If newspapers intentionally mislead those citizens through distortion or suppression of important information, he argued, "the innermost life of our republic is in danger."[109]

And then in 1912, in his influential *Christianizing the Social Order*, Rauschenbusch reiterated those charges, contending that "the newspaper, like all the other higher organs of social life, has gradually come under the control of capitalistic organization and methods." He observed that the time of the great editors such as Greeley, Dana, Halstead, and Medill, who used their papers as instruments of their convictions and the power of newspapers "to lead the people," was nearly gone. Instead, yellow journalism pandered "to the love of excitement and sex passion to increase sales," and otherwise the journalist was the corporations' "hired man" and was dictated to by the paper's advertisers. And because readers had come to have no trust in the paper's editorials, Rauschenbusch asserted, the papers had taken to doctoring the news. He charged that important events involving reformers were ignored or barely covered, while news stories about opposition to "public ownership or direct legislation are so full of facts and so carefully written that we wonder what man in that newspaper office turned out such material, or whether perhaps it was furnished by the press bureau of some big Interest."[110]

And like Gladden and so many other pastoral critics, in many of his writings Rauschenbusch highlighted the power of public opinion and its importance to societal reform. But he observed in *Christianity and the Social Crisis*, "The predatory interests are tampering with the organs which create public opinion." And those interests' efforts were made easy by the fact that journalists had "been 'commercialized' to their inner loss." Thus, he lamented, "The daily press, public opinion, custom, literature, orthodox economic science, and nearly all the forces which shape thought, are on the side of things as they are."[111] Rauschenbusch hinged the need for untainted information to the survival and growth of society. "Publicity and a clear recognition of the facts," he wrote, "have become as essential to the body politic in its complex modern life as free and unobstructed action of the brain is to the physical body. But that is what the great private interests do not want. They invariably resist investigation and seek to paralyze all private and public agencies of scrutiny and publicity."[112]

Rauschenbusch was familiar with this power dynamic from his own work with the laboring classes and his research and writing about the problems of society. One example of this came from his work on the monthly newspaper *For the Right* that he and Baptist minister Leighton Williams began in 1889. Here, again, we have a major pastoral critic of the press working in journalism and then drawing on that experience to inform his views of the modern newspaper. *For the Right* was published between November 1889 and March 1891, and Rauschenbusch used the pages of the periodical to express his views on economic, industrial, and labor issues; on politics; on socialism; on society; on state insurance; on religion and the separation of church and state; and on the Kingdom of God. He also used it to warn about the power of the press and the other agencies that helped create public opinion. For example, he pointed to a new New York City newspaper called the *Daily Recorder* that purported to be independent of any influence on its content. But when the paper began to regularly laud the state's railroad interests, he began to suspect that claim of independence, warning readers that it was clear that the paper was nothing more than a mouthpiece for the railroads and big business that were undoubtedly supporting it.[113]

Ultimately, Rauschenbusch was a reformer but believed that reformers must be reformed themselves before they could succeed in their endeavors. For instance, his pastoral response to the ill conduct of newspapers and newspapermen was a prayer that they reform and see the light. In *For God and the People: Prayers of the Social Awakening* (1910), he composed a prayer titled "For Writers and Newspaper Men." In it God is beseeched to inspire in journalists "a stanch hatred for the making of lies" so that they would not be "used in drugging the mind of the people with falsehood and prejudice" and not pervert the nation. God is also asked to open the eyes of journalists so they could see that "they have a public function in the commonwealth" in which they are "servants of the higher law."[114]

CHAPTER 2

The Sunday Newspaper and the Modern World

> **If there is any sadder sight in nature than a man deliberately sitting down to wallow in a "sextuple" Sunday newspaper, we do not know what it is. The Puritans devised no such tortures for their Sabbath.**
>
> —Rollo Ogden, "Americanizing the English Press"

FROM AROUND 1814 TO 1816, an antiquarian named Ellcee was staying with a friend in the Islington district of London. Each week on Sunday after church services and if the weather was good, Ellcee's friend would say, "Now, my boy, we'll go the round of the papers." Then the two would head off to the Strand, and sometimes to Fleet Street, where the national newspapers were located, reading along the way the billboards headlining the latest news or advertising later editions. "This was a period of great excitement and impatience for news from abroad," he recalled. "When anything important was expected on Sundays the Strand was often thronged, often crowded, by people waiting for second and third editions till late at night." Ellcee's friend counseled him that the *Sunday Observer* and the *Englishman* were the only Sunday journals they could rely on "for original and authentic information." Ellcee recalled several Sundays amid the Hundred Days during Emperor Napoléon I of France's return from exile on Elba to Paris when the demand for news from Europe reached a fever pitch. Large crowds gathered outside the newspaper offices hungry for the latest news, leading to "terrible struggling to get copies" of the *Observer* and *Englishman* as they came out. And on days they made it as far as Fleet Street, the two companions would head to the Chapter Coffee House where they could read the papers.[1]

For our purposes, the key to this narrative was the day each week these two friends would begin their "round of the papers"—Sunday. To the present mind, there is little untoward about traveling about town, socializing at a coffee shop, and reading newspapers after attending church. However, the two friends' weekly adventure belies the invective such behavior and the very Sunday newspapers they sought provoked among the clergy and traditionalists protective of the notion of an inviolable Sabbath. This "profanation of the Sabbath-day" was, one clergyman railed in 1822, a "national wickedness" that had to be suppressed.[2] Two years before the expression of this clergyman's wrath, John Poynder, a British lawyer and theological writer, had already begun the work to suppress. He published an entire book on the "divine origin, and perpetual obligation, of the Sabbath" and on how the Sunday newspaper violated the Sabbath to the detriment of the nation. "These Papers are emptying our Churches and filling our public houses. They are demoralizing and secularizing the minds of thousands, who would otherwise be 'rendering to God the things that are Gods.' . . . These Journals excite and keep alive a spirit of impiety, insubordination, and discontent," he argued. His book included a short address he sent to every member of Parliament. In it Poynder accused the Sunday newspapers of causing both "infidelity and irreligion" and "disloyalty and sedition." These and similar condemnations in the 1820s were early volleys in a decades-long struggle against the Sunday newspaper in both Britain and America that would extend into the twentieth century. But most certainly, the Sunday newspaper found "its most congenial home" in the United States, as John Charlton, a Canadian member of Parliament, observed in 1896. The Sunday paper's effect on religious and moral life had been "disastrous." It was, Charlton charged, just as renowned newspaper editor Horace Greeley had described it, a "social demon" because it "secularizes the Sabbath."[3]

This, then, is the subject of this chapter—the decades-long conflict between the established traditions of religion and the modern juggernaut that was the Sunday newspaper. And it is not too much to say it was a juggernaut. For instance, in 1882, one writer observed that the Sunday paper had begun only "yesterday, yet it has spread like prairie-fires, until it has captured nearly every city in the land."[4] And in 1894, the Reverend Alexander MacKay Smith, the archdeacon of New York, sadly recognized that the Sunday paper had by then become a "permanent feature of our landscape." Driven by the lure of profit, he lamented, newspaper proprietors had created and foisted on the reading public "this Frankenstein of the century, the fifty-page Sunday issue, to bewilder, to fascinate, to at last overpower and enslave, the ninety-nine out of every hundred."[5] Smith also warned that "the Sunday newspaper has arisen within a generation" and was "one of the greatest dangers to the Churches which has ever threatened them."[6]

To that point, historian John Ferré has described the turn-of-the-century Protestant critics' realization that the Sunday newspaper was "a sign of Protestantism's diminishing authority over the American polity." And Jeffery A. Smith has observed that Sunday newspapers were at the core of a struggle in the late nineteenth century over the rationale for observation of the Sabbath.[7] These facts alone certainly led to much consternation reflected in the discussions and debates about the Sabbath and the Sunday paper. However, that the discussion and debate over many decades of struggle ultimately end in the general acceptance of the Sunday newspaper as a part of society is only part of the story. Within that discourse are issues surrounding the tension between the secular and the sacred as an armature of the struggle between the forces of modernity and those opposed to the destabilizing of traditions—reflected most substantively in the Sunday newspaper's expansive redefinition of news. Indeed, the Sunday newspaper was a vehicle of modernity that offered sustenance to a growing modern sensibility.

For example, let's return to our introductory vignette. First, it tells us something about the generalization that people within a modern society have an almost instinctual, genomic hunger for news. Indeed, as Whitelaw Reid, the longtime editor of the *New York Tribune*, observed, people simply have a constant "craving to know" what is going on in their world. And as Pamela Shoemaker has hypothesized, we are "hard-wired for news" because of the evolutionary advantage of our proclivity for surveilling our environment. Our author describes scenes on the streets of London not unlike the public clamoring for news a century later in both Britain and America for the four days after the sinking of the *Titanic*, when little or no news was available. Another illustration comes from French author and journalist Max O'Rell who recalled in 1890 being on a steamer a hundred miles off the coast of America when the pilot boarded his ship with a stack of New York papers. "After being dead to the world for nearly a fortnight, we passengers pounced upon them." Still, if we spend a bit more time with this narrative about this journey through the streets of London and beyond the newsmongers to the Chapter Coffee House, we hear the soundings of a defeudalized modern world in which, as Habermas contended, "the privatized individuals coming together to form a public also reflected critically and in public on what they had read, thus contributing to the process of enlightenment which they together promoted."[8] This, of course, is Habermas's public sphere embedded in a lifeworld. It is also representative of the determination of the denizens of modernity to know about the world in the formation of public opinion as a wedge to leverage policy in a democracy—and, ultimately, upset the cart of tradition.

But also within the caveat about seeking out "original and authentic information" and in the struggle in the streets for the popular papers are early notions of press accountability and an understanding of quality as it applies to news—and, for our purposes, news untainted by any market or ideological constraint. In that demand for quality is defined the importance of the press and its news to a modern, democratic society. And in that is evident the newspaper's mission made manifest. That is, among newspaper readers even in early-nineteenth-century London, readers were cognizant that the quality of news content was key to the correct understanding of the world. And from this brief narrative, it is apparent that the perception was that some papers had mastered what several decades later the Reverend Benjamin St. James Fry, a journalist and publisher turned Methodist clergyman, called "intelligent journalism." That was a journalism, Fry theorized, that offers a "well-digested account" of what was going on in the world—both public affairs and the intellectual thought of the day that was "re-shaping the political, social and religious institutions of our times."[9]

However, that was exactly the problem. For several decades in the nineteenth and early twentieth centuries, the critics of the Sunday newspaper both in Britain and in the United States repeatedly sounded the alarm that societal institutions were not only being reshaped but also replaced. Through the mediation of the newspaper—the Sunday edition especially—the secular was elbowing aside the sacred. And as a vehicle of modernity, it was unmooring the traditions of the past and casting them adrift. In 1882 the Reverend George T. Rider, a well-known teacher and writer on religious subjects, offered a representative summary of this critique of Sunday journalism. Rider was no fan of the daily newspapers that in a spiral of dysfunction "promote and feed gossip-hunger." But more worrisome to Rider was the rapidly spreading Sunday newspaper—"a masterpiece of diversion and entertainment," whose design "is the triumph of seductive art. Memorable verses; brilliant tales and novelettes, racy gossip, with salacious flavorings of mischief and scandal in high and low life, sea-flittings and watering-place delights, oddities and outlandish provincialisms, provide a whet and stimulant in every column." And he pondered the fact that theaters, saloons, and most places of business were closed on Sunday, yet, somehow, journalism continued to be allowed to profane the Sabbath "in its greed of gain." He asserted that while to some seemingly innocuous, Sunday journalism was having more ill effect on religion than all the "anti-Christian eccentrics and revolutionists" of the day. Indeed, "It is avowedly and offensively secular. It is a direct and deliberate bid for the popular eye and ear in competition with the pulpit."[10]

Here, then, in this essay is a fairly representative summary of the litany of criticism of Sunday journalism over the decades: it was a profanation of the Sabbath, it manifested the growing tension between the secular and the spiritual, it was competing with the pulpit for dominance in society, its appeal to the increasingly literate and curious public was such that it was spreading like a plague, and this modern phenomenon's very existence stemmed from the fact that the newspaper was driven by the commercial impulse to the detriment of its prophetic role in society.

Finally, one key element rests in the subtext of Rider's complaint about the Sunday newspaper's mastery of a format for "diversion and entertainment." The first question we might ask is this: Diversion from what? Broadly answered by many pastoral critics over the decades, it was a diversion away from the sacred and down a path of the secular—made more egregious by the fact that it occurred on the holy Sabbath. Indeed, the Sunday newspaper was a smorgasbord of offerings extracted from an increasingly complex modern life. It was, as one writer in 1889 described it, "a great mosaic" of news that was "secular, worldly, of the earth earthy."[11] I will argue more fully later that the criticism of Sunday journalism was fundamentally a conflict between tradition and the slow reveal of the liminal upheavals of a modern world. Thus, prophetic journalism's role as "guides of conduct"[12]—as the Reverend Washington Gladden described it—had been revised to match the times. The Sunday newspaper—this "great mosaic"—was a product of an "age of innovation," and its prophetic role was now seen as a road map to the modern world.[13]

The Growth of the Sunday Newspaper

Writing in 1907, Frank Foxcroft, a poet and editor of the *Living Age*, observed that the previous quarter century had seen a tremendous growth in the Sunday newspaper, and he attributed this growth to several conditions of the modern industrializing age. They included "reduced cost of paper, the introduction of the linotype and other labor-saving printing-machines, cheap processes of illustration through the use of photography, the lowering of telegraph tolls, the development of the newspaper 'syndicate,' and the increasing lavishness and energy of American advertisers." He noted that advertising on Sunday had become so popular among commercial interests that daily papers were forced to put out Sunday editions because much of its Monday through Saturday advertising had been diverted to Sunday. Still, given all this admiration of technological and business prowess, Foxcroft complained that the Sunday newspaper "is ill-suited to Sunday because ordinarily it makes no recognition whatever of the sacred character of the day, but is wholly given up to secular interests and amusements."[14]

Foxcroft identified many of the recognized impetuses for the Sunday paper. As Raymond Williams noted, any discussion about communications or media or journalism begins with the history of the printing press from 1700 until now.[15] It was the introduction of steam printing in 1814 and its effect on increasing the ability to print more copies in a shorter time and then the exponential technological innovations in printing production—along with the attendant rise of a consumer culture and the improvements in literacy, the postal networks, and transportation infrastructure—that drove the production of the voluminous Sunday papers.[16] And to fill those pages, they began to report on the wider world. Gerald Baldasty observes that before the American Civil War, the topic of half the reading matter in metropolitan newspapers was politics. After the war, the definition of news had been expanded to include crime and courts, accidents, society, women, and leisure activities such as sports. They had become, a Minneapolis pastors association complained in 1886, the "scavengers of the nation." Still, by 1890 British newspaper editor Sir Robert Donald observed that "American journalism has reached its highest development in the Sunday newspaper." Donald noted that the Sunday paper was ubiquitous, especially in New York, where busy men would settle down with it for a long read in the morning. "Everywhere you see people reading. . . . The benches in Union and Madison Squares are occupied with readers. Central Park, on a fine Sunday forenoon, contains hundreds of students of this secular Sunday literature. In the trains, in the street-cars, in waiting rooms, and on the pleasure boats, the same spectacle meets one."[17]

The date of the first Sunday newspaper in Britain is the subject of some dispute, according to an 1874 summary on the topic. The first Sunday paper, *Johnson's Sunday Monitor*, began publishing in London in either 1778 or 1780. The 1778 date came from a publication known as *Timperley's Encyclopedia of Literary and Typographical Anecdote*. That date was incorrect, however, the writer asserted. The actual date was 1780, and in that case the first Sunday paper was the *British Gazette and Sunday Monitor*, which began on

March 26, 1780. The paper lasted until 1803, and its success prompted the founding of "several rivals" over the following years.[18]

There is also some dispute in the literature about the beginnings of the Sunday newspaper in America. Newspaper historian Frederic Hudson notes that there were no Sunday papers in the United States before 1825, when the *Sunday Courier* began publishing at the Tontine Coffee House, at Wall and Water Streets in New York City.[19] It lasted, however, only a few months. More than a dozen other Sunday papers were begun before the Civil War, but most failed because of what one writer summarizing the tenth US Census in 1880 called the "prevailing sentiment against" them. Historian Wayne Edison Fuller says the first Sunday newspaper appeared for a short time in 1796. Before the Civil War, some of the larger cities had Sunday papers filled with inconsequential odds and ends of information and some news.[20] One nineteenth-century critic called them "rubbishy affairs," filled with "stories or gossip, or chat about sports and society."[21] The first continuously published Sunday sheet of any substance was the *Sunday Herald*, which James Gordon Bennett began publishing on a permanent basis in 1841, despite the denunciations against him for doing so.[22]

Still, Sunday newspapers were few and far between early in the nineteenth century, and up to 1860 those that existed were "largely incidental" to the production of the daily.[23] Michael Schudson has cited statistics that in 1842, one in twenty-six New Yorkers bought a Sunday newspaper. But the thousands of Irish and later immigrants flooding the country did not bring with them the Puritan conservatism about observing the Sabbath, and by 1850 with the Irish immigration, one in nine New Yorkers bought Sunday papers. Those demographic changes, along with the printing of special Sunday editions during the Civil War—"when news from the seat of war was too momentous to wait a day," as one British newspaper editor observed—habituated readers to seven-day journalism and opened the door for publishers to introduce or continue the practice.[24] Readers' growing reliance on Sunday papers "doubtless weakened the regard of both publishers and readers for the Sabbath," one observer noted. Indeed, the Reverend Charles Augustus Stoddard noted in 1910, "The Civil War made the first great changes in Sabbath observance; and then the Sunday newspapers invaded all of our households; the growth of riches changed many citizens and destroyed the simplicity of family life."[25]

After the war, many of the papers continued to publish Sunday editions that were not that much different from the daily papers. Even after the Civil

War, however, because of daily newspaper publishers' "lingering respect" for the Sabbath, there were only about fifty Sunday editions in 1870.[26] In 1880 Sunday newspapers were published by 11.6 percent of the nation's dailies—a total of 113.[27] In that decade the Sunday paper was revamped into the model we are familiar with today—multiple topical sections, enterprise stories, features, and much advertising. By 1889 half of New York newspaper readers bought Sunday newspapers,[28] and in 1890 more than 250 daily papers in urban areas had Sunday editions—and those papers filtered out into rural America, where they elbowed aside the rural weeklies and the Christian newspapers.[29] Following the Spanish-American War in 1898, most other daily newspapers across the country began to add Sunday editions.[30]

It was, then, the Civil War and the accompanying recognition of the popular mass demand for news that sparked a transformation in the practice of journalism. An editorial in 1901 marking the fiftieth anniversary of the *New York Times* affirms this point. Before the war, newspapers appealed to only a small and often elite segment of society. "The alarms and anxieties of the civil war created a state of public feeling out of which were born the modern theory and practice of newspapermaking. The editors and publishers of New York then learned that the news is the life and soul of a newspaper: that large expenditure in collecting and transmitting news is eagerly reimbursed by the public, . . . and prosperity is the ability to satisfy the demand of the people to know what is going on in the world." After the war, the New York papers had thousands more readers, and New Yorkers "had acquired the habit of newspaper reading."[31] And in this demand by the reading public for news of the modern world and in the money to be made by satisfying that demand are two elements that drove the development of highly profitable Sunday papers.

A Violation of the Sabbath

In 1894 the Reverend C. George Currie, rector of Christ Church in Baltimore, said he recognized that the Sunday newspaper had become an institution, with "nine men out of every ten" taking the paper into their homes. Yet he was one who still protested the Sunday newspaper as a violation of the Sabbath. "It is always dangerous," he warned, "to go tinkering with the foundations of things; and the Lord's Day is one of those foundations." Currie's defense of the holy day was not a new argument but new words representative of many before him. The Sabbath's original purpose, he insisted, was to purify "men's minds by weekly contact with the ideals of another world." History showed, he wrote, that without some weekly relief from the secular world, life became imbued with the material world's "selfishness and earthiness that fill the mind for six days of the week."[32]

What we have, then, is a struggle between two forms of mediation. One was the influential—and seemingly unstoppable—Sunday newspaper of recent origin. And the other was the perceived tradition of the Sabbath, which was, Currie argued, "coeval with the race itself" and at the core of our very existence.[33] However, this latter adamant belief in the deep roots of Sabbath observation was debatable. In 1880 James Freeman Clarke, an American theologian, writer, and editor, observed that for Christians, there really was no Sabbath to be observed. "Only in England and America, among the descendants of the Puritans, and only in religious phraseology, is Sunday called the Sabbath." To that point, historian Jeffery Smith has argued that keeping holy the seventh day was encoded in American's religious DNA from the time of the Sabbatarian colonists who enforced the stricture and enacted laws proscribing work, recreation, and travel on Sunday. Historian John S. Gilkeson has observed that in both the United Kingdom and America, the custom of observing the Sabbath originated in the religious revivals of the late eighteenth and early nineteenth centuries. However, he noted, the observance of the Sabbath in America was not really formalized until the struggle to ban work, travel, and recreation began with the Post Office Act in 1810, which allowed for mail delivery on Sunday. The Sabbath crusade failed to overturn the act. But it did find victory in creating an ethos by "quietly molding the opinion of shopkeepers, artisans, and other members of an emergent middle class." Thus, Gilkeson wrote, though the crusade failed, "strict Sabbath observance became rooted in Protestant culture."[34]

A no more eloquent defender of the Sabbath than Ralph Waldo Emerson once wrote, "The old Sabbath, or Seventh Day, white with the religions of unknown thousands of years, when this hallowed hour dawns out of the deep—a clean page which the wise may inscribe with truth—the cathedral music of history breathes through it a psalm to our solitude."[35] Emerson also argued that mankind needed that one day of rest and meditation to make order out of the chaos of life and "to check this headlong racing and put us in possession of ourselves once more."[36] Here, Emerson is making the two arguments entwined with the majority of the discussion about—and the source code for the tension between—the Sabbath and Sunday newspapers. The latter is one of instrumentality—of the defined benefit to mankind that the Sabbath offered in both church attendance and a short severance from the distractions of daily life. The other is laced with the notion of the ineffable. Reverend Currie described this as "the ideals of another world." The Reverend Joseph Cook saw it as achieving, through the quiet contemplation of a Sunday, "the summit of our natures, until we behold God, and by looking into His face, are changed into the same, from glory to glory." Similarly, Reverend Alexander MacKay Smith believed this respite gave "the soul a chance to say whether it exists." The ineffable was, essentially, the intimations of the unseen too great for our small minds to adequately express or conceive—but present and available to us in our quiet and contemplative Sabbath devotions far from the distractions of modern life—of which the Sunday paper was the apogee. Randolph Tucker, a lawyer, author, and attorney general of Virginia in the late nineteenth century, described this tension between the secular and sacred as a struggle to think about something other than the "dreary gloom of a cheerless materialism" in order to "reach the nobler contemplation of those invisible realities which, through faith, lift us to a higher life."[37]

These concerns are echoed in these and a litany of similar sentiments that the Sunday newspaper "feeds and stimulates the sensuous rather than the moral and spiritual life"[38] and that through it "men will live entirely in the brain and despise the heart,"[39] regularly intermingled in the decades of discursive elaboration on the topic. Particularly relevant to our discussion here—and arguably a culmination of the decades of discourse—are the thoughts of the late Avery Dulles, a Jesuit priest, theologian, and cardinal of the Catholic Church. This short disquisition reveals the struggles of both the past and the present between the news media and religion. Writing on the relationship between the two, Dulles held that a natural antagonism existed between religion and the secular media. That antagonism could be explained and talked about but never entirely eliminated because of the news media's demand for the new thing, controversy, and simplicity. Ultimately, the tension between the two institutions is grounded in the "nature of the church's message and the communicative powers of journalism," wrote Dulles, who then identified seven points of contrast between religion and the news media. The first of these is that while religion is a "mystery of faith," the press is investigative and iconoclastic and does not revere mysteries. Also, religion seeks to hold to the past and "cherishes stability and shuns innovation," but the press feeds on novelty. Too, the press focuses on disagreement and conflict, while religion's goal is "unity and reconciliation." And the very spirituality of the church's actions and pronouncements is simply not "sufficiently concrete to make good copy." In addition, journalism in democratic societies views events through a democratic lens, which means the press has "a built-in bias against the authoritative teaching of popes and bishops." Furthermore, the very subtlety and complexity of nuanced matters of theology run counter to the news media's need for the "short, simple and striking." Dulles's outline in 1994 could be considered the end point of a decades-long thread of discussion. For example, just over a century before, the Reverend David James Burrell, pastor of the Marble Collegiate Church in New York City, pointed to similar distinctions between the pulpit and the press. While the two were often compared and contrasted, they were very distant relatives, if related at all. That was because the church, Burrell declared, was "of divine ordinance" and had nothing to do with expounding on secular truth. Instead, the church "is a living organism through which the divine energy is being applied."[40]

Still, as early as 1879 there were those who had begun to see the Sabbath as doomed in the modern world. An editorial in the *Christian Union* bluntly stated, "The Puritan Sabbath is gone: not threatened; not going; but gone. There may be communities which lie anchored outside the channel of the nineteenth century and preserve the oldtime Sabbath repose because they are not in the new-time secular rush and hurry. . . . [B]ut the New England Sabbath of the seventeenth century exists only as its forts and stockades exist, in curious monumental remains."[41]

Condemnation and Defense of the Sunday Newspaper

In 1843 Charles B. Tayler, a Church of England clergyman and a prolific nineteenth-century writer on religion, published a didactic sermon novel titled *Katherine*. The novel partly deals with Katherine's relations with her father and brothers and her efforts to wean them away from their enthrallment to the Sunday newspaper. At one point Katherine attends church, where the pastor's sermon rails against the Sunday newspaper. Here, we can see the tension between promotion of the sensual to the detriment of the spiritual:

> I would speak on a subject about which every minister of the gospel has need to lift up his voice in every pulpit throughout the land. I fear, alas, that none of us are sufficiently aware of the influence which Sunday newspapers are insensibly gaining in every grade of society; an influence utterly opposed to the

> spirit of the gospel, the practice of the gospel, and the godliness which should distinguish the people of the living God as their peculiar character. All that is of the carnal mind, all that is of the corrupt world, all that is earthly, sensual, devilish, continue to make this poisoned tide, which is by degrees advancing and overwhelming the fairest and brightest tracts, nay all the fields of human society in this nominally Christian land; and what is this reading of Sunday newspapers, what is it, but the most wretched substitute for the sweet and holy enjoyment of Sabbath peace?

Katherine then returns home and confronts her father in an epiphany of awareness about what the pastor described as the "deadly influence" of the Sunday paper. She now understands, she tells her father, "Why, and how, the spirituality of your views and sentiments had dwindled away; how the warmth and zeal of your love to God had grown so cold!" The cause is the Sunday newspaper, she laments, which has "been allowed to supersede, and at last quite set aside, the Holy Bible."[42]

In illustrating the condemnation and the defense of the Sunday newspaper over the decades through many kinds of mediated forms—including the novel and other works of fiction[43]—we are discussing what contemporary British social theorist John Thompson has described as the "corrosive impact of public scrutiny and debate" through the "discursive elaboration" of mediated messages.[44] Those messages at the core of ideology formation and the dismantling and re-embedding of traditions are received through different media and then "adapted and dispersed to an ever-widening circle of secondary recipients."[45] Those messages both for and against the Sunday paper ran the gamut from newspaper articles,[46] trade journal articles,[47] and essays to spoken and published sermons,[48] pastoral letters,[49] editorials,[50] memoirs and biographies,[51] the published proceedings and resolutions of religious conventions,[52] and letters to the editor.[53]

Probably nowhere is the distinction between the mission and the market made clearer than in the attacks upon and defenses of the Sunday newspaper. I could go on at length about those many attacks from many tangents on the Sunday paper. But one mediated form, a letter to the editor of the *New York Times* in 1902, will suffice to demonstrate much of the gist of the condemnation of Sunday papers. In that letter, the Reverend Samuel Ward Boardman, a past president of Maryville College in Tennessee, outlined the essential indictments of the Sunday newspaper that had often been raised in the previous century. His list of charges came long after the

Sunday paper was an established part of life in America. Still, Boardman argued that the Sunday newspaper was harmful to society and needed to be discontinued because it violated God's command to keep the day holy; work to produce and sell it robs those workers of "needed and commanded rest"; it violates laws proscribing such manufacture and trade on Sunday; it, in breaking laws, leads to other violations of law such as gambling, drinking, "and grosser sins"; in its disobeying of God's law it undermines all parental and civil laws; it corrupts youth by encouraging them to break God's law; it is not a work "of necessity or mercy" and thus is not allowed; it works to decrease church attendance; it takes time away from prayer and reading and studying of the Bible; and it encourages skepticism.[54]

I could also go to great length listing the many defenses of Sunday papers from many different sources. But a handful of editorials from the *Washington Post*—one of the staunchest defenders of Sunday journalism in the late nineteenth century—will serve to set down the standard markers of this defense. At the same time, this defense offers a representative summary of the efforts of some advocates of the Sunday newspaper to find the "concord of this discord"[55] between the market and the mission by drawing one into the other. Essentially, in its many forms it is a defense that the Sunday paper was here to stay as "an ineliminable feature of modern life,"[56] as it acted as an expansive educator and a liaison between religion and the public. Simply put, the dogma and creeds of the church were no longer sufficient to prop up those who had begun to lose their footing in the increasingly "complex civilization of the age."[57]

The *Post* had a complicated relationship to the Sabbath. Not to be too cynical, but we could guess this had something to do with this liminal period when most newspapers understood that the advertising-filled Sunday editions were a financial boon, that many people held other ideas about the role of Sunday activities, and that it wanted to avoid offending its many readers who were churchgoers or, at least, avowedly religious. On the one hand, the *Post* rejected the restrictions on leisure activities as "unauthorized and misleading." Yet it declared that the "Christian Sunday was a day of rest and self-improvement, of reflection and spiritual communing." To that point, it was opposed to a "secular Sunday" and instead promoted the Sunday paper as an adjunct to religiosity in that it offered a synoptic account of the modern world and the brotherhood of man.[58] And, in fact, the *Post* argued that journalism—especially Sunday journalism—made readers more religious by broadening their awareness of the modern world.[59] The

Post rejected the argument that the Sunday paper was a desecration of the Sabbath. Besides rebuffing the "zealous pretensions of all narrow-minded Sabbatarians," the *Post* held that "a good Sunday paper is a public benefit" as a permanent feature of life in the modern world. And, the editorial writer observed, the progress of human life was the goal of all religions. Thus, the Sunday paper's advantages in this respect were many. "It is the link of intelligent intercourse between distant countries. It sets forth the latest truths respecting the complex problems of life,"[60] as it uses facts to discuss the "questions of government and society, of art, science, and religion." And finally, it just was not possible any more to hold the view that "ignorance is in all cases the mother of devotion."[61]

The Sunday Paper's Acceptance

The increasingly "complex civilization of the age" referred to above was one factor responsible for the growing relaxed attitude toward the proscriptions of the Sabbath, a writer for the *Lutheran Observer* asserted in 1903. All the amenities of modernity—the abundant availability of consumer goods, the wider range of leisure activities, and improved transportation facilities such as the trolley—led even the "sincerest Christians" to spend time on the Sabbath in ways they never would have thought of doing ten and twenty years before. And certainly, one of those activities was reading the Sunday paper.[62] Indeed, there is much literature over the years in the same kinds of media described earlier where the Sunday paper was criticized that now acknowledged it had become an accepted fact of life.[63] Illustrative of this acceptance was a summary of the tenth US Census of 1880 that observed that in the previous ten years, "much of the popular prejudice against the Sunday sheet has been overcome," and some of those papers were the most profitable in America. The writer also observed that Sunday journalism in America had developed to a much greater degree than in England or Europe.[64] In fact, the distinction between the reception of the Sunday newspaper in Britain and America is particularly apt in our discussion of the slow reveal of its acceptance in the States, as, over time, the prejudices against Sunday journalism had largely disappeared by the late nineteenth century. For example, when a nationwide debate began in Britain over the Sunday newspaper in 1899, the *Washington Post* wondered at the protest. It noted that it would surprise many in America, except those "familiar with the insular conditions and limitations of English life, the stolid conservatism of English character, and the natural horror with which John Bull regards whatever is to him 'new under the sun.'"[65] The *Nation* magazine pointed to its sense of déjà vu, recalling that the same arguments against such papers were hashed over in the post–Civil War seventies in America.[66] And the trade journal *American Printer and Lithographer* took this opportunity to note that in just one generation, Americans' view of Sunday newspapers had changed considerably. "At first there was opposition, then tolerance, and later, when the quality was greatly improved, tolerance became positive welcome."[67]

The *Christian Advocate* took special interest in the battle surrounding the *Daily Mail*'s and the *Daily Telegraph*'s unsuccessful attempts to publish Sunday papers in Britain and then contrasted those with the success papers in the United States had in publishing and popularizing Sunday editions even in the face of withering criticism. In Britain Christians across the country refused to subscribe to either paper both on Sunday and during the rest of the week, with the result that one news agent reported he sold fifteen hundred fewer papers. The Synod of the Presbyterian Church of England resolved to no longer patronize the two papers, and it advised Presbyterians to not advertise in the publications. Other religious and local institutions passed similar resolutions. Labor also joined in, with "one great union" resolving that "every Sunday school officer, teacher, and scholar" would refuse to buy or read any paper connected with Sunday publishing. In addition, library companies ended their subscriptions, as did members of the Workingmen's Lord's Day Rest Association.

The writer observed that the history of the Sunday newspaper in the United States was wholly different. Some papers did publish on Sunday, but the larger ones did not, including the *New York Tribune*. But when the *Tribune* and other major papers began to publish on Sunday, "there were a few jets of indignation, and some platitudinous resolutions," with a handful of Christians announcing they would not advertise in papers that printed a Sunday edition. "The Sunday papers inserted religious articles. They had no trouble in buying the services of some ministers of each denomination. They humbugged a large number who 'did not care for,' but did not refuse, pay, into the belief that they could do good by contributing to them." In addition, the writer complained, the proponents of Sunday editions framed the debate such that those in the clergy who were in favor were described as "progressive and liberal," while the opponents were spoken of as "narrow."[68]

However, Whitelaw Reid's justification for why the *New York Tribune* began a Sunday edition is a much different explanation than that above—and it is instructive in explaining the relaxing of attitudes toward Sunday papers. Reid, the *Tribune*'s editor, president, and chairman, gave his explanation in a speech to the Bromley Foundation at Yale University in 1913. In his speech, he pointed to the hypocrisy of those opposed to Sunday journalism—of those who "approved of this refusal to print a Sunday paper." Reid said he began to point out to those who congratulated him that all his regular readers were simply leaving him and going to his competitors on Sunday. He then would ask: "'By the way, what paper do you read on Sunday?' Then came stammering and hesitation, to be sure; but not once, during the years this went on, did I fail to find that, with the single exception of some of the clergy, the men who were exhorting me to continue setting a noble example for Sabbath observance by not publishing on Sunday, were themselves quietly gratifying their own craving to know what was going on by reading some Sunday paper!"[69]

The Sunday Newspaper as a Vehicle of Modernity

Simply put, the voluminous Sunday newspaper was a vehicle of modernity. Up to this point, these first three chapters have discussed the effects of industrialization and the growing complexity of a once much simpler life, the commodification of news, the growth of commercialism in daily life, and the creation of a consumer culture. While I should not overgeneralize about the effect of Sunday journalism, I can also agree with communication scholars Sandra Gabriele and Paul Moore, who insist that the Sunday newspaper was more than a vehicle of modernity, but "part of the emergence of modernity." By that they meant, "The newspaper animated modernity, establishing a link between the mass market and the democratic public sphere." Anthony Giddens has observed that modernity is the structure of social life that arose in the seventeenth century and was hinged to notions such as the "information society" and the "consumer society."[70] I earlier noted the complaints about the Sunday paper's "secularizing tendency" in its promotion of materialism to the detriment of the spiritual.[71] But let's set aside the "consumer society" implications of modernity that cascade from the pages of advertising-filled Sunday papers. Instead—because this is the core of the pastoral criticism of the press—I will focus on the aspect of the "information society" in which a questioning ethos of doubt and skepticism prevails and out of which grew the modern communications industry and the market forces that struggle to constrain journalistic conduct and content: the news. Thus, for our purposes, I will draw on Bishop James Edward Lesslie Newbigin's declaration in *Truth and Authority in Modernity* (1996):

"Modernity is distrustful of authority. It was born in a movement of emancipation from what were seen as external authorities, and its appeal was to the freedom and responsibility of the individual reason and conscience to judge between rival claims to truth."[72]

Therefore, to say the Sunday paper was a vehicle of modernity means it was "a great mosaic" using that invention of modern journalism that Alan Trachtenberg describes as "a language of mass intelligibility" to reveal the synoptic accounts of modern life while describing, informing, enlightening, and counseling readers about their increasingly complex modern world.[73] As the cliché goes, we can agree that if the Sunday paper did not exist, someone would have to invent it so that the denizens of the nineteenth century and beyond could better understand and cope with their changing world. Indeed, as an editorialist for the *Christian's Penny Magazine* argued as early as 1834, the Sunday newspaper was an invention of "this age of innovation."[74] We can also agree that the Sunday paper, as Reverend Boardman complained, "encourages skepticism"[75] and that it promotes the dominance of "the objective spirit over the subjective"[76] in much the way Kant described the imperative motto of the Enlightenment as having "the courage to use your own understanding!" In other words, dogma issued by traditional authorities would no longer suffice as untested doctrine. That was because, historian Arthur M. Schlesinger observed, "medieval American history" ended with the Civil War, followed by "the great economic revolution which swept through the nation at high tide from about 1860 to 1880 and willy nilly projected America into Modern Times."[77] In the five decades after the war, one late-nineteenth-century writer observed, "our hurrying, widening national life" had become "diversified" and enormously complex.[78] More than a decade later, in 1906, the Reverend Francis R. Beattie, professor of systematic theology at the Louisville Theological Seminary, declared, "The entire world had gone through an enormous cultural and technological upheaval, with government growing larger and more complex, the use of machinery multiplying, business practices becoming byzantine, and transportation infrastructures undergoing a revolution." Indeed, Oscar Wilde once observed, "Modern life is complex and relative," and to understand the complex requires the "subtlety of nuances, of suggestion, of strange perspectives," while the relative "requires background."[79]

In Wilde's analysis, I would argue, is evident the very reason journalism exists—especially Sunday journalism. The Sunday newspaper did not exist simply as an ad-bloated vehicle for the market. Instead, it was primarily a vehicle of modernity that offered a journalism that interpreted the events of the world and offered background as it reported on both the center and the periphery. It was a journalism that, as Jane Addams argued, offered "a realization of the experiences of other people" and an "identification with the common lot which is the essential idea of Democracy."[80] The Reverend Robert A. Holland, rector of St. George's Church in St. Louis, felt similarly. In a series called "The Sunday Newspaper" presented at the 1894 Congress of the Protestant Episcopal Church, Holland blessed the Sunday paper for saving millions of "poor souls" from ignorance. It did so, he said, "by drawing their interest in the world's daily life to an ampler reading than workdays permit about that life's progress—its science, its art, its literature, its politics, its religion. The Sunday newspaper is their one book, their sole library, their museum, their art gallery, their Pantheon of contemporary genius."[81]

That having been said, I would pause to note that an editorial writer for the *Detroit News* in 1896 argued that the "kaleidoscopic view" of contending sermons representing a mosaic of interests—when taken as a whole—was evocative of the Sunday newspaper itself:

> The various pulpit discourses contained a little of politics, a little of stage gossip, a little of religion, a little of society, a little of advertising, a little of literature, and a little of various other elements that go to make up the Sunday newspapers. In addition there was a great deal of editorial comment, and opinionated matter that could hardly be classified. One preacher denounced the theater as a cesspool of immorality and vice. Another warmly commended the theater as a power in the upbuilding of humanity. One scored the newspapers and another took the view that even the Sunday paper is a great moral agent. It is evident that the ministers of Detroit have never held a caucus, and determined just what their composite belief is. It may be taken for granted that the authors of the multi-moral sermons yesterday are all sincere Christians, and all conscientious in their efforts to uplift humanity. The disagreement is merely on the means to the end, and should be comforting to everybody. With such a multiplicity of beliefs, nobody should experience any difficulty in finding the kind of doctrine that suits him, and here is where the resemblance of the various sermons to a Sunday newspaper is again in evidence.[82]

Finally, one eloquent proponent of the Sunday newspaper in its relation to the modern world was the Reverend Julius H. Ward, for many years literary editor of the *Boston Herald* and a widely known clergyman of the Protestant Episcopal Church of New England. In the late nineteenth century, Ward saw the Sunday newspaper as "a new force in American life" and a natural expression of the powerful daily press driven by the demands of modernity. Ward saw in this modern society the coming to power of new forces that were once marginalized and the consequent increase in communication between different classes of society. Thus, the newspaper was seen as a much-sought-after communicative tool of public opinion. Ward believed the newspaper was not only a rival to the pulpit but much better at reaching the public because a growing number of people found the Sunday paper "more attractive than anything the Church has to offer." Indeed, he held, the changes in how Sunday was then being observed and the growing pluralistic society created the path to the Sunday paper, which "represents the largeness of contemporary life." Thus, the Sunday paper was filling a demand by the public that "the evolution of modern life had already created." Ward understood the clergy's antipathy to the Sunday paper, with its confrontation with the traditions of Sabbath observance and the fact that it had not yet developed into the ideal of what it could one day be. Yet Ward was reconciled with the Sunday paper, which was usually much better than the daily. And his acceptance of Sunday papers appears to have been influenced by the fact that he saw them as the "secular and religious" educators of the public in a changing modern society that was increasingly much more complex in its diversity. The Sunday paper, he wrote, "indicates clearly and truly the relative condition and movement of the world." It is, he insisted, "one of the chief agencies for the transformation of modern society."[83]

The Sunday Newspaper as a Fact of Modern Life

John Thompson has argued that traditions never quite disappear from the modern world, but their standing in society is transformed. "They become less taken for granted and less secure as they are increasingly exposed to the corrosive impact of public scrutiny and debate." With this scrutiny and debate, their truths no longer go unquestioned, and if they survive, it is in new forms. For the church, the Sunday newspaper and the chaotic bricolage of modernity it promoted and embodied challenged its long-established integrative power. That is, the increasing pluralism of a complex, modern world fashioned by the effects of a new capitalist order rent the fabric of the social integration of society that the church had stitched together over the centuries. It felt threatened by the usurpation of a tradition—the Sabbath as a constituent of faith as the keystone of society. Thus, it justly worried about what that meant for modern civilization. Yet, possibly, the Sunday newspaper was simply removing the veil from a notion similar to Charles Tilly's argument that societies are constructed "fictitious entities."[84] We can see some realization of that in the ultimate breakdown of resistance to Sunday newspapers. But there certainly remained a distinction on a sliding continuum between a minority who continued to oppose the Sunday newspaper as "the great disintegrator of religious faith, religious thought, religious zeal"[85] and those who had accepted the Sunday newspaper as an "indispensable adjunct and factor in our modern civilization."[86] Considering these two ends of that dialectic—both from 1889—we can appreciate contemporary intellectual historian John Patrick Diggins's surmise that "from the point of view of the modern mind the truths of the past may have been little more than fictions, yet they worked only to the extent they went unquestioned."[87]

Finally, as I have noted, to best understand the history of the progress of any sort of social or cultural artifact, it helps to look at critical junctures. In this case, the tension between the Sunday newspaper and the forces of religion was a slow reveal over many decades. An example of the first hints of this juncture can be found in an essay from 1822 in which an anonymous British clergyman identified the Sunday paper as a "national wickedness" that profaned the Sabbath. What is striking here in this screed against the Sunday paper is that we can find in it an early collision of forces and an early recognition of the first inklings of modernity's effect on the growing tension between the spiritual and the secular. The writer pointed to improvements in transportation and the increased use of carriages and stagecoaches—even on Sunday—that added to the spread of the profane Sunday paper into the countryside. And, he noted, "As the general demand for information has increased, in proportion as education has been diffused, London is thus subject to a far greater breach of the Sabbath than its own demand for news, however great, would require." Certainly, the writer could not avoid the even then common complaint that Sunday newspapers tempted the multitudes "to absent themselves from public worship." And more perversely, the news and literature of those papers both tended "to secularize the mind" and to create a culture of contempt that questioned authority. These papers, he complained, oppose "the existing order of things" and censure and criticize every action of government—"thus fostering in the minds of their readers a contempt for constituted authorities, and a morbid habit of referring every instance of public distress to the incapacity or corruption of our governors."[88] Here, in so many words, we have an early recognition that the Sunday newspaper with its disparate topics, its often irreverent news and views that questioned truths and raised doubts, was a latchkey into the enlightened modern world—for the modern mind is a skeptical mind and Sunday newspapers were breeding a questioning and skeptical public.

CHAPTER 3

The Press, the Pulpit, and Public Opinion

> **The formation of an enlightened Christian public opinion, to which kings give heed and demagogues bow, is due largely to the quill driving propensities of the English, and, in respect to secular affairs, it has ultimately proved a factor in civilization not second to the pulpit.**
>
> —The Reverend Edward Payson Tenney, *Contrasts in Social Progress*

THE REVEREND CHARLES W. CASSON had a decision to make about his future course in life. The son of a Methodist minister, he himself spent a year preaching at a Methodist church but resigned because he came to disagree with the religion's theological standards. He then spent three years working in social reform in Massachusetts and then some time in England, where he studied the country's social and industrial problems. In 1898 he became a Unitarian minister.[1] However, by 1912 he concluded that journalism was the profession in which he could do more for society, and he stepped down from the pulpit to become the editor of a daily newspaper. "I expect to do vastly more good as an editor than as a minister," he told his congregation. The nation's newspaper-industry trade journal, *Editor & Publisher,* found this to be a logical career choice for Casson. That was because the role and responsibilities of the pulpit and the press dovetailed in many ways. The journalist—like the minister of a church—"is at once the Father Confessor and surgeon to the body politic." Indeed, much as a minister to a flock concerned with progressive and moral uplift, the journal editorialized, "America's greatest journalists are characterized by simplicity, purpose, self-sacrifice and an intensely religious spirit under perhaps a rough and uncouth brusqueness."[2] This, then, was an expression of the notion of collaboration between the pulpit and the press and assimilation of one to the other that not that many years before had rarely been expressed. Or if it was, it was the incessantly stated formulaic pairing of "press and pulpit" in discussions of the moral suasion of public opinion in which the former was invariably subsidiary in importance to the latter.[3]

Casson's career change and the journal's reaction to it in 1912 reflect how religion imbued the daily life of journalists and newspapers of the late nineteenth and early twentieth centuries to a degree unlike anything today.[4] For instance, Charles Ellwood, one of the leading sociologists of the early twentieth century who researched and wrote about the social problems of the era, observed as late as 1920, "The majority of those connected with the press are church members and especially those in responsible positions." And the newspaper trade journal the *Fourth Estate* noted that "there is not a business in the world which is so generally conducted in the interests of morality, of religion, and of right living as the newspaper business." And just a year before Casson's career change, the Reverend James B. Wasson, chaplain of the Strangers Welfare Fellowship in New York, reaffirmed both the passing of the baton from the pulpit to the press and the religiosity of most journalists in an essay titled "The Editor as a Preacher." In it he expressed the oft-noted contention that while the power of the pulpit and the pastor had waned, that of other agencies—such as the newspaper editor—"is practically the only preacher who is listened to to-day by the masses of the people."[5]

Public Opinion and the News

In *A Dictionary of Religion and Ethics* (1921), social philosopher James H. Tufts pointed to an issue of morality that involved using the press to influence public opinion. "Discussion and argument is of course the proper method of reaching a public decision," he wrote, "but the most effective means for influencing public opinion seems to be, not argument or discussion, but what appears under the form of news or other material which is intended to shape opinion without encountering the opposition which a professed argument would meet."[6] Tufts's acceding to the power of news in these matters undoubtedly stemmed from the recognition that in the modern complex world in which the population had swelled by millions, a scenario in which discussion and argument were employed among the public for social change would be difficult to achieve. However, left unsaid here is that because the news utilized to help sway public opinion could not be tested in a discursive to-and-fro, it must be as faithful to reality as possible. In other words, the news offered to the public must not be bent to the heliotropic influence of the market or market-driven ideological forces.

Certainly, the gravitational force that slowly drew the pulpit into the orbit of the press was the power to effect social change through public opinion—what Abraham Lincoln called "public sentiment." Lincoln, who knew a thing or two about creating a conducive ethos,[7] once observed that public opinion was the driving force of democracy, that "public sentiment is everything. With public sentiment, nothing can fail; without it, nothing can succeed. Consequently, he who moulds public sentiment, goes deeper than he who enacts statutes or pronounces decisions." Around that same time and an ocean away, Anthony Trollope, the novelist and observer of the changes roiling British society during the Victorian era, understood how public opinion could galvanize reform—a theme that appears in many of his works. One scholar has suggested that Trollope had concluded that "more people were coming to believe that conduct was good or bad, not in God's eyes, but in men's. Trollope thought they were transferring their reverence for God and his supposed dictates to public opinion." In his novel *Phineas Finn* (1866–67), Trollope analyzed the effects of public opinion. In one scene after a debate over tenant rights, a radical member of Parliament expounds on the additory nature of public opinion's effect on social change: "Many who before regarded legislation on the subject as chimerical will now fancy that it is only dangerous, or perhaps not more than difficult. And so in time it will come to be looked on as among the things possible, then among the things probable;—and so at last it will be ranged in the list of those few measures which the country requires as being absolutely needed. That is the way in which public opinion is made."[8]

Trollope well understood the crucial part newspapers played in molding public opinion,[9] and by 1895 Methodist minister John R. Creighton observed that the newspaper had become the primary source "not only for the news, but for direction in thought and opinion." The newspaper, the reverend contended, had become "the historian of our daily life, while forming public opinion, influencing legislation, dictating politics, changing dominant parties, and, whether it be the daily, weekly, monthly, or quarterly issue, representing the institutions, philosophies, literatures, foibles, and habits of men the world over." And across the Atlantic, the Reverend Edmund McClure, the editorial secretary for the Society for Promoting Christian Knowledge in England, described the "almost complete dislocation of spiritual from temporal motives in all efforts for the bettering of society" in which the press rejected the pulpit as a participant in the discussions about the issues of society, while the pulpit was "seemingly contented with little more than its weekly opportunities of influencing popular opinion" through its sermons. This dislocation, McClure declared, began with Gutenberg and the invention of printing that saw the pulpit gradually cede its power over public opinion to the press until in some parts of Europe in the late nineteenth century, "the Church is hardly to be reckoned as a social influence at all." The solution, then, lay in co-opting the press, McClure wrote. "If the Press has come to displace so largely other methods of spreading knowledge, surely every effort should be made to use it for the advancement of the kingdom of God," he argued.[10]

Similar sentiments about the newspaper as arbiter of public opinion were expressed by many observers over the decades.[11] For instance, Washington Gladden had thought much about the power of public opinion—which he once called "the motive power of the Republic of God"[12]—and the newspaper's vital role in its formation.[13] Indeed, to just that point, sociologist Edwin L. Earp related the account of a missionary recently returned from the Philippines who observed, "'In the Philippines there is no public opinion, because there is no way of creating it. They have no newspapers.'" Thus, Earp contended, it was vitally important to create "the proper means of communication that will make an enlightened and intelligent public opinion possible."[14]

That was Washington Gladden's belief, and in *Ruling Ideas of the Present Age* (1895) he devoted an entire chapter to public opinion and in it discussed its connection to the church and the place of the daily press as an agent of public opinion. At one point, he asserted, "In order that no injustice may be done, that the Demos may not degenerate into a mob and destroy the righteous with the wicked, there is need that the citizens should possess the intelligence from which may spring a rational public opinion." Therefore, Gladden argued, creating and disseminating a healthy public opinion was the principal duty in society because it was the ground from which democratic institutions were nurtured. However, Gladden noted, as he wrote during the height of the Industrial Revolution, the age of "money-making" and the acquisitive individual's concern for his personal and private endeavors weakened public opinion because he no longer had time for public affairs unless they affected his private interests. "In such a case, we have nothing that can properly be termed public opinion; we have a great mass of conflicting and quarreling private wishes and aims, but no real concern for the common weal."[15]

Consequently, sociologist Charles Ellwood stressed, religion must work to create "an effective public opinion" to foster a public conscience about how people should live together in order to bring about a "Christian world." As Gladden described the difference between sane public opinion and unwise, ill-guided "public prejudice and public passion," Ellwood made the distinction between public opinion and "public sentiment and popular emotion," and in doing so he employed a democratic theory of rational discourse leading to the right path. That was because, he wrote, "public opinion is concerned with social changes, with making new social adjustments. Its strength and durability consist in its degree of rationality and in the fact that it is formed through deliberate and open discussion." Ellwood called for the use of several agencies to create an effective public opinion, including "oral discussion" with friends and neighbors individually and in discussion groups and instruction in the public schools. But, he observed, the "most powerful agencies" in creating public opinion were the daily and weekly newspapers.[16]

This primacy of the press is revealed most specifically in the literature of exposure of the socially conscious investigative reporters of the era whom President Roosevelt pejoratively dubbed the "muckrakers." Their work overlapped that of the advocates of the Social Gospel in its application of a Christian ethic to society as part of the progressive reform movement. In his seminal history about the rise of the Social Gospel movement, Charles Howard Hopkins observed that its roots could be found in the Gilded Age's ill effects on the social world—essentially the same impetus for the muckrakers. To that point, historian Bruce J. Evensen reveals this journalistic religiosity in his distillation of seven notable muckraking reporters and his exploration of the "spiritual seeking" of S. S. McClure, the founder of one of the primary muckraking periodicals, *McClure's Magazine*, which Richard Hofstadter described as "completely representative of the average thought and sensibility of the muckraking movement."[17] As late as 1917, this interstitial warp and woof of the pulpit and the press was still strong in an interfaith commission report on strategies for publicizing church news in the secular press. The fifteen members of the committee included religious leaders, magazine and newspaper editors, publishers, and university officials. Among them were such notables as Social Gospel advocate the Reverend Charles Stelzle, renowned *Detroit Times* editor James Schermerhorn, and Talcott Williams, the son of Congregationalist missionaries, a former journalist, and a renowned journalism educator and dean of the Pulitzer School of Journalism.[18]

Still, this is not to belie the litany of many years of criticism of newspapers emanating from the pastorate. A common theme of that pastoral criticism was the call for a structural change in the moral laws that journalists followed.[19] For example, in 1894, the Reverend Addison Moore, himself a former newspaperman, delivered a sermon titled "News and Newspapers" to his flock that reflects well the duality of opinion surrounding the views of the press. Moore had some good things to say about the modern newspaper's benefits to mankind, including its positive effect on the morals of the nation by deterring crime through the threat of publicity. But, on the other hand, he did not like that "the newspaper looks upon itself as a common sewer of our social life."[20] Indeed, the press's free-range use of its power often engendered the pulpit's enmity toward what one critic called the "self-elected priesthood of the newspaper press."[21] One early example of the pulpit's anger comes from the early 1700s, when Thomas Fleet's *Boston Evening Post* published a sermon on "free grace" by John Wesley, an Anglican minister and Christian theologian. Almost immediately, the Reverend John Morehead mounted the pulpit and "not only thundered against the unfortunate Fleet, but against the printing-press also."[22] And as noted earlier, continuing the tradition of pastoral enmity toward the press, in the early eighteenth century James Franklin began publishing the "overtly heretical" *New-England Courant*.[23]

This tradition of press-pulpit alienation reached a high point in the 1830s with the first mass-appeal newspapers—the penny press—and with the "moral war" against James Gordon Bennett's "lively, saucy, and spicy" *New York Morning Herald*.[24] The irony here is that the *Herald* became the first newspaper to gather and report news about religion and the first to publish the leading sermons from the previous Sunday.[25] Historian Frederic Hudson observed that the *Herald* gave over one to two pages each Monday to "the important sermons preached on the previous day, not only in New York, but in Boston, Philadelphia, Washington, Cincinnati, and even in Dublin and in London!" That meant that the words heard by one to two thousand people on Sunday were read on Monday by a half-million people from any number of denominations.[26] However, in expanding the notion of what was news by reporting and publishing the first newspaper stories about such things as the annual meetings of different religious groups, Bennett raised the ire of both the pastorate and their flocks.[27] Rather than "welcoming the publicity, the clergy and the religious press treated it as sacrilege," one of Bennett's biographers noted.[28] It also did not help that Bennett's satires of the church were seen as blasphemous.[29] Thus, convincing the pulpit that the press could serve any kind of Christian function did not come easily to many in the pastorate. As one ecumenical report noted in 1912, the press and pulpit had long looked at each other through a lens of accumulated prejudices. "There has been an alienation and a lack of sympathy between these forces in society," the report claimed. "The church has felt that the press was thoroughly materialized and impervious to her idealism. The press has looked upon the church as being aloof from real life and too much occupied with her theological hair-splitting and subjective experiences." And as another report noted in 1917, "Reporters are looked upon as intruders instead of friends."[30]

Aside from the newspaper's intrusions into the affairs of religion, the perceived insults to the church, and the seemingly unbridgeable rift between the materialistic secular press and the ideals of the spiritual, the pulpit's criticism also coalesced around a distrust of the partisan press and a disgust with sensationalist and often salacious journalism—both of which were seen as subverting the true mission of newspapers. For instance, an early and representative sounding about the dereliction of partisanship and sensational journalism appeared in the monthly magazine the *Green Mountain Gem*. In an editorial rant titled "Dignity of the Press" (1842), the magazine complained that the powers of the newspaper press—"this great fulcrum of the world"—had been subverted to "base party servility, coarse and low vituperation, and to promulgation of doctrines and sentiments, alike destructive of good morals and that high tone of dignity and elevation, which by its legitimate use, it is destined to inculcate and establish." The press, too, the writer lamented, was guilty of a sensationalism beyond the pale of its rightful dignity. "Fabulous and false reports and rumors are published for the truth, and disgusting and obscene crimes are depicted in detail, and the Press is prostituted by the support of the most unholy and disgraceful theories of the day."[31]

Of course, these criticisms were largely indictments of the press drawn from anecdotal experience. Accordingly, in 1888 Henry R. Elliot, founder and editor of the *Church Economist* magazine, turned to statistics to determine whether the clergy's assertions that newspapers were irreligious and subordinated their mission to the market were contraindicated by the reality of the newspaper's content. To do so, Elliot conducted two content analyses of the kinds of news appearing in the daily press. One looked at the New York City dailies. The other covered a group of "representative newspapers" published elsewhere. His studies began to adduce the importance newspapers attached to religion as news. But he then broadened his analyses to also look at other topics, to include "crimes, athletic sports, the markets, theaters, labor, and editorials." Elliot argued that his statistics revealed the definition of news as it applied to modern journalism in the context of a commercial enterprise. Elliot's findings for twelve morning and afternoon dailies in New York City over three days—Friday, Sunday, and Monday—revealed the average ratio of religious news to the total as 3.5 percent, with the percentages ranging from a high of 7.5 percent to a low of 1 percent. The second study extended its analysis to several major cities over two days; the morning papers in each city were considered a unit. Elliot found the national average for coverage of religion was 5 percent, with the highest—Boston and St. Louis—at 7 percent and the lowest, Cincinnati, at 3 percent. In addition, Cincinnati joined New York in leading in the space devoted to crime—14 percent.[32]

From these statistics, Elliot attempted to discern the attitude of the editors toward religion. He observed that the general opinion, which was "well founded," was that the secular press was no friend of religion. For instance, he observed that "base-ball and horse-racing news is reported with great care and fullness, while the leading religious events are either ignored altogether or indifferently reported." That was so, he conjectured, because readers sought out those papers that did the best job of offering "full, prompt, and sympathetic treatment of theatrical, sporting, and market news." The same was not true, however, for those interested in news about religion, because "religious people, as such, do not discriminate in their patronage of newspapers with a corresponding exactness." Thus, Elliot argued, the most successful papers were those that were able to divine what the reading public wanted in its newspapers.[33]

It is within both the approbation and the condemnation of the newspaper over the decades that we can tease out two things. One was the slow reveal of religion's ceding its power to the press—what one writer for the *Outlook* called "a strong, good moral agent, whose influence was also far-reaching and decisive."[34] To that point, religion was conferring to the press the role of agent of societal reform as an educator of public opinion vital to society and the maintenance of democracy. The second was the attendant appeal for press reform—for a new news ethic as an essential component of the modern newspaper's role and responsibility to society, as it called for the press to reject the market's leavening effect on the mission of the newspaper and instead interpret the news for readers and advocate for reform and moral uplift.

Certainly, this subsidence of the church's primacy in the area of public opinion and the enlargement of the perceived role of the press in society were no sudden sea change. But ultimately, they ended with the pulpit's general acquiescence. And, it should be noted, it was a pulpit driven by the powerful and progressive Social Gospel movement that recognized it needed to employ the most modern of means in its effort to apply Protestant religious principles to solve the nation's social ills. The demographic changes brought on by the nation's industrialization and population shifts had much to do with this waning of influence, as church attendance dropped and the public looked elsewhere for guidance. The Reverend William C. Skeath summed this up in 1919 when he lamented the decline in church attendance and "the masses of the passively religious who have closed their ears to the sermon subject and their doors to pastoral visitation." Indeed, historian John Ferré observed that religion's voice had been diminished even more by the fact that religious publications had fallen far behind the secular press in readership, as their circulation dropped by four-fifths between 1900 and 1930. Thus, Ferré suggested, "Ministers began to eye secular newspapers as the most efficient and effective means of outreach," despite their decades-long disapproval of and lack of confidence in the moral suasive capabilities of the secular press.[35]

Those concerns partly stemmed from a debate about whether the modern newspaper as it existed was really "the proper means of communication that will make an enlightened and intelligent public opinion possible," as sociologist Edwin Earp observed. For instance, the Reverend Madison Clinton Peters of the Bloomingdale Reformed Church in New York City confidently contended that the newspaper reached everybody "not only as a news-teller, but also as an oracle. It not only reflects public sentiment, but also shapes it." While Peters believed the newspaper could both reflect and shape public opinion, Professor John William Mears of Hamilton College, a clergyman and former editor of *American Presbyterian*, was less sanguine about the newspaper's good effect. He argued in an essay titled "Position of the Secular Press on Moral Questions" (1880) that it had become doubtful, given the policies of the secular newspaper, "whether those of us who are seeking to promote the moral welfare and advancement of the people can rely upon the help of this powerful agency in carrying out our plans."[36] His analysis—and a similar evaluation by Gladden fifteen years later—is especially interesting for two reasons. One, it reflects a common debate over the years about the competing roles of a newspaper—whether as a passive mirror of life or an activist advocating for progress. And second, embedded in this argument are the clashing notions of the market versus the mission of newspapers.

In his essay, Mears boiled down the standards of journalism of his time to one of two positions—either "that of leading public opinion to positions in advance of those now held" or "that of faithfully representing the present attitude of the public conscience and of justifying it to itself." Similarly, in his disquisition on the newspaper and its role in opinion formation, Gladden identified two theories about the function of the newspaper. Some, he observed, insisted the newspaper simply reflected public opinion. Others held that "the newspaper is supposed to generate public opinion." He pointed to one of the world's most prominent and profitable newspapers, the *Times* of London, which followed the theory that the newspaper's sole objective was "to understand and express public opinion."[37] However, that the better theory for society was that a newspaper should "instruct and guide public opinion," as Gladden maintained, echoed the pulpit's argument for a reform-minded journalistic ideal that defined news as interpretive and advocatory. It also reflected the acknowledgment that such journalism was being practiced and thus was feasible. Indeed, if we set aside for the moment issues of yellowness and sensationalism, this is an approach to journalism not unlike one of the competing, but failed, journalistic paradigms of the late nineteenth century—William Randolph Hearst's "journalism of action" that was participatory in nature and acted as an advocate and change agent.[38] Also, recall here the journalism of William T. Stead and his description of a "true journalism of the governing and guiding order, as distinguished from journalism of the mere critical and paragraph-quilting species," and *Collier's* editor Norman Hapgood's contention that the press must represent "moral freedom, disinterested thought, genuine enthusiasm for progress and for principles."[39]

But in reality, Gladden lamented, the tendency was toward the theory that the newspaper reflected public opinion because journalism was defined more as a business in which profit was the principal consideration. That meant the business office of a newspaper dictated policy on journalistic conduct and content. Therefore, its guiding rule was that newspapers "conform to the prevailing public sentiment, and not to antagonize it." To that point, Mears understood financial success had to be a consideration of any publication. However, he declared, "The calling of the journalist is surely too exalted to be subordinated to merely material considerations. Its functions are too near the heart, the conscience, the springs of the moral life of humanity to be classed as wholly mercantile and to be controlled by mercenary motives."[40]

This expression of a higher-order journalistic function uncorrupted by the marketplace was certainly not a one-off. Indeed, despite his own well-publicized misgivings about the secular press, the Reverend Charles Sheldon believed the modern newspaper owed "a debt to civilization which it ought to pay." That was because, he observed, historically it had been the church and the "Christian citizen" who had been expected to aid in "the regeneration of mankind." But that was such "a tremendous job" that the newspaper as instigator of public opinion needed to help. "The modern newspaper could, and I believe it will, make a wonderful contribution to the final brotherhood of the race, and with the Church and home and school and state help bring in the millennium." This expression is apparent in Talcott Williams's declaration that "the newspaper is the conscience of the people." It is also evident in Gladden's contention that because the press had become the "principal agency for the creation of public opinion," the very health of society and the nation depended on a sound public opinion. "The sacredness of the function of the press is therefore obvious," Gladden declared. "It is pledged, by all that is precious in our national life, to tell the truth; to help the people to see things as they are." And the Reverend J. E. Smith echoed this stance in an essay called "The Secular Press and Morality" (1888) that appeared in *Zion's Herald*, a widely distributed Methodist journal. Smith acknowledged the power of the press in "moulding public opinion and in forming the public taste." The problem was the newspapers published as news accounts of events and crimes not fit for publication. Smith wrote that a newspaper is a business with investors who seek dividends—and the test or failure of the paper is its ability to make money, to which all else is subordinated. "This is the rock on which the highest purpose and the greatest usefulness is split." However, Smith held, "The first object of the true journalist cannot be to make money. . . . He should see to it that his whole influence is upon the side of truth and purest morality."[41]

Journalism as Coadjutor to Religion

Reform and moral uplift were the subjects of many a book, article, tract, sermon, and conference proceeding. This impulse involved a complex stew of progressive-minded trepidation triggered by "our seething national life"[42] that included qualms about the ramifications of what Walter Lippmann called a modern "complicated civilization";[43] worries about war;[44] shock at the conduct of Gilded Age corporations that had "neither a soul to be saved nor a body to be damned";[45] concerns about the future of democracy, given the millions of immigrants flooding the nation and the forces of anarchy brought over from Europe and unleashed in the face of corporate misconduct, which spawned the call for Americanization and educating the masses in the values of American democracy;[46] and the outright predictions of a second civil war.[47] These advocates for reform and moral uplift included members of the clergy both inside and outside the Social Gospel movement, religiously oriented and reform-minded sociologists and economists, self-identified socialists both in and out of the clergy, and members of the press.

More than one scholar and religious advocate has described the natural integration of the press and pulpit going as far back as Christ's disciples. Church publicist Herbert Heebner Smith wrote in 1915 that Saint Paul established "the first religious and civic uplift newspaper when he had his friends carry letters to the various young churches which he had founded. These letters of advice and counsel were read to the people in lieu of sermons." Gladden described Saint Paul's Epistles as a "rich elaboration" of the Christian canon and as a kind of news that spread the word of Christianity. However, it was not only the pastorate that saw incipient journalism in the letters of Paul. Walter J. Shepard, the renowned political theorist, noted in 1909 in a discussion about public opinion and its power for change and reformation that journalism was derived from "conversation and correspondence." And, he pointed out, the first journals were nothing more than letters one person duplicated and sent out to others. Similarly, this was the journalistic function of the Epistles of Saint Paul, who "had there been a religious weekly . . . would have published them as articles."[48] This is a notion further elaborated on by contemporary religious scholar Joanna Dewey, who asserted that Saint Paul's use of the written word in what was then an oral world helped move the Christian faith into the authoritative world of text.[49]

The Reverend Simeon Gilbert, editor of the *Advance*, a Congregational weekly, observed in a Chautauqua lecture in 1881 that it should be kept in mind that journalism existed long before newspapers and that the newspaper was simply one product of journalism—that it was "journalism reduced to print, and by aid of the modern miracle of the press, multiplied fast enough to be strewn among the people thick as the buds of spring." For example, he pointed to the ancient relics then being found in the deserts that were laced with iconography and inscriptions that were partly examples of journalism. So, too, were the communicative efforts of the biblical prophets, "who were the journalists of their time," offering truth to the public, "for, the world wants to know; there are always those who want to be known; and there have always existed some means of making popularly known the more notable transactions of the time."[50]

For historian David Paul Nord, journalism—the act of reporting news—has even more complex roots in religion. He observed that Puritan New Englanders were expected to maintain an "informed participation in public affairs." That meant that from the first moment, New Englanders were ensconced in the world of the "Word—and of printing." And for New Englanders, current events were hinged to the notion of divine Providence. And news of such events involved what Nord describes as "reportorial empiricism" and "authoritative interpretation." The former was empirical, but "eclectic and reportorial, not systematic and scientific." It involved the collection, ordering, and citation of information from sources. "Such a methodology was empiricism without science. It was, in a word, journalism." Nord argues that news was teleological because everything that happened did so because it was part of God's plan. In addition, the notion of divine Providence adhered to the seventeenth century's version of the popular press—the "ballads, chapbooks, almanacs." And once the first newspapers began operation in the early eighteenth century, "the news system" based in the teleological and "reportorial empiricism" established by the seventeenth-century Puritans was there to be co-opted. Ultimately, secular journalism divorced itself from religion, as news lost all its importance as a teleological event and became "just the news," with little or no meaning beyond the fact that the news was about interesting occurrences.[51]

Historian Doug Underwood made a similar argument. He contended that the early clergy and religious proselytizers who defended freedom of the press were working in the "tradition of the world's first 'journalists.'" Underwood linked the writings of men such as Quaker activist George Fox back to the tradition of the Hebrew prophets and forward to contemporary advocatory journalists and columnists who espouse progressive causes. Underwood contended that "Fox's writings are representative of a raw and inspired expression that I call 'prophetic journalism'—a journalism of passion, polemic, and moral opinion that has come to exist alongside the modern ethic of objectivity and the commercial elements of profit making that dictate so much of what journalism constitutes today."[52] Still, recall that prophetic journalism as a model beleaguered by a commercialized press is not a new notion. The daily press's responsibility toward "truth and purest morality" was one theme of the criticism of the press by many inside and outside the church—including Gladden, who saw the subjection of the modern newspaper's teaching function to the constraints of the market as a "lack of prophetism," which he described as a "supreme allegiance to truth" in an attempt to be "guides of conduct" for the reading public.[53]

Gladden's argument that the press was a subsidiary coadjutor to the church in its efforts to sway public opinion is embedded in American history in comments such as that the "press ranks second to the pulpit";[54] "The press is next to the pulpit in the ministry of Truth";[55] "The Press should be the chief ally of the Pulpit";[56] "The Press can never be the Preacher's master, but it may and should be his indicator";[57] the press is "the natural alliance between the newspapers and the churches";[58] and "Journalism will never be a substitute for the free utterance of living thought."[59] The Reverend Matthew Simpson, the bishop of the Methodist Episcopal Church in New York, reiterated that notion in 1879 in a speech to students at Yale College. In it he weighed the balancing act between the pulpit and press. He described the latter as both "one of the most powerful agencies" and an "offspring" of Christianity, whose role was one of informing and guiding society. The press and pulpit, he argued, should not be rivals or enemies. "Each has its proper sphere, and the exaltation of one does not diminish the glory of the other." Simpson acknowledged that even in 1879, there were those who argued that the press had supplanted the pulpit because print had taken precedence over the oral society of the past. However, he asserted, the press may deliver messages, but they are not messages grounded in the speaker as witness to the truth. More than three decades later, Smith, the church publicist who wrote about how religion could employ the secular press to spread its message, insisted it was possible to make the press "a warm ally" to the church. It was necessary to do so, Smith observed, because "this is preeminently the age of newspaper readers rather than of church goers."[60]

The advocates of religion recognized that if it were to play a part in controlling the forces of change and participating in the morally charged reform movement of the era, the pulpit did need a friend. That was because a falling rate of churchgoing in the early twentieth century signaled the declining influence of religion and the growing influence of the press. As Judge Samuel J. Miller told the National Conference of Unitarian and Other Christian Churches in 1889, "The Christian ministry of the present day has a rival in the line of its own pursuit, in the press, in the newspaper, in the pamphlet, in the magazine."[61] One response to that decline was the creation of a whole new field of endeavor like that of Ernest Eugene Elliott, a graduate of a school of church advertising who wrote and consulted about the problems of the modern church. In a book titled *How to Fill the Pews* (1920), Elliott noted that because so few members of congregations attended church on a regular basis, the church was no longer an educator of public opinion. That was an assertion made thirty years before by Henry W. Grady, a renowned southern journalist and orator who contended, "The vast majority of people do not go to church, but all intelligent people read the newspapers."[62]

To be sure, this subsidence of the pulpit's influence reflected the nation's transformation. America was rapidly moving from a largely agrarian-based society to a complex modern life with an educated populace based in urban centers and sustained by industrialization. It was a time, as one clergyman noted in 1896, in which the newspaper represented "the new communication, as the industrial city represents the new production."[63] In fact, historian Henry Steele Commager observed that the era saw such an alteration in the social fabric that an ethical problem emerged "from the attempt to apply the individualistic moral code of the eighteenth and early nineteenth centuries—a moral code in which good and evil were significant terms, and responsibility personal—to the complex, impersonal practices of a twentieth-century economic order."[64] One aspect of this transformation was the increasing literacy rates and the growing number of affordable newspapers and periodicals overseen by much-better-educated editors.[65] For example, Census data show that from 1890 to 1920, the number of press venues increased from 16,948 to 21,012. And from 1870 to 1920, the number of people classified as journalists increased by nearly 550 percent, from 5,286 to 34,197, while at the same time the number of clergy rose by just over 190 percent, from 43,874 to 127,270. In addition, from 1890 to 1915, the number of primary and secondary students increased from 12.7 million to 19.7 million, and the population of university and technology college students rose from 55,687 to 216,636.

Another contributor to the undermining of the traditional American way of life and to the subsidence of Protestant influence over public opinion was the enormous influx of immigrants, many of whom adhered to non-Protestant religions or to no religion at all.[66] US Census data confirm this. For example, while the number of members of religious bodies rose from

20.6 million in 1890 to nearly 33 million in 1906, particularly notable was the shift in religious adherents. In 1890 Protestants made up 68 percent of the total. By 1906 that number had fallen to 61.6 percent, as the number of adherents of the Roman Catholic Church nearly doubled and rose from 30.3 percent to 36.7 percent of the total. Meanwhile, between 1890 and 1910, the nation's population grew from nearly 63 million to just over 101 million. That was a nearly 60 percent increase, a good proportion of it driven by immigration. Indeed, according to Census figures, the foreign-born population more than quadrupled between 1850 and 1900, from more than 2.2 million to nearly 11 million—topping out at a little more than 13.5 million in 1910.

These changes in demographics did not go unnoticed by Protestant leaders. For example, clergyman Josiah Strong noted in 1893 a link between the increasing population of the cities and the concomitant falloff in churchgoers. Strong observed that in just a decade, several cities had grown three to four times the size of what they had been in 1880 and that Chicago had doubled to 1 million residents. The cities, then, were becoming the "centre of civilization, and the source of moulding influences." Given that, Strong worried that the Christian church was not growing enough to keep pace and maintain its influence. Strong outlined how in fifty of the nation's largest cities, six of the major denominations had fallen from 12.67 "inhabitants to one communicant" in 1840 to 20.14 per communicant in 1890. That meant these denominations had "grown only 63 per cent as rapidly as the population during the past half-century." And, Strong pointed out, this was occurring during a time when "men are growing more and more sensitive to public opinion." Indeed, as the Reverend William Payne Shriver, superintendent of the Immigration Department of the Board of Home Missions of the Presbyterian Church, observed in 1913, it was not to an organized religion that the growing immigrant population turned for guidance. He noted that at the end of 1912 in the United States and Canada, there were 538 newspapers printed in twenty-nine foreign languages and that the press was one of the forces that "powerfully shapes and molds" the life of the immigrant.[67]

The Tipping Point

In 1889 William Samuel Lilly, a writer and secretary to the Catholic Union of England, asserted that most people read nothing else but newspapers, which had become "the direct sources of those floating opinions which have drifted in their minds, wherewith they judge all social and political problems." The journalist, he reported, had taken over the role once filled by the preacher, who was limited to teaching about religion. "The pulpit has been obliged to resign to the press the instruction of the people in secular affairs," he argued. Lilly's observation about the displacement of the pulpit by the press follows a thread of discourse that had begun long before and carried on long afterward.[68] For example, five years before Lilly's declaration, Matthew H. Buckham, president of the University of Vermont for nearly forty years who held degrees in both law and divinity,[69] described the secular press "as the most powerful agent in forming public opinion." His essay "Lay Theology" appeared in the liberal and progressive *Andover Review.* Buckham suggested that the better newspapers and magazines had begun treating religion with "seriousness and thoroughness," which indicated that readers were interested in the subject as mediated through a lay publication. Buckham went on to observe that the time when the pulpit "dictated opinion on all the secular concerns of man" was now over and that it was now "restricted to spiritual matters."[70]

Still, this review of the writings and discussions of the religious leaders about displacement reveals neither unanimity nor unequivocal acceptance. To use a contemporary coinage, there was still considerable pushback. In it, however, a creeping acquiescence to the shift in power over public opinion to the newspaper press is apparent. But it was often a reluctant acceptance tinged with caveats about channeling the press toward a conduct grounded in Christianity. Much of this pushback was driven by two faults that many in the religious community had difficulty ignoring as others called for making newspapers the vehicle of religious messages. One was the perception that newspapers regularly distorted the truth because they were enthralled to partisan political parties. The other was that newspapers were the hostages of commercial interests, which led to salacious sensationalism, invasions of privacy, the advertising of socially unacceptable products or promotion of social sins, the bending of truth to appease the market and ideological interests, and the failure to advocate for reform and moral uplift.

One of those who saw little hope in co-opting the press to aid in social reform was socialist-leaning Baptist clergyman and church historian Henry Clay Vedder. He argued that while the press should be a noble calling, it was, in reality, "one of the vilest." Newspapers told not the truth but a "version of events" that did two things—please readers and not offend advertisers. "The business of the press as a disseminator of news is seriously impaired by this commercialism, and the proper function of the newspaper, as teacher and prophet, is nearly gone," Vedder lamented. In fact, in 1887, in the Reverend Newell Woolsey Wells's call for the creation of a Christian daily newspaper (the subject of the next chapter), we hear both his acknowledgment of the secular press's primacy in matters of public opinion and his own dissatisfaction with them as venues of moral uplift. Wells described the daily newspapers of the nation as "moral agents." But the problem was, newspapers represented "an accommodation of conscience to the average conscience of the communities" in which they published. Therefore, Wells urged the creation of "an able, clean, Christian daily" that would be a secular, not religious, journal that would apply the principles found in the Bible to public questions, promote the sanctity of the Sabbath, and defend and be fair to the church.[71]

However, most observers agreed that creating a Christian daily newspaper would be a fruitless endeavor because of the expense and the complexity of the newspaper business. The better option was to change the ethos of the existing secular press. Victor S. Yarros, an American anarchist, lawyer, and author, believed just that, calling any such effort to create a Christian daily "futile." Instead, he held, what was needed was "a moral, high-minded, clean, and honest newspaper press—a press that will not prostitute truth to selfish interest." Yarros acknowledged that there were a few newspapers that approached that ideal, but the question was "How is their number to be increased?"[72] The pulpit believed it had the answer. It believed it retained the moral suasive power to influence the conduct of the press. For example, in 1897 the annual letter to editors from the Religious Society of Friends' Committee for the Purification of the Press noted evidence showing that earlier efforts at reforming the press had paid dividends. Therefore, according to the letter, the effort was to be continued because the press was a powerful molder of character and the nation's welfare depended on it.[73] And, it appears, those outside the pulpit were open to such persuasion. For instance, Talcott Williams told one congregation, "One of the efforts of the Christian church ought to be to supervise, and if need be, change the moral tone of the newspaper."[74] This openness to change also appeared in an editorial in the newspaper industry's major trade journal about the nationwide distribution of fliers in an effort to purify the press by the Friends' Press Association. *Editor & Publisher* wished the association success in its effort and acknowledged that there were "plenty of opportunities for improvement among the newspapers of the country. The press is what the people make it.

If they want a pure press, a clean press, they will get it and any effort toward that direction is laudable."[75]

To just that point, one key representation of the disenchantment with newspapers and the belief that they could be reformed appeared in 1897. A committee appointed by the New York Ministers' Association to formulate a way of counteracting "the pernicious influence of the so-called 'New Journalism'"—a reference to the sensationalist yellow press of the time—issued its report. In it the group noted that the daily press's power for good or evil was "vast." Therefore, in a community where most of the population opposed vice and crime, "there should be a moral tone sufficient to influence the press to a degree adequate to make it upon the whole an elevating force." The report acknowledged the economic fact that competition among newspapers promoted huge expenditures to scoop competitors and report stories that "work serious harm"—to include detailed reports on divorces and domestic scandals. The report did not say a paper should leave out such stories. But it called for a redefinition of news. For instance, items about arrests, trials, executions, and divorces should be kept as short as possible "and the result prepared in the spirit of one regretting the necessity of mentioning them at all." In summary, the Ministers' Association appealed to the press "to use the great powers in its hands to help men to do right and to make it hard for men to do wrong."[76]

Ultimately, the culmination of this conversation—and arguably the tipping point toward large acceptance of the notion that the press had replaced the pulpit as arbiter of public opinion—appeared in 1912 in a nearly two-hundred-page report titled *The Church and the Press*. Earlier that year, the Men and Religion Forward Movement—an organization that Walter Rauschenbusch called "the most comprehensive evangelistic movement ever undertaken" in America—held its Christian Conservation Congress at which it established the Commission on Publicity. The commission members included several prominent newspaper and advertising executives. The report was the first effort by American churches to offer a scientific, national examination of the relationship between the pulpit and the press. And its one abiding question was "Can we ally two such forces in even a small way?"[77]

Much of the information in the report was gathered through questionnaires sent to the members of the Men and Religion Congress, the primary secular and religious newspapers, and ministers and laymen. And as its introduction notes, the questionnaires prompted a renewed national interest in both the secular and the religious journals in the pulpit's use of the press to publicize its mission. The authors of the report observed that it came at a time when those involved in the work of the church were "groping after new and better ways" of communicating their message. "The sentiment is widespread that while the truth of the Message has not changed, the new times demand the most modern methods of conveying the Good Tidings to all men."[78] And rather than paraphrase the nuanced argument of the report's authors, I offer two paragraphs that reveal two points that manifest a culmination of religion's views of the press by 1912. One was how the authors attached the needs of publicity for the church to the criticism of—and calls for reform of—the extravagances of the public press. The other reiterates the conviction that the newspaper was a public utility. And implied here is the notion that the newspaper must first heed the demands of this communitarian mission as a public servant before those of the market:

> The public press is being called upon, as perhaps never before, to give an account of itself, and to prove itself worthy of the confidence of the public. The extent of the distrust of the daily newspaper that is abroad in the land should give pause to all editors and publishers, and lead them to a self-examination like unto that which the church is undergoing. What thoughtful persons believe concerning a newspaper really determines that paper's value in all its departments. It is no idle dream that both press and church, in these new and reorganizing times, should, in all brotherliness and mutual respect, cooperate to the advantage of each other in the service of the great public, to which both are indispensable.
>
> Neither the press nor the pulpit will come to its own until each recognizes with intelligence and enthusiasm not only its own opportunity but also the obligation of the other in making wholesome and strong the life of the commonwealth. It is this community of interest and of responsibility that constitutes the natural alliance between the newspapers and the churches.[79]

The report offered several strategies that churches could use to spread their message through the secular press. The authors noted, as others had, that what the newspapers wanted were human interest stories—and what could be more interesting than stories arising from the many religious movements then ongoing in America? These movements unquestionably were of great news value, the report argued, because they "have to do with the breathing, pulsating life of flesh-and-blood men and women; they give the lie to the misleading statement, quoted by one of our correspondents,

'If it is not sinful it is not news.'" In addition, there was news interest in the ideas that emanated from the churches, the report contended. It then went on to chide any preacher who would "attack from his pulpit hobble skirts[80] and false hair." News of his criticism would certainly make its way into print, but that would do more harm than good since it was not representative of the church's position on the social, economic, and political issues of the day.[81]

Finally, a core argument of the report was that the church needed to employ the press to spread the word of religion. That was because in the modern age of literacy driven by compulsory education, the press was the primary way people became acquainted with the ideas that were the ground from which public opinion grew. The press had access to the public "as no other teacher," the report observed. "Backed by organized business sagacity and persistency, and reached for by a newfound hunger in the reading public, the press is the omnipresent publicity means at the disposal of the moral forces of the land." This displacement of the pulpit by the press, the report acknowledged, was a realization the church had finally come to recognize. Thus, the day had come that the press and pulpit must collaborate, the authors argued, because the task facing religion was "so vast" that it needed every ally in its struggle. The church needed, the report declared, to cooperate with "the awakened conscience of the American press," which was "the greatest of all modern institutions of publicity in the world's uplift."[82]

And it is here in aiding "in the world's uplift," and in the New York Ministers' Association's appeal to the press "to use the great powers in its hands to help men to do right and to make it hard for men to do wrong," and in Gladden's earlier lament for the modern newspaper's "lack of prophetism," and in the Reverend Henry Vedder's description of the newspaper's mission "as teacher and prophet," and in Wells's insistence that newspapers were "moral agents" that rests a theme—an enjoinder—common to much of the pulpit's publicly stated conferrals of the role of agent of education and moral uplift to the press. It is an attendant counsel about the press's role and responsibility to society as an attempt to influence newspaper conduct and challenge the notion of journalistic objectivity with its roots in the commercial side of newspapering. Indeed, much of this discourse revealed the pulpit struggling to define newspapers as "a people's university"[83] and "a highly human, ethical and personal form of social service"[84] and news as interpretive and advocatory,[85] as the press was elevated to "a higher moral standard" and wielded on the "side of righteousness."[86]

One representative example of this was Methodist minister John R. Creighton, who wrote in the *Methodist Review* in 1895 that a discussion of the press, pulpit, and pew was "timely," given the exigencies of the era—the "woe of humanity"—and because "nothing could withstand this trinity of forces in regenerating the world." The "triple agency" of the press, pulpit, and pew could work together to encourage uplift and progress toward a moral world. And, in fact, Creighton predicted, if the press did not join in this effort, the result would surely be "social convulsions and civil and religious strife such as the world has never seen." Rather than publishing sensationalist and salacious news items intended to titillate, the secular press needed to expand its coverage of news to "a fuller presentation of social reforms" and anything else that worked for moral uplift. Still, Creighton was encouraged by the recent criticism of the secular press by the better periodicals of the day pointing to just this absence of ennobling news. Additionally, he was heartened by news that the journalistic world was indeed in conversation about how to improve its conduct in the kinds of stories it reported for fear of losing thousands of readers who demanded a better class of news. And, Creighton believed, journalism could be helped along by a concerted public opinion—especially by members of the pew who could guide and support "the rising public sentiment" opposed to the evils of journalism.[87]

Finally, we cannot divorce the call for a press purged of its degrading elements from the call for an interpretive and advocatory journalism grounded in moral uplift—in the gospel of social justice and service promoted by the Social Gospel movement and other reformers. Recall, for example, clergyman and professor John William Mears's insistence on the need for a secular press that led "public opinion to positions in advance of those now held." In fact, religion's powerful criticism of the newspaper press over many decades was one tangent of discourse in a national debate leading to the coalescing of thought and the development of journalistic normative standards. This is evident as early as 1909 in the Christian leanings of the founders of Sigma Delta Chi, the forerunner of the Society of Professional Journalists, a national organization dedicated to high standards of journalistic conduct. Indeed, the group's founders were all Methodists who approached the founding of the honorary fraternity with a missionary zeal. "It was done," historian Judith Buddenbaum contended, "for the purpose of making journalism a force for good in society. That underlying purpose developed as much from the Methodist concept of mission as from the progressive's notion of reform."[88]

Here, again, are the overlapping of the goals of the press with those of the pulpit. This is especially well represented by the American Society of Newspaper Editors' adoption of the Canons of Journalism, the first nationwide code of ethics for the profession in 1923, which was imbued with the echoes of decades of pastoral criticism.[89] And also apparent is the newspaper industry's acknowledgment of the pulpit's cession of power over public opinion to the press and the burden of responsibility adhering to that transfer in *Editor & Publisher*'s paean to journalism guided by the Canons—"a beacon light of promise to those who would make it their means of serving mankind."[90]

CHAPTER 4

The Call Goes Out for a Christian Daily Newspaper

An interesting question, half literary, half ethical, is being discussed in English and American newspapers. It is—the need and feasibility of a "Christian Daily."

—"Highways and Byways" (October 1899)

The expensive experiment of religious people in starting the *New York World*, and the *New York Daily Witness* would seem to indicate that Christian readers in New York will not support a daily paper that has "Piety" written on every page. They look upon a daily paper termed "Christian" as they do upon a hotel called "Temperance"; while approving the more excellent institution, they patronize the other one.

—The Reverend John Bancroft Devins, "Founders Day at Lafayette College"

IN OCTOBER 1920, THE ANNOUNCEMENT went out that the *American Daily Standard*, a Christian daily newspaper, would soon begin publication in Chicago. The paper would not be published on Sunday, and it would be "Christian in character, moral in tone, independent in politics, non-partisan and non-sectarian. Stories or narrations of scandal, vice and crime shall not be given prominence and shall be excluded so far as practicable. Prominence shall be given to news of value in promoting the welfare of the state, the church and the home." In one of many responses to this news, the *Decatur (IL) Daily Review* observed that a newspaper of this sort "has been thought of and discussed and talked about for twenty-five years or more, but it is only now that anything definite has been done toward actually getting it out."[1]

This latter statement, of course, was inaccurate on more than one count. First, there had been other attempts at establishing Christian daily newspapers in America. The most obvious was the *Christian Science Monitor.* In fact, A. J. Bucher, editor of the *Christian Apologist,* observed that despite what one might think of the Church of Christ, Science, it must be conceded it was publishing something "all the Christian churches in the United States combined have thus far failed to produce, namely, the publication of a daily newspaper edited in a thoroughly Christian spirit." It was a paper, Bucher observed in 1929, that for many years had offered clean, quality domestic and foreign news and lead editorials while advocating for and supporting reform movements. And it did this while keeping church advocacy in the background. At the same time, it rejected the "shouting headlines" and the "professional newspaper fiction" of contemporary daily journalism. This paper was, Bucher argued, a template for the American Federation of Churches, which, if all members would cooperate, could publish a successful Christian daily newspaper, "which is one of the most crying needs of the present time."[2] Second, the observation that discussion about a Christian daily had been going on for more than twenty-five years was off by many decades. The conversation calling for a Christian daily began in earnest in midcentury, not long after the establishment of the first secular and market-driven penny newspapers.

This tension over the mission of the newspaper between the sacred and secular—between a demand for a sermonesque interpretative advocacy in the name of moral uplift and individual and societal reform versus a market-driven adherence to neutral objectivity and the expansion of news to the margins of propriety—was often evident in pastoral critiques of the press. And these were often constructed around the recognition that the newspaper was an engine or a force for both good and evil.[3] These arraignments of the press and religion's consequent call for a Christian daily newspaper that would fulfill the mission of newspapers manifested the centuries-old tension between the secular market and the sacred ideals of the church. Barbara Tuchman in her dissection of the fourteenth century described this struggle as "the conflict between the reach for the divine and lure of earthly things," which was the fundamental issue of the Middle Ages. "In economic man," she noted, "the lay spirit did not challenge the Church, yet functioned in essential contradiction. Capitalist enterprise, although it held by now a commanding place, violated by its very nature the Christian attitude toward commerce." For instance, Saint Jerome is reported to have said, "A merchant can seldom if ever please God." And the fifth-century bishop Saint Augustine wrote, "Business is in itself evil."[4]

This discord between the church and commerce continued down through the centuries and dovetailed with the newspaper as it gradually became a powerful commercial force in society. For instance, a speaker in 1851 told an audience that "Christ will never get the advantage of trade, and take his place in the world, until he has possession of the daily press; and by the grace of God, I engage that he shall yet have a daily paper that will compete with any in existence."[5] Similarly, Washington Gladden noted that essayist Thomas Carlyle had likened newspaper publishers and editors to the mendicant friars of the past who appeared outwardly to be holy men but who internally harbored what Carlyle had called a "hunger for terrestrial things." It was, Gladden argued, "this 'hunger for terrestrial things' that now so often dulls the message of our newspaper censors, and keeps them silent in presence of the most flagrant misdoing of their patrons or their fellow partisans."[6]

To that point, in 1860 the religious weekly *Circular* criticized an editorial in the *New York Tribune* that made a distinction between earthly and spiritual realms in relation to the daily press. The weekly called the distinction a "low and false view" of the interaction between religion and daily life. It held that "the curse that rests upon society to-day, is, that men have left God and religion out of their daily affairs."[7] That was largely because, Lyman Abbott recalled fifty-five years later, the previous decades of radical change in the religious life of America had been driven by the "democratic movement of the time." For example, he noted, there was a growing attitude among educated men and women to reject a theology that espoused the doctrine of the inherent depravity of all men and women—that all were "wholly disposed to evil." Abbott observed that in the modern democratic society, court procedures were based on the belief that people tend to tell the truth, business was based on a credit system grounded in honesty, and the electoral process was based on the belief that "in spite of prejudices and passions," voters would be "disposed to see the truth and act in accordance with it." Thus, Abbott continued, "The questions in which the people were interested were not theological but sociological; they were questions, not of future salvation for the few, but of social salvation for all. The questions of slavery, of reconstruction in the South, of public education, of the treatment of the immigrant, of the abolition of poverty, of the cure of crime, of the emancipation of women and children from tasks unfitted or too great for them, of the redemption of the cities and the factory towns from the slums, absorbed the public mind."[8]

And with the "public mind," a key factor in this reformation of the litany of social issues Abbott outlined was public opinion—mediated less and less by the pulpit and more and more by the secular press. The *New York Evangelist* observed this as early as 1851. The religious newspaper, which was founded in the early 1830s as an antislavery publication that promoted "revivals and missions, temperance, and other reforms,"[9] declared that the newspaper had become "Bible, church and priest" and that "much of the power once claimed and wielded by the confessional and pulpit, has been silently given over to this priesthood of letters." The writer pointed to the press's increasing power over public opinion and noted that very few people did not feel its influence in their judgments about the world. The *Evangelist* maintained that religion was failing to employ the press—"God's great gift to our modern era"—and that a Christian daily, even if not the most popular of publications, would still be an influential and powerful force for good. It went on to hope that one day someone would try the experiment.[10]

The problem was, nearly all attempts at such an experiment, the *Zion's Herald* remarked more than forty years later, had "invariably failed."[11] One exception, but only for a short time, was the *New York Daily Witness*. It was a sister publication of the *Montreal Witness*, founded by journalist and temperance reformer John Dougall in 1846 as a religious and temperance weekly. In 1860 a similar daily edition was added. Dougall found such success with his venture that he regularly spoke at religious gatherings and talked with the editors of religious weeklies to promote the founding of Christian dailies, but could find no one interested in taking the chance.[12] Finally, in 1871 he began the *New York Daily Witness*, which—never profitable—lasted until 1877, leaving Dougall with a loss of two hundred thousand dollars. He was forced to downsize the publication to a weekly.[13]

The *American Daily Standard* followed a similar but much shorter path. It closed its doors after only ninety days. Reaction from the journalistic profession to the closure was both quick and biting. The paper, whose policy was to avoid sensational news and, as one writer noted, published "only what the editors believed would be for the best interests of the people," did not appeal to enough readers to attract advertisers.[14] Indeed, the *Waterloo (Iowa) Evening Courier* suggested the *Standard*, which tried to "operate without giving prominence to accounts of crime has suspended publication. Doubtless for the lack of news to print." The lesson to be learned here, the *Ogden (Utah) Standard-Examiner* declared, is that the daily paper "is merely a reflection of the desires of the people who subscribe for it. That is a lesson every publisher has to learn." Finally, the newspaper trade journal the *Fourth Estate* observed, "For years and years ministers of the Church, either singly or in meeting assembled, have complained that the newspapers devoted too much space and prominence to reports of crime and scandal and many of them thought that when the 'Christian' paper started that Christian people would drop the other 'vile' dailies and flock to the new *Standard*. But they didn't." Still, the newspaper trade journal declared, the fact that the *Standard* had "given up the editorial ghost" should not be blamed on the church or Christian readers. Instead, the closure just showed that "the preacher should stick to his ministerial duties and not try to tell editors what to put in their papers."[15]

Such a distinction between the roles of the press and pulpit—between the secular and the sacred—was a view with which the Reverend Charles H. Parkhurst wholeheartedly agreed. Parkhurst, a renowned social reformer, outlined the distinction between the press and pulpit when it came to "human uplift" in a series of Lyman Beecher Lectures delivered in 1913 before the Yale University Divinity School. The pulpit's "prime mission," he observed, was emancipating people from sin, and that was an endeavor at which the secular press would never succeed. Certainly, Parkhurst was ready to admit, the better newspapers did foster morality. "But morality is not religion and does not carry in it the flavor of religion's essence." And the pulpit could not rely on the "moribund" religious journals to contribute to "the evangelizing of the world." Furthermore, he had no more respect for similar journals that attempted to enliven their pages by becoming magazine-like and "padding with secularity." Thus, Parkhurst argued, the moral suasive power of the unaided pulpit was made more clear by the difficulties in creating a paper that would "serve as a kind of legible pulpit." That was because there were three essential components of a successful religious journal—"three that are rarely found in combination,—an unlimited amount of capital, an inexhaustible supply of brain and a rich infusion of the evangelical spirit." Parkhurst went on to note that it was easy to criticize journalism, and it would not be fair to ignore the contributions the better newspapers and magazines made to society. But for Parkhurst, the realpolitik embedded in any discussion about a newspaper doing the work of—or even aiding—the pulpit in its duties lay in the principal mission of the secular press—"to make money, and no man ever does an ideally good thing when the prime motive is shekels." The reality was, he argued, that "an ideal newspaper cannot be issued in an unideal world and have the business pay."[16]

The Roles and Rituals of Newspapers

Still, despite Parkhurst's admonition, what we have here in this call for a Christian daily newspaper over many decades is an assemblage of like-minded advocates across both space and time who believed that the newspaper was a vital tool for maintaining society. Why they believed so is well explicated by historian Joad Raymond in his work *The Invention of the Newspaper: English Newsbooks, 1641–1649*. Raymond explores the advent of the emerging desire for news of recent events and emphasizes that "news is a constituent of communication, and communication binds together societies and cultures." And news, as the American Tract Society similarly argued in 1850, can create a continent-wide "fraternal neighborhood."[17] In fact, while many Protestant churches saw newspapers as an evangelical tool to target nonbelievers, one of the main functions of these papers was to reach out to adherents and cultivate a group identity.[18] Indeed, a religious publication acted as a binding agent, creating a "textual community" across wide geographic areas and broadening the reach of religion.[19] Scholar of rhetoric James A. Herrick describes such a grouping as a community of discourse that permits "people to think and act with unity to address a wide range of serious social problems," a community that can run efficiently without the members actually knowing one another.[20]

Similarly, and especially applicable to our purposes, is Benedict Anderson's definition of nations as "imagined communities" in which the members are largely unknown to one another, "yet in the minds of each lives the image of their communion." And one of the instruments that helped create and sustain these "imagined communities" was the newspaper. At one point, Anderson refers to Hegel's diary entry that "reading the morning newspaper is the realist's morning prayer. One orients one's attitude toward the world either by God or by what the world is. The former gives as much security as the latter, in that one knows how one stands." Anderson describes this act of reading in the privacy of the "lair of the skull" as a "mass ceremony," because "each communicant is well aware that the ceremony he performs is being replicated by thousands (or millions) of others of whose existence he is confident, yet of whose identity he has not the slightest notion."[21] It is then not a long walk to see how newspapers could be instruments of creating and sustaining "imagined" religious communities among strangers across wide geographic areas. For example, the ritual ceremony of reading newspapers has been likened by more than one scholar to the prescribed calendrical reading of the *Book of Common Prayer* as a means of promoting "an ideal of social simultaneity."[22] Indeed, the preface to the prayer book makes note of the importance of just this binding simultaneity: "And where heretofore there hath been great diversity in saying and singing in churches within this realm . . . Now from henceforth, all the whole realm shall have but one use."[23]

From this we cannot help but be reminded of James Carey and his assertion that news acts as ritual. Carey held that this ran counter to the conventional way of looking at communication through the lens of "the economic worldview" in which it was seen as a way of transmitting messages across geographic space as part of a control mechanism. "However, primordially and politically, the origin of communication is at one with the origins of ritual and religion: not the transmission of intelligent information but the construction and maintenance of an ordered, meaningful cultural world that can serve as a container for human action—a world of time rather than space."[24] Yet, Carey lamented, a review of the history of modern communications revealed how both information and meaning had become products of the market. One key case in point, as I noted earlier, is the rite of the notion of objectivity—a "commercially grounded strategy of reporting"[25]—that arose with the commercialization of the newspaper industry and the professionalization of journalism. To remain neutral and inoffensive to advertisers and readers, commercially minded objectivity eschewed the earlier value-based journalistic practice of criticism and interpretation. And here, then, in the demands of the commercial aspect of the values-bereft secular newspapers that began to shoulder aside what historian C. John Sommerville describes as "religion as the 'master text' of English culture"[26] is the constant core constituent of the pulpit's critique of the press and the prompt that propelled its desire for a daily paper that would, the Reverend O. A. Kingsbury, editor of the religious monthly the *American Messenger*, assured, "give its picture of the daily doings of the world as those doings appear from the Christian point of view."[27]

Penny Papers and Press Criticism

It was the mass-appeal penny papers sustained by advertising that began to emphasize profit as the principal purpose of the press. Benjamin Day's success with the *New York Sun*—founded in 1833—spawned many other penny papers in New York and across the country.[28] And as they spread and became a recognized social force, the early hints of a desire for a Christian daily began to be heard. Indeed, the very existence of the penny papers had at least two effects. They showed that it was entirely feasible to launch a successful daily newspaper—even, possibly, a Christian daily. For example, an editorial in 1854 in the *Christian Intelligencer* linked the irreligious penny papers to the need for the wealthy members of the churches to establish a Christian daily. "We believe it would be not only a profitable investment of capital, but a most effectual way of subserving the interest of religion," the editorial declared.[29] In addition, the penny papers' radical redefinition and expansion of news came to be seen as a pernicious influence on society. In fact, the penny newspapers were a rupture in the old ways of doing journalism. Rather than the "sixpenny journals of Wall Street, with meagre supplies of news" that catered to select and wealthy clientele and few people could afford, most people could afford a penny paper and its broad-swath accounts of the news of the world.[30]

The penny papers offered a larger target for press criticism than the political partisan journals of the time, which were often condemned for their barbed and nasty exchanges.[31] As early as 1836, a writer who identified herself only as "A Mother" said she did not allow the "daily penny papers, filled with the envenomed shafts of infidelity," to "defile my sanctuary."[32] That same year, one religious journal worried about the widening effects of the "irreligious penny papers" that were even then selling fifteen to twenty-three thousand copies daily in New York City, hundreds of which were being shipped by steamboat outside the city. The writer asserted that these penny dailies, "which say nothing in favor of religion," were "filled with news (manufactured or real,) tales, politics, murders, police reports, fires and fun" and were "greedily devoured by Christians," producing "an alarming disrelish for religious reading, even the Bible itself."[33] And just a few months later, the financially struggling *Christian Advocate and Journal* told its readers in a fund-raising editorial that "tracts, pamphlets, and penny papers, tending to vitiate the taste and corrupt the morals of the community, are flooding city and country, while our press can utter but a feeble voice through the medium of this class of our publications to countervail their influence."[34] By 1841 that viral spread of the penny dailies with the advent of improved transportation technology worried a writer for the *Boston Weekly Magazine*, who noted that Boston was at the time only twelve days from Europe. "The happy security which distance once gave to our country is gone; our continent is dragged from its moorings, by the force of steam, and we now breathe the atmosphere of the European press." The writer complained that within an hour after a steamship arrived from England, at least four city newspapers were printing news "reeking with the spirit of European society."[35]

Still, such complaints could do little to keep the penny press from spreading and influencing society. Mary White Ovington, the renowned suffragette, journalist, and cofounder of the National Association for the Advancement of Colored People, saw that influence up close. Ovington spent much time in the tenements of New York City, and in 1904 she described how much the cheap sensationalist dailies had become a part of life for many people, who read little else. She pointed to the "omnipresence of the sensational penny paper. It was on the table in nearly every home that I entered, its jokes were a part of the vocabulary of the streets, and its latest robbery or murder was a subject for frequent discussion."[36]

Calls for a Christian Daily

Despite the obvious difficulties of a Christian daily succeeding, the call for such a publication was largely driven by the pulpit's dissatisfaction with the secular press's participation in a changing modern society in which religion no longer held sway. Ultimately, the Christian daily was seen as a much-needed ameliorative response to a modern, industrializing, and fracturing society that the daily newspaper press had helped create. Certainly, that desire stemmed from the fact that, whatever their demographic, Americans enjoyed reading newspapers. Indeed, first-time visitors to America saw this right away. In 1890 the Reverend Howard Crosby recalled Rabbi Max Lilienthal's shock on arriving in America when he saw even carriage drivers reading newspapers. He was quoted as saying, "This is indeed the country of the future, where every one, however humble, reads and judges of all that is going on for himself." Thus, Crosby argued, it was important to create a Christian daily newspaper because Americans were a "reading people" who distilled a worldview and formed a public opinion through what they read. Crosby believed such a daily's primary goal would be "not to make money, but to uphold the nation in truth and right." Here, Crosby is arguing for a Christian daily because he believed the press should be directly used in "support of moral legislation."[37] But others, for the most part, viewed a Christian daily as less a purposeful tool of direct action and more as an instrument in sustaining and reforming society in general and making manifest the Kingdom of God on earth.[38] For instance, in an address to the Tenth International Conference of the Evangelical Alliance in 1896, the Reverend Sylvester F. Scovel, president of the University (now College) of Wooster, described the press and its "highest manifestation"—the metropolitan daily press—as "one of the world's greatest moral and social forces." Given the moral and social power of the press, he declared, Christianity must find a way to own and wield this power by establishing an "ideal Christian daily newspaper."[39]

These views are illustrative of many in and outside the pastorate over many decades as industrial-driven modernity took hold who saw a need for a Christian daily. Probably the most renowned advocate for establishing a Christian daily was the Reverend Charles M. Sheldon, who gained worldwide notoriety in 1900 when he became the editor of the *Topeka Capital*, which he edited for a week as Christ would have.[40] (The following chapter will examine this event in detail.) Indicative of the interest in the subject, the experiment drew international attention, and the *Capital*'s circulation of 11,000 swelled to more than 363,000,[41] as it was printed in four cities and distributed all over the world.[42] The Congregationalist minister, a prolific writer of books and magazine articles, was also active on the speaking circuit. And while on the circuit, Sheldon would call for the pulpit in towns with ten or more churches to come together and endow such a paper. "I do not mean simply a paper that would have good things in it, but a paper that would have a positive program for positive building up of the kingdom of God in this world."[43]

Still, Sheldon's argument in 1900 for a Christian daily had precedents that went back at least five decades.[44] In 1851 the *Third Annual Report of the Oneida Association* (the Oneida Association was a religious utopian community) asked whether Christ should have a voice in this world. "Shall we have a press, a free and inspired organ, through which he may speak, and suitably represent himself?" All the other many interests of society had their daily papers, "But where are God's facts set forth? Where is Christ represented in the public press?" The report went on to question why Christ should be relegated to the religious papers only. "Why, for instance, should he not have a daily press that will carry his name, and power, and presence, into the very world where we live, and where he is needed? We see no way for him to get the advantage of Satan, and take his place on the throne of the world, until he gets possession of the daily press." The following year, a writer for *Circular*, a publication of the Oneida Association, argued that such a paper could certainly be "sustained; it must be—it is one of the predestined facts of this time, just as much as the steamboat and locomotive."[45]

In 1887 the editor of the *Christian Advocate*, who argued that a Christian daily newspaper was "greatly needed," observed that earlier failures offered a lesson in how to succeed. For example, not one denomination could support such a paper, he said. It would have to be ecumenical and deal with general news and many different subjects with which any single church "had no direct connection."[46] And indeed, the following year the New England Conference of the Methodist Episcopal Church passed a resolution calling for the establishment of just such a unified Christian daily. The resolution said:

> Whereas, The power of the press has become almost unlimited in this country in the education of the people, on all great financial, civil, social, and moral questions; and
>
> Whereas, It has signally failed, with few exceptions, to meet the demands which a moral and religious public has a right to make upon it, fostering those institutions which help to perpetuate ignorance and vice, encouraging practices which tend to degrade and brutalize men, allying itself to those associations and practices which aim to destroy the body, debase the intellect, desolate the home, and ruin the soul, and which is ready to sacrifice the dearest interests of society for the sake of filling its own coffers; therefore
>
> Resolved, 1. That we, the members of the New England Conference, believe the time has come for the establishment of a daily secular paper that will strive to remedy this evil, be safe and helpful to the family, hold a high moral tone, and dare to advocate the truth on all those great moral questions which are vitally connected with the public good.
>
> Resolved, 2. That we earnestly desire all kindred bodies in our own and other denominations to co-operate with us in this great work, and that with a view to this end we appoint a commission of five to co-operate with similar commissions of other bodies when so appointed to take action in this important matter.[47]

Defining a Christian Daily

So what exactly would a Christian daily newspaper entail, and what was its intended mission? To that point, in 1899 the *New York Times* noted that in that city, an effort to create a Christian daily newspaper had ended in a dispute among the promoters as how to define such a daily. "One believes that

Christianity consists in the omission of all racing news and all mention of divorce cases. Another man thinks that such matters should be mentioned in a Christian paper in order to warn its readers of the dangerous pitfalls of life." The *Times* story held with the latter position, noting that Christianity that "ignores the existence of vice and crime has not accomplished very much so far." Still, by the late nineteenth century—after decades of industrialization and urbanization, the growth of the corporation and the labor movement, the escalation in class inequities, and the governmental, judicial, and corporate malfeasance of the Gilded Age grounded in a general corruption and an adherence to a Darwinian laissez-faire view of economics—the mission of a Christian daily began to be seen as a tool of societal reform. The Reverend O. A. Kingsbury in an essay titled "A Christian Daily Paper" (1887) held that the news in such a paper would be filtered through the lens of a Christian view of the world. Kingsbury recalled that one Philadelphia divine would open his paper each morning and say, "'Now I will see how God is governing his world.' If he could say this of the ordinary paper, much more will it be true of the Christian daily; for while the great body of facts to be recorded is essentially the same for all, the point of view, the perspective and proportion, the explanation will be different." He went on to observe that the "ideal Christian daily would be really a newspaper." It would offer stories about what happened in the world during the previous day. Still, he wrote, this of course raised the question of "what is news" and, given the constraints of time and space, what news was given primacy. Kingsbury urged that the news report offer a wide swath of daily occurrences, but avoid the trivial and focus on what was really important.

> This would include reports of crimes; but it need not include the details; nor need it be that elaborate telling of the story that shall pander to a morbid curiosity or stir and feed a prurient imagination. Nor need they occupy much space. But these things are facts—grim and unpleasant, to be sure—but still facts in the world's history, and therefore they should be recorded. Otherwise we would be in danger of underestimating the evil that is in the world, and as a consequence would be by so much unfitted to meet that evil.

Here, in calling for a Christian daily, Kingsbury was not overtly attempting to influence journalistic conduct and content of the newspaper in the redaction of daily occurrences—except for such "artificial happenings" as sporting and dramatic events.[48]

Ultimately, the many notions swirling around the idea of a Christian daily came together in 1899 in the *Chautauquan* in a definition that illustrates the concerns about the press and the news ethic ideal hinged to a Christian daily: "By a Christian daily is meant a newspaper that would apply the Christian standard to news as well as theoretical questions, that would print nothing calculated to shock the religious and moral sense, and dwell on the hopeful, bright, inspiriting aspects of life." Therefore, the *Chautauquan* proposed removing or reducing "the sensational, the criminal, the unpleasant features which the 'yellow' press delights and revels in." Still, however, if a Christian daily were to cover such things as art, literature, music, politics, sports, and industrial events much as the secular press, how would it be different from any "clean, dignified, carefully edited paper?" the journal asked. "Newspapers cannot preach religion and morality, but there is every reason why they should be conducted on high principles, and when so conducted they are moral and religious in the deepest sense of the terms."[49]

Many in the pastorate also argued that a Christian daily was economically feasible if the right model were established. On the one hand, some argued, compromises about the journalistic ideal would be needed in order to "strike the happy mean between the two extremes, so that whilst having good literary form it will attract the uneducated."[50] For instance, the Reverend Edgar Powell of LaPorte, Indiana, held that while Christians needed, as soon as possible, to develop a plan that would lead to a Christian daily paper, those plans should take into consideration that "such a press must be established and maintained strictly on its news and business merits." On the other hand, the Reverend Sylvester F. Scovel rejected the argument that a barrier to such a daily was the enormous amounts of capital needed for such an effort by equating a daily paper with the common endeavors of the church—Christian education, missions, and charities. "The money can be found for anything which clearly proves its own supreme importance as a reforming, ameliorating, uplifting, converting agency, able to reconcile man to God." Scovel also discounted the concern that a Christian daily would have a problem attracting readers by equating such a paper to the building of a church that then attracts worshipers. "Just as men have come to hear all the counsel and comfort and correction of the Word of God, so will they read it when it comes to them. They know that the right way of looking at everything is the Christian way. They want to know more of that way in its details. Their own needs and dissatisfactions will bring them to welcoming the Christian Press. They will want it for their children. They will choose it because it is the best." Less sanguine was Whitelaw Reid, the longtime editor of the *New York Tribune*, who saw little chance of creating a successful Christian daily—though it was his hope that the press was essentially Christian, "in the sense that it loves good, and hates evil and assails it." Still, Reid believed, the idea of a Christian daily would "never die out, for there is too much unsophisticated goodness in the world, and too much sophisticated selfishness eager to prey upon it."[51]

Finally, however, the question was whether such a paper—no matter how well balanced—could succeed in modern America. As noted above, the track record for success was not good. Even the much-lauded *Christian Science Monitor*, which began life in 1908, has had its own existential crises. Mary Baker Eddy founded the *Monitor* as a means of reaching "many homes with healing, purifying thought."[52] And Archibald McLellan, the *Monitor*'s first editor, noted that the primary reason for its existence was not whether it would be financially successful. "It seems to us that the more important questions are whether such a paper is needed, and whether it can be made effective for civic righteousness and the uplifting of humanity." Here, McLellan appeared to be relying on the endowment of the church. Still, by 1922, the *Monitor* was in financial trouble after losing 80 percent of its subscribers, according to documents surrounding a lawsuit between church directors and the trustees of the church's publication society.[53] And it should be noted that by 2009, with losses running into the many millions a year, the paper ceased printing daily and instead turned to the Internet and began publishing a printed weekly edition.

Given the many past failures to establish a daily Christian newspaper, in 1897 the *Homiletic Review* quickly put a damper on talk among New York City clergymen about beginning a Christian daily by pointing to the irony of the *New York World*, which began as a religious daily but was by 1897 "one of the leaders of 'yellow journalism.'"[54] Yes, added the *Washington Post*, "how utter has been the failure of the enterprise, how wide the departure from the original idea, how complete the extinction of the holy light." *Zion's Herald* suggested that the failures of such papers stemmed from the vast sums of money needed to sustain a metropolitan daily and the fact that the secular daily had a wider audience, while the religious daily was made for a distinct class. Given that smaller audience, the religious daily must raise its price, which in turn narrowed its audience even more. "The religious daily, in a word, cannot compete with the secular." The rationale for this goes back to the core tension between the sacred and the secular market-oriented newspaper business. "The secular daily carries all kinds of news, and sells to every class of people for that very reason," *Zion's Herald* observed. "The secular daily advertises everything, even some exceptionable things. Vice is a better advertiser than virtue. . . . Here we can see why a religious daily cannot compete with a secular."[55]

This was a fact of life that many observers had been acknowledging for decades.[56] An expression of the consensus came as early as 1860, around the time of the founding of the *New York World*, in an editorial in Horace Greeley's *New York Tribune*. The paper took on the distinction between the secular and the sacred. It argued that while it revered all things holy, it did not believe that the business aspects of a newspaper appealed "to the religious convictions or the religious prejudices of the community" and that a paper that attempted to do so would not succeed. Simply put, "all things holy" should not be made "a matter of trade," the *Tribune* argued. To support its point, the editorial pointed to the separateness of the sacred from the "commercial spirit"—which ran counter to the concept of the immanence of God in all things that would become one of the core beliefs of the Social Gospel movement later in the century. "Men have relations to the religious but they also have relations to the world," argued the editorial writer, who went on to say that there was a separate world of daily affairs in which even the most devout of men needed the intelligence of the newspaper to instruct them about world events that could affect them in the course of business. The editorial also observed that there was a great difference between the weekly and the daily newspaper. "The former belongs to the family and may very properly be made an aid to religious reflection and serious thought." But the daily newspaper is a business enterprise concerned with daily life. It "is a reflection of the news, the crimes, the amusements, the thousand and one incidents which make up the daily affairs of the world, and which are of interest to every body." The two cannot be melded together, argued the editorial writer, who contended, "It is this commingling of things sacred and common at which the mind revolts, that renders the success of a religious daily journal impossible. It has never yet succeeded, though often attempted."[57]

CHAPTER 5

The Sheldon Edition and Journalism's Responsibility to Society

If the churches of this city, or any other city in this country, realized their real power in the matter of wealth sufficiently to carry on such a paper, and in the matter of ability to equip it and make it what it ought to be, I do not know that there is any other one agency which the church might produce more powerful to help the cause of Christ in the world today.

—The Reverend Charles M. Sheldon, "Some Opportunities Before the Church of Today"

When a man has eaten his meat highly spiced for a long time, he will not suddenly conceive a fondness for plain food. Yet the force of the example may be such as to inspire some effort on the part of the better papers to still further improve their tone. And among the many who are now reading Mr. Sheldon's paper out of curiosity, some may perceive its superiority to their favorite "yellows." And in this way, not suddenly, but very slowly, a change may be wrought.

—David A. Curtis, "'As Jesus Would Run It'"

ON NOVEMBER 3, 1899, TOPEKA, Kansas, was the site of an event that attracted the interest of the entire town and the site of the inception of a weeklong undertaking five months later that would attract the attention of the nation and the world. The event on November 3 was the return of the Twentieth Kansas Infantry from fighting in the Philippines. The town turned out for a welcome-home military parade and presentation of a sword ornamented with gold, silver, and diamonds to General Frederick Funston. During the ceremony, a group of people gathered to view the proceedings from the home of the mother-in-law of Frederick O. Popenoe, the principal owner of the *Topeka Daily Capital*. Included in that group was the Reverend

Charles M. Sheldon, the pastor of a Topeka Congregationalist church who was famous nationally and internationally as the author of the best-selling sermon novel *In His Steps; or, What Would Jesus Do?*, which was about a group of people, including a newspaper editor, trying to live and work as Jesus would. In the course of the parade and ceremony, discussion turned to the editing of newspapers and sensational journalism, to which Sheldon, a well-known critic of the daily press, was adamantly opposed.[1] The discussion had been prompted by a description in Sheldon's novel about an editor who tried to run his newspaper as he believed Jesus would have managed it. "It was the general opinion expressed by the friends who were discussing the subject that any such attempt was so visionary that it could not be carried out in actual practice," Sheldon recalled. At some point, Popenoe asked the reverend if he would edit the *Capital* for a week. Sheldon thought he was joking, but Popenoe insisted he was in earnest and then outlined the terms under which the pastor would become an editor. The two came to an agreement, and the second week in March 1900 was designated for the experiment.[2]

That event, for that is certainly what it became, would ultimately garner a great deal of publicity, attract hordes of correspondents from the nation's newspapers and magazines, and push the *Capital*'s average circulation of a bit more than 11,000 to more than 363,000, as it was printed in Topeka, Kansas City, Chicago, New York, and London and distributed all over the world.[3] And its very existence would also prompt one commentator for the secular press to describe the experiment as one of "national importance"[4] and the exultations of a Christian periodical that exclaimed: "In the history of American journalism, it will probably be many years before there will be another week as important as that of March 12 to 17—the week of the Sheldon Edition of the *Topeka Capital*."[5]

But was it? Undoubtedly, one reason the writer for the Christian periodical was beaming was that an exemplar of a Christian daily newspaper had come to pass, if for only one week, as a possible harbinger of things to come. The longing for such a paper, as noted earlier, had often been written about and discussed by the nation's pastorate and theologians as something society needed. Still, despite the few ringing hallelujahs in favor of Sheldon's weeklong effort, the general consensus of commentary in the aftermath—and there were reams of it—from both the press and the pastorate, and even the publisher of the *Topeka Capital*, was that Sheldon's daily paper edited from a "Christian point of view" was a failure.[6] However, even accepting that was the case, Sheldon's editing endeavor offers a wealth of historical data—condensed in a short duration of time—that displays the pulpit's, the press's, and the public's critical articulations about the newspaper's true mission as a fulcrum of society. In doing so, it offers a clear view of one of the contributory influences on journalistic normative standards in the early twentieth century. This is especially so because in Sheldon and his highly publicized work as an editor for one week, the stars align. That is, his very existence as a well-known author and articulate critic of the press and society, his editing experiment as a heightened expression of a stream of pastoral criticism of the press, and the concentration of discussion and debate surrounding his experiment about the role and responsibility of the commercialized press "succeeded in causing an 'arrest of thought' on the very important subject of the influence and responsibility of the daily newspaper," one writer asserted.[7]

Therefore, this chapter's focus is not simply a scenario of the event, as a few other studies have done to one degree or another.[8] Instead, it probes the national debate about the mission of newspapers. Indeed, this distillation of discourse sparked by the Sheldon Edition offers further evidence as to the ongoing conferral of the role of agent of education and moral uplift from the pulpit to the press. But aside from the pulpit's acquiescence to a new reality—that in a growing industrializing nation, it no longer held the reins of power over public opinion—this concentrated national conversation also shows the pulpit attempting to influence newspaper conduct. In this debate we can hear its representatives challenging the notion of journalistic objectivity grounded in commercialism as it struggled to redefine news as interpretive, advocatory, and redactive in order to comport with a journalistic ideal grounded in social justice and service.

Who Was Charles Sheldon?

As noted in chapter 1, the Reverend Charles Sheldon arrived as pastor of a Topeka, Kansas, Congregational church in 1889 as a thirty-two-year-old graduate of Brown University and Andover Theological Seminary. He had been influenced by the Social Gospel movement of the time, which was an effort to engage American Protestantism in the problems of labor and changing society in the modernizing industrial age. In addition to his Topeka church, Sheldon was also pastor for several Washburn College students. In order to keep their interest, he began writing religious novels that he would read chapter by chapter to the students.[9] The fictionalized sermon stories explored in narrative form the church's role in contemporary life. Many of these were also published in *Advance*, an obscure religious periodical based in Chicago. Few people took notice. But after Sheldon published *In His Steps* as a novel, sixteen other publishers also brought it out as a book because of a defect in the copyright. It ultimately, according to one estimate, sold six million copies in the United States and overseas.[10]

The plot of *In His Steps* was fairly straightforward. A man in dire straits shows up at a church and in front of the congregation condemns the economic and social system that has put him on a downward spiral. He then faints and later dies. All of this affects the congregation greatly, and the minister asks his parishioners to volunteer to begin living life differently by always asking before acting "What would Jesus do?" and then following those dictates. One of the people who volunteers is a newspaper editor named Edward Norman, and through him Sheldon put into form his ideas about how a newspaper should be edited. In sum, such a paper would reject sensationalism and yellow journalism (which then was at its height), society news, sporting events (especially boxing), and advertising for any item—for example, liquor—that could injure a reader.[11]

Sheldon's novel may have been a success not because of its literary quality, which most critics have noted was not very high, but because it reflected the thoughts and needs of its times. Indeed, the *Congregationalist* observed that Sheldon's books contained little in the way of literary value and that his effort at newspapering was deficient, but the popularity of both indicated he had found a connection to the "thoughts and questionings touching a better social order that are in every one's mind today."[12] In addition, poet, essayist, and magazine editor Edward Sanford Martin believed the popularity of *In His Steps* said something about the times in which he lived. Martin observed that the consensus was that Christianity "does not affect conduct nearly as much as it might and should," given the fact that it was viewed by few people as a means of escaping damnation. "But surely there was never more attention paid than now to its possibilities as a means of solving the great fundamental questions of civilization, and bettering a world distraught with greed and competition, and pestered with inequalities of condition, disparities of opportunity, war-ships, armies, taxation, oppression, and sin."[13]

In His Steps also became a primary text for Christian organizations such as the Christian Endeavor Societies, the Epworth League, and the Baptist Young People's Union, whose members regularly discussed "What would

Jesus do?" in relation to both personal and public issues. In addition, Sheldon was also a star on the lecture circuit. As part of his lectures, he would bring up the state of the daily press in America and his frustration that it failed to fulfill its duty to be a moral agent. It was in this context that Sheldon attended a Christian Endeavor Societies convention in Detroit in 1899 where fifteen thousand people were in attendance. Sheldon was one of the chief speakers. According to Herbert S. Houston, a past president of the Advertising Federation of America and the former general manager of the Sheldon Edition, "He electrified the eager throngs with the proposal that what the world needed to guide people to spiritual living was a newspaper, conducted as Jesus would have conducted it." That proposal, Houston recalled, prompted the newspaper press to respond as though to a challenge, and almost immediately the papers were filled with news and editorials "expressing widely differing views."[14]

Sheldon's own views of newspapers were not unique but reflected the current of discussion about the secular press by the clergy both before and after the Sheldon Edition.[15] He certainly had a point of view typical of public figures of the time about the press, whether they were clergy or not. His was developed both through his many years of being in the public eye and consequently the subject of press coverage—much of it both misinformed and mendacious, he complained[16]—and through a social-reformist lens that saw both the power for good and evil wielded by newspapers that could be employed as a tool of moral uplift.[17] Indeed, Sheldon's view of the role of editors was grounded in acting as a censorious gatekeeper. Two journalists who were able to gain access to Sheldon just before he began his editorship were Frank Pitts MacLennan, editor and proprietor of the *Topeka State Journal*, and William Allen White, the nationally renowned editor of the *Emporia (KS) Gazette*. The two men visited Sheldon in the *Capital* office abandoned for the week by J. K. Hudson, the editor of the *Capital*. In discussing what was news, Sheldon gave what MacLennan described in a story that appeared in both the *Journal* and the *New York Herald* as "a remarkable statement." He told the men that he "believed the editor should give his readers, not what they want, but what he thinks they need." And again, reflecting a paternalistic view of editorship, Sheldon added, "My boy wants my razor, but I will not give it to him, of course."[18]

Sheldon held the pronounced view that the modern newspaper owed "a debt to civilization." Here, again, is an example of the view that a paradigm shift had taken place in a rapidly growing, diverse, and complex industrializing nation—that the power and responsibility of the pulpit had been conferred to the press. And the standard argument was that conferral included a codicil obliging the press to act with conscience about the effect of its conduct and content. Historically, Sheldon argued, it had been the church and the "Christian citizen" who had been expected to aid in regenerating mankind. But given the enormity of the changes taking place in society, he held, that new arbiter of public opinion—the newspaper—was "under the high command of God to help regenerate the world."[19] Sheldon believed that the modern newspaper could contribute "to the final brotherhood of the race, and with the Church and home and school and state help bring in the millennium."[20] Thus, he suggested, the daily newspaper and every other kind of periodical "have just as much of a duty to give the people the thing they need instead of what they want, as the minister has to give his people what they need instead of what they want."[21]

Still, could a newspaper really be run as a Christian daily, given the moral constraints of commercialism? Sheldon believed so. In November, before it was announced that he would take over the *Capital*, Sheldon addressed the question "Is Christianity, as Christ lived it and taught it, practical?" in an essay in the *Ladies' Home Journal*. In it he delineated the loss and gain of applying a Christian view of the world to the practical affairs of life, most especially business, in which profit and the accumulation of money were seen as the keys to success. Sheldon was a harsh realist about the outcomes of such a policy of life and business, predicting a loss of money, power, and status for anyone who committed themselves to that path. And in understanding his thinking, we can comprehend that, while acknowledging the Sheldon Edition's faults, he believed it was a success despite the overwhelming consensus that it had failed in its mission. Here, Sheldon argued, "If a man's definition of life is 'success,' in the sense of making money, then, of course, Christianity ceases to be practical as soon as obedience to its teachings brings loss of money." But, he contended, after the loss from applying Christ's teachings to "every-day life," the gain would be much more because of "a readjustment of commercial life on a basis of love to mankind." Certainly, he wrote, such a readjustment would in all likelihood lead to the worst financial panic ever. Sounding much like a socialist, which he claimed not to be, Sheldon noted that once the dust settled after the panic, the world would be better off, because "love in business would lose less money, and actually distribute the real earnings of toil among a far greater number of human beings, than is possible under the present system."[22]

Sheldon Edition Announced

On January 23, 1900, the *Capital* devoted the entire front page and half of page 2 to announce that Sheldon would oversee the paper for a week in March. "Unhampered, he will dictate its policy; edit its news columns; control its advertising. In a word, he will embody his idea of what a Christian daily newspaper should be," the announcement declared. An extravagant editorial that ran the same day in the *Capital* proclaimed, "It is to enable this modern-day prophet to further illustrate his far reaching plan of adjustment that *The Capital* has been gladly placed at his disposal."[23]

The paper that Sheldon was to take over was fairly typical of the dailies of the time. It was partisan—in this case Republican—and would publish telegraphic news, editorials related to current events, stories about local events, fashion news, stock-market reports, and, on Sunday, a full page of society news and a page of sporting news. In addition, its advertising columns included ads for department store sales, theatrical performances, sports events, ladies' hosiery and undergarments, and patent medicines. In fact, among the many things that Sheldon believed to be unchristian and he would ban during his editorship were these ads for what he—and many other critics—considered bogus medicines.

And as part of the lead-up to the Sheldon Edition, in February the *Capital* published two letters—one from Sheldon and one from Hudson, the editor of the *Capital*. These two letters were essentially a discrete debate over the role of newspapers in society. And evident in them is the issue that would lie at the heart of much of the criticism of the Sheldon Edition. In his letter, Sheldon explained the distinction between a Christian newspaper and a religious newspaper and said that he would undertake to make the *Capital* the former. He observed that a religious newspaper fails to give all the news and its editorial space is given over mainly to discussions of religious matters. "A newspaper should give all of the news, and in order to be conducted as a Christian newspaper should give news in such a way that it will entertain and instruct its reader without appealing to their baser passions, as so many of the newspapers of this age do."[24]

Meanwhile, Hudson, who wrote that he would not participate in the experiment, defended the press of his day:

> The modern secular daily newspaper must be published everyday, give all the news of all the world, and be made for all the people who read. This does not prevent the tone, politics and policy of the paper from being clean, honest and courageous in all questions affecting the rights and interests of the people,

> the state and the union. While the American daily press is no higher intellectually and morally than the people it is made for, it stands today as the most powerful protector of communities against crime, tyranny and corruption of officials, and as the greatest promoter of all public enterprises, and in my judgment making it conform to certain restrictions and limitations in order to bring it within the idea of a Christian daily would detract from, rather than add to, its influence and usefulness.[25]

The Press and Pulpit React

Given that Sheldon was a well-known author with stated views on the press, it is not surprising that his experiment immediately became grist for commentary from both pastoral and secular sources. A week after the announcement, anticipating the wide interest this event would garner, the influential religiously oriented and reform-minded weekly the *Independent* said that while it would watch the experiment with interest, it was sure there were already many other journals in the land "whose aim is as high as Mr. Sheldon's." Still, it observed, "Newspaper ethics generally needs all the elevation that Mr. Sheldon's example might suggest."[26]

On the first day of publication, nearly every daily in the country devoted a considerable amount of space to stories about the Sheldon Edition. Commentary came from all corners of the country, and what follows is a representative reaction to the proposed experiment. For the clergy's part, in sum they believed one week would be too short a time to prove anything, that no one person could say what Jesus would do with each piece of news, and that they were, for the most part, satisfied with how the better newspapers were conducted. The Reverend J. S. Stone, rector of St. James Episcopal Church in Chicago, said it appeared Sheldon was, one, not aware of the "high standards" of most of the nation's newspapers and, two, that his theory of newspapering would be bound for failure. "A paper that should undertake to publish but a part, and a limited part of the news of the day at that, could scarcely be called a newspaper," Stone said.[27]

Meanwhile, the nation's daily and weekly press had its own ideas about the efficacy of the proposed experiment. And here is evident—in this concentrated moment—a distillation of discourse surrounding the tension between notions of a pronounced journalistic ideal and the commercial exigencies of the business office. For instance, the *Independent* editorialized that the Sheldon Edition was needed to awake people to the "sad neglect of the Christian ideal" by the daily press. The editorial declared: "Sensation, sensation, anything, true or false, to filch a penny; advertisements known to be lies, meant to deceive; pretended news invented by imaginative reporters; attractive descriptions of vicious performances on the stage or encounters in the ring—all these are so frequent in the daily press that it has almost come to be thought that an absolutely pure daily paper is as impossible as Sunday-school politics."[28] Also evident in this discourse are journalists grappling with a definition of news as constitutive of a largely unformed notion of press responsibility. For instance, critical of the state of newspapers, the *Weatherford (TX) Democrat* said the experiment was one of "national importance" in the hope that another way could be found to publish a paper without the economic driver that requires publications to "please and entertain every class of readers."[29]

Still, passages in articles and editorials defending the press as a moral institution were myriad and reveal the tension between those with different perspectives. For instance, the *Chicago Inter Ocean* rejected the charge that newspapers were "not run along Christian lines." Equally, the *Chicago Times-Herald* argued that the secular press was Christian because "its influence tends toward the exaltation of Christian ideals in business, in politics and in society."[30] Closer to home, Edgar Howe, editor of the *Atchison (KS) Globe* and an author of some repute, was angered by Sheldon's statement that most newspapers were not conducted as Jesus would. "By what right or authority does Rev. Sheldon assume to sit in judgment upon the editors of this country?" Howe railed. "It looks to me like a piece of consummate gall for one who knows nothing about the newspaper business to attempt to instruct those who have spent their lives learning it. . . . I contend that the average newspaper of to-day is conducted along Christian lines. It is conscientious, fair, truthful, and enterprising. Newspapers which are not so do not succeed. I also contend that the newspaper has done more for civilization than the clergy."[31]

Finally, indicative of the kind of press coverage the Sheldon experiment was garnering, the Sunday before the reverend began work, a front-page story noted that on Saturday correspondents from across the country, in addition to the stories they put in the mail, had telegraphed from Topeka a total of 35,167 words. But, the story noted, the dispatches "were composed largely of gossip, as Mr. Sheldon has not yet made public his policy."[32]

Sheldon Takes the Reins

However, Sheldon did begin to make his policy known the next day. Twenty newspaper correspondents along with the staff of the *Capital* awaited Sheldon that first day. In the meeting, he told the correspondents there would be no interviews because he had a lot of work to do. "I hope you will all take me seriously. This is not play for me. It is perhaps the most important week in my life," he told them. Sheldon then asked his entire staff for its support in his endeavor, including, as a favor to him, no smoking, drinking, or use of profanity in the building. Apparently in defense and in anticipation of the reams of criticism he would face, Sheldon included in his first edition an editor's prospectus in which he noted the subjectivity of publishing a paper as Jesus would: "If a thousand different Christian men who wished to edit Christian dailies should make an honest attempt to do so, the result might be a thousand different papers in very many particulars."[33]

Reports about his commandments to the staff, his own words about the paper in the first issue, and his later reminiscences reveal something of his news policy and the impetus for it.[34] To begin, reporters were barred from using slang words or phrases in their stories, and he also ordered that all editorials and articles other than small items be signed by the person who wrote them. He also insisted that reporters, after interviewing, submit their article to the person they interviewed and then bring him a copy of the subject's written approval. "If a man does not wish to be interviewed, accept his first refusal as final, and never insist."[35] Sheldon also banned all theatrical news because he opposed the "demoralizing tendencies of the stage."[36] And, he ruled, the *Capital* would not print sports news unless it was "clean, healthful amateur athletics."[37]

After the first edition had been published, Sheldon met with the many correspondents in town covering the weeklong event. He told them he tossed out several police items because his "idea of publishing crime is to go more into its causes. . . . In some cases I may publish more of these things than in others in order to comment on them editorially." In addition, he had published a list of divorces but left out the names, in order to allow the judge and himself to comment on the reasons for the breakups.[38] Sheldon defined "news as any event worth knowing or telling published in the right proportion to its importance."[39] In other words, news was "anything in the way of daily events that the public ought to know for its development and power in a life of righteousness." For example, one editor might perceive reports about some "unusual battle" of much less importance than the "usual daily destruction being caused by liquor." Therefore, Sheldon continued, the *Capital* during his week would contain what he felt were "the most vital issues that affect humanity as a whole" in an attempt to "influence its readers to seek first the Kingdom of God." More concretely, he intended that "all prize fights, scandals, crime, vice, or human depravity, if printed," had "to be defined as evil, and an attempt made in each case to discover and name the cause and remedy," especially if that cause was drink. Crime stories, especially, had to "avoid all horrible details of the actual event," a rule that would be quickly tested after the suicide of a former *Capital* employee who was also the son of a US senator from Kansas.[40] Indeed, a comparative analysis about how the Sheldon Edition covered the suicide with the coverage of another Topeka paper offers an articulate elaboration of how Sheldon's news ethic differed from that of most mainstream dailies of the time. And I should note here, Sheldon's dictates in regards to this story are, in fact, the standard policy today of most mainstream newspapers that rarely report on suicides—and only then the barest facts if the death is of a public figure or created some kind of public spectacle that needs explanation.

The suicide of the son of Kansas senator William Alfred Peffer during the week of the Sheldon Edition was one example of his nonsensational mode of news gathering and reporting. Sheldon gives an account of the incident in his biography in which he recalled that the younger Peffer was working in the advertising section of the paper at the time of his death, though others have noted that Peffer had been let go the Friday before Sheldon took over. The Sheldon Edition published the basic facts of the suicide and a note the young man had left, along with a note of condolence from the paper's staff.

> The news of the suicide reached one of the *Capital* reporters before we received it in the office, and I remember he came running in with it to me asking for instructions as to going right up to Senator Peffer's home and interviewing the family to get inside facts about the affair. I not only refused to let any reporter go to the house, but I turned down a lengthy account of the matter which came up from Kansas City in which there was a detailed description of the room where the young man was found, and more than a hint at some tragic motive other than the reason given in the note he left for his father. It seemed to me at the time and does yet and always will, that such a human tragedy should be reported, if at all, in the briefest and most sympathetic manner. I see nothing to be gained by relating the ghastly details of human frailty and sin.[41]

Meanwhile, the *Topeka State Journal*'s Peffer suicide story was a bit more typical of the kind of salacious exploitation that Sheldon opposed. It topped its story with a six-deck headline: "How He Died. Sherman Peffer

Committed Suicide by Taking Morphine. Secured a Room at a Cheap Lodging House. Note for His Father. Only Explanation Given Was That He Was Tired. Worked on *Capital*, but Was Discharged Last Week." The account of the story was taken from the *Kansas City Journal* and began with the entire suicide note, which ended, "Father—I do not like to do what I am doing; but I am tired." The story went on to describe the scene, the box that had contained the morphine he used to kill himself, and what was found on his body. It then recounted his activities up to the point of his suicide and then the discovery of his body by a chambermaid.[42]

Sheldon's News Judgment

The issues after the first day followed pretty much the same pattern as the first. Sheldon found much of his material in other papers, books, and pamphlets about the progress of socialist movements and the "ethics of socialism," reforms, the negative influence of the corporate trusts, the causes of crime, the success of Prohibition laws, and the dangers of the saloon.[43] In fact, Sheldon believed many crimes were directly traceable to alcohol consumption. He recalled how he once clipped and saved from six newspapers over a six-day period any stories about crime and disorder caused by drink. "It made a roll which, when unwound in the church, stretched clear across it," he recalled.[44]

For the week, the *Capital* was eight pages with about twenty columns of advertising and thirty-six columns of news. The following is a summary of what appeared in the Sheldon Edition on that first day.

The first page began with a prayer by Bishop John H. Vincent of the Methodist Episcopal Church. Other stories dealt with the evils of war, the evils of liquor, a collection of interviews with prominent Kansans about the success of the state's Prohibition law, and the need for philanthropists to build homes for consumptives. However, the lead story goes to the heart of the pastoral understanding of the power of the press as an advocate. The story described a famine in India that was threatening the lives of fifty million people. The story also called for aid from "Christian America," and in a week, Sheldon later boasted, he had raised one hundred thousand dollars. But in addition, farmers donated a carload of corn, the railroads hauled it to New York free of charge, and the *Christian Herald* paid for its passage by ship to India.[45]

The second page included an editorial on the India famine, an editorial by a Korean missionary, an article describing the stock market as "a gambling hell" that went on to note that the paper would include only stories about sales and deals that had been completed, a letter from a reverend in the Philippines, a column of excerpts from daily and weekly Kansas papers, a column of reviews of new books, and an editorial titled "The Ideal Christian World."

The third page contained wire and Kansas news and included one and a half columns on antisaloon and antitrust laws. All the major news stories were signed and included a paragraph of commentary by Sheldon.

The fourth page gave space to Topeka-area news, including a plea made for national Prohibition; a concert given by the Woman's Home Missionary Society; news of a Young Men's Christian Association meeting; an article about a meeting of school principals to discuss organizing an anticigarette league; a county election brief; a council meeting story; preparations for a Chautauqua; a story about two train engineers doing ministerial work along the train line; and a quarter column of religious notes. The page also included a list of divorces—though the divorcing couples went unidentified—and comment about their causes from a judge who said he believed that "men and women do not consider the serious responsibility that marriage involves." Here, also, we can find a representative example of Sheldon's bracketed commentary that he placed at the end of many of the articles. "The cause for most of the above divorces would probably be found in an absence of Christian definition of marriage," he wrote.[46]

The fifth page included four articles from contributors that dealt with Kansas industries, opposition to acquiring the Philippines, how kindergartens had progressed, and reports from area colleges.

No advertisements appeared in the first five pages. Pages 6–8 contained advertisements, and noticeable were the kinds of advertising that were missing, especially if, for instance, we look back a year in the *Capital*. Gone from the Sheldon Edition were ads for performances at the New Crawford Theater, ads for corsets because Sheldon did not believe women should wear them, and, most glaringly, ads for patent medicines. For example, during the corresponding week a year before were ads for such things as Cupidene, a "vegetable vitalizer" that promised "Manhood Restored"; Ajax Tablets that promised to cure "all nervous diseases"; McElree's Wine of Cardui, taken to cure "female troubles"; and Brou's Injection to cure "the most obstinate cases of Gonorrhea." Dell Keizer, business manager of the *Capital*, noted that Sheldon rejected all medical advertisements. Of course, Keizer said, some of the medicines were effective remedies, "but there are others which are spurious." If Sheldon had been in charge of a newspaper permanently, he would have the time to investigate those medicines "to see which are meritorious and which are not." Because he had doubts about "corsets being proper wearing apparel," Sheldon rejected all underwear and corset advertising because he wanted nothing to do with anything that might be questionable. He also excluded all theatrical advertising because he had not the time to investigate any of them to determine their merits.[47]

Finally, to avoid publishing a Sunday edition but to morally fulfill his contractual obligations, Sheldon issued a Saturday-evening edition that lacked anything approaching news. Instead, it was composed almost entirely of Bible quotations. "I learned afterward that a great many subscribers confessed it was the first time they had ever read the Bible!" Sheldon recalled many years later.[48]

Nation Reacts to Sheldon Edition

As soon as the first edition hit the presses, religious publications, the clergy, trade journals, magazines, and newspapers across the country began offering their evaluations, which continued for weeks after that last Saturday-evening edition was put to bed and Sheldon had returned to his church.[49] And in this commentary, aside from the criticism from most that the paper was a failure and from a few that the experiment was the "greatest advertising scheme" ever,[50] we can hear the distillation of a nationwide debate about the newspaper's mission at the center of the conversation surrounding journalism in the early twentieth century. For instance, in one representative criticism, an editorial in the *Outlook* observed that Sheldon "seems to think that the editor should decide what the people ought to know and give them only that. We have more faith in the people and less in the editors, and would, therefore, have the paper tell its readers all that is going on in the world that has any significance, and employ his editorial judgment, first in determining the relative importance of different events and news in giving them such interpretation as he thinks just and right."[51] Still, even months later, Sheldon continued this debate when he told a packed audience at the New York Avenue Presbyterian Church in Washington, DC, that newspapers devoted too much space to crime, which gave the public "the idea that the world is getting worse and worse." He recalled that when he asked a city editor to try a one-week experiment in which he published no stories of crime and published only good news, the editor responded: "'Goodness isn't news.' But nevertheless I firmly believe that the time will come when every large city has a Christian daily, not a religious paper, but a live daily, printing the news of the day, but keeping back what we don't want."[52]

Ultimately, that stance was the core of much of the criticism of the Sheldon Edition. In fact, one cogent rebuttal came from another Kansas newspaper, the *Salina Union*. It rejected Sheldon's policy of ignoring the details of crime but giving the cause. In this rejoinder, again, is a representative illustration of the clash of definitions of news. One definition, which involved a patrician and paternalistic component, called for both a solicitous redaction of information to protect the sensibilities and moral fiber of readers while offering a subjective interpretation of that news item. The other was a much broader view that held—as John Milton and John Stuart Mill argued—that a diversity of topics and sources creates a marketplace of ideas from which readers could derive some sense of truth, some picture of reality in an increasingly complex and modern world.[53] "Modern papers," the *Union* continued, "give details because details nearly always give the cause. Details of a murder often lead to the detection of the murderer. Prize fights have grown in public disfavor by the publication of details. Crooks have been driven from the path of dishonesty by the publication of details of their methods." Here, the *Salina Union* was defining news from a utilitarian facticity perspective that interwove a notion of the press's responsibility to society that was essentially the same as Sheldon's. But unlike Sheldon, the *Union* held that people could be made better by being given all the facts, not if some facts—or entire stories—were held back. To that point, the *Union* observed, "Even the church has its Satan and its Hades to prove that the path of the transgressor is lined with brimstone, and many churches give 'the details' concerning Satan's personality and the temperature of his resort."[54]

But in the minds of those who discussed it, was the Sheldon Edition really a newspaper? The *Topeka Capital* offered its own verdict, which was that "it goes without saying" that Sheldon's effort was not a newspaper as defined by most people. He shunted aside what was accepted as news by most readers in favor of trying to "mirror the times more in a historical than a journalistic sense" by offering his readers "the great moral, religious and humanitarian activities of the age instead of the small ephemeral happenings."[55] Similarly, the *Congregationalist* criticized Sheldon for turning the *Capital* into the equivalent of a religious pamphlet or, at most, given his advocacy of certain reforms, little more than a "periodical issued by reform organizations."[56] One comment that well summed up the evaluations of the many commentators on the experiment was that of renowned reporter

Gilson Willets. Writing in the *Christian Herald and Signs of Our Times*, Willets argued, "As a strictly religious paper, it is a success; but as a newspaper, in the minds of all correspondents here, it is a disappointment."[57] Indeed, one New York editor, commenting on the first issue, noted that all of the important news of the day was missing. "Not a line about bubonic plague at San Francisco, the dreadful tenement house fire at Newark, N.J., the wounding of eight American soldiers in the Philippines, the advance of Roberts on the Orange Free States, the discord of Republicans on the Porto Rico questions, the death of the Italian boxer, Guydo, who died as the result of a blow struck by James Jeffries in a fistic contest."[58] Rather, one writer for the *Rochester (NY) Post-Express* said, the Sheldon Edition had a haunting similarity to some "old friend," but he could not place it. Then it struck him: it looked a lot like a paper issued by a newspaper after a labor strike. "The editors are worried and cannot write anything of value; the fresh news and the daily advertisements have to be put aside because they cannot be set up; and the columns are filled with 'standing matter,' gentle and harmless miscellany that has been accumulating for weeks, awaiting the order to be 'killed,' and with stuff borrowed from yesterday's issue of an esteemed contemporary."[59]

On its surface, that witty barb was a criticism of the Sheldon Edition. But embedded in that sly analysis was the notion of journalism as a profession—often entwined with a recognition of the effect on news content by a newspaper's financial liabilities. The modern newspaper was no longer the product of individual entrepreneurs such as James Gordon Bennett Sr., who spent just five hundred dollars to start the *New York Herald* in 1835. It was now no place for amateurs like Sheldon but an industry whose employees required education, training, and experience to do the job well. It was that notion of journalistic professionalism that was reified in the headlined debate before the Sheldon Edition and in the many postmortems afterward.[60] For instance, a writer for the *St. Louis Republic* declared, "Careful, thoughtful presentation of the news is the work of the daily newspaper. Suppressing and waste-basketing this news does not suffice."[61] And then the next day, William Allen White observed that Sheldon had failed because he lacked training for what he was attempting to do. Editing, he insisted, "is as much a profession as doctoring."[62]

The Newspaper's Mission

Still, the Reverend Charles L. Kloss of Webster Groves Congregational Church in St. Louis, Missouri, said he liked Sheldon's paper for the idea it represented—that "the same responsibility that rests on the pulpit is laid on the newspaper."[63] That is, the Sheldon Edition, though a failure, had succeeded through the fusion of publicity in underscoring the newspaper's importance to society and its constitutive responsibility to act as a moral agent in aiding the uplifting of society. But, the *Independent* lamented, Sheldon's version of a newspaper was too "preachy." In other words, it argued, a newspaper should be "religious, because its purpose is to do good, but it need not talk very much religion."[64] The *Independent* also published a lengthy postmortem essay by Washington Gladden, one of Sheldon's fellow Congregationalist ministers, that was both complimentary and critical. And between those positive and negative poles lies a proposed definition of news values, but one knitted with an argument that one mission of newspapers in their responsibility to the public was an interpretive and advocatory function that bordered on a kind of proselytizing by the press. Gladden observed that the Sheldon experiment offered "some attractive features," including the absence of many offensive items. He also admired the focus on temperance questions and that many social questions "have been treated with vigor; the ethical aspects of all such questions have been clearly and strongly presented; the application of the Christian law to problems of society and politics has been fearlessly made; and there has been not a little earnest talk of a genuinely evangelistic character."

However, Gladden observed, those attributes should not dispel the notion that a Christian daily newspaper could not succeed. Thus, he observed, there was no point to subsidizing such a paper if no one would read it. Gladden noted that unlike the Sheldon Edition, a Christian daily paper must offer all the news, to include the "filthy details of vice and crime," because what greatly interested people was news. As well, Gladden would publish theatrical news but written not from the point of view of the box office but as a work of dramatic art. Gladden, drawing on his years of newspaper experience, went on to note, "The newspaper cannot undertake to dictate to the people what they shall be interested in; the fact that they are deeply interested in anything whatever is a matter with which it must concern itself. It may be necessary to show them that the thing which they care so much about is a thing unworthy of their thought; keen criticism of popular fads and social tendencies is one of the newspaper's great functions."[65]

Ultimately, this national debate about the press revealed a continuum of thought about the nation's press. At one end of this sliding scale were those who believed the press had a responsibility to society in educating its public opinion and protecting and reinforcing its moral fiber. At the other end were those who believed that a newspaper's success was defined by profit and whose maxim was "give readers what they want." Filling in the spectrum were shades of both that sought some sort of balance between those two poles. From his statements and actions, one can conclude that Sheldon was at one extreme of the continuum. His stance rejected profit as the sole arbiter of success. It was, essentially, a sermonizing, paternalistic, and interpretive view of editorship that confronted notions of journalistic objectivity driven by the commercial aspect of newspapers. For example, Sheldon once said, "I think the editor should assume the position of a father toward a child."[66]

Here, then, in the debate about the Sheldon Edition we have in microcosm—in a fusion of interests—a discussion that paralleled the then ongoing national conversation among journalists and nonjournalists about the press reflected in stories about the event, sermons from the pulpit, and editorials and essays that appeared in newspapers, religious periodicals, magazines, and the newspaper trade journals. As we have seen to this point, there was nothing new about this conversation. However, for a few weeks around the turn of the century, the Reverend Charles M. Sheldon's eminence, his well-known views about the press, and his weeklong experiment suddenly coalesced and gave prominence to this often random and diffuse conversation.[67] This is evident in the *Outlook*, which wrote that the event was "a somewhat sensational method of calling the attention of the country to the truth that there is and ought to be some other standard of journalism than commercial success," in the *Congregationalist*'s observation that "this implied reflection upon American journalism is the most surprising phenomenon in connection with the Sheldon experiment," and in the Reverend Gladden's assertion that "Mr. Sheldon's experiment in journalism is significant, quite as much through the comments which it has excited as through the suggestions which it has made."[68]

Also evident in the discourse surrounding the Sheldon Edition's effect on journalism is the tension between the critics' indictment of profit as a measure of success and the assertion that the role of agent of education, interpretation, advocacy, and moral uplift had been conferred to the press by the pulpit. For example, *Zion's Herald* said Sheldon's failure should teach readers to appreciate the average daily. "Too long has it been the practice of a certain clique to deprecate and decry it. Why should anybody take the exceptional 'yellow journals' as the representative of the daily paper? Such judgment is as unjust as it is unintelligent. In moral standards, in ability, comprehensiveness and enterprise the American press is unrivaled. The daily paper enlightens, absorbs, and largely directs the life of our people."[69] Yes, the *Christian Observer* agreed, but it was not yet so ready to extol the beneficence of the American press, holding that there was still much room for correction. One possible solution, the *Observer* counseled, was that "if the love of God and the love of our fellowmen, instead of the love of money, were the animating spirit of the press everywhere it would advance the people in everything that makes life worth living." That was because, the *Observer* asserted, the press's influence reached into every corner of society. Therefore, "A high standard, religious and moral, of the secular press would be very advantageous to the whole community both as affecting the personal character and the business interests of the people."[70]

But many on both sides of the issue agreed that the Sheldon Edition had triggered a "world-wide discussion" about the newspaper and its role and responsibility to society.[71] Indeed, the *Topeka Capital* afterward asked whether Sheldon's efforts, despite his failures, had benefited the newspaper profession. While many commentators inside and outside the clergy considered Sheldon's experiment a failure, its "widespread interest" had taught editors to "look to the public more closely, to perceive more plainly the duty they owe to their constituents and to the world," one writer observed. "It has had the effect also of teaching the readers of newspapers that criticizing a newspaper and producing a newspaper are different. It has taught them some of the difficulties under which the work of a daily newspaper is done. It has made newspaper readers wiser, as it has taught publishers that the reading class is demanding a constantly higher moral standard." Similarly, the Reverend John P. Brushingham of First Methodist Church in Chicago observed that Sheldon had "raised the question whether the secular press should be simply a mirror to reflect the world's face for twenty-fours or should exercise a sense of discrimination?"[72] And one analyst for the *Christian Observer* noted that while the Sheldon Edition was certainly a failure as a daily newspaper, it had prompted as many as a million readers and hundreds of editors and publishers to give serious thought to "whether the moral standard of the press of the country cannot be elevated." Given that fact alone, the writer professed "hope that it will set many Christian men, who are engaged in journalistic work, to think seriously on the question whether their Christianity may not be carried into their daily work on a much larger scale."[73]

CHAPTER 6

The Social Gospel and the Mission of Newspapers in the Modern World

> **The great mass of our newspapers and periodicals make no profession of religion, and this vast enginery of the press is yet to be moved and directed by Christian forces. This is one of the kingdoms of the world that will one day belong to Christ. The time will come when the leaves that fall in myriads from the power-presses, and that fly on the morning trains with tidings from the ends of the earth, shall be for the healing of the nations.**
>
> —Washington Gladden, "Christian Journalism"

WASHINGTON GLADDEN, "THE FATHER OF the Social Gospel" movement, believed that economic issues did not originate outside the ambit of the organism known as society. He rejected the belief that they had no connection to morals and that Christian principles should not be taken into account when considering issues of economics.[1] In fact, the condemnation of classical economics and unregulated competition in which the metric for success was solely pecuniary was a constant theme of the growing social Christianity movement of the era. Instead, as Lyman Abbott put it, the "new political economy" they were seeking to create concerned itself with the maintenance of society and dealt "with man as an intellectual and moral being."[2]

One of the earliest and most important discussions of this issue was Gladden's *Working People and Their Employers* (1876), a book historian of the Social Gospel movement Charles Howard Hopkins observed "became one of the first mileposts set by American social Christianity." In his preface, Gladden offered an early dismissal of any objection to bringing to bear "the truth of the New Testament" upon the then ongoing struggles between labor and capital. These disputes were larger than simple economic issues, Gladden argued, and thus "it is plain that the pulpit must have something to say about them." Here, then, were the beginnings of the reform era. As historian Henry May observed, before Gladden and his generation, the Protestant religion had been anchored "to the theories of divinely-sanctioned laws, the depravity of the poor, the futility of collective action, and the other dogmas of clerical laissez faire." However, May noted, the "early Social Gospel leaders shattered the hold of the old, confining doctrines."[3]

The Social Gospel and the News

To understand the Social Gospel and its struggle with the newspaper press over journalistic conduct and content—the news—we need to first have some understanding of both the context of the times and how the movement was a product of those times.

Context of the Times

The Social Gospel arose during the Gilded Age and reached its height during the Progressive Era.[4] Certainly, at this point there is no need to again rehash the societal ills of and the impulses for reform and adjustment during the raw industrialization of America before and after the turn of the last century. Earlier chapters have delineated these.[5] Suffice it to say this was an era in which people were, first of all, rethinking the dominant theory of laissez-faire economics. Indeed, the clashing notions of unrestrained capitalism versus Progressive Era calls for more government oversight, regulation, and even outright socialism were at the heart of the conversation of the age. This is especially so as it relates to the Social Gospel's view of an interconnected, organic society in which service and social responsibility were key. This critique of laissez-faire economics is one indicator of an era in which people were reconsidering their connections to one another. They were also responding to what journalist and philosopher Walter Lippmann described as a "complicated civilization" and the anxiety brought on by the rupture of old ways. "We are unsettled to the very roots of our being," Lippmann wrote, and "we don't know how to behave when personal contact and eternal authority have disappeared. There are no precedents to guide us, no wisdom that wasn't made for a simpler age. We have changed our environment more quickly than we know how to change ourselves."[6]

An attempt to promote just such a change and make manifest the notion of an interconnected society was the subject of the Fifth General Convention of the Religious Education Association in 1908. The convention included presentations by such Social Gospel stalwarts as Abbott and Gladden. Its focus was discovering and developing a social conscience, for it was such a conscience, historian Donald K. Gorrell observed, that "would produce a sense of social responsibility, social justice, and social morality that in turn would find expression in moral-reform and political-reform societies, in social settlements, in philanthropic groups, and in churches."[7] The description of the era in a convention presentation by a Harvard theology professor, Francis G. Peabody, was indicative of this. "Never in human history were so many people, rich and poor, learned and ignorant, wise and otherwise, concerning themselves with social amelioration, dedicating themselves to philanthropy, organizing for industrial change, or applying the motives of religion to the problems of modern life." Peabody pointed to a new expression that had arisen to describe society—the "Social Organism."[8] That term and permutations of it denoted a nonindividualistic view of a diverse but interrelated society from which arose the notion of social responsibility or a social conscience. And that notion was central to the demands the pulpit put on the press.

Two primary facets of life in America were the impulse for the notion of a social conscience and the seedbed of religion's reset in how it perceived the source of social problems and how to address them. One would be the city with its heaving tenement slums and masses of alienated and often irreligious working-class residents who were often the fuel for anarchy. The other was the soulless corporation—"the seat and source of our present troubles," Walter Rauschenbusch asserted in 1912. These two promontories of society were consubstantial with the other and were the result—as Hopkins and Ronald C. White noted in a discussion about the many prompts for the Social Gospel—of the country "moving from muscular energy to mechanical power, from individualism to collectivism, from farm to factory, and from the village to the city."[9]

Certainly in history, the city has been viewed as foreign and detrimental to life. But the onslaught of industrialism did much to heighten the city's disrepute. This view of the city is evident as early as 1853 in the Reverend Edwin Chapin's work *The Moral Aspects of City Life*. Chapin, a Universalist minister, author, renowned lecturer, and social reformer, described the "nether world" of the city long before the postbellum industrialization and urbanization of America as a "swimming mist of hideous transactions." The Reverend Josiah Strong, one of the "prophets of the new social message," described the city as both "the nerve center of our civilization" and its "storm center." Writing in his best-known and influential work, *Our Country: Its Possible Future and Its Present Crisis* (1891), Strong used census data to show that during the half century before 1880, the population in cities had grown four times more than in rural areas. And in the process, he warned, the city had "become a serious menace to our civilization," as all the dangers of modernity were "enhanced, and all are focalized."[10] More than a quarter century later, the Reverend Charles Stelzle, described in the *New York Times* as the "livest wire in present-day Christianity," also used the trope of the city as storm center in his work *Christianity's Storm Centre: A Study of the Modern City* (1907). Stelzle, who had advanced to the upper echelons of religious life in America, came to his subject with a depth of experience. Born in a tenement, he began working in a sweatshop at the age of eight, and when he headed the Presbyterian Department of Church and Labor, he hung his machinist's certificate in his office.[11] Stelzle recognized that America was "rapidly becoming a nation of cities." He argued that the forces of the city were challenging and undermining the church, which was the superstructure of society and "the principal factor in social progress."[12]

But aside from the threat to the church, the avarice of corporations in dealing with the workers helping them to accumulate great wealth was "centering in the city forces which may some day undermine every institution which stands for the peace and prosperity of the nation."[13] In his index of indictments of the city in which, he argued, the workingman's "hell is here and now,"[14] Stelzle arraigned the "recklessness of great corporations in the violation of law and in the total disregard of the interests of the common people."[15] This charge is illustrated in Rauschenbusch's seminal work on the Social Gospel, *Christianizing the Social Order* (1912). He pointed to the home-based handicraft system that existed before capitalism when prices for goods were "fair and reasonable" and the goal was not to achieve excess profit. But in contrast, modern society was "dominated by owners and organizers of industry and commerce" whose sole goal was profit. These men, he asserted, were "the masters of Business but the servants of Profit." Meanwhile, Richard Hofstadter has observed that the disdain for the corporation had its roots in the antecedent to the Progressives, the Populist movement that held that "the great business combinations, being the only centers of wealth and power, would be able to lord it over all other interests and thus to put an end to traditional American democracy."[16] To that point, the National People's Party platform, adopted at Omaha, Nebraska, on July 4, 1892, is at its core an indictment of the collusion between government and corporations to the detriment of the public welfare. And included in that arraignment were the nation's newspapers, which were, the platform alleged, "largely subsidized or muzzled," thus silencing public opinion to the benefit of corporations and to the detriment of the public, small business, and labor.[17]

After about 1900, the Populist and Progressive movements conjoined, though Progressive thought, Hofstadter wrote, was "more informed, more moderate, more complex." And unlike the Populist movement that rallied around the cry for the "destruction of the money power," the Social Gospel movement was more interested in redeeming it into a Christlike ethic. For example, Rauschenbusch held that when profit was simply a "fair reward" for labor and service, then it was morally sound. But, he argued, when profit came "at the expense of others, and without their willing consent, it rests on power and not on right," and Christians were not morally obligated to respect it. Rather, it was incumbent on Christians "to aid society in tracing this parasitic tribute to its sources and preventing its further absorption."[18]

One contemporary historian who has traced its source is Alan Trachtenberg. He has argued that the causality at the root of that indictment was the very change in the meaning—and the ideas—surrounding the word *corporation*, which had moved from a communitarian notion of public good to a pecuniary notion of private gain. In fact, this concept of a society as a communal organism versus the individualistic self-interested whose measure for success was profit "untroubled by human considerations or moral scruples," as Rauschenbusch asserted, was a dialectic notion at the crux of the debate about the role of newspapers in the life of society. It is evident in such plaints about the loss of "mercy and fraternity"[19] and the attempt to reclaim "a solidaristic conception of social life."[20] Trachtenberg noted that the word *corporation* refers to any association of individuals bound together into a corpus, "a body sharing a common purpose in a common name." Historically, he observed, the purpose of the corporation was usually either communal or religious. Examples of such corporate structures were boroughs, guilds, monasteries, and bishoprics in Europe. Trachtenberg wrote that such corporations were viewed much as we view nonprofits today—that their whole reason for being was the public good. Even as late as the Civil War in America, only special acts of the state legislatures could grant a corporate charter—"and then for purposes clearly in the public interest." But in postbellum America all that had changed, and by 1913 Christian idealist Woodrow Wilson cautioned, "The truth is we are all caught in a great economic system which is heartless. The modern corporation is not engaged in business as an individual. When we deal with it, we deal with an impersonal element, an immaterial piece of society." And at the heart of Wilson's complaint was that the world had changed, but the law had not changed apace. And the laws that would deal with this new form of corporation were based on an old system that could do nothing to "prevent the strong from crushing the weak."[21]

The Social Gospel Movement

So the question, to begin, is this: What was the Social Gospel? And the answer, as the Reverend John A. Patten noted in 1920, is both anchored to a fundament and adrift in the context of the times in which the question was asked because "every age calls for its own emphasis."[22] However, the movement's "permanent truths may be expressed in such phrases as social justice, the brotherhood of man, universal peace, and the like," wrote Patten, for many years the editorial secretary and literary superintendent of the British and Foreign Bible Society.[23] Indeed, those are notions that can be enveloped in the Social Gospel's theology that saw "God as a Social Being, closely identified with humanity, rather than an isolated Being, 'at an infinite distance'"; that held that the human community was to be "understood in the light of racial religiousness, rather than racial depravity"; and that saw "Sin as Social Injustice."[24] And just as economic issues were no longer seen as lying outside the sphere of society, neither were religion and its role in the lives of men and women. Instead, God was immanent, and the concept of the "social" was the armature for a new theology in which "the hand of God is on the whole life of man, physical as well as spiritual."[25] At the risk of oversimplifying, the "New Theology" was "the religious articulation of the social movement" that, as one writer noted in 1908, "is now taking place in every country of the civilized world toward universal peace and brotherhood and a better and fairer distribution of wealth."[26] One contemporary scholar has described this notion of immanence as a fusion of the religious and secular and "the abandonment of a God conceived primarily as a transcendent judge, and the embrace of the world itself as the prime locus of salvation."[27]

That notion is reflective of the Social Gospel advocates' rejection of the idea that poverty was associated with moral depravity, which prompted them to replace the old-line Protestant effort at saving individual souls with the struggle to change society. Especially illustrative of this were the thoughts of renowned sociologist the Reverend John Bascom, an academic moral philosopher, the fifth president of the University of Wisconsin in the mid-1880s, and one of the chief proponents of the Social Gospel movement.

Bascom's philosophy was informed by Darwin's theory of evolution. Thus, no longer was the world to be viewed in terms of individual sin—a consequence of racial depravity[28]—but instead society was seen in all its warp and woof of embedded relationships.[29]

We have already observed the context of the times in which the entanglements of society—rather than the individual—were seen as the core of the problems roiling the world around the turn of the last century. This is illustrated by the concerns of Walter Sheldon, one of the leading spokesmen for the ethical culture movement and leader of the Ethical Society of St. Louis, who warned in 1896 that there had never been a time "when true civilization was in greater peril." To address this crisis, he called for religion to "adjust itself to these new conditions. Instead of looking away from earth it must concentrate its attention upon the practical side of daily life and everyday needs."[30] Two years later, another adherent to the Social Gospel, the Reverend Samuel D. McConnell of Holy Trinity Church in New York, looked at the radical changes in population, technology, and infrastructure creating a modern society that was discarding God's eternal verities[31] and that more and more had little room for churchgoing. Writing in the popular *Outlook* magazine, he cautioned, "The percentage of non church-goers in the community has been steadily increasing for more than a generation, and with the last ten years we have seen some which looks like 'the letting out of waters.'" In that, he meant that if the church did nothing to halt the outflow, the loss of congregants would increase exponentially. Similarly, other Protestant leaders had observed how the changing demographics were affecting the church. The Reverend Josiah Strong pointed to a link between the increasing population of the cities and the decreasing number of churchgoers. Strong was concerned that the church was not growing enough to maintain its influence. What this portended, McConnell argued, was a "revolution"—a "profound reversal of social habit" many centuries old, which meant society no longer regarded the church in the way it did in the past. Given this situation, the question boiled down to this: "How shall the Christian Church adjust her discipline and her methods to modern society?"[32] At its essence, that was what the Social Gospel movement was attempting to address—and, consequently, the secular newspaper would come to be viewed as one of the modern methods of persuasive communication with society leading to reform and moral uplift.

This waning in religion's hold on life in America as arbiter of public opinion stemmed from the fact that the nineteenth century had been a crucible of change—from the small-unit economic drivers of the farm or home-based business to, in just a few decades, a full-blown industrial revolution that created what European theologian Willem A. Visser 't Hooft described as a "modern capitalistic industry with all its baffling problems for Christian ethics." Likewise, Rauschenbusch—whom renowned muckraking journalist Ray Stannard Baker once called "a true prophet of the times"—pointed to the "destructive tendencies of modern life," such as industrialization, that had "trampled down the human considerations of mercy and fraternity which had to some extent prevailed, and created a general temper of lawlessness and ruthlessness." Yes, agreed an editorial that same year in the *Biblical World*: "As individuals we are kind and just, as a society we are heartless and tyrannical. Our whole pitiless competitive wage system is crushing men, women, and children, and nobody is to blame." The editors of the publication included two key figures in the Social Gospel movement—William Rainey Harper and Shailer Mathews—and their editorial went on to argue that "the real nature of sin in the modern world . . . is social as well as personal."[33]

Thus, this was the temper of the times in which the Social Gospel movement found a footing. "It is clear," Visser 't Hooft observed in his pioneering study of the Social Gospel movement, "that the time was ripe for a reassertion of the social implications of Christianity. Though the nation as a whole was confessedly attached to the Christian church, its every-day life, especially in the economic sphere, had been reshaped and in this process the church had had no influence and taken no lead." Visser 't Hooft noted that in the face of the classical economics model of unrestrained business espoused by the eighteenth- and nineteenth-century economic theorists, the Social Gospel movement constituted "the one most important attempt made to transcend the individualistic notions of these last centuries and arrive at a solidaristic conception of social life." Historian Hopkins affirms that its roots and this notion of social solidarity could be found in the Gilded Age, spawned by a sea change wrought by industrialism and its effects on society and by scientific thought's impact on Protestantism. Thus, within that frame of social solidarity, the advocates of the Social Gospel applied Christ's teachings and the notion of salvation to society as a whole. The "social element," Hopkins observed, was a strain of reformational action that ran through Christianity and preceded Christ, most notably evident in "the high moral aspirations of the Hebrew prophets," who were essentially social reformers.[34]

Consequently, Strong observed, "the churches began to see that they have a mission to society as well as to the individual," as the country began to move into what he called in 1902 "the next great spiritual awakening."[35] That movement had its roots in the early nineteenth century's Second Great Awakening, which had rejected the precepts of the First Great Awakening from a half century before that had largely focused on redeeming the souls of individual sinners. During the second, social reform became an important part of Protestantism in America. Abbott, one of the earliest advocates of the Social Gospel, argued that in this new movement, there was a growing attitude among educated men and women to reject a theology that advocated the doctrine of the inherent depravity of all men and women—that all were "wholly disposed to evil." One of the early precursors of this notion was a series of lectures titled "The Kingdom of Christ on Earth" in 1870 by Samuel Harris, the president of Bowdoin College and later professor of systematic theology at Yale. In those lectures he argued that civilization's ills could be cured only "by obedience to the Christian law of service."[36] In other words, men and institutions—such as newspapers—had a responsibility to serve society.

By the last decade of the nineteenth century, one of the ideas of the Social Gospel coming to be accepted was the immanence of God, which leveled the wall between the sacred and the secular. And it also leavened the Social Gospel notion of human solidarity. "The vision of God unfolding himself in human institutions lent religion a new immediacy, expanded its sphere of activity and reinforced the organic bonds integrating the individual with society," argued Hopkins, who observed that the Gospel would affect society by converting the character of individuals, who would, in turn, lead to a transformation in society. Rauschenbusch argued, "The earth is even now the habitation of God, and it is ours to make it wholly so. It is not a place to be spurned, but a home to be loved and made clean and holy." One great exponent of this notion of social solidarity was Gladden, who declared in 1897 that some in the church still "greatly failed to grasp and enforce this central truth." Rather, they viewed religion as a "special and separate interest" disconnected from worldly affairs. This, then, allowed the church to view business, politics, and amusement as "separate realms with codes of their own which religion could not question." Instead, Gladden held, "There is no more reason why a minister of the gospel should be prayerful, and unselfish and consecrated than there is why the superintendent of a factory or the manager of a newspaper, or a bank, or the president of a trades-union, or the member of a city council, or a legislature should be prayerful and unselfish and consecrated; each is God's servant, whether he will or no."[37]

Finally, by the early twentieth century, most American preachers and teachers of any influence were well ingrained in the principles of liberal theology and the Social Gospel,[38] which found support across denominations. For example, the Social Gospel movement's pioneers included Josiah Strong and Charles Sheldon, Congregationalists; Walter Rauschenbusch, a Baptist; Edward Everett Hale, a Unitarian; and an Episcopalian, George Hodges. And by 1912, nearly all of the better theological seminaries had a chair devoted to "Social Ethics" or "Christian Sociology."[39] In addition, the abundant work of Social Gospel advocates of every stripe appeared in the pages of published sermons, periodicals, books, conference proceedings, trade journals for the newspaper industry, and the secular weekly and daily press. Indeed, as Hopkins observed, the clergy "were among the leading diagnosticians of the industrial maladjustments" of the Progressive Era.[40]

The Social Gospel and the Progressive Movement

Because the two movements for reform—the Social Gospel and Progressive—overlapped in the early twentieth century, it is easy to see them as interchangeable in their goals and aspirations and in their perceived solutions to the ills of society. For example, historian Dorothea Muller has observed that both progressives and advocates of the Social Gospel viewed society as an organism as a means of emphasizing "the interdependence of man in the new industrial age."[41] But it would be a mistake to believe the Social Gospel was wholly knitted to the Progressive movement and the muckrakers' literature of exposure, as both grew up and defined themselves over the decades. For example, two contemporary scholars argue Social Gospel advocates held that "if the system were reformed through democratic legislation, the kingdom of God would be present." However, one counter to that assertion are the words of Shailer Mathews, the dean of the University of Chicago Divinity School. Writing in 1899 in the *American Journal of Sociology*, Mathews held, "The church must recognize that its fundamental mission is religious-dynamic, and not regulative."[42]

Thus, given this seeming confusion, it is necessary to briefly tease out the distinctions between the two movements because those subtle differentiations can get lost in the clangor of calls for reform. While much of the conversation of the era and beyond indicates the recombinant nature of the two movements' cooperative efforts, they were not clones. To that point, one contemporary scholar argues that the Social Gospel movement, from its inchoate roots onward, went from tentative criticism of the economic system to an active participant with the forces of progressivism.[43] That would tend to make one think that the two movements were indistinguishable.

The notion that both movements were consubstantial is also seemingly confirmed by two key influences: the Social Gospel's connection with the growing field of social sciences in response to a changing modern society and religion's formal entry into the arena of social action with the adoption of *The Social Creed of the Churches.*

The Rise of Social Sciences

The Social Gospel's association with the emerging social science profession can be seen in the fact that many of its practitioners included social Christians. One example comes from the pen of Josiah Strong. He wrote in 1893 that "we have come upon the sociological age of the world; that we shall not have social peace and ought not to have it until we have social righteousness—until right relations have been established between man and man." Strong believed that the masses had left the church because it had failed to recognize its "social mission" in this new era. Thus, he argued, the church needed to find new methods to work for humanity—and those methods were the ground from which sociology grew. Indeed, in his analysis of the growth of the Social Gospel and sociology, J. Graham Morgan observed that both sociology and the Social Gospel grew in response to a changing society that "rendered individualistic interpretations" of life insufficient for dealing with social problems. Sociology and the Social Gospel were coeval, and sociology was nurtured by the Social Gospel. For instance, recall that Abbott, Gladden, and twenty-two other ministers—under the leadership of Richard T. Ely—helped to establish the American Economic Association in 1885.[44]

To that point, Morgan argued that the adherents of both were reacting to "the more extreme forms of socialism, communism, and anarchism" and thus were more liberal than revolutionary. And even while some within the Social Gospel tended to range from liberal progressives to those who called for the abolition of capitalism, Morgan noted that both factions agreed on the "relevance of religion to everyday life."[45] To more clearly illustrate, of the 298 professors who taught sociology in 1900, nearly one-third of them had studied theology, and most of them were ordained ministers.[46] And Hopkins, in his history of the Social Gospel, also noted that the movement was "a happy ally" of both sociology and reform in the collection and publication of "sociological data for reform purposes." Hopkins went on to assert:

"Prominent social scientists lent their influence, wrote books on social Christianity, and evangelized for reform in the name of religion and of science; some outlined the social character of religion and its institutions and attempted to evaluate its place in modern society in terms of valid sociological concepts. And in this period the churches developed the techniques of social service to such a degree that in the eyes of professional organizations they came to occupy a significant place among the nation's agencies of social welfare."[47]

However, one representative example of the tension between the doctrines of the Social Gospel and the demands of social scientists as it relates to reform can be found in the Reverend John Marshall Barker's work *The Social Gospel and the New Era* (1919). In this book, Barker, a professor of sociology at Boston University's School of Theology, called for more in the way of direct action on the part of the church. And he took to task those who believed such direct action by the "church in its corporate capacity" to create a "new social order" was incompatible with the spiritual work of the church. Barker saw the church as a powerful institution that could work as a change agent. He argued, however, that it had failed "to see that both spiritual power and an ethical program are essential to a full orbed Christian life. . . . The fact that personal redemption is the key to social reconstruction does not warrant the neglect of concerted social activity in behalf of the Kingdom." Barker's complaint was that the church focused too much "upon man rather than upon his wrongs and his economic and social condition." He thought little of the church's abiding hope that by becoming "right with God," men would then amend their social and economic behavior. "However," he asserted, "this central purpose of the Church in no wise relieves it of the responsibility to champion the cause of those seeking to improve their economic and social condition."[48]

The Social Creed

The other influence was the adoption of *The Social Creed of the Churches* in 1908 by the Federal Council of the Churches of Christ in America, which officially represented thirty-three denominations comprising nearly all the nation's mainline Protestant churches. This declaration of principles was the product of the council's Church and Modern Industry Committee and was, one early-twentieth-century scholar noted, "the first crystallization into concrete demands of the common conviction of the Protestant churches concerning their duty in the field of social and industrial relations" and "the deliberate and conscious entrance of the Church upon the field of social action."[49] The creed called for direct action in alleviating the societal ills created by the industrializing of America, including ending Sunday working hours, abolishing child labor, and creating disability insurance for workers injured on the job. Still, while on its face the creed appeared both progressive and secular, it had substantial religious underpinnings, and more than one effort was made to make that clear. For example, William Monroe Balch, a Methodist minister and former secretary of the Methodist Federation for Social Service, included an entire chapter in his book *Christianity and the Labor Movement* (1912) to an exegesis of *The Social Creed*. In it he essentially articulates the link between the Progressive's call for direct social action and the notion of social justice grounded in the teachings of Christ undergirding that call. He argued that "social justice, no less than private morality, must be the uncompromising demand of the Church."[50]

Meanwhile, many clergymen and theologians, while recognizing the overlap of the Social Gospel and Progressive movements, made distinctions in which the efforts of each lay outside the circle of their agreement. Historian Donald Gorrell has observed that Gladden, Rauschenbusch, Strong, and Mathews all argued in their writings that although the Social Gospel was concerned about social conditions, the church's task was not working for social reforms but "the redemption of society." Certainly, the Reverend John Patten, writing in 1920, did not see how the church could find an advantage in injecting itself into a question of economics. The clergy had no expertise in this area, he argued. "But," Patten noted, "economic problems have moral and spiritual aspects, and the church may play a powerful though indirect part in bringing about a reconciliation" in which the employee and employer would come to understand their moral obligations to each other. The church could do so, he argued, by standing "for such principles as justice between employer and workman," which went to one of the central themes of the Social Gospel that saw "Sin as Social Injustice." In 1889 Gladden and two other advocates of the Social Gospel argued that the world had changed and that the church needed to change, too, in order to adapt to the new problems of society. "The old notion," they wrote, "was that the spiritual order was something wholly distinct from, and almost antithetical to, the moral and social order of this world; the new conception is that the spiritual order is realized in the moral and social order of the world."[51]

At the prospect of oversimplifying for clarity's sake, we can put into relief this distinction between what was essentially the Progressives' call for changing the superstructure of society versus the Social Gospel effort to change the inner structure of each person—and thus society. One place this is made clear—and at the same time reveals the overlap—is the contrast between the reform-minded Christian idealist Woodrow Wilson and the sentiments of the advocates of the Social Gospel. In 1913 Wilson complained that the law was inadequate in trying to hold the modern corporations accountable for their behavior in such things as an employer's liability for injuries to his employee on the work site. "Our laws still deal with us on the basis of the old system. The law is still living in the dead past which we have left behind." Given modern conditions, Wilson rejected the old Jeffersonian notion of "the best government was the government that did as little governing as possible." That theory once worked when life was simpler, he argued. "But we are coming now to realize that life is so complicated that we are not dealing with the old conditions, and that the law has to step in and create new conditions under which we may live, the conditions which will make it tolerable for us to live."[52] Here, Wilson was talking about the Progressive notion of updating the laws of men to comport with a new age.

However, Gladden reflected the Social Gospel tenet that there was something much more subterranean and spiritual about changing society than questions of economic method. He outlined in *The Church and Modern Life* (1908) the substantive differences between the Social Gospel advocates' approach to social change and that of Progressives in general. The church, Gladden held, was not concerned "with the machinery of society, but with the moral motive power." Here, Gladden is speaking to the creation of an ethos from which change would flow. That meant, he wrote, that the church sought to "invigorate the moral life of men, and trusts that reinforced life to make its own economic forms." For example, he argued, "When employers and employed are all filled with the spirit of Christ, the wage system will not be a system of exploitation, but a means of social service."[53]

And as late as 1922, Harry Emerson Fosdick, a follower of Walter Rauschenbusch, saw a correlation between Christian ethics and efforts at social progress. But in his book *Christianity and Progress* he argued, "The idea of progress can defeat itself no more surely than by getting itself so believed that men expect automatic social advance apart from the conquest of personal and social sin." He also held that those within the Progressive movement failed to understand the power of sin and believed too much in political change and "social palliatives instead of radical cures for our public maladies." Change toward a more decent world, Fosdick insisted, required not a reset in external circumstances but "a radical change in men's thinking." And that thinking, wrote sociologist Charles Ellwood, required the church to create a public conscience about how people should live together in order to bring a "Christian world" into being. "If we want a Christian world, we must have in their place Christian mores, Christian institutions, Christian civilization, a Christian environment in brief, in which the Christian life will come as easily and naturally to individuals as national loyalty and patriotism do now." Finally, as historian Stanley K. Schultz has noted, "Democracy, in muckraking thought, was more than an organization of government, more than an economic system; it was a moral force." Thus, the muckrakers hardly ever participated in politics. "They hoped by exhortation and moral suasion to enlist their countrymen in a moral crusade." But unlike the advocates of the Social Gospel, while the muckrakers' work was hinged to moral ideals, they were largely secular in their outlook. Schultz asserts, "The writers thought of man primarily as a being dependent only upon himself, rather than as the special creation of an absolute God, playing out on the stage of the world the drama of human dependence on the divine will."[54]

Two examples should well illustrate this moral but secular outlook of the mind of Progressive reformers. For example, reform-minded newspaper mogul E. W. Scripps once admitted, "I cannot recall the time when I was not what is commonly called an atheist. I do not believe in God, or any being equal to or similar to the Christian's God. . . . Yet when I called upon myself to classify myself as to what school of philosophy or religion I belong to, I have had no doubt but that I should be classified as a Christian. My morals, or my moral convictions, are those common to members of the Christian religion." And then Frederic Clemson Howe in his *Confessions of a Reformer* (1925) recalled, "Physical escape from the embraces of evangelical religion did not mean moral escape. From that religion my reason was never emancipated. By it I was conformed to my generation and made to share its moral standards and ideals. . . . This is, I think, the most characteristic influence of my generation. It explains the nature of our reforms, the regulatory legislation in morals and economics, our belief in men rather than in institutions and our messages to other peoples."[55]

The Social Gospel's View of the Role of the Press

With that summary of the Social Gospel and the times in which it arose, we can begin to understand what gave the advocates of the movement purchase to think they could influence the press. At its most fundamental, it was sustained by the notion of the immanence of God in all things. This was a notion that went back to the prophetic conception of the Hebrew prophets in which "right moral conduct" was the essential basis of religion and the binding compound of a new social order of community solidarity and a perfected world that sought, the Reverend John Marshall Barker declared, both "justice and mercy." Barker emphasized that the modern Christian conception foresaw the founding of a "divine order in society" in which God's spirit is part of every human endeavor and in which "men will obey God's will in all their industrial and social relations." In addition, he asserted—and this is a key to regarding the Social Gospel and its view of journalism as one more societal institution needing reform—"Wherever Christian principles are infused into the social fabric, they become more or less fixed moral factors in society."[56]

The Reverend George Davis Herron, a Congregationalist minister and a nationally known and influential Social Gospel preacher, put this concept of immanence and all that it meant for the secular institutions of society into much more stark relief. Here, Herron is gathering together many of those institutions, including the newspaper. And bound up in his view of the secular and the sacred are religion's rationales that necessity supported its belief that it must—that it had the right—to influence the news ethic of the press. Herron argued, "The day is coming when the homes, the shops, the stores, the social clubs, the newspapers, the corporations, the political caucuses, that have not for their sacred purpose the making of men divine will be regarded as out of place in a world that has been redeemed by the Son of God and nourished by the life-blood of his saints. There is no such thing as a secular affair in the universe of God."[57]

It is not a far step from this airy notion of the newspaper "making of men divine" to the more widely accepted contention that its sacred mission was to act as a moral agent. Indeed, one of the leading lights of the Progressive movement—William Jennings Bryan—reiterated that notion in a speech to as many as two hundred newspaper journalists at a dinner in his honor in New York City in September 1906.[58] Bryan held that there was a "great moral awakening" then ongoing in America that the newspapers must participate in and that required journalists to quit "the selling of consciences for a salary." Bryan's pronouncement on the press was not a new idea. Writing in 1892, the Reverend Newman Smyth, a scientist, theologian, and one of the key liberal Protestant ministers along with Gladden, asserted that the modern newspaper was a venue through which "the public conscience may be educated, or by which it may also be debased and misled." Still, he insisted, the daily press was a career field in which Christians may exert the power for change. "Through the incessant influence of an intelligent and honorable journalism, all good causes may be helped rapidly forward on their way of conquest."[59] Here, Smyth is insisting that journalism done with principle and intelligently was an agent of reform by informing and creating sound public opinion.

Similarly, the Reverend E. D. Weigle, a Lutheran clergyman and advocate of the Social Gospel, was representative of the view that modern times needed "the adoption of methods unknown to former times"—that is, employing the secular press—because the pulpit could not stand by and watch without acting against the forces that were harming society. This was a view of the role of the church, Visser 't Hooft observed, that was traditional in its scope. Because religion was such a large part of life in the United States, it was accepted that the church had a part in influencing how to address the moral issues arising from the social and political problems of the day. "The church therefore has always felt free to influence public opinion on matters where it felt convinced that important principles of moral and religious life were at stake."[60] And key to any reform of society lay in public opinion. However, as I have set forth in earlier chapters, religion no longer held sway over public opinion and had, over time, ceded the role of agent of education, moral uplift, and reform to the newspaper.

Still, religion's effort to use the press for reform was not unique—and in that fact we can see the pulpit's historical view of the press that gave the advocates of the Social Gospel precedential purchase to think they could influence its conduct and content. In fact, Lyman Abbott observed, reform often had a sociological rather than a theological basis. Many of the questions to be answered, he wrote in his memoirs, "were questions, not of future salvation for the few, but of social salvation for all." Looking back into the past and then moving forward, Abbott noted these sociological issues included slavery, reconstruction, education, immigrant rights, poverty, crime, labor issues involving women and children, and "the redemption of the cities and the factory towns from the slums." All these issues, he recalled, "absorbed the public mind"[61]—meaning these issues became the focus of public opinion in which the newspaper played a part. The notion that the press had a role as agency of reform with such issues of public opinion had historical precedent going much further back than the late nineteenth century. For instance, as early as the 1830s abolitionist William Lloyd Garrison saw a role for both the church and newspapers in his battle to end slavery. In addition to the distribution of antislavery tracts and periodicals, he vowed to "enlist the pulpit and the press in the cause of the suffering and the dumb."[62] Similarly, in 1866, the *Atlantic Monthly*, in a paean to abolitionist editor Gamaliel Bailey, made just this point. Any historian, it said, who argued that the firing at Fort Sumter started the war would be wholly off the mark. "The battles fought in the press, pulpit, and forum, in ante-war days, were as much agencies in the great conflict as the deadlier ones . . . and it is the proud distinction of the early partisans of freedom to be recognized now as the pioneers of the advance-guard of the armed hosts who at last won the victory for humanity."[63]

Still, determining what prompted Social Gospel advocates to criticize the press and then attempt to influence its news ethic requires a consideration of a number of factors. Earlier chapters have delineated the perceived failures of the newspaper press. Therefore here I will offer only a brief but representative synopsis of those shortcomings of the press from a newspaperman of more than twenty years who summarized this criticism in 1894 as follows: the daily press "transcends the bounds of liberty and runs into license," "it is sensational and unreliable," "it assails private character in a wanton manner," it gives too much "prominence to reports of evil doings," its policy is too often driven by "its own selfish interests," "it panders to vicious appetites and idealizes crime," and it fails to give enough attention to "moral and religious movements and church happenings."[64] And illustrative of religion's view grounded in the notion of social responsibility was the critique of the Reverend John Bascom. In an influential book titled *Sociology* (1887), Bascom argued that the press was the "crier rather than the evangelist of our time." Consequently, he argued, "If society is to win any real inspiration, it must look for it to the pulpit, not to the press." Equally, John Rogers Commons, a professor of economics and social science at Indiana University and secretary of the American Institute of Christian Sociology, believed that because of its conduct and content, the newspaper could not be true to the mission of reform. In *Social Reform and the Church* (1894), he wrote, "I long to see the day when the leadership in the social movements of our time will be taken from the lawyer and the newspaper and given to the Christian minister. We cannot expect to have a society based on righteousness so long as our social philosophy is given to us by editors and lawyers."[65]

Here are arguments in which we can tease out representative examples of the chief held prejudices about newspaper sensationalism and the commercial and partisan influence on journalistic conduct and content that represent well the strains of thought about the press in the late nineteenth and early twentieth centuries—especially when thought was given to the press replacing the pulpit.[66] One illustrative example of this was an editorial in the *Christian Advocate* in 1901 that observed that the newspaper had come to compete with the church "as a modifier of morals." But the church, the writer asserted, often found that the newspaper did more harm than good with its drumbeat of salacious news, its lack of seriousness in writing about the "more solemn things" (especially "its flippant references to suicides"), and its giving too much coverage and thus credence to "pulpit buffoons" and church scandals that created a distrust of religion in general.[67] These were old complaints, going far back before the rise of yellow journalism in the 1890s. For instance, the Reverend W. N. M'Elroy, writing in the *Christian Advocate* in 1890, called for criminalizing the deception and venality of the newspaper press. "Is it not the chief enginery of evil, and the greatest source of corruption in our midst?" the reverend asked. "And is the excuse, that the newspaper is conducted for the money there is in it, any more valid than that of the gambler, the saloon-keeper, the counterfeiter, or the horse-thief, the purchased voter, or the bribed judge or juryman?"[68]

Still, many in the Social Gospel movement saw the need to co-opt the press because—as noted above—it was a powerful arbiter of public opinion at the core of social reform. But in a caveat to that acknowledgment was the movement's call for the nation's press to align its conduct and content to the needs of society as a socially responsible institution—a thread that runs through decades of discourse by advocates of the Social Gospel. At its base, the argument went, the conscience of the secular press was burdened by the demands of profit, which led to such bêtes noires as sensationalism, invasions of privacy, salacious reporting, and—worst of all—distortions of truth. This latter complaint can be seen in high relief in the Social Gospel's and the Progressive movement's confrontation with the corporation in which they largely came down on the side of the labor movement of the time. And in that rests a critique of the press and its conduct and content. The notion of a "religion of solidarity" declared by Protestant reformers and the title of an essay that utopian visionary Edward Bellamy wrote at the age of twenty-four in 1847 but never published in his lifetime "was often a living experience" within the labor movement.[69]

However, among the foes of labor, along with employers and the government, were many "of the most aggressive and influential" of the mainstream newspapers, charged Samuel Gompers, the founder of the American Federation of Labor and an assiduous analyst of the press coverage of labor.[70] Indeed, the leaders of big business were better known through the press than the leaders of the labor movement.[71] Labor leaders asserted that the press's opposition to labor—or at best a reluctant coolness and reportorial ignorance that contemporary scholars describe as "symbolic annihilation"[72]—largely stemmed from the fact that publishers and owners of newspapers viewed labor issues through the distorted lens of an employer and thus spoke "for vested interests and predatory wealth."[73] One brief editorial by Gompers in the *American Federationist* in 1894 titled "Labor News and Labor's Views Suppressed" well illustrates this. In his editorial, Gompers insisted that news about labor was as important as any other institution the modern newspaper covered. But, he lamented, "What is happening is that the news of this great sphere is being gathered and published from the point of view of employing and commercial interests and the whole business of gathering the facts and the views in this great sphere of life is developed and centered on that side of the argument."[74]

Gompers's essay was written in 1894. His critique of the press was later given substance in the exhaustive *Report on the Steel Strike of 1919* by the Commission of Inquiry of the Interchurch World Movement. The report noted the history of the "hostility of the press giving biased and colored news" and observed that "most newspapers, traditionally hesitant in reporting industrial matters, failed notably to acquaint the public with the facts, failed to take steps necessary to ascertain the facts, failed finally to publish adequately what was brought out by the brief investigation of the U.S. Senate committee." The report concluded with several recommendations. And again, here we have religion attempting to influence journalistic conduct and content—this time in a formal report by an influential coalition of churches. Those recommendations called for, among other things, the press to "free itself of the all too well founded charge of bias, favoring capital as against labor and redeem its power as a promoter of truth and a formulator of public opinion by searching out all the facts in regard to industrial questions and publishing them without fear or favor."[75]

In their 1920 examination of the distorted press coverage of the Bolshevik Revolution, Charles Merz and Walter Lippmann described the church coalition's report as an example of "resistance to the newspaper reports of that strike." Indeed, they argued, newspapers should expect that readers would no longer simply write letters to the editor in complaint of some press malfeasance. Instead, Merz and Lippmann declared, "They will speak through organizations which will become centers of resistance." Such centers of resistance, the authors held, are "powerful engines of criticism" that would no longer accept the distortions of news surrounding contentious questions. "With that fact the profession of journalism will have to make a reckoning."[76]

I would argue here that the Social Gospel movement was just such a powerful center of resistance over many years. And in speaking of the Social Gospel's view of and demand it put on the press, three things become relevant here for our purposes. The first is the fact that many of the leading lights in the Social Gospel movement had experience in journalism in some form, including Lyman Abbott, Washington Gladden, Charles Sheldon, and Walter Rauschenbusch—all of whom understood the power of the press as adjuncts to or as part of their ministries. That journalistic experience alone presupposes a face-to-face confrontation with the conditions of society from the ground up, leading to a synoptic regard for life in America, an understanding of the power of the press over public opinion and for promoting reform, and an appreciation for the commercial and political agents of influence that could affect journalistic conduct and content.[77] The second is that the Social Gospel movement's new applications and adoption of new methods manifested themselves in many ways, the most noticeable of which were its proselytizing reform efforts through sermons, books, magazines, essays, conferences, study courses, tracts, and the pages of the daily newspaper. And third is the felt view about the organic interdependence of society and God's immanence in all the connected structures of life and that the Christian ethic had to be applied to every institution of society.[78] Thus, the press was viewed both as a social instrument to spread the word and as an institution in obvious need of reformation if it were to properly inform the public.

Here, then, we have what is essentially a critique of the purpose of journalism. One articulation of the importance of looking at purpose comes from *A Theory of Discourse* (1971) by James Kinneavy. He argued that "the aim of a discourse determines everything else in the process of discourse." And, he asserted, with all discourse there are four aims, with the aim of journalism and news usually being referential—meaning journalists attempt to portray reality.[79] And in the portrayal of reality—in getting at the truth at the heart of things—rests the core of that struggle between the Social Gospel and the profit-driven newspaper. For what purpose, what mission, did newspapers exist? Was it for profit only, which meant that they gave readers only what they wanted[80] rather than "the thing they need," as the Reverend Charles Sheldon put it? Or was their purpose more along the lines of Gladden's call for a "prophetic function" in which newspapers acted as teachers and guides by offering untainted news along with interpretation to properly inform and advance public opinion while drawing as true a picture of reality as possible? This, as we will recall, was a notion elaborated on by the Reverend John William Mears, whose analysis is reflective of the two views of the function of the newspaper. Mears summarized these functions in two theories—as either the prophetic objective "of leading public opinion to positions in advance of those now held" or the commercially influenced effort at "faithfully representing the present attitude of the public conscience and of justifying it to itself."[81] It is the former theory that emphasizes the primacy of the interpretive and subsequent advocatory aspects of journalism that the proponents of the Social Gospel believed were integral to the true mission of the newspaper press.

Interpretation and Advocacy versus Objectivity

What was meant by a news ethic grounded in interpretation and advocacy and how that appeal might conflict with the newspaper's adherence to uncolored or unbiased news and then later to the notion of objectivity was succinctly illustrated in a comment on a discussion in the *New York Evangelist* in 1898 about four former journalists with the same country weekly who had become ministers. The writer noted, "Certainly no reader of the daily press can deny that an infusion of more preacher and preaching would not injure its moral tone, however much it might interfere with political or business schemes."[82] To that point, there was nothing really radical about that writer's view because, as I noted in chapter 3, the newspaper had a long tradition as a coadjutor to religion—often as a kind of publicist for a point of view not unlike the politically partisan journalism of the nineteenth century. The example that Washington Gladden and other Social Gospel advocates often gave as a forerunner was Saint Paul's Epistles as a type of news that broadcast the word of Christianity, as they were read as sermons to Christian communities across Asia, Greece, and Italy.[83]

In addition, a counterweight to the perceived dominance of the counting room of the press and evidence that the newspaper could well serve as a moral agent in an age of reform was the success of those Progressive muckraking journalists of the early twentieth century who saw religion as a primary driver of reform. For example, Progressive Era icon William Allen White held that the church "was the only organization in which purely social functions of life, the altruistic forces, find recognition. I think the job of the church today is to make a public opinion that will so revolutionize our industry, commerce, and political life that it will be possible for a man to live a generous, useful Christian life without hurt or harm to himself or his family." Contemporary scholar Bruce J. Evensen has observed that "White's hope, and the hope of his fellow foot-soldiers, was that social justice would become a permanent part of economic and political institutions as people came to develop the 'Christ' that was in them." This belief, Evensen argued, was the product of the muckrakers' evangelical indoctrination when young, the later effect of Darwinian thought on those beliefs, and then the resultant effort to fuse their faith to the problems of society extant in their times in order to "solve the fundamental injustices of their era." This notion is made more concrete by renowned muckraking reporter and editor Lincoln Steffens, who argued that the original muckrakers were the Hebrew prophets of the Old Testament, and, as one Steffens biographer has noted, those muckraking reporters at the turn of the last century were imbued with "a high moral and ethical purpose that they associated with the Prophets and Apostles." Indeed, in 1909 the editor of *Everybody's Magazine* described them as "evangels of the new era."[84]

To that point, both Evensen and Doug Underwood have noted the intertwining of the work of several well-known muckrakers—such as Steffens and Upton Sinclair—the reform politics of the Progressive Era, and the Social Gospel movement. For instance, Evensen has observed that it was the muckrakers' rejection of orthodox religion and an adherence to the social justice precepts of a social Christianity grounded in the Bible and especially the Sermon on the Mount that "informed their work." In general, the muckrakers recognized the role that "moral regeneration and moral consensus played in creating a human community in which democratic institutions could be allowed to work." And, he added, Ray Stannard Baker argued that "individual salvation" and "community salvation" were "complementary and reciprocal."[85] Similarly, Underwood has shown that the muckrakers acted as "secular preachers," as they followed an American tradition of crusading reform journalism in which "journalists are allowed to step outside the methodology of objective news reporting and openly advocate for cleaning up corruption and doing away with injustice." Still, as this goes to the heart of our earlier discussion about the distinction between the Progressive and Social Gospel movements, Underwood argued that few muckrakers "saw Jesus as the political radical that Steffens and Sinclair did." Instead, most muckrakers believed in capitalism and wanted to reform it.[86]

Still, it should be noted that much of the work of the muckrakers appeared not in the newspapers but in the more independently minded magazines of the era that were less beholden to market and ideological forces. Arguably, that fact largely stemmed from the growing profit orientation of the newspaper press that began with the introduction of the first penny papers in the 1830s. In 1895 the Reverend John Bascom analyzed the mainstream press's relationship to social reform. In an explication of various social forces that made up American society, he echoed the common complaint that the newspaper's evils arose from the fact that it "primarily represents a money, and not a moral, interest." And from this fact cascaded a blindness that allowed for the trivial rather than the truth, Bascom contended. For one, the influence of outside interests ensured that the daily press was antagonistic toward any social reform—at least until it attained a foothold and became a powerful fact of life. The problem a reform movement early in its life faced was opposition from newspapers that would repress facts, that would apologize for or hide violence done against reformers, and that would blame the reform movement for any violence stemming from its efforts. In addition, the irreverent tone of the daily paper's headlines and stories led to a state of affairs in which the dismissal "of things decent, pure, and reverent is accepted as stripping off the disguises of hypocrisy. A confusion of good and evil thus arises, very slow of correction." Ultimately, in Bascom's arraignment of the daily press, the broadest charge leveled against it and a word that encompassed all other accusations was "secularization." The press's duty, Bascom held, was to truthfully interpret the world to its readers. But instead, the press emphasized "transient and sensuous impressions" for its readers. "Interests which touch the higher nature, the deeper and more controlling current of events, the ethical renderings of the world, are lost sight of, and men drift onward, unmindful of the past disasters of the world or of the portents of coming evil."[87]

Like so many other of his peers in the Social Gospel movement, Bascom was calling for a daily journalism of interpretation. But others in the profession had a different notion. For example, likening the newspaper to a threshing machine that separates the chaff from the wheat from which readers may bake their own bread, Erman J. Ridgway, the president of *Everybody's Magazine*, posited that modern life and modern technology's energizing of the news-gathering function had largely marginalized the interpretive function of newspapers. Instead, he argued, "The ideal newspaper is an emotionless machine; that the function of this machine is solely to give the news; that it attains its maximum usefulness when every wheel in the gigantic machine runs smoothly, grinding out its daily grist of facts without emotion, dispassionate, unswerving, relentless." Alluding to a time when newspapers under the direction of such editors as Greeley and Dana ran editorials that held primacy, Ridgway claimed that newspaper editorials in 1909 no longer had the influence they once did. That was because the audience had changed, and that change was largely due to the newspapers themselves. "Today," he wrote, "the news is collected so rapidly and thoroughly and presented so interestingly and ably that the average man knows more about his times and understands the significance of the news better than did the average editors of 50 years ago. The reader says to the editor: 'If you know of any facts of an earlier day or in the experience of other peoples that will help us to interpret events from today, let us have them. As for your theories, you are welcome to them. We have no time for them.'"[88]

Here, we have a representative view of the journalistic news ethic of modern journalism pretty much fixed in the minds of newspaperdom that still has mainstream currency today and that the advocates of the Social Gospel were attempting to countervail. In this view, news stories were expected to remain value neutral, "at the expense," wrote writer and well-known American anarchist Victor Yarros, "of the substantial and serious matters that underlie the news" versus the traditions of the old journalism of Greeley, Dana, and their peers.[89] Instead, any interpretations of facts were reserved for the editorial page.

We can certainly infer from the many statements of the pastorate that they understood well the marginalization of the editorial from the days of Greeley and Dana and the consequent growing importance of news. Thus, we can see why Social Gospel activists and others outside the movement believed the daily press needed to interpret the news of the modern world. But from the extensive literature left behind—much of it written with the meaning-dampening rhetorical flourishes of the sermon—it is unclear what the general consensus was about their definition of the interpretation of news. What did it involve? And it was not always clear whether the expectations were that news interpretation should be reserved for the editorial page, or if it should actually become part of the warp and woof of individual news stories. Homilies like "Daily journalism should be daily preaching"[90] and Gladden's own slightly airy call for a "prophetism" on the part of newspapers and the revival of the "teaching function" leave some room for wide inference as to the meaning of interpretation and the placement of this function.

One place to look at the Social Gospel's ideas about the news ethic of daily journalism is in two popular religiously oriented weekly papers—the *Independent* and the *Outlook*—which published many of the writings of Social Gospel authors. In an introduction to the *Independent* in 1920, the editors offered readers some advice about the kind of journalism they should choose to read. One "essential of sound journalism," they asserted, was the interpretation of the news along with "the criticism of public men and measures and the advocacy of appropriate action." The editors held that the best national weekly paper must offer "the news and the meaning of it. It must provide him with a running narrative of current events, more comprehensive and comprehensible, more critical and correct than that printed in the dailies, in order that the reader may have the facts in hand on which to form his views." It should also be noted that the editors of the *Independent* included Hamilton Holt, a well-known press critic; Norman Hapgood, author and former editor of *Collier's* at the height of its muckraking journalism; Talcott Williams, the former director of the Columbia School of Journalism; and the Reverend Shailer Mathews, the well-known Social Gospel activist and University of Chicago professor who was also editor of the *Biblical World*, past editor of the *World To-Day*, and director of religious work for the Chautauqua Institution.[91]

Meanwhile, in a similar explanation, the *Outlook* emphasized that its role was "not merely to record events as they occur, but to interpret events in accordance with what its editors believe are righteous principles." And it went on to emphasize this interpretation function more than once in the following:

> *The Outlook* is not a neutral journal because it is not merely a reporter of current events and current opinions. Not even in peace times is *The Outlook* neutral. It does report current events and current opinions, but it believes that such events and such opinions have a relation to life, and thus, in addition to its task of reporting, it points out with cogent argument what it believes the relation of current events and current opinions is to our times, and what, in its judgment, the results of that relation will be to our future. Though *The Outlook* believes that information is essential to all sound thinking and

absolutely necessary for the citizens of a democracy, yet it believes that for the guidance of a democracy interpretation is more essential than information. Every editorial or other article which *The Outlook* publishes is for the purpose not only of information, but also of interpretation. All of its articles must be human documents. It holds that no periodical which records current happenings for the best interests of the community can possibly remain truly neutral after it has a thorough understanding of any public question. *The Outlook* believes that no journal will be forceful, will make its readers think and think desperately hard, will greatly advance the cause of morality and democracy—no journal can accomplish this which merely reports events and opinions. The function of *The Outlook* is to interpret events and opinions.[92]

And finally, one concise and understandable definition of interpretation came from the pen of Rabbi Stephen S. Wise, an activist during the Progressive Era who was committed to social justice.[93] In an essay titled "The Moral Power of the Press" (1910), he wrote that "interpretation is that projection of personality which in turn clothes the skeleton of facts with opinion and comment." Indeed, the press must "resist the spreading notion that the newspaper is to be a mere purveyor of news rather than a bringer of intelligence, that its sole business is to be collector and disseminator of news."[94]

To probe this notion of the interpretive function of newspapers and the general confusedness surrounding it, literary critic Henry Walcott Boynton might be helpful. Boynton, a writer and editor who worked for such publications as the *Atlantic Monthly*, *Bookman*, the *Nation* and the *New York Evening Post* in the late nineteenth and early twentieth centuries, explored this function in his collection of essays *Journalism and Literature* (1904). Boynton described—and here we hear the views of the Social Gospel—what he called "the higher journalism" that "aims to inform and to convince rather than to express." This kind of journalism, he maintained, "displays real erudition, it urges admirable specifics, it produces, in fact, printed lectures on practical themes addressed to the practical intelligence. One perceives a close analogy between the functions of the higher journalist and those of the preacher, the lawyer, and the politician."[95]

It is not difficult to draw a connection between this "higher journalism" and what many in the pastorate described as "Christian journalism."[96] For instance, during a lecture titled "Christian Journalism: Its Idea and Its Ideal" delivered in the Hall of Philosophy at Chautauqua in August 1881, the Reverend Simeon Gilbert held that journalism grounded in Christianity was "distinguished, first of all, by its point of view; second, by what it aims to effect: third, by its guiding principles, its motives, its instruments." Gilbert argued that journalism's responsibility was to reveal and then interpret the events of the day. And interpretation involved first the journalist's selection from an infinitesimal number of facts those that had "the most significant bearings on all that is, or that is about to be." Gilbert went on to maintain, "The Christian sermon and the Christian newspaper aim at essentially the same thing, though in different ways. It is the task of Christian journalism to stimulate the public conscience, to educate the public judgment, to concentrate, form, and formulate the public opinion."[97]

A quarter century later in an essay in the *American Journal of Sociology*, Gilbert essentially disputes Ridgway's contention that all the modern newspaper audience wanted was facts from which they could derive their own interpretations. Instead, Gilbert wrote, "As the general awakening of the social consciousness goes on, it is less and less true that people are interested in the news merely as something new. More and more they are interested, judicially, in the meaning, the character, the ethical and social bearing, of the current happenings, doings, movements, struggles, speculations, and opinions of the day." To just that ethical and communitarian point of view, the Reverend Julius H. Ward, for many years literary editor of the *Boston Herald* and a widely known Protestant Episcopal clergyman, observed that the daily newspaper's mission was no longer to just collect the news. It had become an "interpreter of news." In a particularly apt example of what a newspaper should be, Ward argued that it had advanced to be one part "the pure itemizing" of the nation's first continuously published newspaper, the *Boston News-Letter*, and one part Joseph Addison and Richard Steele's *Spectator*, which commented on British society and life in the eighteenth century and, as other scholars have observed, acted as a civilizing force.[98] And Ward saw great benefit in the secular press casting off the political partisanship that made the search for truth more difficult. But with those papers whose position was "national and constructive, then every question is discussed in the interest of the whole community."[99]

Essentially, what the Social Gospel advocates of an interpretive news ethic sought was that the journalist act as prophet for a new age—what James Russell Lowell described as "the Moses of our nineteenth century." That felt desire was made manifest in Gladden's urging that the newspaper "generate public opinion" and not simply reflect it, in Sheldon's effort to add—through a moral and Christian point of view—interpretive comments to the news of the day, and in the *Outlook*'s insistence that everything it published was "for the purpose not only of information, but also of interpretation."[100] And here, we might make some better sense of Gladden's notion of the journalist as prophet and teacher as it relates to interpreting the news for readers. That sentiment is evident in Gladden's memoir when he prefaces a chapter titled "Newspaper Ethics" with the last few lines of Ralph Waldo Emerson's poem "Celestial Love."

> And they serve men austerely,
> After their own genius, clearly,
> Without a false humility;
> For this is Love's nobility,
> Not to scatter bread and gold,
> Goods and raiment bought and sold;
> But to hold fast his simple sense,
> And speak the speech of innocence,
> And with hand and body and blood,
> To make his bosom-counsel good.
> For he that feeds men serveth few;
> He serves all who dares be true.[101]

And finally, the elucidation of the interpretive function from the perspective of the Social Gospel is made most clear by one of Gladden's peers in the Social Gospel movement, Lyman Abbott, who once described the journalist's role in reporting and writing a story as using "events as a means to elucidate the great laws of the social order."[102] In his book *The Christian Ministry* (1905), he compared the roles of minister and journalist and in doing so explored the parameters of the interpretation of events. Abbott, a longtime journalist and editor himself, insisted, "The office of the journalist is twofold: to report the history of the day, and to interpret its meaning whose significance it endeavors to explain."[103] He lauded the American press for its ability at the former, but when it came to interpretation, Abbott was less encouraged. And here, in his critique, we can hear Bascom's own criticism of the influences on the press that affected journalistic conduct and content. The newspaper's interpretations of events, Abbott held, were often "affected by the demands of its subscribers, by the interests of its advertisers, by the relation of events to its favored political or ecclesiastical organization; and when it escapes all these belittling, if not malign influences, it is still apt to consider the immediate, not the ultimate, the provincial, not the world-wide, effect of the event whose significance it endeavors to explain."

And, Abbott counseled, since the journalist's interpretive function was "so often ignored, refused, or ill performed," it was left to the minister, for whom "the application of eternal principles to current problems may often be his duty, as it was the duty, courageously fulfilled, by the Hebrew prophets." And in this counsel—"In preaching on current events the minister should interpret those events in the light of eternal principles"[104]—can be heard a concise and fairly clear articulation of the Social Gospel's notion that the mission of the newspaper "as a promoter of truth and a formulator of public opinion," as the *Report on the Steel Strike of 1919* termed it, was to educate the public by interpreting the news through a moral lens, limning the far-reaching effects of news events, and advocating for reform as a moral agent.[105]

CONCLUSION

The Meanings of Mission

There is no denying that a widespread feeling exists throughout the land that the newspapers are not what they ought to be.

—John McNaught, "New Way of Living Changing the Press," *New York Times*

Things without all remedy should be without regard: What's done is done.

—William Shakespeare, *Macbeth*

RECALL THE REVEREND GEORGE T. Rider's charge—an iteration of so many others—that there was a "deep and growing belief . . . that there are fundamental failures in journalism, that there are portentous and perilous abuses of function and misconception of duty."[1] Certainly, to speak of such things as the "abuses of function and misconception of duty" or the many variants of that complaint begs the question of whether such indictments of journalism—and its derivatives the newspaper and the press—failed to offer criteria for what was meant by function and duty. Thankfully, that was not often the case. However, problems of interpretation often arise when we evaluate this decades-long conversation and then try to point to a definitive conclusion we can take to the bank.

The ideas found in the conversations about journalism's mission were nearly as numerous as the critics of newspapers and ranged across a profusion of descriptions, proscriptions, and prescriptions. They came at the issue from an array of often overlapping political, ethical, cultural, and religious tangents. They often bordered on the overly idealistic and were written as broad-swath statements in an arch language that leaves the reader peering through the mist in search of meaning. Take, for example, this glib description in an essay titled "The Press—Its Power and Mission" in the *Southern Literary Messenger* in 1853: "A newspaper when properly conducted is a public benefaction. Its daily influence is like the gentle dew from heaven which is felt only in the blessings it brings." In the same vein is Washington Gladden's spacious declaration that the newspaper's principal duty was to create and disseminate a democratic-enhancing public opinion, which "bears the same relation to Christian society that protoplasm bears to life."[2] Likewise, embedded in the decades-long conversation about journalism's mission were similarly indecipherable assertions that the "editor is the alchemist by whom the highest inspiration of the best minds may be transmuted into popular thought and fused into common life"; that the newspaper's role is to "enlighten, advance and uplift mankind,"[3] to "root out evil and establish righteousness in public affairs,"[4] to "create Christian public opinion,"[5] and to work at "moulding public opinion and in forming the public taste";[6] and that "enlightenment is the mission of journalism."[7]

Still, to briefly make explicit some various strains of what critics meant by the mission of journalism, what follows draws out and briefly delineates the meanings of mission by extracting them from the many arguments drawn from the decades of critique. Here, then, is an outline of the meanings of mission drawn from conversations about journalism and the newspaper in society.

The Journalist as a Moral Agent

The primary and one overarching mission in which all others are coterminous but subsidiary adjuncts is that the journalist, and thus the newspaper, must act as a moral agent—as "the moral limelight of the age"[8]—that would aid, as the Reverend Charles Sheldon contended, in "the regeneration of mankind,"[9] that would, in Rabbi Adolph Moses's description, act as a "regenerating moral force,"[10] because it was, the Reverend George P. Eckman believed, "among the most potent forces making for righteousness in modern times."[11] For instance, in a short but cynical fable in the *Outlook*, Edward Carleton described the "printer's devil"—the appellation for a print-shop apprentice—as both a "play on words long since played out" and the "veritable power of evil in the newspaper world." He went by the name "'Power of the Press,' but the name was too big for him. He had a right to only half of it. There was another power of the press—a strong, good moral agent, whose influence was also far-reaching and decisive."[12]

Of course, that was the rub, because as one editor contended, most newspaper owners were the "victims, I am sorry to say, to the passionate materialism of the age."[13] Indeed, the conversation of the age about just this topic was regularly spiced with references to a subservient press robbed of its value as a moral agent and with allusions to the diminution of the newspaper's mission as a moral agent as it attempted to fend off or submitted to the constraints of the market. As early as 1885, Gladden observed that the newspaper, unlike the pulpit, was controlled by its owner, whose sole consideration was making money. Thus, "the incongruity and difficulty of this situation" confronted editors who wanted to do the right thing by their readers. Gladden observed, "When the editorial writer finds himself powerless to smite the local boss for his villainies, because it would deprive the paper of the municipal advertising; when he sees the paper dragged, against his protest, into the support of measures that he knows are mischievous, and of men that he knows are scoundrels, he begins to feel that the newspaper, as 'an instrument of righteousness,' is a poor tool."[14]

As I have noted elsewhere, reference was often made to the editors and newspapers of the past when speaking of the present, and this was no exception when the subject of free moral agency was raised. The transition from the journalism of the past to that of the new in America can be fixed to the midnineties, when in 1896 William Randolph Hearst bought the *New York Morning Journal* and Adolph S. Ochs purchased the *New York Times*, with the death in 1897 of Charles A. Dana, and with the retirement, three years later, of E. L. Godkin, that longtime exemplar of the old journalism.[15] In 1908 Gladden referenced an ideal of the past when he probed the question of newspapers as moral agents. "The press—is that a moral agency?" he asked. At its worst, no, but at its best, "there are few moral agencies more efficient. In the days when newspapers were owned and edited by individuals they were often powerful instruments of righteousness; even in these days they have not all lost the prophetic function." Similarly, one speaker at the dedication of the Fort Washington Monument in New York City extolled the "power of the press as one of the chief conservators of the Republic" and pointed to the debt we owed such editors of the past as James Gordon Bennett, William Cullen Bryant, Charles A. Dana, Horace Greeley, Hugh Hastings, Henry J. Raymond, Noah Webster, and Thurlow Weed, who, as "armed priests," wielded an "unsheathed sword of a free conscience."[16]

However, *Current Literature* questioned, was there then any editor like those of the past "who makes his paper's policy the expression of himself alone?" The problem was, the writer suggested, "The owners of newspapers are business men. They want dividends. They want the business, the commercial ideal, upheld, at all hazards." Still, historian Henry Steele Commager contended, the fillip for the transition from the old to the new journalism could be found in more than just the men at the helm of the press, for it was also "physical, it was economic, it was psychological, it was moral. It was part of the transformation of America itself—of the process of mechanization, urbanization, and centralization, of the concentration of economic control, of the emancipation of women, the broadening of social interests, the standardization, democratization, and vulgarization of culture."[17]

Essentially, moral agency is indelibly yoked to liberty—to freedom to act without the constraints of others' influence or one's own prodding self-interest, and thus a moral agent is anyone able to freely make ethical decisions and act on them or put them into action. Recall the laudatory description of Lyman Abbott—an exemplar of a free moral agent—as a journalist "indifferent to the approval or disapproval of his fellow men providing his conscience approves." We can get some sense of what is meant by this notion of the liberty of a "free conscience" in a letter Thomas Jefferson wrote in 1789 to Francis Hopkinson, one of the signers of the Declaration of Independence. Jefferson said, "I am not a federalist, because I never submitted the whole system of my opinions to the creed of any party of men whatever, in religion, in philosophy, in politics, or in anything else, where I was capable of thinking for myself. Such an addiction, is the last degradation of a free and moral agent."[18]

More than a century later, Henry Watterson, the esteemed editor of the *Louisville Courier-Journal* and the nation's "most widely quoted newspaper writer,"[19] applied this capability to think for oneself to journalism. "The vital ethics—the source and resource—the very soul of journalism—is disinterestedness," he contended.[20] Similarly, Gladden held that the newspaper's role in a community was that of a public teacher, whose number-one qualification was that it "shall be sincere and disinterested." However, he counseled, those were qualities that simply could not exist if a newspaper's "management makes plain the fact that the dollar is the paramount consideration; that it is ready, in the conduct of its business, in the shaping of its policy, to sacrifice decency and honor, and truth and public welfare to revenue."[21]

Here, in speaking of disinterest, both Watterson and Gladden did not mean the notion of journalistic objectivity in which news is offered as facts bereft of values and barren of context or interpretation. Instead, they meant that service to the community was paramount and that in the reporting of news, those in charge of newspapers rejected seeking solely after profit or public office that would reflexively encumber their news report and thus their service to their community. Indeed, an editorial in the *American Lutheran Survey* sought to apportion blame for "the failures of the daily press in the sphere of honest, constructive public service." It went on to note:

> A certain portion of it undoubtedly does rest upon those editors who, notwithstanding the pressure of circumstances, have been willing to sell themselves, as it were, to a service which their own consciences, if alive, could not approve. Men in many lines of activity, especially in "cold business", have done that same thing, and have comforted their consciences with the assurance that they were only doing what they were paid to do, and were not responsible for the wrong in the orders received. Where this is the case men are not acting as independent, responsible moral agents. They only lend themselves to service in machines of which they become parts.[22]

The *American Lutheran Survey*'s critique was indicative of the subtext of much of the religious and secular critical conversation regarding the newspaper and its confrontation between acting with disinterest and acting at the behest of certain interests. That very issue was at the crux of the oft-cited "The American Newspaper: A Study of Journalism in Its Relation to the Public," a fifteen-part muckraking analysis of the newspaper industry by Will Irwin, one of the best-known reporters of the early twentieth century. The series appeared in *Collier's* magazine over fifteen weeks in 1911. In it Irwin argued that the newspaper had grown to such an extent that it had more power to influence public opinion than any other agency and that it had grown by dint of modern technology and shifting social factors into a large commercial enterprise. And because of the growing strength of the commercial side of the press, the commercially driven "business attitude" had surpassed the traditional "professional attitude" in which the newspaper existed as a moral agent to, Irwin declared, "help lead the world and improve it"—what Gladden called the "teaching function." In other words, the reporting and presenting of news that would appeal to as many readers as possible had shunted aside the editorial as the newspaper's chief function. Irwin reiterated just this note the same year his series appeared during a public discussion on the press and morality that included the Reverend Frank Oliver Hall, a Social Gospel advocate and pastor of the Church of the Divine Paternity in New York City. "The ethics of the journalists themselves—the newspaper writers—are constantly going up," Irwin held. The problem was that the ethics of the newspaper business was going down, and the fault lay with the businessman who owned that paper and whose sole motive was profit. Thus, journalists were being directed by men who had "no sympathy with their moral views."[23]

More than once that admonition about the power of business interests to thwart the moral agency of newspapers and their editors and journalists was made substantive and became the topic of conversations in the press. For instance, the *New Republic* in 1918 published a lengthy editorial discussion titled "Independence for Editors" after J. P. Morgan & Company acquired the "highly respected" *New York Evening Post*. The magazine described the *Evening Post* as a "common public enterprise"—an allusion to the newspaper as a public utility. Thus, the editorial suggested, the purchase posed "some interesting and important questions about the ownership of American newspapers and the relation which the ownership should occupy to editorial management."[24]

Similarly, another particularly cogent critical juncture and condensation of conversation distilled this debate over the practicality of corporate control of the news media. In 1925 Victor F. Lawson, publisher of the *Chicago Daily News*, died. In his will he left his estate, including his newspaper, to the Illinois Merchants Trust Company. That meant, one writer noted, "one of the great newspapers" in America was directly controlled by a bank. That very fact prompted "a storm of discussion" both for and against the idea in newspapers in Chicago and elsewhere. One popular financial writer for the *Chicago Tribune* who wrote under the pen name "Scrutator" described this turn of events as "an effort to confer the continuity and impersonality of the corporation upon a form of property that has remained almost as personal as the first primitive enterprises of the capitalist era." Here, the writer noted, this forced marriage of the private and the personal presented "a contradiction" that revealed the limitations inherent in defining and classifying different forms of property. He then called up that notion that the newspaper was like "the great public utilities." Thus, he argued, "In its relation to its readers the newspaper has become subject to the same kind of social obligations that are imposed by law on public utilities and these unwritten obligations have been increasingly observed as newspapers have grown, because the penalty of non-observance is death—death inflicted at the news stands by the withholding of patronage."[25]

At the very least this study of religion and journalism reveals an early form of press accountability in which the press was counseled that it must understand it was "a distinctly public institution bound by the same standards of accountability expected of other public institutions," as two contemporary scholars have defined it. However, this notion was imbued with religion's more articulate contention that newspapers—despite the constraining influence of market forces—must struggle to realize that their primary and overriding mission was to act as moral agents of reform in an age of reform. As earlier chapters have shown, the notion of the newspaper press as moral agent has roots going far back into history. Even renowned writer and indefatigable critic of the press in America James Fenimore Cooper, writing in 1838 during the rise of the penny press, saw newspapers as moral agents that too often had become "the greatest enemies of the race." The press, Cooper held, was essentially balanced on a binary fulcrum between being an "instrument of elevating man to the highest point of which his faculties admit, or of depressing him to the lowest."[26]

That there were many other key figures who had their own complaints about the commercialized press goes without saying, but for our purposes the positions outlined here of the many powerful voices of religion and those much influenced by religion who pointed to the faults of the press in confrontation with its rightful role and responsibility to society are fairly representative. To reiterate, religion held that journalism was a noble, communitarian profession that had been corrupted by the forces of commercialization coming to the fore during the age of industrialization. As Gladden charged, the newspaper, blinded by the dollar, had lost its "supreme allegiance to truth," and, Rauschenbusch warned, its "tampering with the public intelligence is a crime against the common good."[27]

This felt view of many of the critics of the press about the imperative moral agency of journalism manifested the Social Gospel's belief that society was a "Social Organism"[28] in which the immanence of God in all its structures denoted a nonindividualistic view of a diverse but interconnected society. From that rose the notion of social responsibility or a social conscience among all societal institutions—including the newspaper—and thus the demands made on the press were justified.

But in addition, the demands religion made on the press were justified by historical precedent. That is, there exists ingrained within the American consciousness a double-tendency view of self and society that intellectual historian Perry Miller observed "makes every allowance for American individualism, but also holds persons responsible to the common stock." This is an idea found in the tensile dialectic of the mission and the market—in the tension between a newspaper grounded in social justice and service to the community and an unbridled, commodified newspaper whose sole goal is profit. It is an idea that goes as far back into American religious and reform thought as the Mayflower Compact and forward to the many ideological debates of today. For instance, contemporary cultural critic Wendell Berry has observed that the strain of rugged individualism in America "has run mostly to absurdity, tragic or comic." And, he notes, "The tragic version of rugged individualism is in the presumptive 'right' of individuals to do as they please, as if there were no God, no legitimate government, no community, no neighbors, and no posterity."[29]

Berry's analysis in the twenty-first century has its beginnings in America in the rhetoric of the nation's founders, who used the term *virtue* to describe this communitarian notion that sought to rein in a self-interested tendency toward an uncongealed atomistic society. George Mason, the Virginia planter whom John Quincy Adams called "the Father of the Constitution," held that self-interest that opposed the public good was both "mean and sordid" and "extremely shortsighted and foolish."[30] Writing at the beginning of the American Revolution, John Adams maintained, "Men must be ready, they must pride themselves, and be happy to sacrifice their private Pleasures, Passions and Interests, nay, their private Friendships and dearest Connections, when they stand in Competition with the Rights of Society." Similarly, in a June 19, 1814, letter, Thomas Jefferson expanded on that notion, describing man as a "social animal" with "social dispositions" and stating that self-love "is the sole antagonist of virtue, leading us constantly by our propensities to self gratification in violation of our moral duties to others."[31]

A representative and seminal expression of this idea comes from lawyer, author, and social activist Thomas Smith Grimké in 1833 in a speech on the temperance cause. This early American reform effort had, Grimké argued, revealed "the principle of individual responsibility and social influence." It showed, he said, that each is obligated "to combine with others, in promoting not only his own immediate good, but, to the utmost of his ability, the good of his fellowmen." No one individual, Grimké said, could "withhold his own from the common stock of social influence. It is the tax, which the law of his nature, and the higher law of God demands of him."[32]

And then transfused across the decades and informed by the ideology of the Social Gospel is Richard Ely's description of "human solidarity," by which he meant that "our true welfare is not an individual matter purely, but likewise a social affair; our weal is common weal; we thrive only in a commonwealth."[33] Indeed, Ely believed that the economic situation of his time demanded a "wider diffusion of sound ethics." He rejected Herbert Spencer's ethical system of "laissez-faire politics" and "extreme individualism" at the core of the market's drive for profit. Ely described this system as immoral because it promoted the notion that "we are not keepers of our brothers, that each one best promotes the general interest by best promoting his own." Instead, he called for a "more advanced political economy" that cast off this individualistic notion and asserted that "within certain bounds we are obliged to concern ourselves about the welfare of others" and to promote "the welfare of our fellow-men."[34]

But how could this notion of the "common stock of influence" and of a "common weal" manifest itself in the news ethic and conventions of a newspaper—especially one expected to act as a moral agent? Certainly, one worry was a commodified newspaper; its journalism may well create community, but it would be one of atomized consumers awash in consumerist values, not in the values of humanity and commonality as the source of an interstitial community. This pastoral concern with the newspaper as a latchkey to a growing secular consumer culture with its ability to elbow aside the sacred and its culpability in giving impulse to the Sunday newspaper haunts many of religion's critiques. It is apparent, for instance, in the plaint of the Reverend Edwin A. McAlpin of Babcock Memorial Presbyterian Church in Baltimore. In a talk titled "Newspapers" in 1909, he said there were two kinds of newspapers, the "yellow journal," which is filled with fiction and stories about crimes and scandals, and the paper that attempts to give readers a "true account" of news locally, nationally, and internationally. The latter, McAlpin insisted, was what a good paper does best because it "makes all the world kin."[35]

And that meant, the Reverend Walter Rauschenbusch maintained, "We live by faith in one another," because we were no longer simply a nation of individuals, not unlike "a colony of mollusks," but rather we were becoming an interconnected community, "like the body of a man."[36] Indeed, the Reverend Reynold E. Blight warned, the constant issue at the crux of the struggle over news was that outside influence tainted the news, which tended "to corrupt the very heart of the community."[37] Therefore, Rauschenbusch advised, "We have to trust our health officers to test our water supply and the milk brought into the city, for we cannot do it. We have to trust our newspapers to report the facts correctly to us, or a whole city will be misled in its judgment, and will crucify its Christ and elect Barabbas mayor." And, Rauschenbusch emphasized, "Our business men hold a fiduciary relation to the whole community." Thus, Gladden believed, a newspaper's mission was to cultivate a "community of interest and feeling" about social and political issues so that the members of the public could "cooperate intelligently." In other words, men of business were expected to be moral agents, for as Gladden made clear, businessmen—including the managers of newspapers—were each "God's servant, whether he will or no."[38]

That the rhetorical remonstrations of Abbott, Gladden, Ely, Strong, Rauschenbusch, and the many other advocates of religion had some effect on press accountability and on the notion that such complaints could have an effect is evident, for example, in a speech in 1913 by Talcott Williams, dean of the Pulitzer School of Journalism. Williams told the Park Avenue Methodist Church Forum that the church ought to demand improvement in all news publications, whether newspapers or cheap magazines. Williams argued that readers make newspapers what they are. "The newspaper is the conscience of the people. When a man buys a paper he helps to edit it, even if he disagrees with it." And "Christian people" were doing just as much to support the worst journalism, Williams said. "Your protest to the editor, if you make one, receives instant attention and it has immediate effect. But you make few protests. One of the efforts of the Christian church ought to be to supervise, and if need be, change the moral tone of the newspaper."[39]

That religion's grievances about the press over many decades was one tangent of discourse in a national debate leading to the development of journalistic normative standards is best represented by the proceedings surrounding the American Society of Newspaper Editors' adoption in 1923 of the Canons of Journalism, the first nationwide code of ethics for the profession. Aside from the religious intonation in the word *canons*, we can hear reverberations of that pastoral criticism in the Canons' linking journalism to "its obligations as teacher and interpreter," to its "considerations of public welfare," to its "fidelity to the public interest," to "high moral purpose," and to "decency." Even the proceedings leading up to the adoption of the Canons were laced with a similar tone, as the editors in attendance described journalism as "predominantly an instrument of public service" and the proposed code as a "creed" and a "statement of definite moral standards."[40]

All good words, certainly. But I should note that I am not suggesting I have empirically unveiled some form of cause and effect—what Emerson called "the chancellors of God." But certainly, as contemporary historian and economist Deirdre McCloskey argues, ideas—encased within the rhetoric of "the habits of the lip"—do matter in the transformation of the world. This position is not unlike British social theorist John Thompson's description of the "corrosive impact of public scrutiny and debate" through the "discursive elaboration" of mediated messages.[41] Here, we have been exploring the many iterations in the discursive elaboration of ideas about the newspaper's—and by extension journalism's—proper role in and responsibility to society embedded within the conceit of the mission versus the market. For instance, I would point to a particularly relevant discursive to-and-fro in 1891 centered on just this topic, which, at its heart, was grounded in the telling observation—and one we should hold on to even today—that "news is a force and not a commodity."[42]

The contending factions in this convoluted conversation—and that certainly is what it was—involved the newspaper trade journal the *Journalist* and an old-line genteel magazine with little love of the "new journalism"—*Century Magazine*. The *Journalist* reacted to a discussion of the role of the newspaper in an article titled "Conscience in Journalism" that had appeared in *Century Magazine*. The trade journal's editorial was accompanied, on separate pages, by versions of both the article and editorial comments that had appeared in *Century Magazine*. The interesting thing here, also, which reveals the connectedness and elaboration of the discourse about journalism between different publications of the age, is that the *Century* article's author, Eugene M. Camp, said it was written in response to requests from scores of newspaper publishers across the country, "no less than seven of whom bear national reputations," who had read a June 1890 piece by him in *Century Magazine* titled "What's the News?"[43] and to an accompanying excoriating critique of the newspaper press that *Century Magazine* decided to add because Camp's article did not "discuss the moral side of the business of gathering and selling the news." But it went much deeper than that, for, according to the *Century Magazine* editorial, Camp's original effort, "What's the News?," had come in response to an earlier criticism of the newspaper press by the magazine.[44]

Essentially, Camp's article "Conscience in Journalism" was a defense of the publishers of newspapers that recognized that while there were problems with accuracy and sensationalist reporting and all that entailed, in the end even the newspapers' worst critic, if he was to work as a publisher, would quickly be let go for want of skills. "The newspaper of today—I speak of the ninety and not of the ten—is above the mean of the public taste which it serves," Camp concluded. Publishers, he held, attempted to do two things: "they educate the public taste to their standard, and they carry that standard forward as fast and as far as the public permits them."[45]

The *Journalist*, in response, observed that the author "gives us a very rose-colored view of the newspaper publisher who is conducting a newspaper probably somewhere in Utopia." The editorialist countered that publishers "were not border-line 'angels' but only human and were sometimes misguided or just plain venal. Many are almost as high-minded, earnest, honest and conscientious as Mr. Camp would have us believe; others are mercenary, unscrupulous, dishonest to themselves and the public, and a disgrace to a profession which should lead public sentiment to a higher plane, instead of ministering to its debasement."[46]

The *Journalist* also published the accompanying editorial in *Century* by Jack Bennett. His argument in relation to the "moral side" of the newspaper business described a Janus-like view of the two paths down which an editor could proceed. One, the ideal "Journalist," appealed in his pages to a "healthy intelligence and not to depraved taste." In other words, he understands that he is a "self-constituted public servant"—essentially a moral agent—and that "news is a force and not a commodity; a force that brings happiness and injury of punishment to thousands of fellow beings every time he sends to broadcast over his community; and that his license to lend this force is his moral acceptance of the duty of seeing that it is true and that it does not wantonly invade the rights of private persons." However, down that other path is the "Newsmonger," who made "merchandise of other people's affairs to satisfy the curiosity of those who will buy." The Newsmonger, Bennett argued, "recognizes in the public a depraved taste as well as a healthy intelligence and caters to both; he measures the influence of his journal by the number of copies he can sell and not by the effect of his teachings." In other words, his "mission is to print whatever will sell," and his excuse for such pandering was he was giving the public what it wanted. In the hands of such a man, Bennett warned, a newspaper "is the greatest tyranny of the time."[47]

As Stuart Hall has noted, with research into the past, "there are no 'absolute beginnings' and few unbroken continuities." Instead, what confronts such endeavors "is an untidy but characteristic unevenness of development."[48] For instance, a decade after this conversation between the *Journalist* and *Century Magazine*, a similar iteration was persuasively articulated by Charles H. Grasty, the son of a Presbyterian minister and the renowned publisher of the *Baltimore Sun*. And here embedded in this rhetoric are ideas about the endemic tension within a newspaper between the need for financial success and the need to properly serve its readers in which we can hear the antagonism of the two tendencies. Here, also, is an allusion to the moral agency of a newspaper in the oft-repeated notion of the newspaper as a public utility and the dangers that advertising—the paper's main source of sustenance—posed to getting at the truth at the heart of things. Grasty, speaking in the lion's den to the seventh annual convention of the Associated Advertising Clubs of America, cautioned:

> The greatest problem that confronts the daily newspaper is how to maintain the pleasant relations that should and do exist between the ordinary business enterprise and its patrons on the one hand and on the other to eliminate this relationship entirely where it concerns the largest question of the performance of the public functions which belong to journalism. In the newspaper business alone, of all the various branches of human endeavor, it is necessary thus to carry on two conflicting functions. I think that most thoughtful publishers will agree with me in the opinion that the most deadly menace to independent and truthful journalism lies in the power of the advertiser.[49]

To that point, these observations about the mission of journalism by a nationally known newspaper publisher echo the connotation in those passages referenced above in the Canons of Journalism and in the proceedings leading to their adoption. Together, they reverberate with the rhetoric of religion's decades-long call for the press to act as a free moral agent of reform. What that meant, of course, was that the press should reject the straitjacket of uncolored and unbiased news conventions and the notion of market-driven objectivity as the benchmark of ethical conduct. Instead, religious advocates urged, the newspaper as a moral agent should have the courage to express its discontent with the aberrations of the age as it committed to a values-based and interpretive journalism. The efficacy of religion's counsel is evident, for example, in a speech by University of Missouri School of Journalism dean Walter Williams in 1914, in which he expressed a confidence in modern journalism when compared with the old. Williams held: "Old style journalism was that the editor tried to find out when and where 'hell on earth' was going to break loose and have a reporter there to describe it. In the new journalism it is to find out where heaven on earth will start and to have a reporter there to boost it."[50]

The Newspaper as Venue for Values-Based Journalism

In their historical and contemporary examination of journalism ethics, three contemporary media scholars make the assertion that "to be human is, in part, to value."[51] Indeed, I would argue that that very axiom underlies the decades-long conversation among both pastoral and secular critics about the newspaper's mission that cascades from a worldview that sees the journalist as a moral agent. It was a call for a news ethic that gave weight to values-based journalism in which "to record the events of one day throughout the world and to discuss their significance is the function of the newspaper."[52] It was a call to cast off the news conventions of reportorial detachment that led to a separation of facts from values—a separation of "what is" from "what ought to be"—and the castration "of the intellect," as Nietzsche described the suspension of values and "emotions."[53]

Such press critics as the Reverend W. N. M'Elroy promoted a values-based journalism in his repudiation of the notion that the individual's responsibility for immoral acts or negative influences on society ceased "because the actor is hidden away behind an impersonality," such as a business or corporation, which lacked a soul. These sorts of appeals were first heard in earnest as early as the mid-nineteenth century with the rise of the secular and advertiser-driven mass-appeal penny newspapers in the 1830s. Further, recall Josiah Strong's reference to giving "Christian form" to the press. That was—at its most essential—a call for a values-based and ministerial journalism of service, advocacy, and social justice. Seventeen years later, the Religious Education Association adopted what was called "A Declaration of Principles" (1910) that declared that the power of the press should be better used to create an ethos of conduct imbued with "deeper conceptions of duty, character and public service."[54] This formal declaration was representative of many similar appeals over the decades for a values-based journalism.[55] One representative distillation of this view comes from Max Nordan, a German writer and social critic, who argued in an essay titled "Public Conscience" (1905) in *Editor & Publisher* that the newspaper "is the visible embodiment of public opinion. It assumes the rights of the latter, with its judicial power which it wields even in its most fearful form, public contempt and moral annihilation; it takes its place as ally by the side of the objective MUST, and announces itself as the public conscience of the community."[56]

Still, recall Michael Schudson's contention that a news convention that called for the separation of facts from values in news stories gradually took hold from the 1870s to World War I. It was the rise of the notion of journalistic objectivity that clearly made that distinction and prescribed that journalists report the news "without commenting on it, slanting it, or shaping its formulation in any way."[57] Indeed, Schudson asserts, to the objective journalist—who, I would add, had little understanding about the reflexive appropriation of acts of communications—facts "are assertions about the world open to independent validation. They stand beyond the distorting influences of any individual's personal preferences. Values, in this view, are an individual's conscious or unconscious preferences for what the world should be; they are seen as ultimately subjective and so without legitimate claim on other people. The belief in objectivity is a faith in 'facts,' a distrust of 'values,' and a commitment to their segregation."[58]

Thus, that objectivity shouldered aside the earlier journalistic practice of criticism and interpretation in which facts and values commingled might leave one to wonder what prompted the pastorate's prior decades of critique before the concept of objectivity arose. However, note Schudson's assertion that objectivity and its separation of facts from values was a slow reveal from the 1870s onward and my earlier inquiry showing that prewar exhortations also reflected a sentiment that insisted on "absolute impartiality"[59] and that the journalist "keep himself, his prejudices, preferences, opinions, out of the story altogether,"[60] which would imply a journalism devoid of values. But in addition, a long soak in those decades of critique reveals that religion was disenchanted with the attributes of the values—largely those of dominant groups and values systems—that newspapers expressed from the 1890s into the twentieth century while employing the concepts of "unbiased" and "uncolored" to describe their so-called impartial reports of news events. Essentially, religion urged the press to act as a moral agent and forgo the lure of profit as its sole consideration. To do so, it should adopt and promote a value system informed by a communitarian ethic grounded in moral uplift and in the gospel message of social justice, liberation, compassion, and service to humanity promoted by the Social Gospel movement and other reformers.

However, as early as 1893 Gladden charged the newspapers with regularly speaking not in the interest of humanity but "in the interest of capital" in offering "one-sided and distorted representations" of labor's side of any issue. This indictment found support in the research of Edward Alsworth Ross, a renowned sociologist and one of the primary reform writers of the early twentieth century. Ross described the rise of rampant commercialism and then connected it to the distortion and outright suppression of news by the commercially oriented press to the detriment of society. "Those who are business men and nothing more slip easily into the fallacy of rating well-being by dollar income," he charged. "What this type of man most longs for is not welfare, but prosperity. The wealth he habitually considers is bankable wealth. Values that are not pecuniary values strike him as moonshine. His ideal condition is high wages, big salaries and fat dividends; and any movement or policy that stands in the way of maximizing these 'hurts business' and is anathema."[61]

W. S. Lilly, who was active in the Catholic Church and wrote on topics to include religion and politics, held that the very "liberty of the press" demanded a journalism that encompassed values because a journalist may employ a printing press, but that very fact did not "relieve him from the duties and responsibilities attending the communication of thought." Thus, when speaking of the liberty of the press, the "journalist may rightly claim: liberty to state facts, liberty to argue upon them, liberty to denounce abuses, liberty to advocate reforms." This demand was essentially a rejection of neutered "unbiased" and "uncolored" news and then later the rite of objectivity—a "commercially grounded strategy of reporting," as James Carey has noted.[62] Indeed, the notion of objectivity rose with the shedding of partisanship, the growth of commercialism, and the need for a normative refuge to protect journalists from criticism[63] that ran counter to the demands of the pastorate heard most specifically in Gladden's call for the press to act as a guide to conduct with the goal of "truth and purest morality."[64]

Here, I would point to the previous chapter and Samuel Gompers's editorial "Labor News and Labor's Views Suppressed," in which he complained of the newspaper's slanted coverage of labor. Gompers further elaborated on this when he wrote:

> The result which we have before us in the daily newspapers every day is the only result which could possibly emanate from such a condition. In any case where it takes, for example, twelve facts to make a complete presentation of a situation, there can be no complete presentation unless all twelve facts are supplied. If six of those facts are to be had from employers or their agents and the other six must be got elsewhere, and if only the six are got which are to be had from employers or their agents, the picture is but half complete, and a half complete picture is what we are getting from day to day.[65]

Thus, to some degree what religion meant by a values-based journalism was a news ethic in which it was the rule that newspapers draw a "complete picture" of life and strive to create a public opinion informed by, for example, Rauschenbush's notion of the "Christian social ideal" of "justice, democracy, and organized fraternity."[66] Such exhortations were, essentially, a critique of news bereft of values, which gave weight to humanity, and then the later rise of the notion of objectivity.

This was a critique not unlike that of William T. Stead, Jane Addams, and many other critics of the press whose theories of journalism called for the reporting of news to move from the center to the periphery and offer platforms to reveal the intersubjective straits of marginalized others. It was a call for a journalistic practice that spoke pointedly to societal aberrations in order, as Addams held, "to give truth complete social expression" and to offer "a realization of the experiences of other people" and, as Stead argued, to give "utterance to the inarticulate moan of the voiceless" in which the newspaper became "a daily apostle of fraternity."[67]

However, neither of these statements spoke directly to issues of race or gender. Instead, both Addams and Stead are speaking to what was described at the time as the "social cleavage" inherent in society and the impulse for possible "social friction and social conflict"[68]—especially among the laboring classes. The cleavage, an editorialist for the *Public* charged in 1916, was a "class-and-group consciousness," that makes "the vaunted word 'community' capable of being defined only as an ideal. Parties, occupations, clubs, fraternities, churches, newspapers, and even schools draw lines of cleavage all through the rank and file of people."[69]

To that point, it should be noted, the advocates of the Social Gospel largely ignored issues of race and gender in their critiques of society and the press. As Jacob Dorn observed in his biography of Washington Gladden, Social Gospel leaders "were, for the most part strikingly silent on the problem of race in the United States."[70] And as Robert T. Handy has well summarized:

> The proponents of the social gospel did tend to center their attention on the labor-capital problem and to touch upon other causes, including race and woman suffrage, only in passing. They tended to accept the views of race held by progressives generally. Josiah Strong was closer to being obsessed with the idea of Anglo-Saxon superiority than most other advocates of the social gospel, though there was some reflection of his sentiments in what they had to say. As the early social gospel leaders saw it, a major step had been taken for

> the Negro with the abolition of slavery; now it was the turn of wage-slaves to be freed.[71]

I have already pointed to the critique of the mainstream press's marginalization of the labor movement reflected in the analysis of Gompers. Here, Gompers was speaking to what mid-twentieth-century media scholar George Gerbner described as "symbolic annihilation"—the very absence of mention in the media—in which, as Gaye Tuchman later elaborated in "The Symbolic Annihilation of Women by the Mass Media," annihilation could also mean "condemnation" and "trivialization" of the marginalized other. Tuchman's discussion appeared as the introduction to a 1978 book concerned with "the depiction of sex roles in the mass media and the effect of that portrayal on American girls and women."[72] However, concern with this issue of distorted portrayals of women goes far back in history. For instance, as early as 1852 in an echo of Gompers's counsel about seeking out labor papers, social reformer and women's rights activist Susan B. Anthony told the Woman's Rights Convention in Syracuse, New York, that it was only when newspapers edited by women thrived that there would be progress in women's rights.[73] Certainly, over the decades, many women activists expressed concern with the sensational and salacious aspects of the newspapers of the era. For instance, the renowned Frances Willard—educator, reformer, and president of the Women's Christian Temperance Union (WCTU)—believed that the ideal of journalism was "to outline the story of the world's doings to-day that the reading thereof may make the world better to-morrow."[74] As one of the early leaders and thinkers in the Social Gospel movement, Willard shared much of the background, concerns, and goals of the movement, and her journalistic ideal mirrors that of the pronouncements on the press by both Washington Gladden and Charles Sheldon.

However, a dominant theme of discussions about newspapers by women activists focused on the press portrayals of the women's rights, suffrage, and temperance movements. This involved both the creation of publications run by women and efforts to ally with the mainstream press so that it would tell their stories without distortion. For instance, Willard once declared that the WCTU needed its "great weekly newspaper, its books and pamphlets" in order to "open the eyes of the blind." But also the organization's "press department, seeking to reach and utilize the plant of the newspaper, both religious and secular, in every town and village, is one of our mightiest engines of power."[75] That latter point was later affirmed by another official of the WCTU, Susan McWhirter Ostrom. Writing in the organization's official publication in 1918, Ostrom expressed her delight with the WCTU's allies in the press that had published thousands of columns of news about Prohibition and had rejected reams of liquor advertisements in that year. Encouraged by those facts, Ostrom declared that "if we could get the press of the country solidly behind us in our light for prohibition, for woman suffrage and for all the other reforms for which we work, it would not be long until we would be 'looking for more worlds to conquer.' With the dynamic power of the press behind our movement there is no limit to our possible influence for good."[76]

But aside from the press's representations of women and their issues, even more pronounced was the symbolic annihilation of African Americans by newspapers that "ordinarily close their pages to all mention of the black man unless he has been very spectacularly lynched," according to an editorial in the *Crisis*, a magazine published by the National Association for the Advancement of Colored People whose editor was W. E. B. Du Bois.[77] For instance, quoting *Survey* magazine of May 15, 1920, the Chicago Commission on Race Relations in a report on a race riot noted, "The custom of newspapers to ridicule the efforts of colored people is a gratuitous insult that they have to meet on every hand." Indeed, as contemporary historian Gary Dorrien pointed out in *The New Abolition: W. E. B. Du Bois and the Black Social Gospel*, the wave of lynching of African Americans drew support from the press that was "so successful at stunting the conscience of the nation that a human being could be burned to death at the stake in Pennsylvania or Georgia without evoking a horrified reaction."[78]

Certainly, a review of the writings of African American writers and analysts of the age reveals a litany of complaints about their race's marginalization, trivialization, and absence of presence in the press,[79] whose effect was succinctly described by Du Bois when he wrote in *The Souls of Black Folk*: "Herein lies the tragedy of the age: not that men are poor,—all men know something of poverty; not that men are wicked,—who is good? not that men are ignorant,—what is Truth? Nay, but that men know so little of men."[80]

Frederick German Detweiler, an American sociologist and expert on race relations, noted in his book *The Negro Press in the United States* (1922) that a theme that ran through the black press was the concern that an accurate portrayal of African American citizens was absent from the white press and that—again echoing Gompers's advice about news about the laboring class—"to get Negro news in full, you must read Negro newspapers." He observed that "through all the Negro press there flows an undercurrent of feeling that the race considers itself a part of America and yet has no voice in the American newspaper. Members of this group want to learn about each other, they want the stories of their successes, conflicts, and issues told, and they want to express themselves in public." Detweiler then quotes an editorialist from the *Kansas City Call*, who lamented, "Oh, if you could see the story of your struggles honestly and fairly related in the newspapers, if you could find your heart yearning after good will with all men, if your aspirations were met with applause as are those of your neighbors, this would be a wonderful world! But no! You are denied what other men are freely granted and to get your wants you must plan and work."[81]

This lament mirrors Addams's charge that journalists offer "a realization of the experiences of other people" and Stead's counsel that they give "utterance to the inarticulate moan of the voiceless." It is an appeal not unlike the contemporary call by three media scholars for a communitarian ethic that seeks a "press devoted to the telos of civic transformation"—one that would "liberate the citizenry, inspire acts of conscience, pierce the political fog, and enable the consciousness raising that is essential for constructing a social order through dialogue, mutually, in concert with our universal humanity."[82]

The Newspaper as Prophet

Celebrated advocacy journalist and editor William T. Stead believed that for the journalist, there were higher possibilities of service to the public than simply being "the keeper of a peep-show," revealing snatches of "the great drama of contemporary life and history." Instead, there existed within reach a realm of service that entailed a "prophetic aspect" in which the journalist acted as "a missionary and apostle."[83] To be clear, journalism that was "prophetic rather than historical" did not mean attempting to tell the future. Instead, Lyman Abbott advised, rather than simply narrating the week's events, its goal was "to interpret them; to turn the mind of the reader toward the future and help him to see in what direction current history was moving." This conceit of the prophetic was built on the belief that all events could be considered "by their relation to human welfare and human development"—in other words through the lens of humanity. This news ethic, Abbott wrote, was grounded in the example of the Hebrew prophets and the four Gospels.[84] In fact, the very word *prophet* means "interpreter." And the author of a book-length treatise on the prophets of the Old

Testament noted that in Hebrew, it "denotes originally a loud, clear speaker, yet always one who declares the mind and words of another who does not himself speak."[85]

The impetus for the prophetic office, as one writer has observed, was grounded in "dissatisfaction with conditions as they are, doubt that they are as they should be, [and] earnest desire to reconstruct faith and life in terms of the enlarged."[86] Indeed, this very sense of moral outrage was the impulse for the muckrakers and their journalism of exposure of the ills of society in the late nineteenth and early twentieth centuries. Also, here in speaking of journalists as prophets for a new age arises discussion about the divide between the mission and the market. For example, Shailer Mathews contended, a journalist was not a prophet simply because he exposed "social evils." He may be only "a scandalmonger at so much a thousand words." The prophet, the real reformer, was a free moral agent, he held, who "rights wrongs. He does not exploit them commercially."[87]

One of the more well known of the prophetic journalists was Lincoln Steffens, who once responded to a question from a historian to say he was not "the original muckraker"—instead, the prophets of the Old Testament preceded him by many centuries. What prompted the writers, editors, and reporters of the muckraking era was their "finding fault with 'things as they are,'" Steffens recalled.[88] And while most of these journalistic prophets had no formal position in any one religion, that was not an impediment. As Selden P. Delany, a Catholic priest and editor of the *American Church Monthly,* observed, many of the great Hebrew prophets were not ordained—they were laymen. Similarly, the prophets of the Progressive Era were the muckrakers such as Steffens, Samuel Hopkins Adams, Upton Sinclair, Edwin Markham, William Allen White, and Ida Tarbell. "Perhaps," Delany suggested, "some of these prophets do not belong to the body of the Church; but at least they belong to the soul of the Church."[89]

In discussing the prophetic mission of the newspaper and its confrontation with the market forces that would fetter that function, no figure looms larger than Washington Gladden, who made the subject a constant theme of his critique of the newspaper press in America. For instance, in 1885 he told a conference of the American Congress of Churches called to discuss the secular press that it was

> greatly to be desired . . . that the newspaper may rise, by and by, above its present business of reflecting public opinion, and take the leadership of public

> opinion, thus attaining unto prophetic functions and dignities, and basing its messages upon truly religious grounds. The one thing now needed in the secular press is prophetism, clear conviction and brave utterance of truth, whether men will hear or forbear. Something of this we have always had in journalism; but there has never been too much of it, and I almost think there is less of it now than ever before. The influence of the counting-room upon the editorial utterance is far too apparent; it is not often successfully resisted.[90]

Gladden's call for "clear conviction and brave utterance of truth" presaged by several years the rise of the Progressive Era reporting of the muckraking journalists and their literature of exposure. It was a call for free moral agents—acting as prophets—to reveal the social straits of the time and to do so despite the obvious constraints of market and ideological forces and despite the shackles of a news ethic that dictated that stories should be uncolored and unbiased. Certainly, Doug Underwood has observed, this is a news convention that grew up in the Progressive Era and has manifested itself in one form or another for more than a century, as journalists have struggled with the notion of objectivity versus reform, advocacy, constructive criticism, and social change.[91]

We can also see this in the suggestion by Herbert J. Gans in his seminal and often-cited ethnographic case study of journalistic conduct that the enduring values that act as an armature for journalists had their origin in the Progressive movement when reporters and editors were part and parcel of the movement. Their values, he asserted, were consubstantial with the Progressive "vision of a good nation and society." One prominent example that bolsters this assertion is press baron E. W. Scripps's model of progressive, advocatory journalism in the early twentieth century in which he would forsake higher profits in order to stand firm with his progressive ideals.[92]

In his study, Gans lengthily spells out the tension between those parallel notions of prophetic, value-laden journalism and objective, neutered journalism. This is evident, Gans argues, in the fact that objectivity—or its like—allows journalists to ignore the "implications of the news," which protects journalists from their critics. Without the ability to disregard those effects the news could have on sources and others, journalists "would have to begin assessing their own intent and to relinquish their detachment." When values do become attached to news, Gans observed, they do not so much reflect journalists' preferences, but more illustrate reality judgments that are "assumptions built into the considerations that journalists apply."

And to our point, once journalists make such judgments about reality, there is no room left in their stories for the reality judgments of—for example—the poor who exist at the periphery. Nor do they ask, Gans observed, "the kinds of questions about the country that radicals, ultraconservatives, the religiously orthodox, or social scientists ask as a result of their reality judgments." Indeed, Gans goes on to point out, such journalistic values lead to little critique of the capitalist order. Thus, "the enduring values are blind to possible structural faults within the system, which in turn reduces the likelihood of stories that question the legitimacy of the present economic order."[93]

For examples of this deficiency, look to the lack of newspaper coverage in the early twentieth century of the ill treatment of employees by department stores[94]—the source of much advertising revenue—and recall Gompers's complaints about the lack of and distorted coverage of labor by the mainstream newspapers of his time. For a more contemporary example, look no further than the mea culpa by the *New York Times* and the apology by the *Washington Post* in which both papers noted that in their enthrallment to governmental authority and their adherence to a kind of press nationalism (my words), they failed to question the Bush administration's reasons for going to war in Iraq.

The counterpoise to this policy of subservience lies in history—in, for example, the pulpit's call for a journalism of advocacy and interpretation not unlike the stance held more than a century ago by journalistic prophet William T. Stead. His own notable press crusades set the government to act in reviving Britain's sea power and led to the Criminal Law Amendment Act of 1885 that raised the age of consent and outlined the penalties for sexual offenses against women and minors.

The Newspaper as Teacher

In 1892 theologian and scientist Newman Smyth asserted that the modern newspaper was a venue through which "the public conscience may be educated, or by which it may also be debased and misled." And then two years later, editor and publisher William F. Gray wrote that the newspaper had a greater part to play than ever before in the education of the public. "It is more widely read and more universally appreciated," he contended. "It is no longer a mere vehicle of news. It carries in its columns literature, science, religion, politics, all that makes up the daily experience of men and women." And then nearly three decades later, renowned newspaper editor

Arthur Brisbane declared, "Every newspaper should be systematically and persistently an educating power." A year later, *Editor & Publisher* editorialized that "journalism is to all men the great informant and educator." And then three months later, the American Society of Newspaper Editors adopted the Canons of Journalism in which the declaration linked journalism to "its obligations as teacher and interpreter."[95]

Note in the latter passage that teaching is yoked to interpretation. Thus, to speak of the newspaper as an educator, one would be hard-pressed to avoid discussing the interpretive function of news, since education is arguably so much a matter of interpretation. As one English reverend declared in 1883, "Daily journalism should be daily preaching."[96] This call for an interpretive function was a view made both implicitly and explicitly in edicts about the role of newspapers as educators. For instance, in 1910 Rabbi Stephen S. Wise, a social justice activist during the Progressive Era, counseled journalists to contest the article of faith in and outside the newspaper industry "that the newspaper is to be a mere purveyor of news rather than a bringer of intelligence, that its sole business is to be collector and disseminator of news." It was not possible to publish facts about the events of the world "without some intimation of editorial thought or feeling," he held, and journalists, if they were doing their jobs, simply could not be "opinionless and neutral."[97]

That there was a change afoot reflecting the exhortations of the pastorate and the work of the muckrakers was apparent in an editorial symposium titled "What Is News?" in *Collier's* magazine in 1911. One of the participants, newspaper editor W. G. McMurchy, noted that while one kind of news was simply narrative, the dominant form involved an inquiry not unlike editorial comment about "the motives and reasons" behind an incident or event that would open the way to a kind "of newspaper literature which is intended to make people think who are apt not to." Such prosecution of a story, McMurchy contended, was "the heart and soul of that sort of news which some call muckraking, but which, even in the most conservative papers, is more and more being recognized as legitimate news in spite of its inevitable editorial tendencies or even prejudices."[98]

That was because, the Reverend Simeon Gilbert insisted, the social awakening of the Progressive Era meant that the public no longer had much interest in news as merely something new. Instead, Gilbert—in an essay titled "The Newspaper as a Judiciary," in the *American Journal of Sociology*—appealed for the newspaper to act as a judiciary and the journalist to employ a judicial mind subject only to the free moral agency of his or her conscience.[99] It was also a call for a new definition of journalism that echoed the explanatory journalism of the partisan-era newspaper. It was a journalism whose news conventions called for the prosecution of the facts of a story not unlike the proliferation of contemporary explanatory journalism websites[100] and the current calls for contemporary news media to adopt explanatory, contextual journalism as a news convention.[101]

Again, we can hear that interpretation is a role critics saddled the newspaper with, given that it lay solely at the fulcrum between an increasingly complex and modern world and a public beset with making its way in that world. Edward Thomas Devine, a professor of social economy and a social worker known internationally for his social relief work, offered a similar but more concrete counsel. Devine pointed to the advantages to society of newspapers that would write and edit stories "from a social point of view" in which events of public interest were interpreted "to discover their significance in relation to the common welfare."[102]

Still, within the compass of the dialectic of the mission versus the market, recall Gladden's disapproval in 1885 of "the domination of the counting-room over the sanctum" and "the subjection of the teaching function to the business of money-making" by newspapers. These economic considerations were at the core of the modern newspaper's "lack of prophetism," Gladden charged, in which its teaching function had diminished. This was a concern voiced more than three decades later by Frank P. Glass, a past president of the American Newspaper Publishers Association, who observed that modern newspapers had "yielded too much to the spirit of commercialism." Thus, he asked, "Is it not true frequently that the high function of the paper as a teacher and a leader is forgotten in the greed for income and profit?" Certainly, the impulse for both Gladden's and Glass's lamentations was the felt view that newspapers had grown so powerful and had so much influence over the public and common conviction that the press had replaced the pulpit as the public's teacher. "The pulpit," writer W. S. Lilly noted as early as 1889, "has been obliged to resign to the press the instruction of the people in secular affairs."[103]

The above assertions and the formal declaration in the Canons illustrate the long conversation cascading from and consubstantial with the newspaper's mission as prophet—its mission as a teacher[104] that was braided with two impulses, modernity and democracy. In many ways, multiple press critics described newspapers as one of the public's "greatest sources of enlightenment" and the "chief educator of the masses."[105] Indeed, Friedrich Nietzsche in a discussion of the growing power of the newspaper and its mission in society asserted that "in the newspaper the peculiar educational aims of the present culminate, just as the journalist, the servant of the moment, has stepped into the place of the genius, of the leader for all time, of the deliverer from the tyranny of the moment."[106]

The Newspaper's Educative Role in Modernity

As an educator, the newspaper functioned to expose and help right the wrongs of society, to act as a societal binding agent, and to serve as guide to life in an increasingly complex and modern society. Michael Schudson goes so far as to say that the newspaper became the "use-paper"—"a compendium of tips for urban survival." In fact, part and parcel with the sudden urbanization of America, newspapers were becoming the new teachers, as editors and publishers began to take on a new role. For example, Richard Hofstadter contended that the slum sketch, which would briefly outline a story about one or more of the city's poor, became a common newspaper feature that helped solidify an ethos of urban solidarity. And, he goes on to argue, "It was just this interest of the secure world in the nether world that served as the prototype of muckraking." Hofstadter described the newspaper's new role as one of the "village gossip," creating a kind of social cohesion that brought together a sense of human contact and unity in a naturally discordant urbanscape that was "strange, anonymous, impersonal, cruel, often corrupt and vicious." He argued that the newspaper was "creating a mental world" for displaced farmers, villagers, and the thousands of immigrants flowing into the cities.[107]

To just that point, early-twentieth-century sociologist Robert Park observed, "The first function which a newspaper supplies is that which formerly was performed by the village gossip."[108] Park also maintained that for the immigrant, the newspaper became "a window looking out into the larger world outside the narrow circle" of his own community. He contended that the sensational yellow journals of William Randolph Hearst were fundamental in informing immigrants and helping to assimilate them, making Hearst "a great Americanizer." In fact, noted Hearst editor and editorialist Arthur Brisbane, who more than once offered a defense of yellow journalism, insisted that such sensationalism was a mode of journalism that helped get people to think and use their imaginations. "Our people want excitement," Brisbane said. "They must have it. The great daily has two functions:

to teach and to cause thought. There is no doubt that 'yellow' journalism has started millions to thinking who never had done much thinking or reading except along trashy lines."[109]

In a similar but more erudite analysis in 1896 titled "The Ethics of Modern Journalism," French journalist and critic Aline Gorren observed that "the newspaper constitutes by far the greatest factor in the education of countless thousands." Thus, she proposed, the fact that so many newspapers thrived on the "vulgar and commonplace and indiscreet and unenlightened" because of "deep-seated social conditions" offered a social-utilitarian way of reflecting on the newspaper's effect on modern society.

> In reality, do we perceive what the vulgarities of the modern newspaper press actually represent? Do we realize that their personalities are the result of the desperate desire of the new classes, to whom democratic institutions have given their first charge, to discover the way to live, in the wide social meaning of the word? The hour belongs to these classes. Their ideals are becoming more and more the ideals of all masses of society, and what they are chiefly eager for is not ideas but palpable realities. What the man wants who newly finds himself with incalculably increased material opportunities before him is not, at first, thoughts that will strengthen his hold upon the eternal verities. No. It is information that will put him in direct touch with the actualities of the passing hour; information that will teach him all about his environment, and what he is to do there, and how he is to conduct himself in order to keep the place that he has got, and to extend it, to push himself farther on.[110]

One writer who had lived through the industrial transition of America and the rise of those "new classes" was William Torrey Harris, an educator, philosopher, and lexicographer. He pointed out that before the railroad and telegraph made the daily newspaper possible, "each person adjusted himself to his narrow environment through village gossip, which he heard at the neighboring inn or at the clubs. Now, instead of village gossip he reads world gossip, without leaving his fireside or breakfast table." Similarly, another writer of the early industrial age, Richard Grant White, a journalist and a renowned literary, music, and social critic, argued that the "true function" of the newspaper, "even in its lowest stage, is to inform, to enlighten, to place within the knowledge of men the facts which concern their most important interests, ignorance of which may expose them to loss, to perplexing error, and to suffering." In other words, White argued, the journalist is both "a counsellor and a prophet" and in its ideal form journalism "informs and educates; it expands the horizon of men's thoughts and sympathies." It is "the brain of the community, the organ of its collective thought; it is the chief among the active visible forces of modern civilization."[111]

The Newspaper's Educative Role in a Democracy

In 1905 the newspaper trade journal the *Journalist* pointed to the onset of modernity and the challenges of an increasingly complex democratic society, which had shifted newspapers from their former role simply as "gatherers and publishers of news" to a more commanding position in modern life as "forums of the people, the pulpits of Democracy." That judgment was a constant core theme of much of the Reverend Walter Rauschenbusch's critique of the modern newspaper in which he worried about the ill effects of a malign press on democracy. He once observed that "the justice and efficiency of democratic government depend on the intelligence and information of the citizens." If newspapers intentionally misled those citizens through distortion or suppression of important information, he argued, "the innermost life of our republic is in danger." Likewise, W. S. Lilly linked the responsibility of the press to our system of modern democracy, "the great, universal, dominant fact of modern civilization." It is the office of the press, he maintained, to "guide the sovereign people to understand matters of state." The newspapers, Lilly argued, are the people's "guides, philosophers, and friends," teaching them what to think on many relevant subjects. "For the great majority of men, I say, their newspapers—they seldom read anything else—are the direct sources of those floating opinions which have drifted into their minds, wherewith they judge all social and political problems."[112]

Those were sentiments with which both the *New York Journal*'s Arthur Brisbane, a renowned proponent of the efficacy of yellow journalism,[113] and the Reverend Reynold E. Blight, minister of the Los Angeles Fellowship, agreed. Brisbane declared that the newspaper makes "possible democratic government on a wide scale," as it acted as a public square, much like that of the first democracy—ancient Greece. And Blight observed that in the ability to dispense information broadly, the nation's newspapers had surpassed "the pulpit, the school, the forum" in power over public opinion. "It determines the questions of popular interest, sets the trend of public speech, public thought and general customs. The community is dependent on it for information and guidance concerning commercial, social and political matters." Indeed, looking back over the years in the *Ethics of Journalism* (1924), Nelson Antrim Crawford observed that the modern journalistic ideal had grown out of this changing face of America. More people were moving to the cities, he noted, and the problems of governing a growing, fractious population were becoming more complex. Thus, voters could no longer "obtain, through personal observation or investigation, objective facts on which to base" their political decisions. The only agents remaining to present these facts were the newspapers.[114]

Crawford's assertion is one that echoes across the decades in numerous iterations about the newspaper as a vital asset to an engaged and knowledgeable citizenry in a democracy.[115] As Charles Dudley Warner observed in 1890, "If the circulation of ideas has any value, the newspaper is a necessity." That was because the "great service that the newspapers render" in a political democracy was the publicity it presents that "informs the most powerful of all modern engines, public opinion," which affects the course of government. "This great service newspapers render."[116] In 1916 Professor J. T. House distilled in a speech the many arguments for a newspaper press unfettered by partisan or commercial influence. House observed that, "in the modern sense," no nation existed without a press, and there was "no such thing as democracy without a free press." America was not the democratic Athens of the past and its daily, face-to-face gatherings. In a nation as vast as America, those gatherings took place in the nation's twenty-four thousand newspapers and in the process created a "common mind," he asserted.[117] "Each morning from one end of our country to the other, we consider the same questions and so keep alive our national purpose."[118]

These discussions about a newspaper's lubricating effect on the growth and sustenance of democracy were a constant rhetoric of inculcation of an ethos, especially in America, where the press had been since colonial times the crucible of the nation's newly forming institutions. For example, often ignored in discussions about jury nullification in the celebrated case of John Peter Zenger in 1734 was the fact that at the center of the controversy over his *New-York Weekly Journal* were the debates between the *Journal* and the semiofficial *New-York Gazette* about the theory of government appropriate to America. At the heart of that rational-critical debate were the first steps in molding public opinion in America that led to the Declaration of Independence decades later. The *Journal*'s writers stood for the right of the people to have a voice in their government and with rulers being responsive to the people from whom they drew their authority, the right to criticize leaders, the freedom of the press, and the right to jury trials. The *Gazette*, on the other hand, argued for the status quo regime.[119]

This was not an isolated case. Similar political discussions took place over many years in other colonial newspapers, and while their circulations were limited, their influence had enormous consequences. For example, one printer loyal to Britain—Ambrose Serle—wrote in a letter on November 26, 1776, "Among other Engines, which have raised the present Commotion next to the indecent Harangues of the Preachers, none has had a more extensive or stronger Influence than the Newspapers of the respective Colonies. One is astonished to see with what Avidity they are sought after, and how implicitly they are believed, by the great Bulk of the People."[120]

The end of the Revolutionary War did nothing to decrease newspapers as venues of political discussion. Only the subject had changed, and the most notable of these debates was again over theories of government. This time it was the Federalists' and Anti-Federalists' confrontation centering on the new Constitution and the form America's government should take. As before the war, much of this debate was carried on through anonymous letters that, after being published in one paper, were clipped and copied by other papers in a kind of centrifugal spiraling of the discussion across the infant nation.[121] It was that notion, then, passed down as a rhetorical "habit of the lip" through the generations of the American experience—democracy was the offspring of an untrammeled press—that infused so much of the pastoral and secular critics' commentary on daily journalism.

In sum, here in this long conversation could be heard the issues at the fulcrum of the debate over the old journalism versus the new journalism driven by the social context of industrial-driven modernity and a changing American demographic. The "eternal verities" espoused by the elite genteel tradition of the past as the agents of acculturation no longer held any value for the growing middle and immigrant classes. What they wanted, instead, was a news ethic in which the newspaper's pulse-driven and faithful daily account of life at its fullest would bind them to a cohesive community and show them how to live in a changing, pluralistic democracy.

That, then, is a desire that has not gone away. For instance, the digital transformation of the media and the ongoing subsequent upheaval of traditional journalism platforms have prompted discussions that have shone light on this view of the news media's mission. One such revealing critical juncture in a collision between a publication and its public came in 2015 after the Tribune Company dismissed Austin Beutner as publisher of the *Los Angeles Times*. An open letter sent to the Tribune Company's board of directors signed by twenty-four civic leaders, including two former mayors, expressed the concern that Beutner's dismissal made it much more difficult for the *Los Angeles Times* to fulfill its responsibilities to the community. We can hear this communitarian and social-cohesion view articulated in the letter's assertion that a paper's mission is to promote civic engagement by serving "as the voice of a community" and as a space where "citizens can come together to exchange ideas, create and strengthen relationships, and forge consensus on how to make their community a better place to live."

But what is also instructive is that those two dozen civic leaders also recognized the tension between the mission and the market. For instance, the letter acknowledged the *Times*'s "goals are both to serve a community and to oversee a profitable business enterprise." But, the civic leaders added, they agreed with Beutner's "view that the paper's commitment to Los Angeles is a key to its financial success as well." The civic leaders went on to acknowledge that readers could find news from an endless number of digital venues. However, they wrote, the issue was more than ready access to news from anywhere. Instead, "the connection that develops from a media platform's commitment to a community is of tremendous import" because over its 133 years, "the *Times* has helped us come to understand each other, face our challenges and move forward together."[122]

The Struggle for the Soul of Journalism

A review of the literature regarding the conceit of the "soul" when applied to the role of news in society reveals it is a somewhat ineffable notion with assorted, often overlapping, meanings.[123] For example, there was the *New York Times*'s declaration in 1901 that the "news is the life and soul of a newspaper." Or there was this waggish but pithy pronouncement of Sir Henry Irving, a renowned English actor and chairman of the Newspaper Press Fund in Britain, that "the soul of journalism must be prophetic, because it has to do for a curious and wide-eyed public what was done for a much simpler generation by the alchemists and the astrologer."[124]

However, in 1916 Ralph Pulitzer, publisher of the *New York World*, offered a much more intricate elaboration of this conceit over the tension in the struggle with the market to set forth the boundaries of news and its role in society—the subject of many a speech, essay, and symposium and often couched in the question "What is news?"[125] In a speech to the New York Press Club on the newspapers' coverage of Woodrow Wilson's presidential reelection campaign, Pulitzer told the assembled journalists that "the press has a public conscience which it sets above its material advantages." That was because, he said, the "newspaper has not only a body and a brain; it has also a soul." He pointed out that news was more than a daily manufactured commodity. A newspaper's "life-force lies in a higher function," as the news it publishes must be infused with service to society in the form of "public convictions, public principles and public ideals."[126]

This, again, is the understanding that "news is a force and not a commodity."[127] Indeed, as Henry Watterson once advised a gathering of journalists, "The newspaper is not a commodity to be sold over the counter like dry goods and groceries. It should be, as it were, a keeper of the public conscience."[128] That is, rather than as a mere product to satisfy the demands of an expanding readership who began to buy and read the commercialized "penny press" in the United States and the "pauper press" in Britain,[129] news was conceived of as a force for principled social change, for social cohesion, and for helping sustain a just social world. For instance, Walter H. Page, manager of the magazine *Forum*, described the power of the press as transformative. "It is as yet an untamed force, but it is a force for good," he said. "In itself, it is raising the standard of humanity."[130] Similarly, an editorial in Richard Watson Gilder's *Century Magazine* in 1890 titled "Journalists and Newsmongers" spoke to just this point in an askance sort of way:

> The reader is acted upon by the news as by a force; he uses it as a force. Like every other force, news is a power for good or evil, according to the way it is given out and handled. It makes and wrecks private fortunes, destroys the peace of mind of individuals, directs the thoughts of the multitude, and incites to suicide and murder. If a force that has the potency of great good to society is thus capable of doing so much injury to individuals, it would seem as though the shapers and purveyors of it ought to be conspicuous among men for their sense of moral responsibility.[131]

At its most basic, the soul of journalism was allied with what the Reverend Simeon Gilbert called the "general awakening of the social consciousness" in which humanity was beginning to "look upon the world from a more sympathetic and more ethical point of view" and in which, the Methodist minister John R. Creighton maintained, the press must be elevated to "a higher moral standard" and be wielded on the "side of righteousness."[132] The soul, then, is a constituent of the body manifested in the Social Gospel's conviction that society was a "Social Organism."[133] And it is integral to a moral argument about news and the journalist's incumbent service to society in which we can hear soundings in the conceit of the press as a public utility. Indeed, in 1911 Will Irwin, a leading analyst of the newspaper industry in the early twentieth century, observed that the news columns had elbowed aside the editorial page to become the focal point of the power of the newspaper. In a speech titled "Moral Responsibility of the Press" (1911), sponsored by three New York City churches, Irwin told an audience of about a thousand people that whether they realized it or not, much of their view of the world came from the news they read in the paper. "The chief responsibility is thus on the news editor. And the aim of the news editor should be to publish only such things as would be best for the democracy. When the news editors do this, the millennium will come."[134]

Of course, what is "best for the democracy" is a subjective notion and is open to definitional interpretation. As John C. Merrill and S. Jack Odell have observed, because of "journalism's nebulous nature," defining both it and the concept of news is a daunting task.[135] However, if we take the preceding pages in which religion largely took a functional view of the press—its mission and that it was a force and not a commodity—and approach journalism by looking first at its perceived purpose, we can capture an understanding of what was at stake in the struggle over a news ethic a century ago between religion and the profit-driven press and its ideology of objective news. But also, shrugging off attempts to simply define journalism and instead recognizing the importance of its purpose puts into relief the debate and criticism of a century ago that still have currency and remain unsettled even today.

If we were to put the press—both newspapers and periodicals—on a continuum ranging from objective to subjective, there have always been a number of small-circulation, but often influential, publications at the subjective margin that cover such things as religious, political, ethical, and social issues through the lens of an ideology on both the Left and the Right. These would include the monthly and weekly publications that employ an explanatory, interpretive, and value-laden news convention and take sides in advocating for their position as they reject the notion of objectivity and acknowledge their purpose is opinion formation and social or political change or both.

What is new, now, is the digital disruption of contemporary media practices—especially the broader avenues of opportunities to report and publish news on a local, national, and even international stage. It is within these venues—many of them with a considerable audience—that the conventions of news have begun to allow for a broader spectrum of sources to the periphery and for a values-based, explanatory, interpretive, advocatory form of journalism.

Why this would be, I believe, stems from the amorphous nature of digital venues in which space—and even time—no longer circumscribes the presentation of news. In other words, online is a metaphorical horizonless and borderless configuration—what Scott McCloud calls an "infinite canvas"—whose only constraint is the imagination. And that means a wider circulation base, even with a niche interactive engagement with readers who can also influence a news ethic, and fewer proximate powerful market and ideological constraints to covertly or overtly enforce an objective news convention. Indeed, this shift from the more hidebound uncolored, unbiased, and objective mainstream sources of news to the ever-increasing panoply of available online news venues with the moral agency to freely speak their minds is reminiscent of press critic Hamilton Holt's contention more than a century ago that "the moral power of the American periodical press has been transferred from the dailies to the monthlies and weeklies," because magazines were "less subject to local and personal influence."[136]

At the center of such critical discourse about the daily press was the effect on the old ideal of newspapering by what various authors described as "modern journalism" or the "new journalism." In this core argument can be heard the precursors of debates today over the relaxing of regulations on the media. It is an argument with two sides that fits fairly neatly into the conceit of the mission versus the market. One is those who believe the media have an inherent societal influence necessary to our democracy and our life in the modern world through giving venue to the instruction of a multiplicity of voices. The other is those who view the media—to include journalistic endeavors—as nothing more than another commodity never better articulated than in former Federal Communications Commission chairman Mark Fowler's pronouncement in the early 1980s that "television is just another appliance. It's a toaster with pictures." Yet those who oppose deregulation say it is the vertical integration of the commodified media as just another business out of many that leads to suppression and distortion of news in the business's interest rather than in the public's interest—an argument heard a century ago by those who opposed the commercialization of the daily newspaper press.

The commercialization of the newspapers, the commodification of news, and the drive for scarce advertising dollars among those papers a century ago and the whole growing panoply of online news technologies we face today were and are the prompt for changes in the way the news media operate. And as a century ago, within the digital realm advertising dollars are scarce. Today, this transformation is increasingly prompting newspapers—robbed of much of their advertising base by the digital realm—to redefine their business models grounded in "online first, print second," in which journalists must "think differently about how they report, write and present the news."[137]

Meanwhile, online news start-ups are also defining their business models in the search for scant advertising dollars. These business models, however, have proved at times to be a threat to long-standing ethical norms of news gathering and reporting that define journalism and its mission. And if they lead to new news conventions that pay homage to the market rather than the mission, they will, I worry, lead to the distortion of news, the suppression of news, and lost credibility. We can already see the latter in the decline in public confidence in newspapers.[138]

Certainly, there has been a seemingly endless stream of warning signs about the changing new media indicative of this detrimental change. We can see this, for instance, in Emily Bell's admonition that "the free press is now controlled by companies whose primary interests are not necessarily rooted in strengthening public discourse and democracy."[139] We can see this in a 2014 study of journalistic normative standards in the digital age that found that the "blurring of content types, and native ads threaten standards" and questioned whether "legacy guidelines fit the ethos of digital content."[140] We can see this in the call for cooperation between the news and business sides of a publication.[141] We can see this in the various efforts to merge advertising content with news content[142] and the rise of sponsored content—also called native advertising—and the increasing pressure on journalists to also work as advertising copy writers.[143] To extend that one step farther, we can see this in the announcement by the cofounders of *City AM*, a successful British business newspaper, that they were removing the "hallowed wall of 'church and state,' which for generations has divided the newsroom from the advertising department."[144] We can see this in Tribune Publishing's 2016 decision to combine editor and publisher roles at several of its newspapers, including the *Los Angeles Times* and *Chicago Tribune*.[145] That was, one observer quickly noted, "a break from the legacy model"[146] that creates, another observer pointed out, an "inherent conflict" because traditionally publishers "tend to the business of the paper and editors to serving the readers."[147] And finally, we can see this in the Online News Association "Build Your Own Ethics Code" project, aimed at helping "news organizations, startups and individual journalists create codes of ethics that reflect their own journalistic principles."[148]

Thus, as I contended many pages ago, before we continue to transform our present news ethic in the midst of contemporary digital-driven disruption, we need to understand the past as an anchorage for the present to discern and save what is fundamental about the true mission of journalism and to fend off the forces seeking to constrain and commodify the news media. Of course, in the midst of change, I am asking for change that looks to the past. That is, print newspapers, online news sites, and journalists should struggle over the soul of journalism as they hold fast to the originalist notions defined a century and more ago. They should do so by recognizing the following:

1. They are free moral agents who courageously express their discontent with the aberrations of the age, and with an awakened conscience they are free to act without the constraints of others' influence or their own prodding self-interest.
2. They are prophets who consider all events "by their relation to human welfare and human development."[149]
3. They are teachers who inform and educate in order to "expand the horizon of men's thoughts and sympathies."[150]
4. They are citizens committed to a values-based, interpretive, and explanatory journalism grounded in social justice that rejects the constraints of market-inspired objectivity.

I recognize that such epithets as moral agency, prophetism, and even the notion of a newspaper/news site and journalist as teacher may well be seen by some as somewhat lofty and seemingly out of touch with pecuniary reality. But they are expressions that the press critics of the past used to set forth the newspaper's mission in confrontation with the forces of the market. They are rhetorical conceits located in each critic's social-historical context that are meant to offer a handle to help grasp and think about complex ideas. Indeed, as writer Walt Harrington once observed, "The kind of journalism we end up doing is shaped by the way we think about our mission."[151]

However, I hold, there is a power to be had by forthrightly committing to a mission dedicated to the notion of journalists as free moral agents, as modern-day prophets concerned with social justice, as teachers who inform and educate, and as professionals committed to a values-based, interpretive, and explanatory journalism. By proclaiming and holding fast to a mission that declares that "news is a force and not a commodity,"[152] journalists may well begin the road to reclaiming the status of a free and independent press—especially in confrontation with flagrant contemporary criticism and the demands of the market of the expanding digital realm.

Indeed, as I write this, an ethos of blame and sneering derision has been arising around the mainstream news media that castigates and discounts its substantive journalistic efforts as "fake news." At the same time, the American public's trust and confidence that the news media report "the news fully, accurately and fairly" have plummeted to a new low. This, I would argue, has been partly prompted by the fact that the news media, as the conservative *National Review* observes, "has become for the Right what the Soviet Union was during the Cold War—a common, unifying adversary of overwhelming importance"—and that the president of the United States, the birthplace of modern democracy, regularly describes the legitimate news media and its journalists as evil.[153]

Certainly—especially with the growth of the digital realm—no greater point of contention surrounds the conversation about the news ethic of modern journalism in recent years than the enigmatic and overarching notion of objectivity,[154] the rise of which James Carey once attributed to "the struggle journalists faced in defining a place for themselves within the modern system of communication."[155] Indeed, after working for more than twenty years for newspapers in which objectivity was the sole sustaining pillar, I must admit to a degree of squeamishness when talk arises about journalists shrugging off objectivity and acting as advocates and social change agents. But I am certainly not alone. The continuing evolution of the entire news industry has meant that the fundamental notions of journalistic objectivity held dear by many in the mainstream media are still being questioned and critiqued not just by media critics but also by both creators and consumers—and especially consumers. To that point, a handful of examples will suffice to show this and the fact that in the midst of this media transformation, the rules of reporting are still unsettled.

I would point first to that bastion of objective news, *PBS NewsHour*. In 2011 the nightly news show offered a report on one of the Republicans' many efforts to repeal health reform. This was followed by a discussion between then *NewsHour* political editor David Chalian and reporter and anchor Gwen Ifill. At one point, Chalian described the confusion regarding the public's reaction to the health reform bill. The following is an excerpt from the transcription of that discussion:

> GWEN IFILL: Isn't it also confusing because it's hard to know what's true, whether it's a job-killing bill or a job-creating bill? You have Republicans and Democrats just toe-to-toe arguing the exact opposite thing.
>
> DAVID CHALIAN: There's no doubt about that. And—and the fact that there's no sort of arbiter right now works to both sides' advantages, right? They each get to make these points.[156]

Here, I and others would argue, is where the tenuous nature of journalistic objectivity—especially the he-said, she-said format—fails as a model of journalism. Here, in the enforced rigors of *NewsHour*'s vaunted objective mode, Ifill failed to hold Chalian accountable. That is, what did he mean by "there's no sort of arbiter"? I would argue that in this changing, complex, and often fractious world, informed journalists need to act as "arbiters" in such cases. Otherwise, what is the point? That is certainly a position others held in commenting on the story and discussion. For example, one commenter makes a similar point and also raises the issue of market and ideological constraints on the mission of journalism:

> This was pathetic on the part of the two "newspersons." They callously stated that there was no way to determine "the truth" about the benefits of the health care bill. This is unbelievable. PERHAPS THEY SHOULD HAVE HELPED US SEE THE TRUTH!! And that is that the independent government financial office has stated the net result will be to create jobs. And the lies that were stated today on the House floor by Republicans was outrageous—all sorts of plain, common lies about the health care bill. They are very dangerous people and Gwen Ifill did not do us any service by simply saying we could not get at the truth—that in itself was a lie. I wonder if it has anything to do with the fact that these same lying republicans have threatened to cut off funding to PBS??? I wonder. Gad where are humans going to end up?[157]

Part of the critical response of news media consumers stems from the growth and influence of cable networks and, more recently, online news sites. As Michael Scherer, then the White House correspondent for *Time*, observed in 2011, as both have increased in power, "the old popular broadcasters of a centrist, less directly-opinionated type of journalism were supplanted as the primary referee of the national political debate by new, louder voices, who more freely embraced open advocacy, and built niche audiences around shared concerns." Accordingly, in recent years, even the venerable *New York Times* has begun to adjust its news ethic in response to the changing times. Arthur Brisbane, the then public editor for the *Times*, observed that "what some call opinion, others call interpretive journalism." And, he noted, the three public editors before him had been dealing with readers' concerns about "advocacy pieces"—as one reader put it—appearing in the news sections of the *Times*. Brisbane described this as a "morphing of the news"—a trend toward the use of "interpretive material" that the *Times* editors viewed as "desirable and manageable."[158]

Thus, the impulse for this "morphing" of news conventions even within mainstream news venues is the dawning realization that journalists are—as the pastorate of a century ago argued—the public's advocates.[159] Indeed, media scholar Patricia Aufderheide has observed, "We might have passed the point where we can talk about objectivity in journalism with a straight face. Objectivity was always a shortcut. It was a useful little shortcut of a concept to say you should be fair, you should be honest, you should have integrity, you should tell people accurately and responsibly what you think are the important things about what you saw or researched."[160]

In a further step, critics of the constraints of objectivity often observe that advocacy reporting and its like are acquiring credibility. For instance, they note that it was a reporter for the American Civil Liberties Union who helped break the news about the Flint, Michigan, water crisis; that in 2012 a reporter for the progressive-leaning *Huffington Post* won the Pulitzer Prize for National Reporting; and that the following year the advocacy-oriented online site *InsideClimate News*, which covers the environment and politics, won the same prize.

That the niche news media's readers care about the nonobjective news conventions of a publication was made evident after AOL announced its purchase in 2011 of the *Huffington Post*, which exists solely in the horizonless realm of online news. In response, Peter S. Goodman, the editor overseeing business and economic coverage, felt the need to allay readers' concerns that the publication would not back away from its news ethic grounded in interpretation. And in defining news as an interpretive ethic, we can hear echoes of the mission statements of the *Outlook* and the *Independent* that were discussed earlier. Also, the response to the news site's acquisition by a large corporate entity was resonant of concerns raised decades ago by J. P. Morgan & Company's purchase of the *New York Evening Post* and the Illinois Merchants Trust Company's taking control of the *Chicago Daily News*. Goodman wrote, "We are in no way seeking to retreat to the phony version of journalistic objectivity that pretends the truth always lies in the middle, between two generally exaggerated and intellectually-disingenuous extremes." Instead, Goodman argued, objectivity in reporting is based in "a fully open-minded inquiry" in which "we offer a conclusion, and transparently so, with whatever caveats are in order."[161]

Finally, it is of interest that nearly a century or more later in the twenty-first century the "psychic meltdown"[162] of the press sparked by the Internet has induced in recent years a correspondence to the pastoral critiques of the past in a stream of contemporary discussion about how the press—unrestrained by what three media scholars call the "pathology" of objectivity[163]—has a higher function in society that calls for it to "not only educate people about what they can do, but pro-actively lead and encourage behavior change."[164]

For instance, columnist Steve Outing argued in *Editor & Publisher* that the press needed to set aside its "time-honored journalistic practice" of objectivity in order to push for change in the face of global warming. However, Outing then retreated and emphasized he still defended the status quo notion of objectivity that adheres to the press when "sizable groups of people" are on both sides of an issue.[165] Yet, I would ask, if advocacy is a good idea in the case of global warming, what of other issues similarly important to society? It seems that if the press can be made instrumental in global warming, it could function as an informed change agent with other societal problems in which any sense of truth and correct action is lost in a morass of conflicting agendas and perspectives. It is hard to see how this notion of press as guide to conduct could be so limited—a stance with which the pastorate of a century ago would most certainly agree.

Notes

Preface

1. Hazel Dicken-Garcia, *Journalistic Standards in Nineteenth-Century America*, 7.

2. American Society of Newspaper Editors, *Problems of Journalism: Proceedings of the First Annual Meeting, American Society of Newspaper Editors*. The proceedings contain pointed discussions about the role of journalism in society and debates about how to enforce the code of ethics. The Canons of Journalism was revised and renamed the Statement of Principles in 1975.

3. Robert M. Hutchins, *Report of the Commission on Freedom of the Press: A Free and Responsible Press*.

4. Helen MacGill Hughes, *News and the Human Interest Story*, 7.

5. Ronald R. Rodgers, "'Journalism Is a Loose-Jointed Thing': A Content Analysis of *Editor & Publisher*'s Discussion of Journalistic Conduct Prior to the Canons of Journalism, 1901–1922."

6. W. B. Turner, "The American Newspaper," 289.

7. Simeon Gilbert, "Christian Journalism: Its Idea and Its Ideal," 275.

8. Noah Brooks, "The Newspaper of the Future," 569–71, 576.

9. Douglas Birkhead, "The Progressive Reform of Journalism: The Rise of Professionalism in the Press," 123.

10. Gerald J. Baldasty, *The Commercialization of News in the Nineteenth Century*, 140 (quote), 143.

11. See, for example, Mary M. Cronin and James B. McPherson, "Pronouncements and Denunciations: An Analysis of State Press Association Ethics Codes from the 1920s," 890. In their study of state press association ethics codes from the 1920s before the adoption of the Canons of Journalism, Cronin and McPherson found that those state codes reflected several concerns among journalists of the time. They included the increasing number of public relations practitioners—the aftermath of the extensive propaganda efforts during World War I—the revival of sensationalism, and the independence of newspapers from outlier influences such as political parties and business interests. In response, they found, "The codes consistently emphasized the watchdog ideal, public service, truthfulness, and honesty in advertising."

12. George H. Douglas, *The Golden Age of the Newspaper*; George F. Spinney, "Newspaper Methods Yesterday and To-Day," 600 (quote).

13. "Highways & Byways" (December).

14. Chester S. Lord, "Reminiscences of Charles A. Dana and the Old *New York Sun*," 9.

15. Charles R. Williams, "Speech of Charles R. Williams," 54; Frank A. Munsey, "Freak Journalism," 3.

16. Quoted in L. U. Reavis, *A Representative Life of Horace Greeley*, 265–66.

17. George French, *Advertising: The Social and Economic Problem*, 178.

18. "Henry Watterson's Retirement," 164; Walt Harrington, "A Writer's Essay: Seeking the Extraordinary in the Ordinary."

19. See, for example, Richard Hofstadter, *The Age of Reform: From Bryan to F.D.R.*, 152. Hofstadter observes that "Progressivism can be considered . . . as a phase in the history of the Protestant conscience, a latter-day Protestant revival." See also Walter Rauschenbusch, *A Theology for the Social Gospel*, 160. Rauschenbusch argued, "Such a change of attitude toward the ritual institutions of religion, when it has become common, has availed to purge the religion of whole nations of its nonethical inheritances; it has reinforced the progressive elements of society by turning the energies of religion from the maintenance of conservative institutions to the support of movements for political emancipation and social justice. Such a change in religion inaugurates new eras in history."

20. Charles Grant Miller, "The Making of Better Citizens in Brooklyn: Educational Work among the Young and Old Is Only One of the Many Services That Make the *Eagle*," 5; Norman Hapgood, "To *Harper's Weekly* Readers," *Independent*, May 22, 1916, 263.

21. An example of the latter would be James Russell Lowell in the preface to the poem "The Pious Editor's Creed," in that he writes: "He would be the Moses of our nineteenth century." James Russell Lowell, "The Pious Editor's Creed," 200.

22. Quoted in Washington Gladden, "The Relation of Corporations to Public Morals," 624. Such analogies to Mary Shelley's creation were not uncommon. See also "Frankenstein," in *More Copy: A Second Series of Essays from an Editor's Drawer on Religion, Literature, and Life,* by Hugh Miller Thompson; and "The Origin and Growth of Corporations," 468.

23. "The Unity of Christendom."

24. Gladden, "Relation of Corporations," 612, 625–26.

25. Alan Barth, "The Cult of Loyalty," 58. Barth was a longtime editorial writer for the *Washington Post.*

26. Shailer Mathews, *The Validity of American Ideals*, 189; Michael Schudson, "The Objectivity Norm in American Journalism," 149.

27. "History," PBS NewsHour, http://www.pbs.org/newshour/about/history/.

28. See, for example, Turner, "The American Newspaper," 289; "On the Moral Influence of Newspapers," 63; "London Newspapers," 350; "The Mirrors of a Degenerate World: The Daily Press Reflects the Spirit of a Corrupt Generation; It Is a Potent Factor of Evil in the Hand of the Money Power," 6; James Keeley, "Newspaper Work," 77; "The Power of Advertising Is Told by Brisbane," 31; and David Davies, "Mirror of Life," 12; "Newspapers Are the Mirrors of Life Today," 10.

29. Schudson, "Objectivity Norm," 159–60; Richard Streckfuss, "Objectivity in Journalism: A Search and a Reassessment," 973–74.

30. Associated Press, "Mr. Bryan and the Associated Press"; Charles G. Ross, *The Writing of News: A Handbook with Chapters on Newspaper Correspondence and Copy Reading*, 17–18. See also Walter Williams and Frank L. Martin, *The Practice of Journalism: A Treatise on Newspaper Making*, 79–80. Williams and Martin included a version of the entire editorial from the *St. Louis Republic*.

31. Edward Cary Hayes, "The Sociological Point of View," 15. In 1922 Edward Cary Hayes, founder and president of the American Sociological Association, observed that "the sociological point of view is a keen appreciation of the struggle to be objective and unbiased" in order to dispel "partisan conceits and all the manifold bigotries that hitherto go so far toward subjecting human life and social organization to a reductio ad absurdum."

32. Streckfuss, "Objectivity in Journalism," 975.

33. David Croteau, William Hoynes, and Stefania Milan, *Media/Society: Industries, Images, and Audiences*, 131.

34. Streckfuss, "Objectivity in Journalism," 982; Clifford G. Christians, "Fifty Years of Scholarship in Media Ethics," 20–21; Michael Schudson, *Discovering the News: A Social History of American Newspapers*, 6.

35. Schudson, "Objectivity Norm," 159–60.

36. Brooks, "Newspaper of the Future," 569.

37. "A Vanderbilt in Journalism," *Eugene (OR) Register-Guard*, April 30, 1928, 4.

38. William T. Stead, "The Future of Journalism"; Herbert W. Horwill, "W. T. Stead." Horwill, the London correspondent for the *Nation*, observed that Stead was not really a journalist but more a preacher who turned to journalism because the newspaper was better than the pulpit for "spreading his message."

39. Matthew Arnold, "Up to Easter," 638–39.

40. "The Wail of the Has Been," 244.

41. W. H. A. Williams, *H. L. Mencken*, 22.

42. Patrick Collier, *Modernism on Fleet Street*, 123.

43. Meagan Doll, "7 Questions for Craig Silverman on Verification and Rumors."

44. Stead, "The Future of Journalism," 663–64, 670–71.

45. James Carey, "The Communications Revolution"; Ryan Michael, "Journalistic Ethics, Objectivity, Existential Journalism, Standpoint Epistemology,

and Public Journalism"; Maurice Hamington, "Jane Addams"; Jane Addams, *Democracy and Social Ethics*, 9–11.

46. Will Irwin, *The Making of a Reporter*, 164–69.

47. See, for example, Mary M. Cronin, "Trade Press Roles in Promoting Journalistic Professionalism, 1884–1917." Cronin explores *Editor & Publisher*'s campaign from its first publication for a more honest, unbiased, accurate, truthful, and professional newspaper industry. See also Marion Tuttle Marzolf, *Civilizing Voices: American Press Criticism, 1880–1950*. Marzolf explores standards of newspapers and the criticism of them over a seventy-year period, briefly discusses the Canons, and also explores the background of calls for codes of ethics in the newspaper industry previous to the Canons.

48. Henry James, *The American Scene*, 406.

49. Robert Andrews, *The Concise Columbia Dictionary of Quotations*, 139; Ralph Waldo Emerson, *Essays*, 133. This echoes a quotation attributed to Buddha: "All that we are arises with our thoughts. With our thoughts we make the world." Thomas Byrom, *The Dhammapada: The Sayings of the Buddha*, 1.

50. Hofstadter, *Age of Reform*, 185; Deirdre N. McCloskey, *Bourgeois Equality: How Ideas, Not Capital or Institutions, Enriched the World*.

51. Dicken-Garcia, *Journalistic Standards*, 6; George T. Rider, "The Pretensions of Journalism," 471.

52. David A. Curtis, "The New Journalism."

53. James Carey, "Communications and Economics," 67; Brooks, "Newspaper of the Future," 569.

54. "Ethics of the Press." The editor was George F. Milton of the *Knoxville Sentinel* and *Chattanooga News* at a meeting of the Tennessee Press Association in Nashville.

55. Schudson, *Discovering the News*, 98.

56. See, for example, "The *Guardian* View on Press Freedom: The Need for Constant Vigilance," *Guardian*, August 14, 2016, https://www.theguardian.com/commentisfree/2016/aug/14/the-guardian-view-on-press-freedom-the-need-for-constant-vigilance. The editorial asserts, "Journalists do not deserve protection because they constitute a privileged group; they need it because they can show the world as it really is and allow the unheard to find a voice. There is a reason why people so often want to shut them up. Halting print runs, closing down websites, silencing radio stations and blacking out TV screens are all ways of concealing misdeeds, preventing scrutiny or simply blocking alternative viewpoints. But such actions also serve to remind us all why press freedom matters."

57. "Sermon on Newspapers: New York State Minister Appeals for Freedom of the Press."

58. Stephen J. A. Ward, "Why We Need a Radical New Framework for Media Ethics"; Ian Burrell, "BBC Told to Emulate *Buzzfeed* by Producing 'Informal'

Short Videos Where Reporter Acts as a 'Friend,'" *Independent*, November 5, 2015, http://www.independent.co.uk/news/media/bbc-told-to-emulate-buzzfeed-by-producing-informal-short-videos-where-reporter-acts-as-a-friend-a6723216.html; E. A. D., "Newspapers."

Introduction

1. George W. Smalley, "Notes on Journalism," 213.

2. Charles Dudley Warner, "Newspapers and the Public," 198; "Can the Impartiality of the News-Gathering and the News-Supplying Agencies Be Fairly Challenged?," 38; Roger W. Riis, "Are Newspapers Doing Their Duty?," 117.

3. See, for example, George Tucker, "Progress of Population and Wealth in the United States in Fifty Years, as Exhibited by the Decennial Census Taken in That Period," 58. "The newspaper press is thus a most potent engine, both for good and evil. It too often ministers to some of our worst passions, and lends new force to party intolerance and party injustice." See also Moorfield Storey, "The Daily Press," 41. Storey asserted that the newspaper's "power and privileges carry with them great responsibilities, for it can lead or mislead the public." "Preachers Criticize: Prominent Clergymen in Sermons Point Out Evils of Newspapers; New York Minister Finds 39 Per Cent of News Items Are 'Worth While'—Massachusetts Preacher Classes Newspaper Managers with Ananias and Saphira—Methodist Clergyman from Sweden Admires American Newspapers."

4. Hofstadter, *Age of Reform*, 5.

5. Ibid.

6. Josiah Strong, "Why the League for Social Service."

7. "New Way of Living Changing the Press," *New York Times*, March 2, 1913, 10.

8. Lyman Abbott, *The Rights of Man: A Study in Twentieth Century Problems*, 329; American Congress of Churches, *Proceedings: American Congress of Churches, Cleveland, Ohio, May, 1886*, 3; "The Power of the Press: How It Assists in Promoting Christian Welfare; An Interesting Paper on the Influence of the Secular Press on Christian Life," *New York Times*, May 13, 1885, 5.

9. "The Congress of Churches," *New York Evangelist*, May 21, 1885, 4.

10. "The Unity of Christendom," *Christian Union*, May 21, 1885, 7.

11. "Power of the Press," 5.

12. Washington Gladden, "More about the Secular Press," 7.

13. Charles Howard Hopkins, *The Rise of the Social Gospel Movement in American Protestantism, 1865–1915*, 26–27.

14. "American Congregational Theology," 254.

15. Washington Gladden, *Social Facts and Forces: The Factory—the Labor Union—the Corporation—the Railway—the City—the Church*, 224.

16. Quoted in Hopkins, *Rise of the Social Gospel Movement*, 44.

17. Ibid., 44–49, 122, 135.

18. Ernst Troeltsch, *The Social Teaching of the Christian Churches*, 1010; Gary J. Dorrien, *Soul in Society: The Making and Renewal of Social Christianity*, 1.

19. "Agencies of the Church. Needs of the Preacher and Power of the Press. Topics Discussed by the Methodist Ecumenical Congress—Addresses by Bishop R. S. Foster, the Rev. H. P. Hughes, and Others," *New York Times*, October 13, 1891, 8.

20. See, for example, *Official Report of the Proceedings of the Thirteenth Meeting of the National Conference of Unitarian and Other Christian Churches Held at Philadelphia, Pa., October 28–31, 1889*, 12. Samuel J. Miller, president of the National Conference of Unitarian and Other Christian Churches, acknowledged that the church had a rival in newspapers, pamphlets, and magazines, whereas "fifty years ago, the preacher had that theatre to himself." See also J. E. Smith, "The Secular Press and Morality"; George P. Eckman, "Pulpit and Press: Newspapers Are to Be Reckoned among the Most Potent Forces Making for Righteousness—Pulpit May Well Look upon the Press as Its Most Important Ally," 6; and Amory Howe Bradford, *My Brother*, 153. Bradford, pastor of the First Congregational Church of Montclair, New Jersey, wrote, "There are now but few parishes like those in which Jonathan Edwards and Nathaniel Emmons preached to the world from obscure pulpits. He who would influence many men, henceforward, must preach in cities, or have an exceptional opportunity to use the press." Ralph Eugene Diffendorfer, *The Church and the Community*, 163. Diffendorfer asserted, "It goes without saying that the editorial columns, and especially the news sections of American newspapers, are among the greatest, if not the most potent, factors in forming public opinion. In a democracy, people feel that they have a right to the truth."

21. "The Periodical Press," *New York Evangelist*, June 12, 1851, 94; Josiah Strong, "The Present Tendency to World Unity," *Herald of Gospel Liberty*, July 30, 1903, 493; Charles Stelzle, *The Workingman and Social Problems*, 101.

22. Charles Stelzle, "How One Thousand Workingmen Spend Their Spare Time," 764. His study found the following: "Of the 8 to 9 hour group, 96.2 per cent read newspapers; of the 9 to 10 hour group, 93.3 per cent; of the 10 to 11 hour group, 92.1 per cent; of the 11 hour and over group, 78.7 per cent. But while more men of the 8 hour group read newspapers, the 11 hour and over group spend slightly more time in this way. Those engaged in domestic and personal service are lowest in amount of time spent in reading newspapers. Married men spend more time reading newspapers than do single men, although a larger proportion of young men between 17 and 24 read newspapers than do any other age group."

23. "Need a Conscience: Growing Public Demand for Newspaper Guided by Right Principles; Purchasable Press Foe to Liberty and Progress, Says California Minister."

24. "The Church and the Newspaper," 1403; Mathews, *Validity of American Ideals*, 189; "Need a Conscience."

25. "The Modern Novel," *New York Times*, December 23, 1866, 4.

26. Candy Gunther Brown, "Religious Periodicals and Their Textual Communities," 271.

27. Frank Luther Mott, *American Journalism: A History, 1690–1960*, 206.

28. C. Brown, "Religious Periodicals," 271.

29. Grenville Mellen, *The Age of Print: A Poem, Delivered before the Phi Beta Kappa Society, at Cambridge, 26 August, 1830*, 5; David Paul Nord, "The Evangelical Origins of Mass Media in America," 69; Isabelle Lehuu, *Carnival on the Page: Popular Print Media in Antebellum America*, 23.

30. Samuel G. Goodrich, *Recollections of a Lifetime; or, Men and Things I Have Seen, in a Series of Familiar Letters to a Friend, Historical, Biographical, Anecdotal and Descriptive*, 86; Nathan O. Hatch, *The Democratization of American Christianity*, 126.

31. Goodrich, *Recollections of a Lifetime*, 86.

32. David Paul Nord, "Benevolent Books: Printing, Religion, and Reform," 221; Alexis de Tocqueville, *Democracy in America*, 600.

33. John Pressley Barrett, "The Beginning and Beyond: A Brief Study of the Conditions and Ideals Which Gave Rise to the Christian Church," 14–15.

34. *Christian Herald*, "The Pulpit and the Press," 140; Elias Smith, "Address to the Public," 32–33; J. Barrett, "Beginning and Beyond," 14–15; Frank Luther Mott, *A History of American Magazines, 1741–1930*, 1:136; John Weeks Moore, *Moore's Historical, Biographical, and Miscellaneous Gatherings, in the Form of Disconnected Notes Relative to Printers, Printing, Publishing, and Editing of Books, Newspapers, Magazines and Other Literary Productions, Such as the Early Publications of New England, the United States, and the World, from the Discovery of the Art, or from 1420 to 1886, with Many Brief Notices of Authors, Publishers, Editors, Printers, and Inventors*, 54. See also Simon Newton Dexter North, *History and Present Condition of the Newspaper and Periodical Press of the United States, with a Catalogue of the Publications of the Census Year*, 119.

35. E. Smith, "Address to the Public," 32–33.

36. C. Brown, "Religious Periodicals," 276.

37. Horace Bushnell, *Views of Christian Nurture, and of Subjects Adjacent Thereto*, 158–59.

38. American Tract Society, *Home Evangelization: A View of the Wants and Prospects of Our Country, Based on Facts and Relations of Colportage*, 137, 139–40.

39. David Paul Nord, "Teleology and News: The Religious Roots of American Journalism, 1630–1730," 35.

40. Kevin J. Hayes, *The Oxford Handbook of Early American Literature*, 306.

41. Quoted in Willard Grosvenor Bleyer, *Main Currents in the History of American Journalism*, 54.

42. Charles B. Connolly, "The Ethics of Modern Journalism," 453; George Perry Morris, "Young Journalists Worth Knowing," 851.

43. Eric Foner and John A. Garraty, eds., *The Reader's Companion to American History*, 690–91.

44. "Newspapers Honest: Milton A. McRae, of Detroit, Refutes Impression That the Newspaper Has Become Purchasable and Is Controlled by the Advertiser," 8.

45. Walter Lippmann, "Two Revolutions in the American Press," 436; Asa Greene, *A Glance at New York: Embracing the City Government, Theatres, Hotels, Churches, Mobs, Monopolies, Learned Professions, Newspapers, Rogues, Dandies, Fires and Firemen, Water and Other Liquids, & C., & C.*, 131, 133.

46. James D. Startt and W. David Sloan, *The History of American Journalism*, 169–70.

47. Frank M. O'Brien, "The Story of the *Sun* (Part 3)," 292.

48. Baldasty, *Commercialization of News*, 8. See also Frederic Hudson, *Journalism in the United States, from 1690–1872*, 506.

49. Hughes, *News and the Human Interest Story*, 7. The Lippmann quote comes from Walter Lippmann, *Public Opinion*, 321.

50. Bleyer, *Main Currents*, 192, 193.

51. "Independence of the Press: The Position of the 'Times,'" *New York Daily Times*, January 13, 1857, 4; Bleyer, *Main Currents*, 135.

52. Edwin Emery, *The Press and America: An Interpretative History of the Mass Media*, 106.

53. "Independence of the Press," 4.

54. "Independent Newspapers."

55. "Newspaper Independence," 4.

56. "Arraigns the Press. Editor of *Boston Common* Pours Hot Shot into Editorial Ranks. Mr. Richard Gives Instances Showing That Important News Is Sometimes Ignored Because It Might Hurt the Newspaper's Advertising—Declares There Can Be No Freedom until Circulation Makes Bulk of Income."

57. "'The Ideal Newspaper,'" 335; Frank Crane, "What a Publication Owes to Its Readers," 28; Charles Dudley Warner, *The Relation of Literature to Life*, 202; "Newspaper Ethics," 483.

58. Samuel Bowles, "The Independent Press: Its Opportunities and Duties," 40; Villard quoted in "Back to Old Ideals: There Exists Decided Tendency to Reaction, Says Noted Editor."

59. See, for example, "For a Truthful Press"; "Newspaper Accuracy"; "Power and Responsibility"; "Publishers Should Protect the Public"; "Punish the Fakirs"; and "The Middle Course."

60. See, for example, "Creelman on the School." See also "University Training"; and "Joseph Bryan on Journalism."

61. Hamilton Holt, *Commercialism and Journalism*; "Henry Watterson, 'Good Judge and Master of Style.'"

62. Josiah Strong, *The New Era; or, The Coming Kingdom*, 353; "Agencies of the Church," 8.

63. George E. Vincent, "The Press and the People," 12.

64. "Journalists Meet at Madison to Discuss Questions of Timely Interest; Accuracy and Impartiality of Associated Press Reports Indispensable to Its Success, Says Melville E. Stone—Dr. George H. Vincent against Municipally Owned Newspapers—Socialist Gives His Views."

65. Other investigations included William Kittle's series "The Making of Public Opinion" in 1909 in *La Follette's*, articles in *Pearson's Magazine* by Charles Edward Russell that exposed how advertisers influenced the news, and George French's articles on the "masters of the magazines" in *Twentieth Century.*

66. "That Newspaper Conference: Professor Ross Says It Was So Successful Another Will Be Held at Madison in 1913," 12; "Have We a Free Press? This Question Will Be Faced by Newspaper and Magazine Writers at a Conference Arranged by the Extension Division of the University of Wisconsin," 7.

67. Vincent, "Press and the People," 13; *Marsh v. Alabama*, 326 US 501 (1946).

68. Nelson Crawford, *The Ethics of Journalism*, 34.

69. "A Public Servant: The Newspaper Thus Characterized by Dean Williams—'He Serves His Newspaper Best Who Serves His Community Best'—Peculiar Responsibility Rests upon Journalism."

70. See, for example, Leon Nelson Flint, *The Conscience of the Newspaper: A Case Book in the Principles and Problems of Journalism*, 264–65. See also "Clean Journalism: Subject of Simultaneous Address in Ninety-Seven Cities and Towns; Beginning of Wide Movement to Be Conducted under the Auspices of the Christian Science Publishing Co.—News Policy of Clean Journalism Must Be Established through Evolution," 3. The editorial asserted, "It is patent that every editor should uphold the dignity of the press and maintain inviolate the true mission of the newspaper as a public servant in order to make journalism a growing power for good." "The Scripps-McRae Formula," 12. H. N. Rickey, editorial director of the Scripps-McRae League of Newspapers, declared, "The counting room devil is a most persistently tempting devil. To the extent that his blandishments are resisted; to the extent that every question of policy in every department is finally subjected to the acid test of the editorial conscience, to that extent does a newspaper justify its existence as a public servant." Merle Harrold Thorpe, *The Coming Newspaper*, 280. In one chapter, Marco Morrow, the assistant publisher of Capper Publications, argued, "The newspaper is in reality a public service institution, a public utility privately operated." "A Business Man's Opinion of the Press." The businessman observed, "The newspaper is not a free lance as the reading public seems to think, but rather a public servant supported by private enterprises which it also serves."

71. Albert J. Beveridge, "The Journalist as Public Man: How Self Interest Injures the People's Interests," 23; Negley Cochran to B. H. Canfield, July 20, 1909, MSS Coll. 34, Negley D. Cochran Collection, box 1, folder 38, N. D. Cochran

Papers, Toledo-Lucas County Public Library, Ohio; "Dailies Condemned," *New York Times*, January 7, 1911, 1.

72. See, for example, Doris Kearns Goodwin, *The Bully Pulpit: Theodore Roosevelt, William Howard Taft, and the Golden Age of Journalism*.

73. Bleyer quoted in "Condemns Colored News: Prof. Bleyer Compares It with the Adulterated Food Evil"; Williams quoted in "Public Servant," 6; Bowles, "Independent Press," 46; American Society of Newspaper Editors, *Problems of Journalism*, 156.

74. Flint, *Conscience of the Newspaper*, 264–65.

75. "Discusses Newspapers," *Topeka State Journal*, March 12, 1900, 6.

76. "Sunday Religion."

77. "The Sunday Newspaper," *Washington Post*, May 19, 1889, 4.

78. Gladden, "More about the Secular Press," 7; Gladden, *Recollections*, 238; Livy S. Richard, "Publicity and Public Welfare as It Relates to Journalism," 19.

79. Julia Tolman Lee, *The Spirit of Service: Seven Lessons on Christian Stewardship for Class and Discussion Groups*, 5; Clifford L. Barrett, "A New Era of Prayer."

80. Ralph Waldo Emerson and Joel Porte, *Emerson in His Journals* (Cambridge, MA: Belknap Press of Harvard University Press, 1982), 153.

81. Crawford, *The Ethics of Journalism*, 34.

82. "A Declaration of Principles Adopted by the Religious Education Association," 52–53.

83. Joan Cocks, *The Oppositional Imagination: Feminism, Critique and Political Theory*, 103.

84. Robert W. McChesney, "Freedom of the Press for Whom? The Question to Be Answered in Our Critical Juncture," 1434. McChesney notes, "This notion of critical junctures is increasingly accepted in history and the social sciences, and it is has proven especially useful for communication. Most of our major institutions in media are the result of critical junctures, periods when policies could have gone in other directions, and, had they done so, put media and society on a different path." See also Robert W. McChesney, *Communication Revolution: Critical Junctures and the Future of Media*.

85. William Shakespeare, *A Midsummer Night's Dream*, act 5, scene 1, in *Shakespeare: Twenty-Three Plays and the Sonnets*, edited by Thomas Marc Parrott (New York: Charles Scribner's Sons, 1938), 157.

Chapter 1. Six Apostles of the Reformation of Newspapers

1. See, for example, John William Mears, "Position of the Secular Press on Moral Questions," *Independent*, July 29, 1880, 3. Reverend Mears argued that the function of the newspaper was "leading public opinion to positions in advance of those now held."

2. Justin Wroe Nixon, "The Status and Prospects of the Social Gospel," 351.

3. Maurice C. Latta, "The Background for the Social Gospel in American Protestantism," 269; Gladden, *Recollections*, 43–44.

4. Lyman Abbott, *Reminiscences*, 392.

5. Abbott, *Rights of Man*, 329; Lyman Abbott, *The Spirit of Democracy*, 104.

6. George P. Morris, "Religious Journalism and Journalists," 425.

7. William H. Brackney, *Baptists in North America: An Historical Perspective*, 102.

8. Ira V. Brown, *Lyman Abbott, Christian Evolutionist: A Study in Religious Liberalism*, 100–102; Susan Curtis, *A Consuming Faith: The Social Gospel and Modern American Culture*, 152; "The Social Order," 333.

9. Abbott, *Reminiscences*, 326.

10. Robert R. Roberts, "The Social Gospel and the Trust-Busters."

11. Theodore Roosevelt, "American Journalism for Which the *Outlook* Stands," 9.

12. Abbott, *Reminiscences*, 335; Mott, *History of American Magazines*, 435.

13. Abbott, *Reminiscences*, 335.

14. Mott, *History of American Magazines*, 428.

15. Abbott, *Reminiscences*, 335–36.

16. Mott, *History of American Magazines*, 430.

17. Abbott, *Reminiscences*, 336–37.

18. Lyman Abbott, "Democracy throughout the World," 1026.

19. Lyman Abbott, *America in the Making*, 25–26.

20. Quoted in I. Brown, *Lyman Abbott*, 191.

21. Quoted in ibid., 183; "A Frenzied Financial Critic." See as commentary on the *Outlook*'s article "Sensible Estimate of Lawson's Publicity Campaign," *Journal of Insurance Economics* 12, no. 2 (1904): 61.

22. Norman Hapgood, *The Changing Years: Reminiscences of Norman Hapgood*, 171; Horwill, "W. T. Stead."

23. Abbott, *Rights of Man*, 295–96.

24. Willis J. Abbot, *Watching the World Go By*, 138–39.

25. Abbott, *Rights of Man*, 295–97.

26. Ibid., 292, 329.

27. Lyman Abbott, *Christianity and Social Problems*, 361, 180–81, 361–62.

28. Hopkins, *Rise of the Social Gospel Movement*, 27.

29. Washington Gladden, "Christian Journalism," 80.

30. Gladden, "More about the Secular Press," 7.

31. Ibid.

32. Ibid.; Gladden, *Recollections*, 164.

33. Washington Gladden, "Tainted Newspapers, Good and Bad: Address Delivered at Kansas Newspaper Week under the Auspices of the Department of Journalism, University of Kansas, May 10 to 14, 1914," 2–4.

34. Gladden, *Recollections*, 43–44.

35. Gladden, "Tainted Newspapers," 2–4.
36. Gladden, *Recollections*, 272–73.
37. Jacob Henry Dorn, *Washington Gladden: Prophet of the Social Gospel*, 53.
38. Gladden, *Recollections*, 232.
39. Robert T. Handy, ed., *The Social Gospel in America, 1870–1920*, 22–23.
40. Gladden, *Recollections*, 235, 238.
41. Ibid., 232–37.
42. Washington Gladden, *Tools and the Man: Property and Industry under the Christian Law*, 116.
43. Gladden, *Recollections*, 238.
44. Ibid., 211–12.
45. Washington Gladden, *Applied Christianity: Moral Aspects of Social Questions*, 100, 146–48.
46. Gladden, "Tainted Newspapers," 6.
47. "The Social Order," 332.
48. Dorothea R. Muller, "The Social Philosophy of Josiah Strong: Social Christianity and American Progressivism," 183.
49. Walter Lippmann, *A Preface to Morals*, 51–65; J. Strong, *New Era*, 210.
50. Josiah Strong, "An Instructive Experience," 37–38.
51. Muller, "Social Philosophy of Josiah Strong," 183.
52. Josiah Strong, *Our World: The New World-Life*, 77.
53. See, for example, Josiah Strong, *The Times and Young Men*, 230. Strong argued, "Many of the present-day evils are due to bringing the old individualistic spirit over into the new social conditions. The motto of that spirit was 'Every man for himself.' Every angel for himself would ruin heaven. The normal spirit of the new social civilization would express itself in the motto, Each for all and all for each; and this new altruism is inspired by that spirit of service and sacrifice."
54. J. Strong, *New Era*, 280–81.
55. Muller, "Social Philosophy of Josiah Strong," 189; J. Strong, *Our World*, 53.
56. J. Strong, *New Era*, 12.
57. Quoted in Muller, "Social Philosophy of Josiah Strong," 189–90.
58. Roberts, "Social Gospel and the Trust-Busters," 243.
59. Frank Luther Mott, *Golden Multitudes*, 8.
60. Josiah Strong, *Our Country: Its Possible Future and Its Present Crisis*, 69.
61. Josiah Strong, *The Challenge of the City*, 36.
62. Josiah Strong, *Expansion under New World-Conditions*, 225. See also Josiah Strong, "The Increasing Oneness of the World." Strong wrote, "The press is producing an international climate of opinion. Millions now read the same printed page and think the same thoughts under different skies. Science is every day removing something from the domain of opinion (and therefore of

strife) to that of actual knowledge; and every such addition to recognized truth enlarges the common ground where all men may stand."

63. Josiah Strong, "The Present Tendency to World Unity," *Herald of Gospel Liberty*, July 30, 1903, 493; Tocqueville, *Democracy in America*, 600; J. Strong, "Present Tendency to World Unity," 493.

64. Josiah Strong, "Methods of Promoting Arbitration," 212. See also George Washington, *Washington's Farewell Address*, 17. "It is substantially true, that virtue or morality is a necessary spring of popular government. The rule, indeed, extends, with more or less force, to every species of free government. Who, that is a sincere friend to it, can look with indifference upon attempts to shake the foundation of the fabric? Promote, then, as an object of primary importance, institutions for the general diffusion of knowledge. In proportion as the structure of a government gives force to public opinion, it is essential that public opinion should be enlightened."

65. J. Strong, *New Era*, 308.

66. J. Strong, *Our World*, 4.

67. J. Strong, *New Era*, 210, 310.

68. Gladden, "More about the Secular Press," 7; Josiah Strong, *The Twentieth Century City*, 169–70.

69. Benjamin G. Rader, "Richard T. Ely: The Lay Spokesman for the Social Gospel," 73.

70. Abbott, *Reminiscences*, 392; Richard T. Ely, *The Social Law of Service*, 125–40; Richard T. Ely, "Christianity as a Social Force," 552.

71. Fred C. Kelly, "A College Professor with Punch."

72. J. David Hoeveler Jr., "The University and the Social Gospel: The Intellectual Origins of the 'Wisconsin Idea.'"

73. Kelly, "College Professor with Punch," 61.

74. Richard T. Ely, *The Labor Movement in America*, 311–12.

75. Richard T. Ely, *Report of the Organization of the American Economic Association*, 10–11.

76. Richard T. Ely, *An Introduction to Political Economy*, 233.

77. Ely, *Labor Movement in America*, 50, 159, 313–14.

78. Richard T. Ely, "Public Control of Private Corporations," 432–33. See also Richard T. Ely, *Problems of Today: A Discussion of Protective Tariffs, Taxation, and Monopolies*, 138. In a discussion about the resistance to public works projects, Ely charged that "so many of our great newspapers are completely under the control of corporations."

79. Ely, *Introduction to Political Economy*, 257.

80. Richard T. Ely, *Social Aspects of Christianity, and Other Essays*, 76.

81. Ely, *Problems of Today*, 281; Richard T. Ely, "Socialism and the General Welfare," *Independent*, April 23, 1891, 13.

82. Ely, *Labor Movement in America*, 314.

83. Richard T. Ely, *Studies in the Evolution of Industrial Society*, 85.

84. John A. Patten, "The Contribution of the Church to Social Uplifting," 174–75.

85. See, for example, "Magazine Dinner: Periodical Publishers Hear Sensational Speech by Bishop Williams; He Said That 'Big Interests' Control the Daily Press—Francis J. Heney Also Denounced the Newspapers—Colonel Roosevelt Spoke a Kind Word for the Dailies, but Said the Magazines 'Have a Greater Influence in Shaping Public Opinion,'" 1, 4. Williams's speech was reported in all the New York dailies as a leading news item, and reports on his speech were sent out across the country through all the telegraphic news associations.

86. Clyde K. Hyder, "The Press and Public Service," 6.

87. Frank M. Chase, "Charles M. Sheldon, Author, Preacher, Editor," *Dearborn (MI) Independent*, February 4, 1922, 13.

88. Ibid.

89. Charles M. Sheldon, "Some Opportunities before the Church of Today."

90. Charles M. Sheldon, *Charles M. Sheldon: His Life Story*, 81–82.

91. Charles M. Sheldon, *The First Christian Daily Paper, and Other Sketches*, 25.

92. Charles M. Sheldon, *In His Steps: "What Would Jesus Do?,"* 153–55.

93. For a detailed description of the invitation, see George Ellery Crosby Jr., "The Sheldon Experiment." See also Herbert S. Houston, "Truth Drive Began in the Early Days: Past President of AFA Recalls the Notable Sheldon Experiment When *Topeka Capital* Was Edited 'As Jesus Would Have Done It,'" 15. Houston, a past president of the Advertising Federation of America and the former general manager of the Sheldon Edition, recalled that Sheldon "electrified the eager throngs with the proposal that what the world needed to guide people to spiritual living was a newspaper, conducted as Jesus would have conducted it."

94. Mott, *American Journalism*, 575–76.

95. Charles M. Sheldon, "The Modern Newspaper," *Independent*, July 25, 1912, 196.

96. Charles M. Sheldon, "Symposium: Giving the Public What It Wants," 233–34.

97. "American Congregational Theology," 256.

98. Hopkins, *Rise of the Social Gospel Movement*, 60; Brackney, *Baptists in North America*, 102.

99. See, for example, all by Walter Rauschenbusch: *Christianity and the Social Crisis*, 261, 302, 328; *For God and the People: Prayers of the Social Awakening*, 78–80; *Christianizing the Social Order*, 31, 282, 284–86, 359, 432; *Theology for the Social Gospel*, 49, 247; *The Social Principles of Jesus*, 161, 178; and *The Righteousness of the Kingdom*, 170, 249.

100. Rauschenbusch, *Christianity and the Social Crisis*, 302.

101. Rauschenbusch, *Christianizing the Social Order*, 284, 220.

102. Patrick W. Carey and Joseph T. Lienhard, *Biographical Dictionary of Christian Theologians*, 433.

103. Rauschenbusch, *Theology for the Social Gospel*, 49.

104. Rauschenbusch, *Christianizing the Social Order*, 317–18.

105. Ibid., 284.

106. Hopkins, *Rise of the Social Gospel Movement*, 222.

107. Rauschenbusch, *Social Principles of Jesus*, 177.

108. Nixon, "Status and Prospects," 356.

109. Rauschenbusch, *Christianity and the Social Crisis*, 260–61.

110. Rauschenbusch, *Christianizing the Social Order*, 284–85. See also Rauschenbusch, *Social Principles of Jesus*, 160, 276, 284–85.

111. Rauschenbusch, *Christianity and the Social Crisis*, 260, 302, 362.

112. Rauschenbusch, *Christianizing the Social Order*, 282.

113. Quoted in Dores Robinson Sharpe, *Walter Rauschenbusch*, 89–90.

114. Rauschenbusch, *For God and the People*, 78–80. Below is the entire text of the prayer:

> O Thou great source of truth and knowledge, we remember before thee all whose calling it is to gather and winnow the facts for informing the people. Inspire them with a determined love for honest work and a stanch hatred for the making of lies, lest the judgments of our nation be perverted and we be taught to call light darkness and darkness light. Since the sanity and wisdom of a nation are in their charge, may they count it shame to set the baser passions of men on fire for the sake of gain. May they never suffer themselves to be used in drugging the mind of the people with falsehood and prejudice.
>
> Grant them boldness to turn the unwelcome light on those who love the darkness because their deeds are evil. Put into their hands the shining sword of truth, and make them worthy successors of the great champions of the people who held truth to be a holy thing by which nations live and for which men should die. Cause them to realize that they have a public function in the commonwealth, and that their country may be saved by their courage or undone by their cowardice and silence. Grant them the heart of manhood to cast their mighty influence with the forces that make the people strong and free, and if they suffer loss, may they rejoice in that as proof to their own souls that they have fought a good fight and have been servants of the higher law.

Chapter 2. The Sunday Newspaper and the Modern World

1. Ellcee, "Sunday Newspapers," 197–98. Ellcee—also known as Ellcee of Craven Yorkshire—was an antiquary correspondent for *Notes and Queries*, Victorian England's version of Wikipedia.

2. "Presbyter's Appeal to His Brethren the Clergy, on Some of the Prevailing Iniquities of the Times, with Suggestions for Their Suppression," 397.

3. John Poynder, *Observations upon Sunday Newspapers: Tending to Shew the Impiety of Such a Violation of the Sabbath, the Religious and Political Evils Consequent upon the Practice, and the Necessity Which Exists for Its Suppression*, 1, 94–95, 52; John Charlton, "The Sunday Newspaper."

4. Rider, "The Pretensions of Journalism," 479.

5. Church Congress in the United States and Episcopal Church, *Authorized Report of the Proceedings of the Congress of the Protestant Episcopal Church in the United States*, 83.

6. Alexander MacKay Smith, "The Clergy and the Times."

7. John P. Ferré, "Sunday Newspapers and the Decline of Protestant Authority in the United States," 8; Jeffery Smith, "Sunday Newspapers and Lived Religion in Late Nineteenth-Century America," 151.

8. Whitelaw Reid, "Recent Changes in the Press," 2:300; Pamela Shoemaker, "Hard-Wired for News: Using Biological and Cultural Evolution to Explain the News"; "London Awaited the News; Crowds Up All Night to Hear Details of the Disaster," *New York Times*, April 19, 1912, 8; Max O'Rell, "Lively Journalism," 366; Jürgen Habermas, *The Structural Transformation of the Public Sphere: An Inquiry into a Category of Bourgeois Society*, 51.

9. Benjamin St. James Fry, "Religious Journalism."

10. Rider, "The Pretensions of Journalism," 480.

11. Herrick Johnson, "Sunday Newspapers," 116.

12. Gladden, "More about the Secular Press," 7.

13. "Influence of Sunday Newspapers."

14. Frank Foxcroft, "The American Sunday Newspaper," 259, 261.

15. Raymond Williams, *Communications*, 22.

16. For an excellent brief summary of these improvements, see Charles Johanningsmeier, *Fiction and the American Literary Marketplace: The Role of Newspaper Syndicates in America, 1860–1900*, 19–26.

17. Baldasty, *Commercialization of News*, 122; "A Religious Boycott: The City Pastors Declare War upon the Sunday Newspapers," *St. Paul Daily Globe*, March 9, 1886, 8; Robert Donald, "Sunday Newspapers in the United States," 78, 80.

18. William Rayner, "Sunday Newspapers," 121–23.

19. Hudson, *Journalism in the United States*, 337.

20. S. North, *History and Present Condition of the Newspaper and Periodical Press*, 124–25; Wayne Edison Fuller, *Morality and the Mail in Nineteenth-Century America*, 78–79.

21. Rollo Ogden, "Americanizing the English Press," 371.

22. Fuller, *Morality and the Mail*, 78–79.

23. J. Cutler Andrews, *The North Reports the Civil War*, 33–34.

24. Schudson, *Discovering the News*; Donald, "Sunday Newspapers in the United States," 78; Schudson, *Discovering the News.*

25. Wilbur F. Crafts, *The Sabbath for Man: A Study of the Origin, Obligation, History, Advantages and Present State of Sabbath Observance, with Special Reference to the Rights of Workingmen, Based on Scripture, Literature, and Especially on a Symposium of Correspondence with Persons of All Nations and Denominations*, 335; Charles Augustus Stoddard and Edgar Whitaker Work, "Old Memories Revived in the Fourth Church: Anniversary Addresses," *New York Observer*, October 13, 1910, 456.

26. Fuller, *Morality and the Mail*, 79.

27. Alfred McClung Lee, *The Daily Newspaper in America, 1690–1940*, 1:68.

28. Schudson, *Discovering the News.*

29. Fuller, *Morality and the Mail*, 79.

30. Alexis McCrossen, *Holy Day, Holiday: The American Sunday.*

31. "Newspapers Fifty Years Ago," *New York Times*, October 20, 1901, A6.

32. Church Congress in the United States and Episcopal Church, *Authorized Report*, 80.

33. Ibid., 78–80.

34. James Freeman Clarke, "Rational Sunday Observance," 496; J. Smith, "Sunday Newspapers and Lived Religion," 129; John S. Gilkeson Jr., "The Rise and Decline of the 'Puritan Sunday' in Providence, Rhode Island, 1810–1926," 75–76.

35. Ralph Waldo Emerson, *The Works of Ralph Waldo Emerson: Society and Solitude* (Boston: Houghton Mifflin, 1883), 62.

36. Ralph Waldo Emerson, *The Works of Ralph Waldo Emerson* (London: George Bell and Sons, 1904), 431.

37. Church Congress in the United States and Episcopal Church, *Authorized Report*, 78; Joseph Cook, *Vital Orthodoxy: With an Index and Analysis of Contents, and a Symposium on the Christian Soteriology; or, The Question, "What Saves Men, and Why?,"* 137; Alexander MacKay Smith, *The Sunday Newspaper: An Address Delivered before the Church Club of Philadelphia on the Evening of February 26, 1906*, 7; Tucker quoted in Crafts, *Sabbath for Man*, 333.

38. *Missionary Survey* 2, no. 10 (1913): 803.

39. A. Smith, "Clergy and the Times," 207.

40. Avery Dulles, "Religion and the News Media: A Theologian Reflects"; David James Burrell, "Wanted: A Newspaper," 185–86.

41. "The Sunday Question."

42. Charles B. Tayler, *Katherine*, 89, 100.

43. See, for example, Sheldon, *In His Steps*, 155. In chapter 17 of *In His Steps*, the character of Edward Norman writes down eleven rules of conduct to follow in running a newspaper as Jesus would. Number eight on that list was "Jesus would not issue a Sunday edition."

44. John B. Thompson, *The Media and Modernity: A Social Theory of the Media*, 183.

45. John B. Thompson, *Ideology and Modern Culture: Critical Social Theory in the Era of Mass Communication*, 244.

46. See, for example, "Religious Boycott," 8. In 1886 a pastors association in Minneapolis voted nearly unanimously to boycott the Sunday press and to persuade parishioners to do likewise. They pointed to the fact that many readers of the Sunday papers never go to church or give any note to the spiritual part of life, as "Sunday sinks to the common level."

47. "Presbyterians Condemn the Sunday Newspaper," 24.

48. See, for example, A. Smith, *Sunday Newspaper*, 1–12. Alexander Mackay Smith, the archdeacon of New York, in a published sermon on the Sunday newspaper said: "Our accusation against the Sunday paper is that it symbolizes, embodies, multiplies, and encourages all the influences which are crushing out the national rest-day, and stunting the higher development of men," for it was the day of rest that allowed men to "change the current of groveling, materialistic, bestializing weekday thought" and "give the soul a chance to say whether it exists."

49. See, for example, Howard Crosby, "One of Satan's Engines," *New York Times*, November 15, 1885, 2. The Reverend Howard Crosby, a Presbyterian preacher, scholar, and professor, wrote a pastoral letter to the members of the Fourth Avenue Presbyterian Church, warning them of the evils of the "insidiously seductive" Sunday newspaper, a powerful engine employed by Satan that "nullifies all the sacred influences of the Lord's Day." The papers, he cautioned, fill the mind "with thoughts on business, politics, games, theatres, and crimes, (which form the staple of newspaper literature,) at a time when the Lord calls us especially to consider the things that belong to our higher spiritual welfare."

50. See, for example, "The Modern Sunday." The editorial lamented, "It is a cause for regret that so large a portion of the press is engaged in breaking down the observance of Sunday as a religious holy day. Probably nothing has done more to secularize Sunday than the publication of Sunday newspapers. They keep people from church, and thus from the public worship of God, and the services of religion, by offering them agreeable reading matter, the news of the day, and in some cases, coarse wit broadly illustrated with colored cartoons."

51. See, for example, Orlando John Hodge, *Reminiscences*, 142. Hodge noted that "there is no more preaching against Sunday papers, and yet more men stay at home on the Sabbath to read their papers than go to church."

52. See, for example, Presbyterian Church in the U.S.A., *Minutes of the General Assembly of the Presbyterian Church in the United States of America*, 3:22.

53. See, for example, Samuel Wix, "On the Sunday Press," 633. Wix wrote, "It is sad, indeed, at present, to witness, in walking the streets of our metropolis on Sunday, a profusion of political and religious poison, vended at the cheapest

rate, alluring the unemployed, desecrating our Sabbath, corrupting the minds of the rising generation, and plunging multitudes into sedition and every species of political debauchery: multitudes, on the only day that they can have either to receive the contagion of false politics and corrupted principles, or for the happy impressions to be found from religious meditation and instruction."

54. Samuel W. Boardman, "The Sunday Newspaper Condemned," *New York Times*, July 13, 1902, 8.

55. William Shakespeare, *A Midsummer Night's Dream*, act 5, scene 1, in *Shakespeare: Twenty-Three Plays and the Sonnets*, edited by Thomas Marc Parrott (New York: Charles Scribner's Sons, 1938), 157.

56. "The Sunday Newspaper," *Washington Post*, January 5, 1889, 4.

57. "Sunday Religion."

58. "The Sunday Newspaper," *Washington Post*, June 2, 1889, 4.

59. "The Sunday Newspaper," *Washington Post*, January 5, 1888, 4.

60. "The Sunday Newspaper," *Washington Post*, May 19, 1889, 4.

61. "The Sunday Newspaper," *Washington Post*, January 5, 1889, 4.

62. "Sunday Religion."

63. See, for example, "Pulpit and Press to Join," *New York Times*, June 18, 1888, 8. The Reverend Thomas De Witt Talmage wrote, "The fact is, the modern Sunday newspaper is a great improvement on the old Sunday newspaper. What a beastly thing was the Sunday newspaper 30 years ago!"

64. S. North, *History and Present Condition of the Newspaper and Periodical Press*, 124–25.

65. "The Sunday Newspaper," *Washington Post*, February 10, 1889, 4.

66. Ogden, "Americanizing the English Press."

67. "Note and Comment."

68. "Sunday Newspapers," 894–95.

69. Reid, "Recent Changes in the Press," 2:300.

70. Sandra Gabriele and Paul Moore, "The *Globe* on Saturday, the *World* on Sunday: Toronto Weekend Editions and the Influence of the American Sunday Paper, 1886–1895," 342, 344; Anthony Giddens, *The Consequences of Modernity*, 1.

71. "Religious Boycott," 8.

72. Lesslie Newbigin, *Truth and Authority in Modernity*, 11.

73. Johnson, "Sunday Newspapers," 116; Alan Trachtenberg, *The Incorporation of America: Culture and Society in the Gilded Age*, 124.

74. "Influence of Sunday Newspapers."

75. Boardman, "The Sunday Newspaper Condemned," 8.

76. Georg Simmel, "Metropolis and Mental Life," 18. Simmel contended:

> The eighteenth century found the individual in the grip of powerful bonds which had become meaningless—bonds of a political, agrarian, guild and

religious nature—delimitations which imposed upon the human being at the same time an unnatural form and for a long time an unjust inequality. In this situation arose the cry for freedom and equality—the belief in the full freedom of movement of the individual in all his social and intellectual relationships which would then permit the same noble essence to emerge equally from all individuals as Nature had placed it in them and as it had been distorted by social life and historical development.

77. Immanuel Kant, "An Answer to the Question: What Is Enlightenment," 58; Arthur M. Schlesinger, *Viewpoints in American History*, 246.

78. Charles Worcester Clark, "The Day of Rest."

79. Francis R. Beattie, "Christian Ethics and Modern Life," 413; Oscar Wilde, *De Profundis*, 31.

80. Addams, *Democracy and Social Ethics*, 9–11.

81. Church Congress in the United States and Episcopal Church, *Authorized Report*, 76. See also Julian Proctor, "The Future of Newspapers," 122.

82. Quoted in "Two Views of the Sunday Newspaper."

83. Julius H. Ward, "The Future of Sunday Journalism," 395, 389–90.

84. Thompson, *Media and Modernity*, 183; Charles Tilly, *Big Structures, Large Processes, Huge Comparisons*, 21.

85. Theodore E. Schmauk, "The Sunday Newspaper."

86. Johnson, "Sunday Newspapers," 117.

87. John Patrick Diggins, *Pragmatism: Modernism and the Crisis of Knowledge and Authority*, 189.

88. "Presbyter's Appeal to His Brethren," 400–401.

Chapter 3. The Press, the Pulpit, and Public Opinion

1. "Rev. C. W. Casson to Leave City," *Ottawa Citizen*, October 14, 1907, 3.

2. "The Truth Will Prevail."

3. Indeed, a Boolean search of most any digital research database will reveal numerous references to the pairing.

4. See, for example, John Arnold Schmalzbauer, *People of Faith: Religious Conviction in American Journalism and Higher Education*, 7–9. See also Eckman, "Pulpit and Press." Eckman, pastor of St. Paul's Methodist Episcopal Church in New York, argued, "The most influential literary product of our day is the newspaper, and whoever pronounces impartial judgment upon its moral quality must acknowledge that, with some notorious and flagrant exceptions which will diminish in number as society rises in dignity, newspapers are to be reckoned among the most potent forces making for righteousness in modern times." Robert Stuart MacArthur, "Press and Pulpit: Allies in All That Is Noblest in Civilization and Divinest in Humanity; Ideal of Each Is Best Attained When Both Join Hands in Interest of Humanity and Religion," 18. MacArthur,

pastor of Calvary Baptist Church in New York City, argued that the press was an ally with the church and was a "force for righteousness." "Newspaper His Text: Connecticut Clergyman Says That They Are an Ally of Religion." The Reverend Albert C. Dieffenbach declared in a sermon that newspapers, "if well regulated," were "an ally of religion." "Printed Word Has Only Started Divine Mission." "Spirit and Purpose of the Ideal Newspaper as Visualized by George Booth: President of *Detroit News*, in Address at University of Michigan, Makes Impressive Appraisal of Comparative Value of Material and Spiritual Factors in Newspaper Making—Sees Pendulum of the 'Clock of the World' Swinging with Resistless Force toward Brotherhood of Man"; "Newspaper Praised: Chicago Divine Declares Press Is the Latter-Day Autocrat." The Reverend Joseph A. Milburn said the press was more powerful than either the clergy or the legislative bodies. It should not be called the Fourth Estate, he said, but the "Latter-Day Autocrat" as the "distributor of light."

5. Charles Ellwood, "The Formation of Public Opinion: The Principles in Accordance with Which Public Opinion Can Be Formed by the Church Democratically and Effectively," 75; "Newspaper Morality"; James B. Wasson, "The Editor as a Preacher," 7.

6. Shailer Mathews and Gerald Birney Smith, eds., *A Dictionary of Religion and Ethics*, 342. Smith was a professor of Christian theology at the University of Chicago, and Mathews was the dean of the Divinity School at the University of Chicago and one of "the midwives" to the birth of the Social Gospel.

7. Harold Holzer, *Lincoln and the Power of the Press: The War for Public Opinion.*

8. *Political Debates between Abraham Lincoln and Stephen A. Douglas*, 101; Robert M. Polhemus, *The Changing World of Anthony Trollope*, 147; Anthony Trollope, *The Writings of Anthony Trollope*, 290.

9. L. J. Swingle, *Romanticism and Anthony Trollope: A Study in the Continuities of Nineteenth-Century Literary Thought*, 232.

10. John R. Creighton, "Press, Pulpit and Pew," 68–69; Edmund McClure, "The Church and the Press," 509–10.

11. See, for example, Bushnell, *Views of Christian Nurture*, 120–21. Bushnell, an American Congregational clergyman and theologian, observed as early as 1847, "There is no instrument of power, in this age, as we are just beginning to discover, that can be compared with a newspaper." See also George Hodges, *Faith and Social Service: Eight Lectures Delivered before the Lowell Institute*, 32–33. Hodges, a clergyman and dean of the Episcopal Theological School in Cambridge, Massachusetts, in a series of lectures in 1896 before the Lowell Institute, observed that the newspaper was "the people's book." It was affordable and spoke the language of the people, and it was the venue through which the public questions of the day were reported and discussed. Indeed, Hodges drew a parallel between the "great awakening" of the sixteenth century and

the enlightenment and empowerment of the masses in the nineteenth century. Frank Taylor, *The Newspaper Press as a Power in Both the Expression and Formation of Public Opinion*, 10. Taylor wrote, "A sermon, if it is to echo far beyond the walls of a church, must be reproduced in the papers. Quite apart from any original efforts of its own, the press is always in a position to increase or to diminish enormously the effects of other forces." Charles William Eliot, *American Contributions to Civilization, and Other Essays and Addresses*, 308. Eliot, the president of Harvard, contended, "The press has enlarged the public influence of the pulpit by adding the multitude who read the printed sermon to the congregation who listen to it." Robert Collyer, "Newspapers and Modern Life," in *The World's Best Essays from the Earliest Period to the Present Time*, edited by David J. Brewer (St. Louis: Ferd P. Kaiser, 1900), 3:1104. The Reverend Collyer observed that "the newspaper has come to be beyond all doubt more popular and more widely read in this country than the Bible."

12. Gladden, "Tainted Newspapers," 4–6.

13. See, for example, Washington Gladden, *The Christian Pastor and the Working Church*, 433. Gladden extolled the virtues of public opinion to mete out change. In advising churches to regularly hold interfaith community conferences on singular topics, he observed that a product of these conferences—the religious or social conditions of the community—would be news that any "enterprising" newspaper would be glad to print. "The conference would thus assist in enlightening the whole community respecting its own social needs, and could be an effective means of creating an intelligent and wholesome public opinion."

14. Edwin L. Earp, "Discussion," 689.

15. Washington Gladden, *Ruling Ideas of the Present Age*, 210, 199–200. See also Washington Gladden, *The Church and Modern Life*, 213. Gladden believed that the "cynical dishonesties and the brutal spoliations" of high finance and big business so much in the news in the early 1900s would not have existed if so many people did not admire them. Too often, he lamented, the protestations against them had more to do with envy than disgust. "The cure for this evil, as of most others, is found in public opinion; and the church must educate public opinion to reprove it."

16. Ellwood, "Formation of Public Opinion," 73; Gladden, *Ruling Ideas of the Present Age*, 204–7; Ellwood, "Formation of Public Opinion," 75.

17. Hopkins, *Rise of the Social Gospel Movement*, 3; Bruce J. Evensen, "The Evangelical Origins of Muckraking," 188; Hofstadter, *Age of Reform*, 202.

18. "Report of the Sub-Committee on a Department of Religious Publicity."

19. See, for example, "Prays for the Press: Chaplain in Connecticut Senate Asks for Guidance for Newspapers," 2. Chaplain J. F. Sexton offered the following prayer for the press:

> Almighty and gracious God, who has favored our land by causing knowledge to run to and fro, we beseech Thee to strengthen our public press in all things that tend to the enlightenment and betterment of the people. Save our public journals from low standards touching morals and government. Deliver them from sensationalism, untruthfulness, malice, dishonest political measures, personal attacks and the parade of the details of crime and vice. Make them the instruments of good and the defenders of justice, mercy and truth. May they respect morality and honor religion, so that wisdom and knowledge may become the stability of our times. Amen.

See also "The Public Press." In this essay, the press is described as "a mighty engine for good or for evil. . . . The blessings which it is calculated to produce are great, but the evils which inevitably ensue from its improper management are equally so." See "Magazine Dinner." Bishop Charles D. Williams of Detroit, the Protestant Episcopal bishop of Michigan, spoke at a banquet hosted by the Periodical Publishers' Association of America at the Waldorf Astoria Hotel in New York City. Williams told the assembled publishers, including several who oversaw newspapers, that the "daily press is under suspicion in the popular mind. It has come to be believed that big interests—corporate, financial or advertising—control the daily press. For that reason it is losing its influence in the public mind. The periodicals have won over the people." Williams's speech was reported in all the New York dailies as a leading news item, and reports on his speech were sent out across the country through all the telegraphic news associations. "Back to God's Law; Newspapers Must Return to Christ and the Ten Commandments; Bishop McFall Discourses on the Mission of the Press and Says High Moral Standard Is Required—Enumerates Defects of Newspapers and Suggests a Remedy—Four Rules for Guidance of Newspaper Men"; "Preachers Criticize." A roundup of commentary on the daily press included the Reverend Percy Stickney Grant, Episcopalian clergyman and rector of the Church of the Ascension of New York City, who delivered a sermon called "Newspapers and Crime." To make his point, he made use of a content analysis of three months' worth of stories in one of New York's leading dailies that classified stories with the following result: "Demoralizing, 2,285 items; unwholesome, 1,684; trivial, 2,100; worth while, 3,900, or 39 per cent." "Sermon on Newspapers." The Reverend Edwin A. Rumball, in a sermon titled "The Newspaper as an Ethical Force," said, "The first, greatest and perhaps only evil of the press is the power and tyranny of commercialism."

20. "News and Newspapers," 6.
21. "Education," 88.
22. Hudson, *Journalism in the United States*, 80–81.
23. Nord, "Teleology and News," 35.
24. Bleyer, *Main Currents*, 192.

25. "The *Herald*'s Place in Journalism."

26. Hudson, *Journalism in the United States*, 453–54.

27. James Melvin Lee, *History of American Journalism*, 196. For a further discussion about this, see John Ferré, "Protestant Press Relations in the United States, 1900–1930," 515.

28. Don Carlos Seitz, *The James Gordon Bennetts, Father and Son, Proprietors of the "New York Herald,"* 70.

29. Judith M. Buddenbaum, "'Judge . . . What Their Acts Will Justify': The Religion Journalism of James Gordon Bennett," 56.

30. Men and Religion Forward Movement, *The Church and the Press*, 26–27; "Report of the Sub-Committee on a Department of Religious Publicity," 155.

31. "Dignity of the Press." See also "The Press," *Poughkeepsie Casket*, July 30, 1836, 127. One writer asserted that a "fearful tendency" of the press "undermining the beautiful structure of morality and virtue in our land" was the "detailed publication of police reports" in the newspapers. "In these reports, the haunts of prostitution and infamy are unveiled to the eyes of virtue and innocence, and those, perhaps, who never heard or formed any conceptions of these receptacles of sensual degradation with which large cities abound."

32. Henry R. Elliot, "The Ratio of News."

33. Ibid., 99, 106, 99.

34. Edward Carleton, "The Power of the Press," 471.

35. William C. Skeath, *Building the Congregation: A Study of Appeals*, 22–23; Ferré, "Protestant Press Relations," 514–15.

36. Earp, "Discussion," 689; Madison Clinton Peters, *Sanctified Spice; or, Pungent Seasonings from the Pulpit*, 53; John William Mears, "Position of the Secular Press on Moral Questions."

37. Gladden, *Ruling Ideas of the Present Age*, 204–7.

38. W. Joseph Campbell, *The Year That Defined American Journalism: 1897 and the Clash of Paradigms*, 75–87.

39. Stead, "The Future of Journalism," 663–64; Norman Hapgood, "To *Harper's Weekly* Readers," *Independent*, May 22, 1916, 263.

40. Gladden, *Ruling Ideas of the Present Age*, 204–7; Mears, "Position of the Secular Press," 3.

41. Charles M. Sheldon, "The Modern Newspaper," *Independent*, July 25, 1912, 1961; "Asks Church to Aid Press: Dr. Williams Says Members Can Have Influence on Moral Tone of Newspapers"; Gladden, *Recollections*, 238; J. Smith, "Secular Press and Morality," 42.

42. Skeath, *Building the Congregation*, 22–23.

43. Walter Lippmann, *Drift and Mastery: An Attempt to Diagnose the Current Unrest*, 152–53. Lippmann observed, "We are unsettled to the very roots of our being. There isn't a human relation, whether of parent and child, husband and wife, worker and employer, that doesn't move in a strange situation.

We are not used to a complicated civilization, we don't know how to behave when personal contact and eternal authority have disappeared. There are no precedents to guide us, no wisdom that wasn't made for a simpler age. We have changed our environment more quickly than we know how to change ourselves." See also "David Graham Phillips." In this essay, Phillips, a journalist and novelist, argued, "Journalism in this country to-day has been raised to greater heights than ever before. The influence of print was never so pervasive. We have no Horace Greeley—which, as well as anything else, shows the advance. To deal with a complex subject like specie resumption by means of a striking epigram, or with the field movement of armies by dogmatic opinion formed in an armchair, would hardly answer journalism's best requirements nowadays. Those requirements can be answered only by dealing primarily with the facts."

44. See, for example, "Newspapers and War," an outline of William T. Stead's speech in which he lambasted "unscrupulous" newspapers that were attempting to incite a war in Europe. See also Sidney L. Gulick, *The Fight for Peace: An Aggressive Campaign for American Churches*. Gulick was the associate secretary of the Commission on Peace and Arbitration.

45. "Gaynor's Newspaper: New York's Mayor Gives His Ideas on How It Should Be Conducted; Declares That a Small Home Circulation Is Worth a Million in the Gutter—Dwells on the Importance of Truth in All Departments and Advocates Brevity and Simplicity of Statement."

46. See, for example, Mathews, *Validity of American Ideals*. Mathews was dean of the Divinity School at the University of Chicago. See also Philip Davis and Bertha Schwartz, *Immigration and Americanization: Selected Readings*; and "Encourage the Use of English." The latter is an editorial that supported a proposal that called for encouraging foreign-language newspapers to print at least part of their editions "in the language of the United States." It includes a discussion of the need to Americanize the nation's immigrant population.

47. Creighton, "Press, Pulpit and Pew," 68.

48. Herbert Heebner Smith, *Publicity and Progress: Twentieth Century Methods in Religious, Educational and Social Activities*, 15; Gladden, *Ruling Ideas of the Present Age*, 9; Walter J. Shepard, "Public Opinion," 47–48. See also "Greater New York," *Congregationalist and Christian World*, November 11, 1906, 681. In 1906 a church in Westchester, New York, published Saint Paul's Epistle to the Philippians in a newsletter with headlines like those of modern newspapers.

49. Joanna Dewey, "Textuality in an Oral Culture: A Survey of the Pauline Traditions."

50. Gilbert, "Christian Journalism," 275.

51. Nord, "Teleology and News," 13–14, 26, 10, 12, 37.

52. Doug Underwood, *From Yahweh to Yahoo! The Religious Roots of the Secular Press*, 19. See also Schmalzbauer, *People of Faith*, 7, 21. Schmalzbauer also

notes that "such providentialism gave way to literary realism and an emphasis on empirical facts."

53. Gladden, "More about the Secular Press," 7.

54. "Henry Ward Beecher," 862.

55. E. A. D., "Newspapers," 69.

56. John Bancroft Devins, "The New Journalism," *New York Observer and Chronicle*, June 28, 1900, 842.

57. Hugh Reginald Haweis, "The New Pulpit," 173.

58. Men and Religion Forward Movement, *Church and the Press*, 5.

59. "Literary Notices."

60. Matthew Simpson, *Lectures on Preaching Delivered to the Students of Yale College in 1879*, 176–77, 17; H. Smith, *Publicity and Progress*, 13–14, 16–17.

61. *Official Report of the Proceedings of the Thirteenth Meeting of the National Conference of Unitarian and Other Christian Churches*, 12.

62. Henry W. Grady, "The Opportunities of Journalism," 434.

63. Hodges, *Faith and Social Service*, 32–33.

64. Henry Steele Commager, *The American Mind: An Interpretation of American Thought and Character since the 1880s*, 49.

65. See, for example, Samuel H. Lee, "Men of Wealth and Institutions of Learning," 389. The Reverend Lee cited the assertion by newspaper industry critic Henry Holt that "while twenty-five years ago there was hardly a college-bred man in the publishing business, now there is hardly a publishing house that is not presided over by one."

66. For a further explication of this, see Hofstadter, *Age of Reform*, 185. See also Commager, *American Mind*, 189; and Henry Adams, *The Education of Henry Adams*, 237–38.

67. J. Strong, *New Era*, 308, 198–99, 308; William Payne Shriver, *Immigrant Forces: Factors in the New Democracy*, 226.

68. W. S. Lilly, "The Ethics of Journalism," 505. See, for example, Bradford, *My Brother*, 153. Bradford, pastor of the First Congregational Church of Montclair, New Jersey, wrote, "There are now but few parishes like those in which Jonathan Edwards and Nathaniel Emmons preached to the world from obscure pulpits. He who would influence many men, henceforward, must preach in cities, or have an exceptional opportunity to use the press." Diffendorfer, *Church and the Community*, 163. Diffendorfer asserted, "It goes without saying that the editorial columns, and especially the news sections of American newspapers, are among the greatest, if not the most potent, factors in forming public opinion. In a democracy, people feel that they have a right to the truth."

69. "Matthew H. Buckham: President of University of Vermont for Nearly Forty Years," *New York Times*, November 30, 1910, 11.

70. Matthew H. Buckham, "Lay Theology," 155–56. See also S. Lee, "Men of Wealth and Institutions of Learning," 389. The Reverend Lee gave this displacement a positive spin, arguing that it was a good thing for the church. In fact, he

described as "vain" the debate comparing the values and contributions of the pulpit and the press. It was enough to know that the press "relieves the clergy of a great part of their duties in a former time, and leaves them free for a more effective and undivided attention to their own proper work."

71. Henry Clay Vedder, *Socialism and the Ethics of Jesus*, 310–11; Newell Woolsey Wells, "A Christian Daily."

72. V. S. Yarros, "The Press and Public Opinion," 377.

73. "Purification of the Press."

74. "Asks Church to Aid Press." Williams told the Park Avenue Methodist Church Forum that the church ought to demand improvement in all news publications, whether the newspapers or cheap magazines. He argued that readers make newspapers what they are. "The newspaper is the conscience of the people. When a man buys a paper he helps to edit it, even if he disagrees with it." And "Christian people" are doing just as much to support the worst journalism. "Your protest to the editor, if you make one, receives instant attention and it has immediate effect." See also American Society of Newspaper Editors, *Problems of Journalism*, 105. Discussion at the first annual meeting of the American Society of Newspaper Editors about reader influence on the press included the acknowledgment that "on editorial policies the paper influences the reader a great deal, and in turn the reader should influence the editor a good deal in his general point of view, for we are living in an inevitable democracy, whether we welcome it or not, and in no respect is that democracy more assertive than in the field of journalism."

75. "Purifying the Press."

76. "Duty of the Press: Recommendations as to Pernicious 'New Journalism' Adopted by New York Ministers; Against Sunday Newspapers; Everything Tending to Degrade Man or Exploit Vice Should Be Excluded from Advertisements, Editorials, and News Columns," *New York Times*, January 26, 1897, 12. See also "It Is Out," *Topeka State Journal*, March 13, 1900, 1.

77. Rauschenbusch, *Christianizing the Social Order*, 19; Men and Religion Forward Movement, *Church and the Press*, 31.

78. Men and Religion Forward Movement, *Church and the Press*, 1–2.

79. Ibid., 4–5.

80. A style of skirt so narrow at the hem as to impede walking, popular in the 1910s.

81. Men and Religion Forward Movement, *Church and the Press*, 22.

82. Ibid., 25–26.

83. Vedder, *Socialism and the Ethics of Jesus*, 311.

84. "Discusses Newspapers," *Topeka State Journal*, March 12, 1900, 6.

85. See, for example, "The Moral Standard of the Secular Press." The *Christian Observer* argued, "A high standard, religious and moral, of the secular press would be very advantageous to the whole community both as affecting the personal character and the business interests of the people." See also

"American Newspapers: Tremendous Power for Good and Always Found Defending Right." Howard S. Biscoe in a speech, "The History of American Journalism," declared, "There never was a time in the history of our country when the newspapers were more powerful for good, and when they were doing more good than they are now. . . . It is the modern newspaper that serves as the moral limelight of the age. It uncovers and denounces fraud and moral wrong. It is always found defending the right. The great political reforms and the improvements that have been achieved in State and municipal government in recent times have been due to the publicity given them and to their advocacy by the newspapers." H. Smith, *Publicity and Progress*, 20. Smith observed, "The press is waiting, ready to be harnessed, willing to help pull the load, for it knows that thus it is helping to make a better community, helping tie more people to the publication, obtaining a stronger grasp on the interest of the consumers of its product."

86. Creighton, "Press, Pulpit and Pew," 75.

87. Ibid., 68, 77.

88. Judith M. Buddenbaum, "The Religious Roots of Sigma Delta Chi," 213.

89. See, for example, Rodgers, "'Journalism Is a Loose-Jointed Thing.'"

90. "The Profession of Journalism."

Chapter 4. The Call Goes Out for a Christian Daily Newspaper

1. "Print Christian Daily Paper: American Daily Standard to Occupy New Field," *Decatur (IL) Daily Review*, October 24, 1920, 2.

2. Quoted in Lyman P. Powell, *Mary Baker Eddy: A Life Size Portrait*, 233–34.

3. See, for example, George Tucker, *Progress of the United States in Population and Wealth in Fifty Years, as Exhibited by the Decennial Census*, 149. Tucker wrote, "The newspaper press is thus a most potent engine, both for good and evil. It too often ministers to some of our worst passions, and lends new force to party intolerance and party injustice." See also Storey, "The Daily Press," 41. Story described the newspaper as "a great educational force for good and evil."

4. Barbara W. Tuchman, *A Distant Mirror: The Calamitous 14th Century*, 6, 37; Saint Jerome quoted in Richard C. Chewning, John W. Eby, and Shirley J. Roels, *Business through the Eyes of Faith*, 4.

5. Quoted in "Christianity Arming: Memoranda of the Press-Revolution."

6. Thomas Carlyle, *Critical and Miscellaneous Essays*, 194; Washington Gladden, "The Attitude of the Secular Press in America towards Religion," 106.

7. "Religious Journalism."

8. Lyman Abbott, "Reminiscences: Chapter XIX, A Religious Revolution," 753, 757.

9. Hudson, *Journalism in the United States*, 298.

10. "The Periodical Press," 94.

11. "A Religious Daily" (1892), 156. See also "The Late John Dougall," *New York Evangelist*, August 26, 1886, 4; and "Methodist Social Union," *Zion's*

Herald, January 24, 1900, 128. The *New York World* began in 1860 as a religious daily newspaper but did not succeed in that format.

12. George Maclean Rose, *A Cyclopaedia of Canadian Biography: Being Chiefly Men of the Time; A Collection of Persons Distinguished in Professional and Political Life; Leaders in the Commerce and Industry of Canada, and Successful Pioneers*, 304–5.

13. "The Week."

14. "Short-Lived Papers," *Sandusky (OH) Star Journal*, April 14, 1921, 4.

15. *Waterloo (Iowa) Evening Courier*, April 19, 1921, 6; "The Kind of Paper the Public Likes," *Ogden (UT) Standard-Examiner*, March 26, 1921, 4; "Failure of a Religious Newspaper Venture," 18.

16. Charles H. Parkhurst, *The Pulpit and the Pew*, 38–39, 40–41, 113–14.

17. Joad Raymond, *The Invention of the Newspaper: English Newsbooks, 1641–1649*, 2; American Tract Society, *Home Evangelization*, 139.

18. Paul A. Soukup, *Christian Communication: A Bibliographical Survey*, 5–6.

19. C. Brown, "Religious Periodicals," 271.

20. James A. Herrick, *The History and Theory of Rhetoric: An Introduction*, 23. See also Miles Little, Christopher F. C. Jordens, and Emma-Jane Sayers, "Discourse Communities and the Discourse of Experience," 73. These scholars assert, "Discourse communities are groups of people who share common ideologies, and common ways of speaking about things."

21. Benedict Anderson, *Imagined Communities: Reflections on the Origin and Spread of Nationalism*, 6; Georg Wilhelm Friedrich Hegel, *Miscellaneous Writings of G. W. F. Hegel*, 247; Anderson, *Imagined Communities*, 35–36.

22. Claire Elizabeth McEachern, *The Poetics of English Nationhood, 1590–1612*, 15. See also Timothy Rosendale, *Liturgy and Literature in the Making of Protestant England*, 36–37. Rosendale argues that the "conceptual consolidation of the nation" can be seen centuries before Anderson in the *Book of Common Prayer*, "arguably the first book in English to perform the functions that Anderson finds so ideologically significant in the newspaper."

23. William Miles Myres, ed., *The Book of Common Prayer, A.D. 1886: Compared with the First Prayer Book of King Edward the Sixth, A.D. 1549* (London: Griffith, Farran, Okeden and Welsh, 1887), 12.

24. J. Carey, "Communications and Economics," 69.

25. James Carey, "The Communications Revolution and the Professional Communicator," 137.

26. C. John Sommerville, *The News Revolution in England: Cultural Dynamics of Daily Information*, 143. Sommerville observed that until 1700 in England, "religion provided the names, identities, and narratives in which people lived their lives. It offered illiterates and philosophers a shape for their moral and social situation."

27. O. A. Kingsbury, "A Christian Daily Paper," 182.

28. Frank Michael O'Brien, *The Story of the "Sun": New York, 1833–1918*.

29. Quoted in "A Religious Daily Newspaper."

30. Augustus Maverick, *Henry J. Raymond and the New York Press, for Thirty Years: Progress of American Journalism from 1840 to 1870*, 53. See also "A Religious Daily Newspaper," 118. An editorial from the *Christian Intelligencer* described the penny papers as those "conducted on the cheap system," distinguishing them from the more elite limited-circulation papers that appealed to the commercial and business interests and that "seldom enter into families and form part of the reading of the wives and children of their patrons."

31. William Ellsworth Strong, "The Religious Press in America," 447–48. To that point, Strong notes that from the beginning, one of the two goals of the denominations' religious newspapers was "to provide a better treatment of public affairs than appeared in the coarse, partisan press of the day." See also "Critical Notices." The writer complained of "the utter perversion of truth by which the *partisan press* influences the appointment of many to responsible stations." "Garbling and Misrepresentation." The journal complained of "the gross unfairness of a merely *partisan press*." See also "The Partisan Press"; and "The Secular Press." One of the writer's complaints about the secular press was its tendency to use "exciting diatribes for mere partisan effect." W. N. M'Elroy, "The Ethics of the Press." M'Elroy described the partisan press "as much the foes of good order as any other corrupters of the public morals."

32. A Mother, "Practical."

33. "Penny Papers."

34. "The Book Concern."

35. "Dangerous Selections."

36. Mary White Ovington, "The Penny Paper," 280.

37. H. Crosby, "Christian Co-operation," 167–68.

38. See, for example, "Moral Standard of the Secular Press." "Would that this spirit could be infused into all our journals," the *Observer* intoned. "If the love of God and the love of our fellowmen, instead of the love of money, were the animating spirit of the press everywhere it would advance the people in everything that makes life worth living." See also McClure, "Church and the Press," 509–10. The Reverend Edmund McClure, the editorial secretary for the Society for Promoting Christian Knowledge in England, argued, "If the Press has come to displace so largely other methods of spreading knowledge, surely every effort should be made to use it for the advancement of the kingdom of God."

39. Sylvester F. Scovel, "The Duty and Opportunity of Christianity in the Press," 247–48, 251.

40. One genesis of Sheldon's Topeka experiment was his best-selling sermon novel *In His Steps*, which included a critique of the modern newspaper press, which was in turn inspired by William T. Stead's 1894 novel, *If Christ Came to Chicago!* Stead's work included a critique of the daily press in the chapter titled "The Watchmen of the City." See, for example, William T. Stead, "What

Would Jesus Do?," *Review of Reviews* 14 (May 1899): 488. In a review of Sheldon's novel, Stead described *If Christ Came to Chicago!* as "the precursor" to *In His Steps*.

41. *Topeka Daily Capital*, March 25, 1900, 1.

42. Charles M. Sheldon, "A Preacher Edits the News."

43. Sheldon, "Some Opportunities before the Church." This comes from an address to the Boston Congregational Club on September 24, 1900.

44. See, for example, "A Religious Daily" (1873). The journal asked if it was not time to have a "Daily Paper, devoted to Christ and the Truth? We must have a Daily for our own improvement, and to please the living Spirit of Truth." See also Mary Anna Jackson, *Memoirs of Stonewall Jackson by His Widow, Mary Anna Jackson*, 387–88.

45. Oneida Association, *Third Annual Report of the Oneida Association*, 8–9; "The Idea Growing."

46. "Answers to Inquiries."

47. Methodist Episcopal Church, *Official Minutes of the Eighty-Ninth Session of the New England Conference of the Methodist Episcopal Church Held at Milford, Mass., April 4–10, 1888*, 89.

48. W. L. Alden, "London Literary Letter," *New York Times*, August 19, 1899, BR550; Kingsbury, "A Christian Daily Paper," 182–83.

49. "Highways and Byways," 8–9.

50. The London representative of the *Congregationalist*, "An American Editor of a London Weekly," 300. William Thomas Moore, an American-born clergyman who worked in England and the founder and editor of the *Christian Commonwealth*, said, "Such a journal might do splendid work in uplifting and Christianizing the masses of the population."

51. Edgar Powell, "A Christian Daily Newspaper"; Scovel, "Duty and Opportunity of Christianity," 260–61; Whitelaw Reid, "Journalistic Duties and Opportunities," 336.

52. Quoted in Archibald McLellan, "The *Christian Science Monitor*," 505.

53. Archibald McLellan, "Editor's Table"; "More Lawsuits in *Christian Science* Circles."

54. "The Ideal Newspaper," 482.

55. "A Religious Daily Newspaper," *Washington Post*, July 16, 1899, 6; "A Religious Daily" (1892), 156.

56. See, for example, "The Witness," *New Brunswick (NJ) Daily Times*, February 21, 1880. In a reaction to the demise of the *New York Daily Witness*, the *Daily Times* noted that the paper's end was not unexpected, since "people want a news paper, and the 'religious' daily went down in the struggle." See also "Sheldon's Utopian Idea," *Chicago Daily Tribune*, July 9, 1899, 34. The writer asserted that a religious daily newspaper that would present only "the sweet, pleasing side of life" would not succeed anywhere in America. Readers "want to

be amused as well as edified. They want to know something of the sufferings of men as well as their rejoicings." "Why the *Standard* Failed," *Burlington (Iowa) Hawk Eye*, March 27, 1921, 18. Commenting on the failure of the religious daily the *American Daily Standard* in Chicago, an editorial writer asserted that the reading public did not care for the paper's policy of not printing anything about crime and "the shortcomings of citizens." The writer noted that some would say that the paper's failure was "a sad commentary on the reading public." But he disagreed. "The public wants to know what is going on." Readers do not want their newspapers to leave anything out of their news columns. "The *Standard* had high ideals, so have all great newspapers, the difference lies in this: The *Standard* gave the public what the editors of the *Standard* thought the public should read: The successful daily paper gives the public all the news and lets the public decide what it wants to read."

57. Quoted in "Religious Journalism."

Chapter 5. The Sheldon Edition and Journalism's Responsibility to Society

1. John W. Ripley, "Another Look at the Rev. Mr. Charles M. Sheldon's Christian Daily Newspaper," 2–3. See also Sheldon, *His Life Story*, 112–13. In his autobiography, Sheldon described the home as belonging to Popenoe. Dave Meir, "Casual Conversation Touched Off One of Journalism's Most Amazing Experiments," *Topeka Capital*, May 24, 1953.

2. Sheldon, *His Life Story*, 113. Two ironies of note also arise out of this day of November 3, 1899. One was the fact that Sheldon, an adamant foe of war and militarism, was observing a military parade and ceremony on that day. The other was General Funston's own rocky dealings with the press sixteen years later that made news after he sent a telegram to the War Department, notifying it of his plan to oust reporters from the National Guard camps along the Mexican border who wrote false accounts—he described them as a "carnival of lying"—about camp conditions. "Gen. Funston Condemns Lying Correspondents: Newspaper Men Hereafter Found Guilty of Sending Out Untruthful Dispatches Will Be Ordered from Camp—Malicious and Shameless Falsifying Is Charged by Military Authorities," *Editor & Publisher*, August 5, 1916, 4.

3. Charles M. Sheldon, "A Preacher Edits the News," 64.

4. "The Press of the Nation on Sheldon Idea," *Topeka Capital*, February 11, 1900, 10.

5. Gilson Willets, "Pastor Sheldon's Editorial Experiences: How the *Christian Daily* Was Welcomed by the World and How It Looked—Practically Applying the Text: 'What Would Jesus Do?,'" 231.

6. "A Final Word as to the Sheldon Edition," *Topeka Capital*, March 28, 1900, 4. See also "Mr. Sheldon's Christian Daily," 403. The *Congregationalist* described his efforts as a "pronounced failure."

7. "Mr. Sheldon's Experiment," *Friends' Intelligencer*, April 28, 1900, 335.

8. See, for example, Elliott Parker, "Fantasy Theme Analysis: 'In His Steps.'" This paper explores Sheldon's experiment and its linkage to a work of fiction using the theory of symbolic convergence. See also Ripley, "Another Look." This is an excellent summary of the events surrounding the Sheldon experiment, but essentially explores the product in relation to the discourse surrounding whether what Sheldon was doing was actually a newspaper. Sheldon, *His Life Story*. Sheldon's own discussion about the newspaper experiment is nostalgic and mostly laudatory of others and self-congratulatory. See Michael Ray Smith, *The Jesus Newspaper: The Christian Experiment of 1900 and Its Lessons for Today*. This book, essentially an extended monograph, explores the lessons of the past for today. See also Billie Barnes Jensen, "A Social Gospel Experiment in Newspaper Reform: Charles M. Sheldon and the *Topeka Daily Capital*," a detailed but somewhat perfunctory outline of the events surrounding the Sheldon Edition.

9. Jensen, "Social Gospel Experiment."

10. Paul S. Boyer, "In His Steps: A Reappraisal," 60.

11. In chapter 17 of *In His Steps*, the character of Edward Norman writes down eleven rules of conduct to follow in running a newspaper as Jesus would.

12. "The Demand for Christlikeness."

13. E. S. Martin, "New Testament Christianity in Practice," 310.

14. Houston, "Truth Drive Began in the Early Days," 15. See also "A Religious Daily Newspaper," *Washington Post*, July 16, 1899, 6. The *Kansas City Star* opined, "That Mr. Sheldon should believe such an enterprise to be feasible shows that, beyond matters essentially spiritual, he is not a trustworthy or reliable guide."

15. See, for example, "The Power of the Press: How It Assists in Promoting Christian Welfare; An Interesting Paper on the Influence of the Secular Press on Christian Life," *New York Times*, May 13, 1885, 5. See also John William Mears, "Position of the Secular Press on Moral Questions," *Independent*, July 29, 1880, 3; and B. F. Vaughan, "Some Influences of the Secular Press," 551. Vaughan complained that the editors of the modern newspaper were "worldly-minded, pleasure-loving, self-seeking men" and that much of what they put in the newspapers was "not only unprofitable but decidedly impure and unwholesome." W. N. M'Elroy, "The Ethics of the Press," 767. The Reverend W. N. M'Elroy noted that the newspaperman—not unlike the gambler or someone who ran a house of prostitution—had no right to "cater to depraved taste." Creighton, "Press, Pulpit, and Pew," 68. Reverend Creighton opined that aside from the "unwholesome and polluting" press, the largest problem was those newspapers ignored religion "as the basis of national prosperity and individual nobleness of character."

16. See, for example, Charles M. Sheldon, "The Daily Papers and the Truth," 117. Two months after Sheldon finished his stint as the *Capital* editor, he published a two-page grievance about newspapers and their tenuous grasp on truth.

17. See, for example, Charles M. Sheldon, "What Does It Mean to Be a Christian?" Sheldon pointed to the paradox of newspapers that attacked him as "irreverent" in attempting to act as Jesus would, while at the same time on other pages they "printed columns of liquor advertisements, and others which are immoral, all of which are a constant insult to the spirit of Christ himself; to say nothing of the overwhelming quantity of other material printed in these papers that is unchristian to the last degree."

18. "The Last *Herald* Story," *Topeka State Journal*, March 19, 1900, 4.

19. Charles M. Sheldon, "Symposium: Giving the Public What It Wants," 233–34.

20. Charles M. Sheldon, "The Modern Newspaper," *Independent*, July 25, 1912, 196.

21. Sheldon, "Symposium," 233–34.

22. Charles M. Sheldon, "Is Christianity Practical in Worldly Affairs?," 10.

23. "Rev. Charles M. Sheldon to Edit the *Capital*: Author of *In His Steps* Will Assume Entire Editorial and Business Control of the Paper on March 13; To Illustrate His Conception of the Christian Daily Newspaper," *Topeka Capital*, January 23, 1900, 1; "The Sheldon Edition," *Topeka Capital*, January 23, 1900, 4.

24. Charles M. Sheldon, "To the Editor of the Journal," *Topeka Capital*, February 6, 1900, 6.

25. J. K. Hudson, "To the Editor of the Journal," *Topeka Capital*, February 6, 1900, 6.

26. *Independent*, February 1, 1900, 330.

27. "These Are Skeptical," *Topeka Capital*, January 25, 1900, 1. See also "Rev. C. M. Sheldon's Daily Paper." The *Herald* observed, as many others did, that a weeklong experiment was not enough time to prove anything, "but it may be enough to teach Mr. Sheldon all that he needs to know; for there is a great amount of senseless talk about an ideal and Christian daily, mainly from people who know the least about editing papers." The religious journal went on to argue that there were many daily papers in the country that were "practically Christian." "Topics of the Times," *New York Times*, March 16, 1900, 6. The *Times* noted that once it got its hands on "what has been left of the *Topeka Capital*" after it passed through Sheldon's hands, it was immediately disappointed that the reverend had taken more out of the paper "than he has put into it."

28. "Mr. Sheldon's Paper," *Independent*, March 22, 1900, 728.

29. Quoted in "The Press of the Nation on Sheldon Idea," *Topeka Capital*, February 11, 1900, 10.

30. "The Press of the Nation on Sheldon Idea," 10.

31. "Editor Will Teach Preacher," *Washington Post*, January 29, 1900, 8.

32. "They Write of Sheldon," *Topeka Capital*, March 11, 1900, 1.

33. "The Rev. C. M. Sheldon's Newspaper Experiment; The *Topeka Daily Capital* Is Now under His Direction; Tells Staff What He Wants; First Page Will

Contain Articles on the Indian Famine, Militarism, and the Prohibition Law," *New York Times*, March 13, 1900, 9.

34. The outline of his policy comes from Sheldon, "A Preacher Edits the News," 64; Charles M. Sheldon, "Is a Christian Theater Possible?"; Willets, "Pastor Sheldon's Editorial Experiences"; and Sheldon, *His Life Story*, 2.

35. Willets, "Pastor Sheldon's Editorial Experiences."

36. Sheldon, "Is a Christian Theater Possible?" 617.

37. Willets, "Pastor Sheldon's Editorial Experiences."

38. "It Is Out," *Topeka State Journal*, March 13, 1900, 1.

39. Sheldon, *His Life Story*, 97–98.

40. "It Is Out," 1.

41. Sheldon, *His Life Story*, 132.

42. "How He Died," *Topeka State Journal*, March 15, 1900, 6.

43. "Description of the Paper."

44. Sheldon, "Some Opportunities before the Church."

45. Sheldon, "Preacher Edits the News."

46. "Judge Hazen Speaks of Cases in His Court," *Topeka Capital*, March 13, 1900, 4.

47. "It Is Out," 1. See also "Business Men Talk," *Topeka State Journal*, March 13, 1900, 1. Topeka businessman H. A. Auerbach said he was impressed by Sheldon's censorship of the newspaper and believed every newspaper should have an editor of advertisements. "People should be entitled to read the truth in advertisements on every daily paper the same as in the news." However, two other businessmen, D. J. Greenwald and Samuel Barnum, did not like the fact that all the advertising was segregated from the news and placed at the back of the newspaper. Advertisers wanted their ads to run sprinkled among the news so that they would be read, both men said.

48. Sheldon, "Preacher Edits the News."

49. See, for example, "Current Comment," *Ohio Farmer*, March 29, 1900, 284. The *Ohio Farmer* observed that "nearly every journal of any note" had been highly critical of the Sheldon Edition. See also "This Horrible Selfishness," *Washington Post*, March 18, 1900, 6. The *Chicago Chronicle* went so far as to say Sheldon's *Capital* was nothing like a newspaper. "It is a sort of religious symposium, with a few washed-out, expurgated news items scattered through it." "Capitol Chat," *Washington Post*, March 20, 1900, 6. Kansas senator William A. Harris described the Sheldon Edition as a "stale, flat, and unprofitable" newspaper. "Mr. Sheldon's Christian Daily," 403. The *Congregationalist* noted, "He began, continued and ended by subordinating to a great degree the material out of which newspapers are usually constructed—namely, real news." "Sheldon Edition," *Topeka Capital*, March 25, 1900, 9. The Reverend John W. Day of the Church of the Messiah in St. Louis noted that he regretted "the attempt most of all because it is of no help to the press and will injure the standing of Mr. Sheldon's profession." Other St.

Louis pastors were equally castigatory. The Reverend Daniel S. Tuttle, the Episcopal bishop of Missouri, observed that a minister was not qualified to "sit as a censor in the editorial office"; the Reverend E. Duckworth, rector of St. James Episcopal Church, regarded the experiment "as a humiliation"; Rabbi Samuel Sale of the Temple Shaare Emeth called the experiment a "seven days' wonder" that would not "have any effect" on the newspaper world; and the Reverend R. P. Johnston of Third Baptist Church said it "would require some stretch of language to call" the Sheldon Edition a newspaper.

50. "A Great Week for Topeka," *Topeka State Journal*, March 22, 1900, 2.

51. "Mr. Sheldon's Experiment" (March 24, 1900), 658.

52. "Editor Sheldon Here," *Washington Post*, November 14, 1900, 2.

53. See, for example, "Sheldon Edition," *Topeka Capital*, March 21, 1900, 6. The *New York Sun* asked how Sheldon's policy to avoid the "horrible details" of a crime squared with accuracy and truth. "What will Mr. Sheldon do? Will he tell of a murder, for instance, without telling how it is done?" See also F. L. Vandegrift, "F. L. Vandegrift Says Sheldon Edition Fails of Its Mission," *Topeka State Journal*, March 13, 1900, 6. One commentator observed, "Greater good has been accomplished by shocking the public mind than by lecturing it. Witness the crucifixion of Christ, a crime that gave the impetus to the religion that Mr. Sheldon preaches." "Whitman Raps Newspapers: Resents Unfairness and Ignorance but Says True Information Heralds Reform." New York governor Charles S. Whitman said in an interview, "Neither Mayors, nor Governors, nor Presidents can give good government of and by themselves. Every citizen must help, and this aid waits on the education in public matters that only the press can provide."

54. "The Sheldon Experiment," *Topeka State Journal*, March 22, 1900, 2.

55. "A Final Word as to the Sheldon Edition," 4.

56. "Mr. Sheldon's Christian Daily," 403.

57. Willets, "Pastor Sheldon's Editorial Experiences," 230. See also "This Horrible Selfishness," 6. The *Washington Post* described Sheldon's experiment as an "alleged newspaper" and a "travestying of journalism."

58. "An Expert View: What Editor Frank H. Lancaster of New York Says," *Topeka State Journal*, March 23, 1900, 1.

59. "Topics of the Times," *New York Times*, May 24, 1900, 8.

60. See, for example, "The Press of the Nation on Sheldon Idea," 10. The *Lowell (MA) Courier* noted that Sheldon's effort was an example of the "old theory held by Tom, Dick and Harry that anybody can run a newspaper." Apparently, the *Courier* wrote, Sheldon "thinks a newspaper can be run on sentiment and not on business principles." See also "This Horrible Selfishness," 6. The *Chicago Chronicle* pointed to the amateur nature of the paper as the product "of mediocre minds engaged in unfamiliar work."

61. "Sheldon Edition," *Topeka Capital*, March 21, 1900, 6.

62. "Wm. Allen White on Sheldon's Errors," *Topeka State Journal*, March 22, 1900, 2.

63. "Sheldon Edition," *Topeka Capital*, March 25, 1900, 9.

64. "Mr. Sheldon's Paper," 728.

65. Washington Gladden, "Mr. Sheldon's Newspaper," *Independent*, April 5, 1900, 807.

66. "What the Papers Said," *Topeka State Journal*, March 19, 1900, 2.

67. See, for example, Ronald R. Rodgers, "The Problems of Journalism: An Annotated Bibliography of Press Criticism in *Editor & Publisher*, 1901–1923." See also Rodgers, "'Journalism Is a Loose-Jointed Thing.'"

68. "Mr. Sheldon's Experiment," *Outlook*, March 22, 1900, 8; "The Demand for Christlikeness"; Gladden, "Mr. Sheldon's Newspaper," 807.

69. "Sheldon Edition," *Topeka Capital*, March 25, 1900, 9.

70. "Moral Standard of the Secular Press."

71. See, for example, "Scott's Opinion," *Topeka State Journal*, March 22, 1900, 2. While the *Iola (KS) Register* observed that the Sheldon Edition "was not a newspaper," it thought much good would come from the experiment. "The worldwide discussion which the experiment has precipitated has directed the attention of thousands of editors to their own papers, and there can be no doubt that the blue pencil will be more in evidence hereafter than it has been before, both on advertisements and news." It had also prompted readers to look at the papers they allow into their home with a "more critical eye." See also "Sheldon Edition," *Topeka Capital*, March 21, 1900, 6, a roundup of commentary from around the country. In it the Reverend Cornelius H. Patton of the First Congregational Church noted that while it "may not be the most readable" of newspapers, it was enjoyable to read a daily without "the trail of the serpent in it from beginning to end" and without even "one slimy advertisement" in its pages. The good that would come from it was the awareness that Christians were interested in "having journalism properly conducted," which would prompt "our dailies to devote more space to religious, moral and humanitarian matters, and eventually to give larger recognition to Christian ideals in the management of their paper." "Current Comment," *Ohio Farmer*, March 29, 1900, 284. An *Ohio Farmer* editorial writer observed that while "nearly every journal of any note" had been highly critical of the Sheldon Edition, many of them conceded that some of the reforms Sheldon had advocated should be adopted by the daily press. While the people want the news and not religious intonations, "every moral man" recognized that the news should be clean, truthful, and "couched in circumspect language." While Sheldon's rigid policies went down the right path, the writer noted, they were much too extreme. "Mr. Sheldon's experiment was too short to demonstrate anything fully, but it was long enough to suggest some much needed reforms."

72. "Sheldon Edition," *Topeka Capital*, 6.

73. "Moral Standard of the Secular Press."

Chapter 6. The Social Gospel and the Mission of Newspapers in the Modern World

1. Hopkins, *Rise of the Social Gospel Movement*, 26–27.

2. Abbott, *Christianity and Social Problems*, 180.

3. Hopkins, *Rise of the Social Gospel Movement*, 26–27; Washington Gladden, *Working People and Their Employers*, 3; Henry F. May, *Protestant Churches and Industrial America*, 230.

4. The Gilded Age describes postbellum industrializing America, and it extended from about 1865 to 1901. The term comes from the title of Mark Twain and Charles Dudley Warner's book, *The Gilded Age: A Tale of Today*, which satirized the greed and corruption of the era. The dates for the Progressive Era are usually given as 1901 to 1917.

5. See, for a fuller explication, Trachtenberg, *Incorporation of America*. See also Charles W. Calhoun, *The Gilded Age: Essays on the Origins of Modern America*; Howard W. Morgan, *The Gilded Age*; and Hofstadter, *Age of Reform*.

6. Walter Lippmann, *Drift and Mastery: An Attempt to Diagnose the Current Unrest*, 152–53.

7. Donald K. Gorrell, *The Age of Social Responsibility: The Social Gospel in the Progressive Era, 1900–1920*, 82.

8. Henry Churchill King et al., *Education and National Character*, 15.

9. Rauschenbusch, *Christianizing the Social Order*, 156; Ronald C. White and Charles Howard Hopkins, *The Social Gospel: Religion and Reform in Changing America*, 56.

10. Edwin H. Chapin, *Moral Aspects of City Life*, 146–47; "The Social Order," 332; J. Strong, *Our Country*, 179–84.

11. "Churches Unite in Great Publicity Campaign," *New York Times*, October 31, 1909, 6.

12. Charles Stelzle, *Christianity's Storm Centre: A Study of the Modern City*, 18, 13.

13. Ibid., 21–22.

14. "Churches Unite in Great Publicity Campaign," 6.

15. Stelzle, *Christianity's Storm Centre*, 21.

16. Rauschenbusch, *Christianizing the Social Order*, 223; Hofstadter, *Age of Reform*, 225.

17. William Dwight Porter Bliss, *The Encyclopedia of Social Reform Including Political Economy, Political Science, Sociology and Statistics*, 954–56.

18. Hofstadter, *Age of Reform*, 133, 65; Rauschenbusch, *Christianizing the Social Order*, 226.

19. Rauschenbusch, *Christianizing the Social Order*, 223, 167.

20. Willem A. Visser 't Hooft, *The Background of the Social Gospel in America*, 65.

21. Trachtenberg, *Incorporation of America*, 5–6; Woodrow Wilson, *The New Freedom: A Call for the Emancipation of the Generous Energies of a People*, 10–11, 15.

22. Patten, "Contribution of the Church," 174–75. See also May, *Protestant Churches and Industrial America*, 202–3. May notes that the "essential character" of the Social Gospel doctrines developed by Washington Gladden and his generation remained much the same over the years but that they were later "elaborated, reapplied and given more thorough theological exposition by Walter Rauschenbusch and other leaders."

23. Patten, "Contribution of the Church," 174–75.

24. "American Congregational Theology," 256. See also John Marshall Barker, *The Social Gospel and the New Era*, 1.

25. *Proceedings of a Council in Plymouth Church, Brooklyn, New-York, for the Installation of the Rev. Lyman Abbott, D.D., as Pastor, and the Rev. Howard S. Bliss, as Assistant Pastor, Held January 16, 1980: With a Sermon by Lyman Abbot, D.D., on the New Theology*, 45.

26. R. J. Campbell, *The New Theology*, 14.

27. Richard Wightman Fox, "The Culture of Liberal Protestant Progressivism, 1875–1925," 645.

28. See, for example, "The sin of Adam is typical of our sin; the sins of our ancestors result in an evil atmosphere into which we must grow up, there is no inherited guilt, and no racial depravity aside from the totality of individual offences." Justin Martyr quoted in Craig D. Allert, *Revelation, Truth, Canon and Interpretation: Studies in Justin Martyr's Dialogue with Trypho*, 116.

29. John Bascom, *Evolution and Religion; or, Faith as a Part of a Complete Cosmic System*, 8–9.

30. Walter Lorenzo Sheldon, *A Volume of Lectures*, 8–9.

31. See, for example, Ministers of the Unitarian Church, *The Unitarian Pulpit: Discourses on the Christian Spirit and Life*, 268. "Amidst the hurry and the eager chase of life are we losing our hold on God's eternal verities? Are they still realities to us? Do we feel them to be true? Oh! how apt are the holiest things to become mere matters of routine to us, and truths,—great, solemn truths,—that should stir the deep fountains of the soul and transfigure life, to move us no more than the pettiest interests of the world!"

32. Samuel D. McConnell, "The Church in Modern Society," 177; J. Strong, *New Era*, 308; McConnell, "Church in Modern Society," 177.

33. Visser 't Hooft, *Background of the Social Gospel*, 20–21; Ray Stannard Baker, *American Chronicle: The Autobiography of Ray Stannard Baker [David Grayson]*, 256; Rauschenbusch, *Christianity and the Social Crisis*, 202; Rauschenbusch, *Christianizing the Social Order*, 167; "The Social Gospel," 148–49.

34. Visser 't Hooft, *Background of the Social Gospel*, 23, 65; Hopkins, *Rise of the Social Gospel Movement*, 3.

35. J. Strong, *Our World*, 79; Josiah Strong, *The Next Great Awakening*, vi. See also J. Strong, *Our World*, 340, 344, 414, 469.

36. Abbott, *Reminiscences*, 468; Samuel Harris, *Kingdom of Christ on Earth: Twelve Lectures Delivered before the Students of the Theological Seminary, Andover*, 168.

37. Hopkins, *Rise of the Social Gospel Movement*, 124, 8; Rauschenbusch, *Christianizing the Social Order*, 97; Gladden, *Social Facts and Forces*, 223–24.

38. May, *Protestant Churches and Industrial America*, xi.

39. Rauschenbusch, *Christianizing the Social Order*, 21.

40. Hopkins, *Rise of the Social Gospel Movement*, 67.

41. Muller, "Social Philosophy of Josiah Strong," 191. See also Shailer Mathews, "The Significance of the Church to the Social Movement," 617. Mathews asserts, "The Christian ideal of the individual is social. A man cannot conform to the example of Jesus unless his life be joined consciously to others."

42. Robert Jewett and Ole Wangerin, *Mission and Menace: Four Centuries of American Religious Zeal*, 183; Mathews, "Significance of the Church," 607.

43. Roberts, "Social Gospel and the Trust-Busters," 243.

44. J. Strong, *New Era*, 348; J. Graham Morgan, "The Development of Sociology and the Social Gospel in America," 42; I. Brown, *Lyman Abbott*, 102.

45. J. Morgan, "Development of Sociology," 43–44. See also Harry Frederick Ward, *The Social Creed of the Churches*.

46. J. Morgan, "Development of Sociology," 52.

47. Hopkins, *Rise of the Social Gospel Movement*, 257.

48. Barker, *Social Gospel and the New Era*, 11, 99–100.

49. H. Ward, *Social Creed of the Churches*, 5, 9.

50. William Monroe Balch, *Christianity and the Labor Movement*, 80–90.

51. Gorrell, *Age of Social Responsibility*, 73; Patten, "Contribution of the Church," 174–75; "American Congregational Theology," 256; Minot J. Savage, Edward Everett Hale, and Washington Gladden, "Can Our Churches Be Made More Useful?," 382.

52. Wilson, *New Freedom*, 12, 20.

53. Gladden, *Church and Modern Life*, 15.

54. Harry Emerson Fosdick, *Christianity and Progress*, 178–80; Ellwood, "Formation of Public Opinion," 73–74; Stanley K. Schultz, "The Morality of Politics: The Muckrakers' Vision of Democracy," 528–31.

55. E. W. Scripps, *I Protest: Selected Disquisitions of E. W. Scripps*, 178; Frederic Clemson Howe, *The Confessions of a Reformer*, 16–17.

56. Barker, *Social Gospel and the New Era*, 3–4, 12–16.

57. George Davis Herron, *The Christian Society*, 116.

58. "Bryan Says Newspapers Need Moral Awakening; Stop Selling Conscience for a Salary, He Urges; Tells of Early Struggles; Wouldn't Change Places

Now with Rockefeller or Morgan, He Says to Newspaper Workers," *New York Times*, September 2, 1906, 2.

59. "Bryan to the Craft"; Newman Smyth, *Christian Ethics*, 308.

60. E. D. Weigle, "The Ministry and Current Social Problems," 467, 472; Visser 't Hooft, *Background of the Social Gospel in America*, 20–21.

61. Abbott, *Reminiscences*, 478.

62. Quoted in Bliss, *Encyclopedia of Social Reform*, 4.

63. "A Pioneer Editor," 743–44.

64. William A. Spalding, "The Moral Responsibilities of the Press," 270.

65. John Bascom, *Sociology*, 243; John Rogers Commons, *Social Reform and the Church*, 23.

66. See, for example, W. N. M'Elroy, "The Ethics of the Press," 767. See also "The Decay of American Journalism"; "Newspaper Morality"; "Theology and Yellow Journalism: The Bane of the Headline"; "Preachers Criticize"; "Arraigns the Press: Rev. Dr. Brann Points Out Some of Its Weak Points in a Sermon; Attacks the Anonymous Writer—Declares Editorials and Articles Should Be Signed by the Writers—Recommends Law to That Effect—Insincerity of the Semi-Socialist—What Greed Will Sometimes Do"; and "Daily Paper Praised and Also Condemned: St. Louis Clergyman and Ethical Culture Leader at Wide Variance in Their Views as to What Sort of News Should Be Printed—*Globe-Democrat* and *Post-Dispatch* Have Something to Say."

67. "Church and the Newspaper," 1403.

68. M'Elroy, "The Ethics of the Press," 767.

69. Edward Bellamy, *The Religion of Solidarity*; Trachtenberg, *Incorporation of America*, 94.

70. Samuel Gompers, "The Newspapers and Unemployment," 205. See also Trachtenberg, *Incorporation of America*, 98.

71. Trachtenberg, *Incorporation of America*, 80.

72. George Gerbner, "Violence in Television Drama: Trends and Symbolic Functions."

73. Samuel Gompers, "The Lockwood Committee, Mr. Gompers, the Press," 416.

74. Samuel Gompers, "Labor News and Labor's Views Suppressed."

75. Interchurch World Movement of North America, *Report on the Steel Strike of 1919*, 248, 29, 250.

76. Walter Lippmann and Charles Merz, "A Test of the News," 42.

77. Latta, "Background for the Social Gospel." Latta also noted that other leading advocates of the Social Gospel were active in "connectional bodies" (such as Josiah Strong and Charles Stelzle) or professors in theological schools (such as Shailer Mathews and Walter Rauschenbusch).

78. Hopkins, *Rise of the Social Gospel Movement*, 319, 139.

79. James L. Kinneavy, *A Theory of Discourse*, 2, 39.

80. "Public the Editor: Dean Mathews Says Papers Print Just What Their Readers Want."

81. Sheldon, "Symposium," 233–34; Washington Gladden, "Bringing All the Moral and Religious Forces into Effective Educational Unity," 34–35; John William Mears, "Position of the Secular Press on Moral Questions," *Independent*, July 29, 1880, 3.

82. W. S. J., "Detroit Letter."

83. H. Smith, *Publicity and Progress*, 15.

84. Quoted in John DeWitt McKee, *William Allen White: Maverick on Main Street*, 199; Bruce J. Evensen, "The Muckrakers as Evangelicals," 20; Lincoln Steffens, *The Autobiography of Lincoln Steffens*, 357; Justin Kaplan, *Lincoln Steffens: A Biography*, 118; John O'Hara Cosgrave, "Present-Day Opportunities in Literature," 11.

85. Evensen, "Evangelical Origins of Muckraking," 193–95.

86. Underwood, *From Yahweh to Yahoo!*, 79, 76, 81.

87. John Bascom, *Social Theory: A Grouping of Social Facts and Principles*, 9, 110–13.

88. Erman J. Ridgway, "The Ideal Newspaper," *Atlanta Georgian and News*, December 24, 1909, 3. This was published over the entire page 3 of the newspaper, which had requested an essay on this topic. Condensations of the essay later appeared in other widely read publications. For instance, "'The Ideal Newspaper.'" *Current Literature* noted, "The change that is taking place, according to Mr. Ridgway, is that the newspaper is passing from the stage of personal control to that of impersonal news-service, and the great need of the day is not new Greeleys and Danas, but efficient and yet more efficient machinery for the gathering of news." See also "Ideal Newspaper: Is an Emotionless Machine—Its Sole Function Is to Give the News Truthfully and Dispassionately—Editorials Have Not the Influence They Once Had."

89. V. S. Yarros, *Our Revolution: Essays in Interpretation*, 179.

90. Joseph Parker, *The Inner Life of Christ, as Revealed in the Gospel of Matthew*, 365.

91. Editors, "About Ourselves," *Independent*, July 10, 1920, 33.

92. "The Outlook for 1918: A Characterization and a Programme."

93. For instance, in 1914 Wise cofounded the National Association for the Advancement of Colored People.

94. Stephen S. Wise, "The Moral Power of the Press," 410.

95. Henry Walcott Boynton, *Journalism and Literature, and Other Essays*, 19.

96. Though the term *religious journalism* was, at times, used to describe the same idea, that term could also refer to the work of denominational journals, thus creating some confusion about distinctions.

97. Gilbert, "Christian Journalism," 275–76.

98. Simeon Gilbert, "The Newspaper as a Judiciary," 290; Julius H. Ward, "Paper by Rev. Julius H. Ward," 107; George Sampson, *The Concise Cambridge History of English Literature*, 383. Sampson asserts that the two writers acted as the "voice of a new and civilized urban life."

99. J. Ward, "Paper by Rev. Julius H. Ward," 107–10.

100. Lowell, "The Pious Editor's Creed," 200; Gladden, *Ruling Ideas of the Present Age*, 206–7; "The Outlook for 1918," 420.

101. Gladden, *Recollections*, 232.

102. Abbott, *America in the Making*, 147.

103. Lyman Abbott, *The Christian Ministry*, 109.

104. Ibid., 109–11.

105. Interchurch World Movement, *Report on the Steel Strike of 1919*, 250.

Conclusion

1. Rider, "The Pretensions of Journalism," 471.

2. "The Press—Its Power and Mission"; Gladden, *Ruling Ideas of the Present Age*, 189.

3. "Printed Word Has Only Started Divine Mission."

4. "Accuracy the Foundation: Essential to Permanent Newspaper Success, Says St. Louis Editor."

5. Ellwood, "Formation of Public Opinion."

6. J. Smith, "Secular Press and Morality," 42.

7. Alexander K. McClure, foreword to *Journalism: Its Relation to and Influence upon the Political, Social, Professional, Financial and Commercial Life of the United States of America*, by New York Press Club, ii. Alexander K. McClure was then the former editor of the *Philadelphia Ledger*.

8. "American Newspapers."

9. Charles M. Sheldon, "The Modern Newspaper."

10. Adolph Moses, "Democracy and Despotism," 276. Moses contended, "Some of the wisest men and sincerest patriots are at the head of great newspapers and periodicals and through them instruct the people in the duties of the hour, warn them of dangers, chide them for their follies, and create sound public opinion on matters of great moment. The ancient republics had no such regenerating moral force behind them as the press."

11. Eckman, "Pulpit and Press," 6.

12. Carleton, "Power of the Press," 471.

13. A. E. Fletcher, "The Ideal Newspaper."

14. Gladden, "More about the Secular Press," 7.

15. Commager, *American Mind*, 68.

16. Washington Gladden, "Educational Unity of the Moral and Educational Forces," 308; Andrew H. Green, "Scenic Beauties of Fort Washington Battlefield: The American Revolution and the Free Press; An Address by the Hon.

Andrew H. Green, President of the American Scenic and Historic Preservation Society, at the Dedication of the Fort Washington Monument, in New York City, November 16, 1901," 88.

17. "Is Honest Journalism Possible?," 46; Commager, *American Mind*, 69–70.

18. Morris, "Religious Journalism and Journalists," 425; Thomas Jefferson, *Letters and Addresses of Thomas Jefferson*, 77.

19. "Henry Watterson," 841.

20. Henry Watterson, "The Newspapers of New York: Some Reminiscences of the City's Papers, Past and Present." See also "The Attitude of Detachment," *Editor & Publisher*, October 21, 1905, 4. The trade journal observed that a newspaper "is supported by readers who expect it to give them a truthful account of the world's doings day by day, and not to be prostituted to promote the ambitions of any one man or any set of men. It should be unbiased, unhampered by selfish motives, unencumbered by allegiance to any political boss or any ring."

21. Gladden, "Tainted Newspapers," 11.

22. "Are Newspaper Editors to Be Blamed?," 845.

23. Will Irwin, "The Editor and the News," 18; Gladden, "More about the Secular Press," 7; "Press and Morality: Newspaper Ethics Discussed at Union Church Meeting—'Sincerity and Truth Should Be Publishers' Code of Morals'—Power of Newspaper Now Lies in the News Columns."

24. "Independence for Editors," 61–62.

25. William Hayes, "Can a Trust Company Successfully Administer a Great Newspaper? The Experiment of the Illinois Merchants Trust Company with the *Chicago Daily News* Creates Much Discussion."

26. Theodore L. Glasser and Stephanie Craft, "Public Journalism and the Prospects for Press Accountability," 152; James Fenimore Cooper, *The American Democrat; or, Hints on the Social and Civic Relations of the United States of America*, 125.

27. Gladden, "More about the Secular Press," 7; Rauschenbusch, *Christianizing the Social Order*, 284.

28. King et al., *Education and National Character*, 15.

29. Perry Miller, *The Life of the Mind in America: From the Revolution to the Civil War*, 86; Wendell Berry, *The Way of Ignorance, and Other Essays*, 9.

30. Kate Mason Rowland, *The Life of George Mason, 1725–1792, Including His Speeches, Public Papers, and Correspondence*, viii, 404.

31. Massachusetts Historical Society, *John Adams, Samuel Adams, and James Warren: Warren-Adams Letters, Being Chiefly a Correspondence among John Adams, Samuel Adams, and James Warren . . . 1743–1814*, 222; Thomas Jefferson, *The Works of Thomas Jefferson: Published by Order of Congress from the Original Manuscripts Deposited in the Department of State*, 349–50.

32. Thomas Smith Grimké, *Address on the Patriot Character of the Temperance Reformation: Delivered before the Charleston Temperance Society, and the*

Young Men's Temperance Society of Charleston, on Tuesday Evening, 26th February 1833, 29.

33. Richard T. Ely, *Ground under Our Feet: An Autobiography*, 88.

34. Ely, *Labor Movement in America*, 311–12.

35. "Newspaper in Modern Life."

36. Rauschenbusch, *Christianizing the Social Order*, 220.

37. "Need a Conscience." See also Gladden, "Tainted Newspapers," 1–17.

38. Rauschenbusch, *Christianizing the Social Order*, 220; Gladden, *Recollections*, 242–43; Gladden, *Social Facts and Forces*, 224.

39. "Asks Church to Aid Press."

40. "Canons of Journalism"; American Society of Newspaper Editors, *Problems of Journalism*, 156, 82, 18.

41. Ralph Waldo Emerson, *The Prose Works of Ralph Waldo Emerson*, 262; McCloskey, *Bourgeois Equality*; Thompson, *Media and Modernity*, 183.

42. "'Journalists and Newsmongers' Again," 13.

43. "The Century on Journalism: Conscience in Journalism; Open Letter by Eugene M. Camp."

44. "'Journalists and Newsmongers' Again," 13.

45. "Century on Journalism."

46. "The Human Publisher."

47. "'Journalists and Newsmongers' Again," 13.

48. Stuart Hall, "Cultural Studies: Two Paradigms."

49. "'The Goods We Sell': The Business of a Newspaper Is Made Upstairs in the Editorial Rooms—Advertising Will Come—a Newspaper Established in the Family Circle—the Deadly Menace to Independent Journalism."

50. "Editors at Columbia: Missouri University Journalism Week Most Successful since Inauguration; Addresses by Prominent Newspapermen and Women of the Country—Associated Afternoon Papers Organized for Raising of Business Standards and Promotion of Foreign Advertising—Nelson's Talk," *Editor & Publisher*, May 23, 1914, 1026.

51. Clifford G. Christians, John P. Ferré, and Mark Fackler, *Good News: Social Ethics and the Press*, 120.

52. "Draws Vivid Picture of Ideal Newspaper: Louis Wiley, of the *New York Times*, Outlines Policies and Methods of Up-to-the-Hour Journalism—Discusses Awakening of Advertisers to Their Opportunities." Louis Wiley was business manager of the *New York Times*.

53. Friedrich Nietzsche, *The Birth of Tragedy & The Genealogy of Morals*, 256.

54. W. N. M'Elroy, "The Ethics of the Press," 767; J. Strong, *New Era*, 353; "Declaration of Principles," 52–53.

55. See, for example, Richard Grant White, "The Morals and Manners of Journalism." White argued that the journalist is both "a counsellor and a prophet," and in its ideal form journalism "informs and educates; it expands

the horizon of men's thoughts and sympathies." See also Kingsbury, "A Christian Daily Paper," 182. Kingsbury called for a newspaper press that gave "its picture of the daily doings of the world as those doings appear from the Christian point of view." "Moral Standard of the Secular Press." "Would that this spirit could be infused into all our journals," the *Observer* intoned. "If the love of God and the love of our fellowmen, instead of the love of money, were the animating spirit of the press everywhere it would advance the people in everything that makes life worth living." Howard A. Bridgman, "Journalism as an Opportunity for Christian Service," 215; "Must Battle for Progress: Editor Who Stands Still, Is a Failure, Says Florida Writer." Excerpts from an essay by Charles E. Jones—formerly of the *Jacksonville (FL) Metropolis*, in which he argued that journalists "must battle unalterably and everlasting for progress, for morality, for honesty and for improvements along every line that tends to the upbuilding of the State and nation."

56. Max Nordan, "Public Conscience."

57. Schudson, "Objectivity Norm," 150, 159–60.

58. Schudson, *Discovering the News*, 5–6.

59. Associated Press, "Mr. Bryan and the Associated Press."

60. Charles G. Ross, *The Writing of News: A Handbook with Chapters on Newspaper Correspondence and Copy Reading*, 17–18. See also W. Williams and Martin, *Practice of Journalism*, 79–80. Williams and Martin included a version of the entire editorial from the *St. Louis Republic*.

61. Gladden, *Tools and the Man*, 116; Edward Alsworth Ross, *Changing America: Studies in Contemporary Society*, 83.

62. Lilly, "The Ethics of Journalism," 507; Carey, "Professional Communicator," 137.

63. See, for example, Schudson, "Objectivity Norm," 165. See also Gaye Tuchman, "Objectivity as Strategic Ritual: An Examination of Newsmen's Notions of Objectivity," *American Journal of Sociology* 77, no. 4 (1972): 660–79.

64. Gladden, "More about the Secular Press," 7. Gladden argued that the goal of a "moral and religious teacher" is not to make money. "The moment it becomes evident that this is so, his influence is gone. The prime condition of success in this calling is that the mercenary motive shall be consciously and manifestly subordinate. This is not only true of ministers of the gospel, but of all others who seek to be guides of conduct."

65. Gompers, "Labor News," 201.

66. Rauschenbusch, *Christianizing the Social Order*, 397.

67. Addams, *Democracy and Social Ethics*, 9–11; Stead, "The Future of Journalism," 670–71.

68. Edwin Lee Earp, *The Social Engineer*, 49.

69. "The Open Forum."

70. Dorn, *Washington Gladden*, 291.

71. Robert T. Handy, "Washington Gladden: An Introduction," in *Social Gospel in America*, edited by Robert T. Handy, 29.

72. Gerbner, "Violence in Television Drama"; Gaye Tuchman, "Introduction: The Symbolic Annihilation of Women by the Mass Media," 4.

73. *The Proceedings of the Woman's Rights Convention, Held at Syracuse, September 8th, 9th, & 10th, 1852*, 77–78.

74. Jane Agnes Stewart, *The Frances Willard Book*, 19.

75. Anna A. Gordon, *Frances E. Willard: A Memorial Volume*, 142. See also Frances Elizabeth Willard, Carolyn De Swarte Gifford, and Amy R. Slagell, *Let Something Good Be Said: The Speeches and Writings of Frances E. Willard*, 12. In 1875 she urged activists in the temperance movement to "get correct statistics of intemperance in your own town, and have them kept before the people. These will tell more than imported figures. Interest the press in your work. Give your editors facts. Wherever practicable, edit a column in the local newspaper in the interest of reform, and strive, by all honorable means, to enlist the press as our most powerful ally."

76. Susan McWhirter Ostrom, "What the Press Can Do."

77. "'Thieves,' 'Liars' and So Forth," 122.

78. Chicago Commission on Race Relations, *The Negro in Chicago: A Study of Race Relations and a Race Riot*, 521; Gary Dorrien, *The New Abolition: W. E. B. Du Bois and the Black Social Gospel*, 522.

79. See, for example, Irvine Garland Penn, *The Afro-American Press and Its Editors*, 448, 482. Penn, an educator, journalist, and lay leader in the Methodist Episcopal Church, charged, "As a regrettable fact, the white Press of the South is leagued against the negro and his rights, and it is re-enforced by quite two-thirds of the Press of the North and West." Penn also quotes Booker T. Washington: "The white press readily sees our dark side, but is not disposed, as a rule, to go far out of its way to let the world know of the negro's advancement." Reverdy Cassius Ransom, *The Spirit of Freedom and Justice: Orations and Speeches*, 23. "The Negroes who are aggressively fighting for their rights have the press against them and the weight of public opinion. They are branded as disturbers of the harmony between the races, but they have the same spirit that animated the founders of this nation." Irving Garland Penn, "The American Press and the Congress," 565. "What the Negro needs at his back is a healthy public sentiment of a friendly character, which will guarantee him an equal chance in life with those by whom he is surrounded and with whom he lives. . . . It may be said in a sentence that the books written and the editorials published against the Negro, which either ignore or minimize his good deeds and magnify his evil traits, while they make heroes of our rapists and murderers, are for the prime business of creating sentiment against the Negro, which will eventually have as its end the consignment of the Negro to an indifferent place in the nation's esteem." Carter Godwin Woodson, *The Negro in Our*

History, 260. Woodson, an African American historian, author, and journalist, charged, "The local newspapers, by their art of psychological appeal to the race prejudice of the masses, have succeeded in convincing the public that the general cause of these lynchings was criminal assault, but statistics show that ordinary misdemeanors of Negroes have been the sole excuse for three out of every four of these lynchings."

80. W. E. B. Du Bois, *The Souls of Black Folk: Essays and Sketches*, 226–27.

81. Frederick German Detweiler, *The Negro Press in the United States*, 79–80.

82. Addams, *Democracy and Social Ethics*, 9–11; Stead, "The Future of Journalism," 670–71; Christians, Ferré, and Fackler, *Good News*, 14.

83. William T. Stead, "Government by Journalism," 664. See also "William T. Stead: A Character Sketch," 176–77. In a letter to editor John Morley, Stead expanded on his notion of prophetic journalism by observing, "My idea of 'prophetic journalism' is that any man who has to guide the opinions of other men ought ever to have before his eyes the fact that right is right, and wrong is wrong; and that any man or nation who acts wilfully, as if it were not binding upon him to do right, has nothing before him but a terrible looking forward to of judgment to come, certainly in this life, possibly in that which is to come." John Stuart Mill, *Considerations on Representative Government*, 42. John Stuart Mill quoted "a distinguished Hebrew," who once said "that the Prophets were, in Church and State, the equivalent of the modern liberty of the press."

84. Abbott, *Reminiscences*, 335.

85. Georg Henrich August von Ewald, *Commentary on the Prophets of the Old Testament*, 8.

86. William Allen Harper, "Faith and Progress," 680.

87. Shailer Mathews, *The Making of To-morrow: Interpretations of the World To-day*, 177–78.

88. Steffens, *Autobiography of Lincoln Steffens*, 357. See also George French, "The Damnation of the Magazines," 8. French asserted that "insurgency was the editorial motive, and trusts and combines were lambasted with great vigor by the writers who were the prophets of insurgency."

89. Selden P. Delany, "The Clergy and Social Reform," 915.

90. "The American Congress of Churches," 592.

91. See, for example, Underwood, *From Yahweh to Yahoo!*, 21. Underwood noted that "prophetic journalism" from the time of Quaker activist George Fox had rested alongside the "ethic of objectivity and the commercial elements of profit making that dictate so much of what journalism constitutes today."

92. Herbert J. Gans, *Deciding What's News: A Study of "CBS Evening News," "NBC Nightly News," "Newsweek," and "Time,"* 204; Dale E. Zacher, *The Scripps Newspapers Go to War, 1914–18*. See also Gerald Joseph Baldasty, *E. W. Scripps and the Business of Newspapers*.

93. Gans, *Deciding What's News*, 188, 201, 206.

94. Rauschenbusch, *Christianity and the Social Crisis*, 260. See also "The Shackled Editor." An anonymous editorial writer recalled that when he sought to editorially criticize the low pay and maltreatment of his city's department store workers—mostly young women—the publisher blocked him. The stores, his boss said, would organize against the paper and put it out of business. Simply put, the writer asserted, the daily press was "hampered and curbed."

95. Smyth, *Christian Ethics*, 308; "Editorial Responsibility: A Paper Read by William F. Gray before the Mississippi Press Association"; Arthur Brisbane, "The Newspaper of Today," 258; "The Profession of Journalism"; "Canons of Journalism."

96. Parker, *Inner Life of Christ*, 365.

97. Wise, "Moral Power of the Press," 410.

98. "What Is News? A Symposium from the Managing Editors of the Great American Newspapers," 44.

99. Gilbert, "Newspaper as a Judiciary," 290.

100. Recent digital explanatory journalism sites include Vox, FiveThirtyEight, the *New York Times*'s the Upshot, and Bloomberg's QuickTake and the Conversation.

101. See, for example, Thomas E. Mann, "Explanatory Journalism: A Tool in the War Against Polarization and Dysfunction." See also Richard Fawal, "Can Explanatory Journalism Cure the Internet?"; and Jonathan Stray, "Objectivity and the Decades-Long Shift from 'Just the Facts' to 'What Does It Mean?'"

102. Edward Thomas Devine, *Misery and Its Causes*, 258–60.

103. Gladden, "More about the Secular Press," 7; "Is Trend of Today's Newspapers Away from Journalistic Ideals? Frank Glass Charges Business Office Organizations Have Been Perfected at Expense of Editorial Public Service in Past Quarter Century"; Lilly, "The Ethics of Journalism," 505.

104. See, for example, Joseph C. G. Kennedy, *Preliminary Report on the Eighth Census of the United States: 1860*, 102. As early as 1860, Joseph C. G. Kennedy, a Whig politician, lawyer, and journalist, argued, "At the present day the newspaper and the periodical have become "popular educators. . . . Instead of mere chronicles of formal proceedings or passing events they are vast depositories of discussion and information on all topics which engage the thoughts or enlist the activity of men in the figure of society." See also Gilbert, "Newspaper as a Judiciary," 289–97. The Reverend Simeon Gilbert contended that as an agency of education, the newspaper was unparalleled. "Everybody belongs to this university," he said, "and no one ever graduates from it." Gladden, "Bringing All the Moral and Religious Forces," 36. Gladden counted newspapers among the "moral forces," and "the proper work of all these religious and moral institutions and organizations is largely the work of education." "Read the Newspapers: Advice Given to Evening Study Club of Baltimore, by W. K. Barrett." Barrett, a newspaper publisher, said in a speech that newspapers were one of

the public's "greatest sources of enlightenment" and the "chief educator of the masses." "The Profession of Journalism." The newspaper trade journal *Editor & Publisher* asserted, "Journalism is to all men the great informant and educator." William Van Buren, "The Press as an Educator." William Van Buren of the *Lansing (MI) Republican* in an essay, "The Press as an Educator," held that no institution of society wielded more power than the newspaper. "It brings to our doors the profoundest truths of philosophy, the subtlest essence of thought, the flowers of poetry and eloquence, and in all the treasures of knowledge accumulated by the explorer, the traveler and scholar, we are made participants by this powerful dispenser of blessings, which has created a new social, moral and intellectual world, and brought joy and happiness to millions of homes."

105. "Read the Newspapers," 12.

106. Friedrich Wilhelm Nietzsche, *On the Future of Our Educational Institutions: Homer and Classical Philology*, 40.

107. Schudson, *Discovering the News*, 102; Hofstadter, *Age of Reform*, 187–88. See also "Free-lance Writer Gives 'Inside Information on Newspaper Game.'" Ethel M. Colson, freelance writer and former literary editor of the *Chicago Record-Herald* in a talk with students at the University of Illinois, contended, "We have grown too large for the village gossip and too noisy for the town crier, so it is up to the newspaper to keep the people informed." Booker T. Washington, *My Larger Education: Being Chapters from My Experience*, 86. Washington maintained:

> To a very large extent the daily newspapers have merely taken up the work that was formerly performed by the village gossip, or by the men who sat around in the village store, talked politics, and made public opinion. The newspaper, however, does that work on a higher plane. It gives us a world-wide outlook, and it makes a commendable effort to get the truth. Even if, like the village gossip, it puts the emphasis sometimes on the wrong things and spends a lot of time over personal and unimportant matters, it at least brings all classes of people together in doing so. People who read the same newspaper are bound to feel neighborly, even though they may never meet one another, even though they live thousands of miles apart.

108. Robert E. Park, "The City: Suggestions for Investigation of Human Behavior in the City Environment," 606.

109. Robert E. Park, "The Natural History of the Newspaper," 274–75; "Ad Men's Convention." See also "Interesting Debate." Arthur Brisbane said yellow journalism was the future of journalism: "Different kinds of newspapers are necessary for different kinds of people. New York is the only city in the world that does not contain a successful anarchistic or socialistic journal, and this

is due to the fact that 'yellow' journals exist. We are trying to make the more fortunate assist the less fortunate, and we are trying to do this by an appeal to law. We tell the people who are wronged that their redress is in the ballot-box, not in crime."

110. Aline Gorren, "The Ethics of Modern Journalism," 507–10.

111. William Torrey Harris, "The Rationale of the Course of Study in the Common Schools," 357; R. White, "Morals and Manners of Journalism," 840.

112. "The Fulminations of Adostoh"; Rauschenbusch, *Christianity and the Social Crisis*, 260; Lilly, "The Ethics of Journalism," 503.

113. See, for example, "Wants to Be Yellow: Arthur Brisbane Seeks the Top Round in Saffron Journalism." Brisbane, in a speech, recalled, "I addressed a meeting of 100 Presbyterian ministers once, and when they criticized this method of journalism, I told them that when God gets ready to send a storm he creates ugly black clouds which are typified in the paper in black type; the lightning is the red type that they frequently used and the colored supplement on Sunday is the rainbow." See also "'Yellow Journalism' Defined." Brisbane once asserted, "Anything in journalism that is new and successful is yellow journalism, no matter what you or I see fit to call it. A newspaper must be seen, read, understood, and believed. The public must be told what is the matter with it, and it is up to the newspapers to tell them. It is a question of first attracting attention and then saying something that will hold it. Yellow journalism has done this."

114. Brisbane, "The Newspaper of Today," 258; "Need a Conscience"; Crawford, *The Ethics of Journalism*, 37.

115. See, for example, W. S. Lilly, "The Shibboleth of Public Opinion." Lilly asserted, "Our journalists are the prophets of democracy. It is for democracy to insist that they be true prophets and not false." See also "Freedom of the Press: Melville E. Stone's Valuable Address at the Boston Press Club's Anniversary—How Three Great Events in 1811 Have Influenced Modern Journalism—Rise of the Editorial Column—the Future." Melville E. Stone, general manager of the Associated Press, observed that the generally agreed-upon view was that aside from entertainment, newspapers "should, first, furnish the information upon which the citizen may form a judgment for his guidance in both his business and his political relations." "Fighting Fire." An editorial in the journal *Editor & Publisher* held, "The editor, from time immemorial, has been 'selling' democracy to the people—and making his community sterile soil for the propagation of the seeds of anarchy, disloyalty, sedition or insurrection against democratic rule." W. D. Showalter, "A Free Press the First Line of Defense for the World's Democracies: Great Principle, Safeguarding Human Rights, Always in Conflict with Ruling Classes and Special Interests—Popular Governments Still Adhere to Secret Process in Conduct of Public Business"; "The Call of the Nation." A

collection of short articles by journalists and officials emphasizes the theme of the newspaper's responsibility to serve democracy in a time of labor unrest. "Democracy and the Press."

116. Charles Dudley Warner, "Newspapers and the Public," 206.

117. A view earlier espoused by Alexis de Tocqueville, who wrote, "Only a newspaper can deposit the same thought in a thousand minds at once." Tocqueville, *Democracy in America*, 600.

118. "Progressive American Journalism."

119. Bleyer, *Main Currents*, 64.

120. Quoted in ibid., 93.

121. Ibid., 102.

122. Kevin Roderick, "Broad, Villaraigosa, Riordan Sign Protest Letter to *Tribune*."

123. See, for example, "An Appeal for the Truth." "Truth is the very soul of journalism," the journal insisted. "Without truth there is no public confidence, and without the trust and confidence of its readers journalism is powerless." See also Charles M. Coleman, "The Editorial Page," 260. Coleman, managing editor of the *Seattle Post-Intelligencer*, declared, "The editorial page is the heart and soul of the modern newspaper. In it are to be found the spirit that actuates a newspaper, the level of its ideals, the principles for which it fights and strives." Watterson, "Newspapers of New York." Watterson held, "This vital ethics—the source and the resource—the very soul of journalism—is disinterestedness."

124. "Newspapers Fifty Years Ago," *New York Times*, October 20, 1901, A6; Henry Irving, "The Function of the Newspaper," 684.

125. See, for example, "Editor and Pastor Exchange," *New York Times*, January 28, 1900, 1. In an editorial titled "What Is News?" the Reverend Charles Sheldon observed, "A definition of what is news requires a definition of what is not. It is not news, for example, to publish in a Topeka paper the account of a murder trial in California. It is not news to print hearsay. The news of the day is facts. Everything in the nature of supposition should have a column to itself headed 'rumor.'" See also "Columbia Lectures on Journalism: Melville E. Stone Discusses the Topic 'What Is News?' before the Students—Scope of the American Daily—Duty the Press Owes the Public in Furnishing Information—Instructive Journalism Upheld," *Editor & Publisher* (November 29, 1913): 461; "What Is News?," *Editor & Publisher* (July 8, 1922): 24; "What Is News? A Symposium from the Managing Editors of the Great American Newspapers," *Collier's*, March 18, 1911, 22; April 15, 1911, 44; May 6, 1911, 35; May 13, 1911, 42; May 20, 1911, 26; Will Irwin, "What Is News?," *Collier's*, March 11, 1911, 16; "What Is News?," *Outlook*, May 23, 1908, 39; "What Is News?," *Scribner's* 44 (October 1908): 507; and H. B. Brougham, "News—What Is It?," *Harper's Weekly*, February 17, 1912, 21.

126. "Ralph Pulitzer's Witty Speech."

127. "'Journalists and Newsmongers' Again," 13.

128. "Watterson Dinner: Distinguished Editor Guest of the New York Press Club; Pleads for Clean Journalism—Declares That News, Like Victuals, Should Be Served Hot and Savory—Recounts Early Experiences and Tells of Difficulties in Finding Work—Old Virtues Best."

129. Stuart Allan, *News Culture*, 32–33.

130. "The Shoemaker's Last."

131. "Journalists and Newsmongers," 313. A no more ardent opponent of the commercialization and influence on culture of the metropolitan press, Richard Watson Gilder was a poet, reformer, literary maven, and the editor of *Century*, one of the prominent quality genteel monthly magazines.

132. Gilbert, "Newspaper as a Judiciary," 290; Creighton, "Press, Pulpit, and Pew," 74.

133. King et al., *Education and National Character*, 15.

134. "Press and Morality."

135. John C. Merrill and S. Jack Odell, *Philosophy and Journalism*, 66–69.

136. Scott McCloud, *Reinventing Comics: How Imagination and Technology Are Revolutionizing an Art Form*; Holt, *Commercialism and Journalism*, 93.

137. Kristen Hare, "Today at the South Florida *Sun Sentinel*, a Switch to Digital Thinking."

138. Jim Norman, "Americans' Confidence in Institutions Stays Low."

139. Emily Bell, "The Rise of Mobile and Social News—and What It Means for Journalism," 88.

140. Kellie Riordan, *Accuracy, Independence, and Impartiality: How Legacy Media and Digital Natives Approach Standards in the Digital Age*, 4.

141. Xavier van Leeuwe, "How Do We Mend the Unspoken, Harmful Division of Newsrooms and Business Units?"

142. See, for example, Jessica Davies, "The *Independent*'s Hiring Writers to Do Both Native Ads and Edit Content." According to Jon O'Donnell, group commercial director of the *Independent*'s parent, ESI Media, "The thought process behind these new roles is that the writers will be close to the industry they write about, so will be best placed to help brands unlock the audiences that enjoy reading that content. They may not always write the commercial content; this could be done by a member of the commercial team in some cases. But they'll be responsible for the idea and the channels the content is distributed across: video, mobile, social, print." See also Ginny Marvin, "Consumers Can't Tell the Difference between Sponsored Content and Editorial: In a New Study, Consumers Identified Native Advertisements as Articles a Large Percentage of the Time"; "FTC Issues Enforcement Policy Statement Addressing 'Native' Advertising and Deceptively Formatted Advertisements"; Jessica Davies, "Why Trinity Mirror Created Disgusting and 'Purposefully Disruptive' Branded Content for Sky1"; and Jack Murtha and Chava Gourarie, "Do Buzzfeed's Native Political Ads Cross a Line?"

143. Michele McLellan, "A 2016 Snapshot of the Local News Startup Business."

144. Ian Burrell, "'There's No Longer This Church versus State': How *City AM* Is Tearing Down the Editorial/Commercial Divide."

145. "Tribune Publishing Co. Reports Fourth Quarter 2015 Results."

146. Rick Edmonds, "Tribune Publishing's New Management Is in Place—Now How Will They Make Money?"

147. Ken Doctor, "Between the Lines of Today's Big Tribune Reshuffle." See also Lucia Moses, "The Case Against Combining Publisher and Editor Roles." Moses quotes Jacob Weisberg, editor in chief and chairman of *Slate* (but not the day-to-day editor), who argued, "The person who's in charge of the business has a very different mindset—you're trying to bring in business and make friends. In one case you're working for the readers and in the other case you're working for the advertiser."

148. Thomas Kent, "'Build Your Own Ethics Code' for Digital Journalists."

149. Abbott, *Reminiscences*, 335.

150. R. White, "Morals and Manners of Journalism," 840.

151. Walt Harrington, "A Writer's Essay: Seeking the Extraordinary in the Ordinary."

152. "'Journalists and Newsmongers' Again," 13.

153. Art Swift, "Americans' Trust in Mass Media Sinks to New Low"; Rich Lowry, "Trump's Evil Empire: Trump Rode His Mutual Enmity with the Media to the White House."

154. See, for example, Geneva Overholser, "The Inadequacy of Objectivity as a Touchstone." See also Stephen J. Berry, "Why Objectivity Still Matters"; "The *NYT*: We Changed Reality Because Cheney Wanted Us To"; Glenn Greenwald, "Bill Keller's Self-Defense on 'Torture': The *New York Times* Editor Dismisses Debates over 'Torture' as 'Tendentious Political Correctness'"; Gavin Dahl, "'Journalism of Neutrality Is an Illusion' and Inadequate to Democracy, Says Professor"; Glenn Greenwald, "Martha Raddatz and the Faux Objectivity of Journalists"; Jonathan Stray, "Objectivity and the Decades-Long Shift from 'Just the Facts' to 'What Does It Mean?'"; Jack Shafer, "From Tom Paine to Glenn Greenwald, We Need Partisan Journalism"; "NPR Clarifies Cokie Roberts' Role after Anti-Trump Column"; Glenn Greenwald, "The Rise of Trump Shows the Danger and Sham of Compelled Journalistic Neutrality'"; and Rory O'Connor, "A for Activist: No Longer Journalism's Scarlet Letter."

155. James Carey, "Afterword: The Culture in Question," 335.

156. "House Republicans Pass Health Reform Repeal as Democrats Defend Law."

157. Ibid.

158. Michael Scherer, "In Defense of the Mainstream Media"; Arthur Brisbane, "In an Age of Voices, Moving beyond the Facts," *New York Times*, September 4, 2010, http://www.nytimes.com/2010/09/05/opinion/05pubed.html.

159. Paul Raeburn, "The Journalist as Advocate: Is There Any Other Kind?" Patricia Aufderheide, a university professor and the founder of the Center for Media & Social Impact at American University, maintains, "If what we're doing is advocating for the public, that's our job."

160. Quoted in Raeburn, "Journalist as Advocate."

161. Peter S. Goodman, "Beyond Left and Right: It's about Reality."

162. Michael Kinsley, "The Twilight of Objectivity."

163. Christians, Ferré, and Fackler, *Good News*, 119. These three scholars argue, "To be human is, in part, to value; thus the quest for systematic disinterest and disengagement is more akin to pathology than to quality understanding. It signifies moral indifference and disguises the observer's motivations under the prestige of the white lab coat."

164. Steve Outing, "Climate Change: Get over Objectivity, Newspapers." See also Sidney Blumenthal, "Journalism and Its Discontents." Blumenthal notes that as Walter Lippmann observed nearly ninety years ago, "The crisis of journalism cannot be disentangled from the crisis of national government. Government and journalism now share a crisis of credibility, trust, and competence. At the least, the crisis of journalism reveals a changing standard for and definition of 'objectivity.' Journalism, or more precisely, freedom of expression and freedom of the press, has been plunged, as a result of casual, callow, craven, or simply career-minded attitudes, into complicity, tacit and active, with a harsh and secretive administration that seeks to concentrate unaccountable power in the executive and sees itself as above the law and above reproach." See also Howard Kurtz, "The Lukewarm Truth," *Washington Post*, September 17, 2007, http://www.washingtonpost.com/wp-dyn/content/article/2007/09/16/AR2007091601411.html; Peter Johnson, "More Reporters Embrace an Advocacy Role," *USA Today*, March 6, 2007, http://usatoday30.usatoday.com/life/television/news/2007-03-05-social-journalism_N.htm; Saul Friedman, "How the Truth May Be Told by the MSM"; and Bill Carter and Jacques Steinberg, "Anchor-Advocate on Immigration Wins Viewers," *New York Times*, March 29, 2006, http://www.nytimes.com/2006/03/29/politics/anchoradvocate-on-immigration-wins-viewers.html.

165. Outing, "Climate Change."

Bibliography

Primary Sources

Abbot, Willis J. *Watching the World Go By*. Boston: Little, Brown, 1934.

Abbott, Lyman. *America in the Making*. New Haven, CT: Yale University Press, 1911.

———. *Christianity and Social Problems*. Boston: Houghton Mifflin, 1896.

———. *The Christian Ministry*. Boston: Houghton Mifflin, 1905.

———. "Democracy throughout the World." Outlook, August 31, 1912, 1023–28.

———. *Reminiscences*. Boston: Houghton Mifflin, 1915.

———. "Reminiscences: Chapter XIX, A Religious Revolution." *Outlook*, July 28, 1915, 743–60.

———. *The Rights of Man: A Study in Twentieth Century Problems*. London: James Clarke, 1901.

———. *The Spirit of Democracy*. Boston: Houghton Mifflin, 1910.

"Accuracy the Foundation: Essential to Permanent Newspaper Success, Says St. Louis Editor." *Editor & Publisher* (July 9, 1910): 6.

Adams, Henry. "The Press." In *The Education of Henry Adams*, 237–54. Boston: Houghton Mifflin, 1918.

Addams, Jane. *Democracy and Social Ethics*. New York: Macmillan, 1907.

"Ad Men's Convention." *Editor & Publisher* (September 5, 1908): 3.

Allen, Frederick L. "Newspapers and the Truth." *Atlantic Monthly*, January 1922, 44–54.

Allen, Philip Loring. *America's Awakening: The Triumph of Righteousness in High Places*. New York: F. H. Revell, 1906.

"American Congregational Theology." In *International Congregational Council: Volume of Proceedings of the Fourth International Congregational Council Held in Boston, Massachusetts, June 29–July 6, 1920*, edited by Truman J. Spencer, 246–63. New York: National Council of the Congregational Churches of the US, 1921.

"The American Congress of Churches." *Churchman* 51 (May 30, 1885): 592–94.

American Congress of Churches. *Proceedings: American Congress of Churches, Cleveland, Ohio, May, 1886*. Hartford, CT: Case, Lockwood & Brainard, 1886.

"American Newspapers: Tremendous Power for Good and Always Found Defending Right." *Editor & Publisher* (February 5, 1910): 7.

American Society of Newspaper Editors. *Problems of Journalism: Proceedings of the First Annual Meeting, American Society of Newspaper Editors*. Washington, DC: American Society of Newspaper Editors, 1923.

American Tract Society. *Home Evangelization: A View of the Wants and Prospects of Our Country, Based on Facts and Relations of Colportage*. New York: American Tract Society, 1850.

An Appeal for the Truth." *Editor & Publisher* (November 20, 1920): 26.

"Answers to Inquiries." *Christian Advocate* (April 21, 1887): 257.

"Are Newspaper Editors to Be Blamed?" *American Lutheran Survey* 8, no. 27 (1918): 845–46.

Arnold, Matthew. "Up to Easter." *Twentieth Century* 21 (May 1887): 629–43.

"Arraigns the Press: Editor of *Boston Common* Pours Hot Shot into Editorial Ranks; Mr. Richard Gives Instances Showing That Important News Is Sometimes Ignored Because It Might Hurt the Newspaper's Advertising—Declares There Can Be No Freedom until Circulation Makes Bulk of Income." *Editor & Publisher* (November 11, 1911): 1, 10.

"Arraigns the Press: Rev. Dr. Brann Points Out Some of Its Weak Points in a Sermon; Attacks the Anonymous Writer—Declares Editorials and Articles Should Be Signed by the Writers—Recommends Law to That Effect—Insincerity of the Semi-Socialist—What Greed Will Sometimes Do." *Editor & Publisher* (March 30, 1912): 1.

"Asks Church to Aid Press: Dr. Williams Says Members Can Have Influence on Moral Tone of Newspapers." *Editor & Publisher* (February 1, 1913): 9.

Associated Press. "Mr. Bryan and the Associated Press." *Service Bulletin of the Associated Press* (June 15, 1908): 12.

"Back to God's Law; Newspapers Must Return to Christ and the Ten Commandments; Bishop McFall Discourses on the Mission of the Press and Says High Moral Standard Is Required—Enumerates Defects of Newspapers and Suggests a Remedy—Four Rules for Guidance of Newspaper Men." *Editor & Publisher* (May 13, 1911): 3, 6.

"Back to Old Ideals: There Exists Decided Tendency to Reaction, Says Noted Editor." *Editor & Publisher* (February 5, 1910): 5.

Baker, Ray Stannard. *American Chronicle: The Autobiography of Ray Stannard Baker [David Grayson]*. New York: C. Scribner's Sons, 1945.

Balch, William Monroe. *Christianity and the Labor Movement*. Boston: Sherman, French, 1912.

Barker, John Marshall. *The Social Gospel and the New Era*. New York: Macmillan, 1919.

Barrett, Clifford L. "A New Era of Prayer." *New Era Magazine* 26, no. 3 (1920): 268–69.

Barrett, John Pressley. "The Beginning and Beyond: A Brief Study of the Conditions and Ideals Which Gave Rise to the Christian Church." In *The Centennial of Religious Journalism*, edited by John Pressley Barrett, 13–26. Dayton, Ohio: Christian Publishing Association, 1908.

Bascom, John. *Evolution and Religion; or, Faith as a Part of a Complete Cosmic System*. New York: G. P. Putnam, 1897.

———. *Social Theory: A Grouping of Social Facts and Principles*. New York: T. Y. Crowell, 1895.

———. *Sociology*. New York & London: G. P. Putnam's Sons, 1887.

Beattie, Francis R. "Christian Ethics and Modern Life." *Homiletic Review* 51, no. 6 (1906): 413–17.

Beveridge, Albert J. "The Journalist as a Public Man: How Self Interest Injures the People's Interests." *Saturday Evening Post*, November 23, 1907, 23, 28.

Bliss, William Dwight Porter, ed. *The Encyclopedia of Social Reform Including Political Economy, Political Science, Sociology and Statistics*. New York: Funk & Wagnalls, 1897.

———, ed. *The New Encyclopedia of Social Reform*. London: Funk & Wagnalls, 1909.

"The Book Concern." *Christian Advocate and Journal*, September 2, 1836, 6.

Bowles, Samuel. "The Independent Press: Its Opportunities and Duties." *North American Review* 183, no. 596 (1906): 40–46.

Boynton, Henry Walcott. *Journalism and Literature, and Other Essays*. Boston: Houghton Mifflin, 1904.

Bradford, Amory Howe. *My Brother*. Boston: Pilgrim Press, 1910.

Bridgman, Howard A. "Journalism as an Opportunity for Christian Service." *The Intercollegian: Organ of the Student Department of the International Committee of Young Men's Christian Associations of North America and of the Student Volunteer Movement for Foreign Missions* 24, no. 9 (1902): 215–17.

Brisbane, Arthur. "The Newspaper of Today." *Washington Newspaper* 7, no. 9 (1922).

Brooks, Noah. "The Newspaper of the Future." *Forum* 9 (July 1890): 569–78.

Bryan, William Jennings. *The Commoner Condensed*. Vol. 2. Chicago: Henneberry, 1908.

———. "The Moral Awakening." *Saturday Evening Post*, December 15, 1906, 3–4.

"Bryan to the Craft." *Editor & Publisher* (September 8, 1906): 1, 4.

Buckham, Matthew H. "Lay Theology." *Andover Review* 1 (February 1884): 149–59.

Burrell, David James. "Wanted: A Newspaper." In *The Golden Passional, and Other Sermons*, edited by David James Burrell, 183–96. New York: W. B. Ketcham, 1897.

Bushnell, Horace. *Views of Christian Nurture, and of Subjects Adjacent Thereto*. Hartford, CT: Edwin Hunt, 1847.

"A Business Man's Opinion of the Press." *Fourth Estate* (May 21, 1921): 9.

"The Call of the Nation." *Editor & Publisher* (January 15, 1920): 5–6, 9.

Campbell, R. J. *The New Theology*. New York: Macmillan, 1907.

"Canons of Journalism." *Annals of the American Academy of Political and Social Science* 109 (September 1923): 305–6.

"Can the Impartiality of the News-Gathering and the News-Supplying Agencies Be Fairly Challenged?" In *Proceedings of the National Newspaper Conference, July 29–August 1, 1912*, edited by National Newspaper Conference, 36–38. Madison: University of Wisconsin, 1912.

Carleton, Edward. "The Power of the Press." *Outlook*, February 19, 1898, 471–72.

Carlyle, Thomas. *Critical and Miscellaneous Essays*. New York: D. Appleton, 1864.

"The Century on Journalism: Conscience in Journalism; Open Letter by Eugene M. Camp." *Journalist* (July 11, 1891): 12–13.

Chapin, Edwin H. *Moral Aspects of City Life*. New York: Henry Lyon, 1853.

Charlton, John. "The Sunday Newspaper." *Christian Work* 60, no. 1531 (1896): 977–78.

Christian Herald. "The Pulpit and the Press." *Religious Informer* 4, no. 9 (1823).

"Christianity Arming: Memoranda of the Press-Revolution." *Circular*, January 31, 1854, 98.

"The Church and the Newspaper." *Christian Advocate*, September 5, 1901, 1403–4.

Church Congress in the United States and Episcopal Church. *Authorized Report of the Proceedings of the Congress of the Protestant Episcopal Church in the United States*. New York: Thomas Whittaker, 1894.

Clark, Charles Worcester. "The Day of Rest." *Atlantic Monthly*, September 1889, 366–67.

Clarke, James Freeman. "Rational Sunday Observance." *North American Review* 131, no. 389 (1880): 496–506.

Chicago Commission on Race Relations. *The Negro in Chicago: A Study of Race Relations and a Race Riot*. Chicago: University of Chicago Press, 1922.

"Clean Journalism: Subject of Simultaneous Address in Ninety-Seven Cities and Towns; Beginning of Wide Movement to Be Conducted under the Auspices of the Christian Science Publishing Co.—News Policy of Clean

Journalism Must Be Established through Evolution." *Editor & Publisher* (April 1, 1911): 1, 3.

Coleman, Charles M. "The Editorial Page." *Washington Newspaper* 7, no. 9 (1922): 260–62.

Commons, John Rogers. *Social Reform and the Church*. New York: Thomas Y. Crowell, 1894.

"Condemns Colored News: Prof. Bleyer Compares It with the Adulterated Food Evil." *Editor & Publisher* (April 19, 1913): 5.

Connolly, Charles B. "The Ethics of Modern Journalism." *New Catholic World* 75 (July 1, 1902): 453–62.

Cook, Joseph. "Sunday Newspapers." In *Boston Monday Lectures*, edited by Joseph Cook, 132–41. London: Richard D. Dickinson, 1886.

———. *Vital Orthodoxy: With an Index and Analysis of Contents, and a Symposium on the Christian Soteriology; or, The Question, "What Saves Men, and Why?"* London: Richard D. Dickinson, 1886.

Cooper, James Fenimore. *The American Democrat; or, Hints on the Social and Civic Relations of the United States of America*. Cooperstown, NY: H. & E. Phinney, 1838.

Cosgrave, John O'Hara. "Present-Day Opportunities in Literature." *New England Magazine* 39 (September 1909): 9–13.

Crafts, Wilbur F. *The Sabbath for Man: A Study of the Origin, Obligation, History, Advantages and Present State of Sabbath Observance, with Special Reference to the Rights of Workingmen, Based on Scripture, Literature, and Especially on a Symposium of Correspondence with Persons of All Nations and Denominations*. Washington, DC: International Reform Bureau, 1894.

Crane, Frank. "What a Publication Owes to Its Readers." *Editor & Publisher* (November 14, 1914): 428.

Crawford, Nelson. *The Ethics of Journalism*. New York: Alfred A. Knopf, 1924.

"Creelman on the School." *Editor & Publisher* (February 3, 1906): 4.

Creighton, John R. "Press, Pulpit and Pew." *Methodist Review* 77 (January 1895): 68–80.

"Critical Notices." *North American Magazine* 1 (July 1833): 195–98.

Crosby, George Ellery, Jr. "The Sheldon Experiment." *Fame: A Journal for Advertisers* 9, no. 3 (1900): 101–2.

Crosby, Howard. "Christian Co-operation in Relation to the Enforcement of Moral Legislation." In *National Needs and Remedies*, edited by Evangelical Alliance for the United States of America, 163–70. New York: Baker & Taylor, 1890.

Curtis, David A. "'As Jesus Would Run It.'" *Journalist* (March 24, 1900): 646.

———. "The New Journalism." *Journalist* (May 29, 1895): 43.

"Daily Paper Praised and Also Condemned: St. Louis Clergyman and Ethical Culture Leader at Wide Variance in Their Views as to What Sort of News

Should Be Printed—*Globe-Democrat* and *Post-Dispatch* Have Something to Say." *Editor & Publisher* (January 19, 1916): 1004.

Dana, Charles A. *The Art of Newspaper Making: Three Lectures*. New York: D. Appleton, 1895.

———. "The Newspaper and the Art of Making It." *Scientific American Supplement* 39, no. 995 (1895): 15907–10.

"Dangerous Selections." *Boston Weekly Magazine*, March 13, 1841, 205.

"David Graham Phillips." *Editor & Publisher* (March 4, 1911): 12.

Davies, David. "Mirror of Life." *Editor & Publisher* (July 31, 1920): 12.

Davis, Philip, and Bertha Schwartz. *Immigration and Americanization: Selected Readings*. Boston: Ginn, 1920.

"The Decay of American Journalism." *Dial*, April 16, 1897, 237–39.

"A Declaration of Principles Adopted by the Religious Education Association." *Religious Education* 5, no. 1 (1910): 52–53.

Delany, Selden P. "The Clergy and Social Reform." *Churchman* 94 (December 8, 1906): 915–16.

"The Demand for Christlikeness." *Congregationalist*, March 29, 1900, 439.

"Democracy and the Press." *Editor & Publisher* (October 15, 1921): 32.

"Description of the Paper." *Congregationalist*, March 22, 1900, 408.

Detweiler, Frederick German. *The Negro Press in the United States*. Chicago: University of Chicago Press, 1922.

Devine, Edward Thomas. *Misery and Its Causes*. New York: Macmillan, 1911.

Diffendorfer, Ralph Eugene. *The Church and the Community*. New York: Council of Women for Home Missions and Interchurch World Movement of North America, 1920.

"Dignity of the Press." *Green Mountain Gem: A Monthly Journal of Literature, Science and the Arts* 5 (January 1847): 22.

Donald, Robert. "Sunday Newspapers in the United States." *Universal Review* 8 (September 1890): 78–89.

"Draws Vivid Picture of Ideal Newspaper: Louis Wiley, of *New York Times*, Outlines Policies and Methods of Up-to-the-Hour Journalism—Discusses Awakening of Advertisers to Their Opportunities." *Editor & Publisher* (December 23, 1916): 14.

Du Bois, W. E. B. *The Souls of Black Folk: Essays and Sketches*. Chicago: A. C. McClurg, 1909.

Dulles, Avery. "Religion and the News Media: A Theologian Reflects." *America* 171, no. 9 (1994): 6–9.

E. A. D. "Newspapers." *Arcturus: A Journal of Books and Opinion* 1 (January 1841): 69–75.

Earp, Edwin Lee. "Discussion." *American Journal of Sociology* 12, no. 5 (1907): 687–90.

———. *The Social Engineer*. New York: Eaton & Mains, 1911.

Eckman, George P. "Pulpit and Press: Newspapers Are to Be Reckoned among the Most Potent Forces Making for Righteousness—Pulpit May Well Look upon the Press as Its Most Important Ally." *Editor & Publisher* (December 25, 1909): 6–7.

"Editorial Responsibility: A Paper Read by William F. Gray before the Mississippi Press Association." *Fourth Estate* (May 31, 1894): 4.

"Education." *American Whig Review* 12 (July 1850): 87–92.

Eliot, Charles William. *American Contributions to Civilization, and Other Essays and Addresses*. New York: Century, 1898.

Ellcee. "Sunday Newspapers." *Notes and Queries* (March 7, 1874): 197–98.

Elliot, Ernest Eugene. *How to Fill the Pews*. Cincinnati: Standard, 1920.

Elliot, Henry R. "The Ratio of News." *Forum* 5 (March 1888): 99–107.

Ellwood, Charles. "The Formation of Public Opinion: The Principles in Accordance with Which Public Opinion Can Be Formed by the Church Democratically and Effectively." *Religious Education* 15 (April 1920): 73–80.

Ely, Richard T. "Christianity as a Social Force." In *Neely's History of the Parliament of Religions and Religious Congresses at the World's Columbian Exposition*, edited by Walter R. Houghton, 550–54. Chicago: F. T. Neely, 1893.

———. *Ground under Our Feet: An Autobiography*. New York: Macmillan, 1938.

———. *An Introduction to Political Economy*. New York: Hunt & Eaton, 1894.

———. *The Labor Movement in America*. New York: Thomas Y. Crowell, 1886.

———. *Problems of To-Day: A Discussion of Protective Tariffs, Taxation, and Monopolies*. New York: T. Y. Crowell, 1890.

———. "Public Control of Private Corporations." *Cosmopolitan* 30 (February 1901): 430–33.

———. *Report of the Organization of the American Economic Association*. Baltimore: John Murphy, 1886.

———. *The Social Aspects of Christianity, and Other Essays*. New York: Thomas Y. Crowell, 1889.

———. *The Social Law of Service*. New York: Eaton & Mains, 1896.

———. *Studies in the Evolution of Industrial Society*. New York: Macmillan, 1903.

Emerson, Ralph Waldo. *Essays*. Boston: J. Munroe, 1841.

———. *The Prose Works of Ralph Waldo Emerson*. Boston: Fields, Osgood, 1869.

"Encourage the Use of English." *Editor & Publisher* (February 19, 1916): 1118.

"Ethics of the Press." *Editor & Publisher* (April 14, 1906): 7.

"Failure of a Religious Newspaper Venture." *Fourth Estate* (March 19, 1921): 18.

"Fighting Fire." *Editor & Publisher* (February 8, 1919): 32.

Fletcher, A. E. "The Ideal Newspaper." *Independent*, March 29, 1900, 771.

Flint, Leon Nelson. *The Conscience of the Newspaper: A Case Book in the Principles and Problems of Journalism*. New York: D. Appleton, 1925.

"For a Truthful Press." *Editor & Publisher* (May 18, 1907): 8.
Fosdick, Harry Emerson. *Christianity and Progress.* New York: Fleming H. Revell, 1922.
"Founders Day at Lafayette College." *Lafayette* 27, no. 6 (1900): 53.
Foxcroft, Frank. "The American Sunday Newspaper." *Living Age* 255, no. 3304 (1907): 259–64.
"Freedom of the Press: Melville E. Stone's Valuable Address at the Boston Press Club's Anniversary—How Three Great Events in 1811 Have Influenced Modern Journalism—Rise of the Editorial Column—the Future." *Editor & Publisher* (December 21, 1911): 4.
"Free-lance Writer Gives 'Inside Information on Newspaper Game.'" *Fourth Estate* (April 26, 1919): A12.
French, George. *Advertising: The Social and Economic Problem.* New York: Ronald Press, 1915.
———. "The Damnation of the Magazines." *Twentieth Century Magazine* 6 (June 1912): 3–15.
"A Frenzied Financial Critic." *Outlook*, December 24, 1904, 1016–17.
Fry, Benjamin St. James. "Religious Journalism." *Zion's Herald*, August 5, 1891, 1.
"The Fulminations of Adostoh." *Journalist* (July 15, 1905): 196.
"Garbling and Misrepresentation." *National Era* (November 4, 1852): 178.
"Gaynor's Newspaper: New York's Mayor Gives His Ideas on How It Should Be Conducted; Declares That a Small Home Circulation Is Worth a Million in the Gutter—Dwells on the Importance of Truth in All Departments and Advocates Brevity and Simplicity of Statement." *Editor & Publisher* (December 2, 1911): 1, 10.
Gilbert, Simeon. "Christian Journalism: Its Idea and Its Ideal." *Chautauquan* 2, no. 5 (1882): 274–78.
———. "The Newspaper as a Judiciary." *American Journal of Sociology* 12, no. 3 (1906): 289–97.
Gladden, Washington. *Applied Christianity: Moral Aspects of Social Questions.* 1886. Reprint, New York: Arno Press, 1976.
———. "The Attitude of the Secular Press in America towards Religion." In *American Congress of Churches: Proceedings of the Hartford Meeting, 1885*, edited by the Executive Committee of the American Congress of Churches, 99–107. Hartford, CT: Case, Lockwood & Brainard, 1885.
———. "Bringing All the Moral and Religious Forces into Effective Educational Unity." In *Education and National Character*, edited by Henry Churchill King et al., 33–42. Chicago: Religious Education Association, 1908.
———. "Christian Journalism." *Christian Union*, January 26, 1882, 80–81.
———. *The Christian Pastor and the Working Church.* New York: Scribner, 1898.

———. *The Church and Modern Life*. Boston: Houghton Mifflin, 1908.

———. "Educational Unity of the Moral and Educational Forces." *Homiletic Review* 55, no. 4 (1908): 307–11.

———. "More about the Secular Press." *Christian Union*, June 18, 1885, 7–8.

———. *Recollections*. Boston: Houghton Mifflin, 1909.

———. "The Relation of Corporations to Public Morals." *Bibliotheca Sacra* 52, no. 208 (1895): 607–28.

———. *Ruling Ideas of the Present Age*. Boston: Houghton Mifflin, 1895.

———. *Social Facts and Forces: The Factory—the Labor Union—the Corporation—the Railway—the City—the Church*. New York: Knickerbocker Press, 1897.

———. "Tainted Newspapers, Good and Bad: Address Delivered at Kansas Newspaper Week under the Auspices of the Department of Journalism, University of Kansas, May 10 to 14, 1914." *University of Kansas News-Bulletin* (November 30, 1914): 1–18.

———. *Tools and the Man: Property and Industry under the Christian Law*. Boston: Houghton Mifflin, 1893.

———. *Working People and Their Employers*. Boston: Lockwood, Brooks, 1876.

Gompers, Samuel. "Labor News and Labor's Views Suppressed." *American Federationist* 29 (March 1922): 199–202.

———. "The Lockwood Committee, Mr. Gompers, the Press." *American Federationist* 29 (June 1922): 414–20.

———. "The Newspapers and Unemployment." *American Federationist* 29 (March 1922): 204–8.

Goodrich, Samuel G. *Recollections of a Lifetime; or, Men and Things I Have Seen, in a Series of Familiar Letters to a Friend, Historical, Biographical, Anecdotal and Descriptive*. New York: C. M. Saxton, 1859.

"'The Goods We Sell': The Business of a Newspaper Is Made Upstairs in the Editorial Rooms—Advertising Will Come—a Newspaper Established in the Family Circle—the Deadly Menace to Independent Journalism." *Editor & Publisher* (August 5, 1911): 3.

Gordon, Anna A. *Frances E. Willard: A Memorial Volume*. Chicago: Woman's Temperance Publishing Association, 1898.

Gorren, Aline. "The Ethics of Modern Journalism." *Scribner's Magazine* 19, no. 4 (1896): 507–13.

Grady, Henry W. "The Opportunities of Journalism." In *Joel Chandler Harris' Life of Henry W. Grady Including His Writings and Speeches*, edited by Joel Chandler Harris, 434–35. New York: Cassell, 1890.

Green, Andrew H. "Scenic Beauties of Fort Washington Battlefield: The American Revolution and the Free Press; An Address by the Hon. Andrew H. Green, President of the American Scenic and Historic Preservation Society, at the Dedication of the Fort Washington Monument, in New York

City, November 16, 1901." In *Annual Report of the American Scenic and Historic Preservation Society to the Legislature of the State of New York*, by American Scenic and Historic Preservation Society, 83–89. Albany, NY: Wynkoop, Hallenbeck, Crawford, 1898.

Greene, Asa. *A Glance at New York: Embracing the City Government, Theatres, Hotels, Churches, Mobs, Monopolies, Learned Professions, Newspapers, Rogues, Dandies, Fires and Firemen, Water and Other Liquids, &C., &C.* New York: A. Greene, 1837.

Grimké, Thomas Smith. *Address on the Patriot Character of the Temperance Reformation: Delivered before the Charleston Temperance Society, and the Young Men's Temperance Society of Charleston, on Tuesday Evening, 26th February 1833.* Charleston, SC: Observer Office Press, 1833.

Gulick, Sidney L. *The Fight for Peace: An Aggressive Campaign for American Churches.* New York: Fleming H. Revell, 1915.

Hapgood, Norman. *The Changing Years: Reminiscences of Norman Hapgood.* New York: Farrar & Rinehart, 1930.

Harper, William Allen. "Faith and Progress." *Herald of Gospel Liberty*, July 20, 1922, 679–80.

Harrington, Walt. "A Writer's Essay: Seeking the Extraordinary in the Ordinary." *NiemanStoryboard*, March 28, 1997. http://niemanstoryboard.org/stories/a-writers-essay-seeking-the-extraordinary-in-the-ordinary-2/.

Harris, Samuel. *Kingdom of Christ on Earth: Twelve Lectures Delivered before the Students of the Theological Seminary, Andover.* Andover, MA: Warren F. Draper Press, Rand, Avery, 1874.

Harris, William Torrey. "The Rationale of the Course of Study in the Common Schools." In *Annual Report of the Superintendent of Public Instruction Being the Forty-Third Annual Report upon the Public Schools of New Hampshire*, by Office of Superintendent of Public Instruction, 342–59. Manchester, NH: John B. Clarke, 1889.

"Have We a Free Press? This Question Will Be Faced by Newspaper and Magazine Writers at a Conference Arranged by the Extension Division of the University of Wisconsin." *La Follette's Weekly Magazine*, June 8, 1912, 7, 15.

Haweis, Hugh Reginald. "The New Pulpit." *North American Review* 160 (February 1895): 172–84.

Hayes, Edward Cary. "The Sociological Point of View." In *Papers and Proceedings, Sixteenth Annual Meeting, American Sociological Society, Held at Pittsburgh, Pennsylvania, December 27–30.* Vol. 16, *Factors in Social Evolution*. Chicago: University of Chicago Press, 1922.

Hayes, William. "Can a Trust Company Successfully Administer a Great Newspaper? The Experiment of the Illinois Merchants Trust Company with the *Chicago Daily News* Creates Much Discussion." *Bankers' Magazine* 111 (November 1925): 709–13.

"Henry Ward Beecher." *Atlantic Monthly*, May 1858, 862–70.
"Henry Watterson." *North American Review* 841 (June 1908): 841–44.
"Henry Watterson, 'Good Judge and Master of Style.'" *Editor & Publisher* (July 16, 1910): 8.
"Henry Watterson's Retirement." *Nation*, August 17, 1918, 164–65.
"The *Herald*'s Place in Journalism." *Editor & Publisher* (January 22, 1920): 6.
Herron, George Davis. *The Christian Society*. Chicago: Fleming H. Revell, 1894.
"Highways and Byways." *Chautauquan* 30 (October 1899): 8.
"Highways & Byways." *Chautauquan* 30 (December 1899): 234.
Hodge, Orlando John. *Reminiscences*. Cleveland, OH: Imperial Press, 1902.
Hodges, George. *Faith and Social Service: Eight Lectures Delivered before the Lowell Institute*. New York: Thomas Whittaker, 1896.
Holt, Hamilton. *Commercialism and Journalism*. Boston: Houghton Mifflin, 1909.
Horwill, Herbert W. "W. T. Stead." *Nation*, March 17, 1926, 292.
Houston, Herbert S. "Truth Drive Began in the Early Days: Past President of AFA Recalls the Notable Sheldon Experiment When *Topeka Capital* Was Edited 'As Jesus Would Have Done It.'" *Editor & Publisher* (June 27, 1936): 15–16.
Howe, Frederic Clemson. *The Confessions of a Reformer*. New York: Charles Scribner's Sons, 1925.
Hughes, Thomas P. "Sensational Journalism." *Independent*, June 11, 1896, 4–5.
"The Human Publisher." *Journalist* (July 11, 1891): 8.
Hyder, Clyde K. "The Press and Public Service." *Business Philosopher* 19, no. 11 (1922): 5–7.
"The Idea Growing." *Circular*, June 6, 1852, 118.
"'The Ideal Newspaper.'" *Current Literature* 48, no. 3 (1910): 335–36.
"The Ideal Newspaper." *Homiletic Review* 33 (May 1897): 482.
"Ideal Newspaper: Is an Emotionless Machine—Its Sole Function Is to Give the News Truthfully and Dispassionately—Editorials Have Not the Influence They Once Had." *Editor & Publisher* (January 1, 1910): 6.
"Importance of Truth in All Departments and Advocates Brevity and Simplicity of Statement." *Editor & Publisher* (December 2, 1911): 1, 10.
"Independence for Editors." *New Republic*, August 17, 1918, 61–63.
"Independent Newspapers." *Editor & Publisher* (February 21, 1903): 6.
"Influence of Sunday Newspapers." *Christian's Penny Magazine*, August 16, 1834, 263.
Ingersoll, Robert G. "Henry M. Taber's 'Faith or Fact,' and Its Suppression." *Free Thought Magazine* 17 (July 1899): 390–95.
Interchurch World Movement of North America. *Report on the Steel Strike of 1919*. New York: Harcourt, Brace, 1921.
"Interesting Debate." *Editor & Publisher* (February 2, 1907): 7.

Irving, Henry. "The Function of the Newspaper." In *Modern Eloquence*, edited by Thomas B. Reed et al., 681–85. Philadelphia: J. D. Morris, 1901.

Irwin, Will. "The Editor and the News." *Collier's*, April 1, 1911, 18–19, 28–29.

———. *The Making of a Reporter*. New York: Putnam, 1942.

"Is Honest Journalism Possible?" *Current Literature* 46 (January 1909): 46–48.

"Is Trend of Today's Newspapers Away from Journalistic Ideals? Frank Glass Charges Business Office Organizations Have Been Perfected at Expense of Editorial Public Service in Past Quarter Century." *Editor & Publisher* (July 2, 1921): 13.

Jackson, Alexander, ed. *Sunday Rest in the Twentieth Century: Containing an Account of the International Sunday Rest Congress at St. Louis; the Various Papers and Addresses Presented at It; Sketches of the Societies Which United in Holding It; and Portraits and Autographs of the Leading Advocates of Sunday Rest*. Cleveland: International Federation of Sunday Rest Associations of America, 1905.

Jackson, Mary Anna. *Memoirs of Stonewall Jackson by His Widow, Mary Anna Jackson*. Louisville, KY: Prentice Press, 1895.

James, Henry. *The American Scene*. New York: Harper & Brothers, 1907.

Jefferson, Thomas. *Letters and Addresses of Thomas Jefferson*. Edited by William B. Parker and Jonas Viles. Buffalo, NY: National Jefferson Society, 1903.

———. *The Works of Thomas Jefferson: Published by Order of Congress from the Original Manuscripts Deposited in the Department of State*. Edited by H. A. Washington. New York: Townsend MacCoun, 1884.

Johnson, Herrick. "Sunday Newspapers." *Our Day: A Record and Review of Current Reform* 3, no. 14 (1889): 114–26.

"Joseph Bryan on Journalism." *Editor & Publisher* (April 7, 1906): 4.

"Journalists and Newsmongers." *Century Magazine* 40 (June 1890): 313–15.

"'Journalists and Newsmongers' Again." *Journalist* (July 11, 1891): 12–13.

"Journalists Meet at Madison to Discuss Questions of Timely Interest; Accuracy and Impartiality of Associated Press Reports Indispensable to Its Success, Says Melville E. Stone—Dr. George H. Vincent against Municipally Owned Newspapers—Socialist Gives His Views." *Editor & Publisher* (August 3, 1912): 1, 16–17.

Keeley, James. "Newspaper Work." In *The Making of a Newspaper*. Seattle: University of Washington Press, 1913.

Kelly, Fred C. "A College Professor with Punch." *American Magazine* 79, no. 4 (1915): 61.

Kennedy, Joseph C. G. *Preliminary Report on the Eighth Census of the United States: 1860*. Washington, DC: Government Printing Office, 1862.

Kimball, Arthur Reed. "The Invasion of Journalism." *Atlantic Monthly*, July 1900, 119–24.

King, Henry Churchill, et al. *Education and National Character.* Chicago: Religious Education Association, 1908.

Kingsbury, O. A. "A Christian Daily Paper." *New Englander and Yale Review* 47 (September 1887): 182–88.

Lee, Julia Tolman. *The Spirit of Service: Seven Lessons on Christian Stewardship for Class and Discussion Groups.* New York: Fleming H. Revell, 1922.

Lee, Samuel H. "Men of Wealth and Institutions of Learning." *New Englander and Yale Review* 42 (June 1888): 379–420.

Lewis, Abram Herbert. *Swift Decadence of Sunday: What Next?* Plainfield, NJ: American Sabbath Tract Society, 1899.

Lilly, W. S. "The Ethics of Journalism." *Forum* 4 (July 1889): 503–12.

———. *On Shibboleths.* London: Chapman and Hall, 1892.

———. "The Shibboleth of Public Opinion." *Forum* 10 (November 1890): 256–63.

Lippmann, Walter. "The Basic Problem of Democracy." *Atlantic Monthly,* November 1919, 616–27.

———. *Drift and Mastery: An Attempt to Diagnose the Current Unrest.* New York: Mitchell Kennerley, 1914.

Lippmann, Walter, and Charles Merz. "A Test of the News." *New Republic,* August 8, 1920, 1–48.

"Literary Notices." *Evangelical Magazine and Missionary Chronicle* 8 (January 1878): 36.

"London Newspapers." *London* 5, no. 122 (1843): 337–52.

The London representative of the *Congregationalist.* "An American Editor of a London Weekly." *Congregationalist,* August 29, 1895, 300–301.

Lord, Chester S. "Reminiscences of Charles A. Dana and the Old *New York Sun.*" *Saturday Evening Post,* July 30, 1921.

Lowell, James Russell. "The Pious Editor's Creed." In *The Complete Poetical Works of James Russell Lowell.* Boston: Houghton Mifflin, 1896.

MacArthur, Robert Stuart. "Press and Pulpit: Allies in All That Is Noblest in Civilization and Divinest in Humanity; Ideal of Each Is Best Attained When Both Join Hands in Interest of Humanity and Religion." *Editor & Publisher* (April 29, 1911): 18–19.

"Magazine Dinner: Periodical Publishers Hear Sensational Speech by Bishop Williams; He Said that 'Big Interests' Control the Daily Press—Francis J. Heney Also Denounced the Newspapers—Colonel Roosevelt Spoke a Kind Word for the Dailies, but Said the Magazines 'Have a Greater Influence in Shaping Public Opinion.'" *Editor & Publisher* (January 14, 1911): 1, 4.

Martin, E. S. "New Testament Christianity in Practice." *Harper's Bazaar,* April 15, 1899, 310–11.

Massachusetts Historical Society. *John Adams, Samuel Adams, and James Warren: Warren-Adams Letters, Being Chiefly a Correspondence among John Adams, Samuel Adams, and James Warren . . . 1743–1814*. Boston: Massachusetts Historical Society, 1917.

Mathews, Shailer. "The Development of Social Christianity in America during the Past Twenty-Five Years." *Journal of Religion* 7, no. 4 (1927): 376–86.

———. *The Making of To-morrow: Interpretations of the World To-day*. New York: Eaton & Mains, 1913.

———. "The Significance of the Church to the Social Movement." *American Journal of Sociology* 4, no. 5 (1899): 603–20.

———. *The Validity of American Ideals*. New York: Abingdon Press, 1922.

Mathews, Shailer, and Gerald Birney Smith, eds. *A Dictionary of Religion and Ethics*. New York: Macmillan, 1921.

Maverick, Augustus. *Henry J. Raymond and the New York Press, for Thirty Years: Progress of American Journalism from 1840 to 1870*. Hartford, CT: A. S. Hale, 1870.

McClure, Edmund. "The Church and the Press." In *Official Report of the Church Congress Held at Birmingham on October 3rd, 4th, 5th, and 6th, 1893*, edited by C. Dunkley, 506–12. London: Bemrose & Sons, 1893.

McConnell, Samuel D. "The Church in Modern Society." *Outlook*, January 15, 1898, 177–80.

McLellan, Archibald. "The *Christian Science Monitor*." *Christian Science Journal* 26, no. 8 (1908): 505–7.

———. "Editor's Table." *Christian Science Journal* 26, no. 1 (1908): 571.

McQuaid, Bernard J. "The Decay of Protestantism." *North American Review* 136, no. 315 (1883): 135–52.

Mears, John William. "Position of the Secular Press on Moral Questions." *Independent*, July 29, 1880, 3.

Mellen, Grenville. *The Age of Print: A Poem, Delivered before the Phi Beta Kappa Society, at Cambridge, 26 August, 1830*. Boston: Carter and Hendee, 1830.

M'Elroy, W. N. "The Ethics of the Press." *Christian Advocate*, November 20, 1890, 767.

Men and Religion Forward Movement. *The Church and the Press*. Vol. 7 of *Messages of the Men and Religion Movement, Complete in Seven Volumes, Including the Revised Reports of the Commission Presented at the Congress of the Men and Religion Forward Movement, April, 1912, Together with the Principal Addresses Delivered at the Congress*. New York: Association Press, 1912.

———. *Messages of the Men and Religion Movement*. New York: Association Press, 1912.

Methodist Episcopal Church. *Official Minutes of the Eighty-Ninth Session of the New England Conference of the Methodist Episcopal Church Held at Milford, Mass., April 4–10, 1888*. Boston: Alfred Mudge & Son, 1888.

"The Middle Course." *Editor & Publisher* (May 19, 1906): 4.

Mill, John Stuart. *Considerations on Representative Government*. London: Savill and Edwards, 1861.

Miller, Charles Grant. "The Making of Better Citizens in Brooklyn: Educational Work among the Young and Old Is Only One of the Many Services That Make the *Eagle*." *Editor & Publisher* (February 12, 1921): 5, 14.

Ministers of the Unitarian Church. *The Unitarian Pulpit: Discourses on the Christian Spirit and Life*. London: Edward T. Whitfield, 1857.

"The Mirrors of a Degenerate World: The Daily Press Reflects the Spirit of a Corrupt Generation; It Is a Potent Factor of Evil in the Hand of the Money Power." *Flaming Sword* 13, no. 45 (1899): 6.

"The Modern Sunday." *New York Observer and Chronicle* 82, no. 31 (1904): 82, 133.

Moody, Dwight Lyman, and L. T. Remlap. *"The Gospel Awakening," Comprising the Sermons and Addresses, Prayer-Meeting Talks and Bible Readings of the Great Revival Meetings Conducted by Moody and Sankey. Also the Lives of D. L. Moody, I. D. Sankey, P. P. Bliss. And Sermons and Addresses by Rev. G. F. Pentecost, Joseph Cook, D. W. Whittle, and Frances E. Willard*. Chicago: Fairbanks and Palmer, 1885.

Moore, John Weeks. *Moore's Historical, Biographical, and Miscellaneous Gatherings, in the Form of Disconnected Notes Relative to Printers, Printing, Publishing, and Editing of Books, Newspapers, Magazines and Other Literary Productions, Such as the Early Publications of New England, the United States, and the World, from the Discovery of the Art, or from 1420 to 1886, with Many Brief Notices of Authors, Publishers, Editors, Printers, and Inventors*. Concord, NH: Republican Press Association, 1886.

"The Moral Standard of the Secular Press." *Christian Observer*, March 21, 1900, 2.

"More Lawsuits in *Christian Science* Circles." *Christian Century* 39, no. 1 (1922): 57.

Morris, George P. "Religious Journalism and Journalists." *Review of Reviews* 12, no. 4 (1895): 413–29.

———. "Young Journalists Worth Knowing." *Congregationalist and Christian World*, December 9, 1905, 851–53.

Moses, Adolph. "Democracy and Despotism." *American Magazine of Civics* 9, no. 4 (1896): 261–76.

A Mother. "Practical." *New York Evangelist*, February 6, 1836, 26.

"Mr. Sheldon's Christian Daily." *Congregationalist*, March 22, 1900, 403–4.

"Mr. Sheldon's Experiment." *Friends' Intelligencer*, April 28, 1900, 335–36.

"Mr. Sheldon's Experiment." *Outlook*, March 24, 1900, 657–58.

"Mr. Sheldon's Paper." *Independent*, March 22, 1900, 728–29.

Munsey, Frank A. "Freak Journalism." *Printers' Ink* (June 29, 1898): 3–4.

"Must Battle for Progress: Editor Who Stands Still, Is a Failure, Says Florida Writer." *Editor & Publisher* (April 24, 1909): 18.

"Need a Conscience: Growing Public Demand for Newspaper Guided by Right Principles; Purchasable Press Foe to Liberty and Progress, Says California Minister." *Editor & Publisher* (August 13, 1910): 6, 16.

"News and Newspapers." *Fourth Estate* (October 11, 1894): 6.

"Newspaper Accuracy." *Editor & Publisher* (July 10, 1909): 8.

"Newspaper Ethics." *Current Literature* 23, no. 6 (1898): 483–84.

"Newspaper His Text: Connecticut Clergyman Says That They Are an Ally of Religion." *Editor & Publisher* (February 5, 1916): 1049.

"Newspaper Independence." *Editor & Publisher* (December 16, 1905): 4.

"Newspaper in Modern Life: Baltimore Clergyman Gives His View of Their Opportunities." *Editor & Publisher* (April 24, 1909): 7.

"Newspaper Morality." *Fourth Estate* (February 16, 1898): 6.

"Newspaper Praised: Chicago Divine Declares Press Is the Latter-Day Autocrat." *Editor & Publisher* (October 8, 1910): 2.

"Newspapers and War." *Editor & Publisher* (April 20, 1907): 4.

"Newspapers Are the Mirrors of Life Today." *Fourth Estate* (November 4, 1922): 10.

"Newspapers Honest: Milton A. McRae, of Detroit, Refutes Impression That the Newspaper Has Become Purchasable and Is Controlled by the Advertiser." *Editor & Publisher* (May 15, 1909): 8.

New York Press Club. *Journalism: Its Relation to and Influence upon the Political, Social, Professional, Financial and Commercial Life of the United States of America*. New York: New York Press Club, 1905.

Nordan, Max. "Public Conscience." *Editor & Publisher* (November 25, 1905): 4.

North, Helen Marshall. "What Americans Read." *North American Review* 150, no. 4 (1890): 533–35.

North, Simon Newton Dexter. *History and Present Condition of the Newspaper and Periodical Press of the United States, with a Catalogue of the Publications of the Census Year*. Washington, DC: Government Printing Office, 1884.

"Note and Comment." *American Printer and Lithographer* 28, no. 4 (1899): 164.

O'Brien, Frank M. "The Story of the *Sun* (Part 3)." *Munsey's Magazine* 62 (July 1917).

Official Report of the Proceedings of the Thirteenth Meeting of the National Conference of Unitarian and Other Christian Churches Held at Philadelphia, Pa., October 28–31, 1889. Boston: Geo. H. Ellis, 1889.

Ogden, Rollo. "Americanizing the English Press." *Nation*, May 18, 1899, 370–71.

Oneida Association. *Third Annual Report of the Oneida Association*. Oneida Reserve, NY: Leonard, 1851.

"On the Moral Influence of Newspapers." *Boston Weekly Magazine*, October 26, 1839, 62–63.

"The Open Forum." *Public* (December 29, 1916): 1234.

O'Rell, Max. "Lively Journalism." *North American Review* 150, no. 400 (1890): 364–69.

"The Origin and Growth of Corporations." *Spectator*, October 6, 1906.

Ostrom, Susan McWhirter. "What the Press Can Do." *Union Signal: A Journal of Social Welfare* 44, no. 1 (1918): 11.

"The Outlook for 1918: A Characterization and a Programme." *Outlook*, November 14, 1917, 420.

Ovington, Mary White. "The Penny Paper." *Outlook*, January 30, 1904, 280–83.

Parker, Joseph. *The Inner Life of Christ, as Revealed in the Gospel of Matthew*. New York: Funk & Wagnalls, 1883.

Parkhurst, Charles H. *The Pulpit and the Pew*. New Haven, CT: Yale University Press, 1913.

"The Partisan Press." *The Round Table: A Saturday Review of Politics, Finance, Literature, Society and Art*, August 18, 1866, 40.

Patten, John A. "The Contribution of the Church to Social Uplifting." In *Volume of Proceedings of the Fourth International Congregational Council Held in Boston, Massachusetts, June 29–July 6, 1920*, edited by Truman J. Spencer, 171–76. New York: National Council of the Congregational Churches of the US, 1921.

Penn, Irvine Garland. *The Afro-American Press and Its Editors*. Springfield, MA: Willey, 1891.

———. "The American Press and the Congress." In *The United Negro: His Problems and His Progress: Containing the Addresses and Proceedings the Negro Young People's Christian and Educational Congress, Held August 6–11, 1902*, edited by I. Garland Penn and J. W. E. Bowen, 565–79. Atlanta: D. E. Luther, 1902.

"Penny Papers." *Christian Secretary*, February 6, 1836, 15.

Peters, Madison Clinton. *Sanctified Spice; or, Pungent Seasonings from the Pulpit*. New York: Wilbur B. Ketcham, 1893.

"A Pioneer Editor." *Atlantic Monthly*, June 1866, 743–51.

Political Debates between Abraham Lincoln and Stephen A. Douglas. Chicago: Burrows Brothers, 1894.

Powell, Edgar. "A Christian Daily Newspaper." *Homiletic Review* 57, no. 1 (1909): 81–82.

"Power and Responsibility." *Editor & Publisher* (March 25, 1905): 4.

"The Power of Advertising Is Told by Brisbane." *Editor & Publisher* (January 27, 1917): 31.

Poynder, John. *Observations upon Sunday Newspapers: Tending to Shew the Impiety of Such a Violation of the Sabbath, the Religious and Political Evils Consequent upon the Practice, and the Necessity Which Exists for Its Suppression*. London: J. Hatchard and Son, 1820.

"Prays for the Press: Chaplain in Connecticut Senate Asks for Guidance for Newspapers." *Editor & Publisher* (March 25, 1911): 2.

"Preachers Criticize: Prominent Clergymen in Sermons Point Out Evils of Newspapers; New York Minister Finds 39 Per Cent of News Items Are 'Worth While'—Massachusetts Preacher Classes Newspaper Managers with Ananias and Saphira—Methodist Clergyman from Sweden Admires American Newspapers." *Editor & Publisher* (December 17, 1910): 3.

Presbyterian Church in the U.S.A. *Minutes of the General Assembly of the Presbyterian Church in the United States of America*. New York: Presbyterian Board of Publication, 1903.

"Presbyterians Condemn the Sunday Newspaper." *Editor & Publisher* (June 2, 1917): 24.

"Presbyter's Appeal to His Brethren the Clergy, on Some of the Prevailing Iniquities of the Times, with Suggestions for Their Suppression." *Christian Observer* 71, no. 247 (1822): 393–403.

"The Press." *Poughkeepsie Casket*, July 30, 1836, 127.

"The Press—Its Power and Mission." *Southern Literary Messenger* 19 (September 1853): 561–64.

"Press and Morality: Newspaper Ethics Discussed at Union Church Meeting—'Sincerity and Truth Should Be Publishers' Code of Morals'—Power of Newspaper Now Lies in the News Columns." *Editor & Publisher* (February 25, 1911): 13.

"Printed Word Has Only Started Divine Mission." *Editor & Publisher* (May 28, 1921): 21, 24.

Proceedings of a Council in Plymouth Church, Brooklyn, New-York, for the Installation of the Rev. Lyman Abbott, D.D., as Pastor, and the Rev. Howard S. Bliss, as Assistant Pastor, Held January 16, 1980: With a Sermon by Lyman Abbott, D.D., on the New Theology. Brooklyn: n.p., 1890.

The Proceedings of the Woman's Rights Convention, Held at Syracuse, September 8th, 9th, & 10th, 1852. Syracuse, NY: J. E. Masters, 1852.

Proctor, Julian. "The Future of Newspapers." *North American Review* 149, no. 392 (1889): 122–24.

"The Profession of Journalism." *Editor & Publisher* (June 5, 1923): 5.

"Progressive American Journalism Should Abandon Mob Psychology: Paramount Ethical Demand Is That Every Legitimate Interest of Society Should Be Fairly Represented in the Daily Press—Partisanship Cannot Be Played upon with Safety—American People Can Be Aroused to Interest in Every Vital Movement." *Editor & Publisher* (March 4, 1916): 1183.

"The Public Press." *Rutgers Literary Miscellany* 1 (April 1842): 56–57.
"A Public Servant: The Newspaper Thus Characterized by Dean Williams—'He Serves His Newspaper Best Who Serves His Community Best'—Peculiar Responsibility Rests upon Journalism." *Editor & Publisher* (February 18, 1911): 6.
"Public the Editor: Dean Mathews Says Papers Print Just What Their Readers Want." *Editor & Publisher* (July 31, 1909): 8.
"Publishers Should Protect the Public." *Editor & Publisher* (August 24, 1901): 4.
"Punish the Fakirs." *Editor & Publisher* (February 22, 1902): 8.
"Purification of the Press." *Lend a Hand* 18, no. 1 (1897): 73–74.
"Purifying the Press." *Editor & Publisher* (August 22, 1908): 3.
"Ralph Pulitzer's Witty Speech." *Fourth Estate* (July 8, 1916): 32.
Ransom, Reverdy Cassius. *The Spirit of Freedom and Justice: Orations and Speeches*. Nashville, TN: AME Sunday School Union, 1926.
Rauschenbusch, Walter. *Christianity and the Social Crisis*. New York: Hodder & Stoughton, 1907.
———. *Christianizing the Social Order*. New York: Macmillan, 1912.
———. *For God and the People: Prayers of the Social Awakening*. Boston: Pilgrim Press, 1910.
———. *The Righteousness of the Kingdom*. Nashville, TN: Abingdon Press, 1965.
———. *The Social Principles of Jesus*. New York: Association Press, 1920.
———. *A Theology for the Social Gospel*. New York: Macmillan 1917.
Rayner, William. "Sunday Newspapers." *Notes and Queries* (March 7, 1874): 121–23.
"Read the Newspapers: Advice Given to Evening Study Club of Baltimore, by W. K. Barrett." *Editor & Publisher* (January 29, 1910): 12.
Reavis, L. U. *A Representative Life of Horace Greeley*. New York: G. W. Carleton, 1872.
Reid, Whitelaw. "Journalistic Duties and Opportunities." In *American and English Studies*. New York: C. Scribner's Sons, 1913.
———. "Recent Changes in the Press." In *American and English Studies*, by Whitelaw Reid, 281–310. New York: C. Scribner's Sons, 1913.
"A Religious Daily." *Circular*, March 10, 1873, 1.
"A Religious Daily." *Zion's Herald*, May 18, 1892, 156.
"A Religious Daily Newspaper." *Christian Advocate and Journal*, July 27, 1854, 118.
"Religious Journalism." *Circular*, September 27, 1860, 138.
"Report of the Sub-Committee on a Department of Religious Publicity." In *The Manual of Inter-Church Work*, edited by Roy B. Guild, 149–68. New York: Commission on Inter-Church Federations of the Federal Council of the Churches of Christ in America, 1917.

"Rev. C. M. Sheldon's Daily Paper." *Zion's Herald*, January 31, 1900, 137.

Richard, Livy S. "Publicity and Public Welfare as It Relates to Journalism." In *Sagamore Sociological Conference*, edited by Sagamore Sociological Conference, 19–22. Sagamore Beach, MA: Sagamore Sociological Conference, 1912.

Rider, George T. "The Pretensions of Journalism." *North American Review* 135, no. 312 (1882): 471–83.

Riis, Roger W. "Are Newspapers Doing Their Duty?" *Independent* 112 (March 1924): 117–19.

Roosevelt, Theodore. "American Journalism for Which the *Outlook* Stands." In *Outlook Editorials*. New York: Outlook, 1909.

Ross, Charles G. *The Writing of News: A Handbook with Chapters on Newspaper Correspondence and Copy Reading*. New York: Henry Holt, 1911.

Ross, Edward Alsworth. *Changing America: Studies in Contemporary Society*. New York: Century, 1912.

Rowland, Kate Mason. *The Life of George Mason, 1725–1792, Including His Speeches, Public Papers, and Correspondence*. New York: G. P. Putnam's Sons, 1892.

Savage, Minot J., Edward Everett Hale, and Washington Gladden. "Can Our Churches Be Made More Useful?" *North American Review* 148, no. 3 (1889): 372–85.

Scovel, Sylvester F. "The Duty and Opportunity of Christianity in the Press." In *The Jubilee of the Evangelical Alliance: Proceedings of the 10th International Conference Held in London, June–July, 1896*, edited by A. J. Arnold, 247–62. London: J. F. Shaw, 1897.

Scripps, E. W. *I Protest: Selected Disquisitions of E. W. Scripps*. Edited by Oliver Knight. Madison: University of Wisconsin Press, 1966.

"The Scripps-McRae Formula." In *University of Missouri Bulletin*. Columbia: University of Missouri, 1914.

"The Secular Press." *Christian Advocate*, July 2, 1868, 212.

"Sermon on Newspapers: New York State Minister Appeals for Freedom of the Press." *Editor & Publisher* (November 20, 1909): 5.

"The Shackled Editor." *Collier's*, April 14, 1913, 22.

Sheldon, Charles M. *Charles M. Sheldon: His Life Story*. New York: Doran, 1925.

———. "The Daily Papers and the Truth." *Outlook*, May 12, 1900.

———. *The First Christian Daily Paper, and Other Sketches*. New York: Street & Smith, 1900.

———. *In His Steps: "What Would Jesus Do?"* Chicago: Advance, 1899.

———. "Is a Christian Theater Possible?" *Independent*, March 14, 1901, 616.

———. "Is Christianity Practical in Worldly Affairs?" *Ladies' Home Journal*, November 1899, 10.

———. "The Modern Newspaper." *Independent*, July 25, 1912, 1961.

———. "A Preacher Edits the News." *Christian Herald* 21 (March 1946): 64.

———. "Some Opportunities before the Church of Today." *Congregationalist* 85, no. 40 (1900): 459.

———. "Symposium: Giving the Public What It Wants." In *The Coming Newspaper*, edited by Merle Thorpe, 223–47. New York: Henry Holt, 1915.

———. "What Does It Mean to Be a Christian?" *Congregationalist and Christian World*, October 10, 1903, 505.

Sheldon, Walter Lorenzo. *A Volume of Lectures*. London: Macmillan, 1896.

Shepard, Walter J. "Public Opinion." *American Journal of Sociology* 15 (July 1909): 32–60.

"The Shoemaker's Last." *Journalist* (May 17, 1890): 8.

Showalter, W. D. "A Free Press the First Line of Defense for the World's Democracies: Great Principle, Safeguarding Human Rights, Always in Conflict with Ruling Classes and Special Interests—Popular Governments Still Adhere to Secret Process in Conduct of Public Business." *Editor & Publisher* (July 3, 1919): 13.

Shriver, William Payne. *Immigrant Forces: Factors in the New Democracy*. New York: Missionary Education Movement of the United States and Canada, 1913.

Simpson, Matthew. *Lectures on Preaching Delivered to the Students of Yale College in 1879*. London: Richard D. Dickinson, 1879.

Skeath, William C. *Building the Congregation: A Study of Appeals*. New York: Methodist Book Concern New York, 1919.

Smalley, George W. "Notes on Journalism." *Harper's New Monthly Magazine* 67 (July 1898): 213–23.

Smith, Alexander MacKay. "The Clergy and the Times." *Harper's New Monthly Magazine*, January 1889, 206–14.

———. *The Sunday Newspaper: An Address Delivered before the Church Club of Philadelphia on the Evening of February 26, 1906*. New York: Woman's National Sabbath Alliance, 1906.

Smith, Cornelius B. "The Daily Press and Public Morals." *Churchman* 53 (January 30, 1886): 136–37.

Smith, Elias. "Address to the Public." In *The Centennial of Religious Journalism*, edited by John Pressley Barrett, 29–34. Dayton, Ohio: Christian Publishing Association, 1908.

Smith, Herbert Heebner. *Publicity and Progress: Twentieth Century Methods in Religious, Educational and Social Activities*. New York: George H. Doran, 1915.

Smith, J. E. "The Secular Press and Morality." *Zion's Herald*, February 8, 1888.

Smyth, Newman. *Christian Ethics*. Edinburgh: T. & T. Clark, 1892.

"The Social Gospel." *Biblical World* 40, no. 3 (1912): 147–51.

"The Social Order." In *International Congregational Council: Volume of Proceedings of the Fourth International Congregational Council Held in Boston, Massachusetts, June 29–July 6, 1920*, edited by Truman J. Spencer,

321–41. New York: National Council of the Congregational Churches of the US, 1921.

Spalding, William A. "The Moral Responsibilities of the Press." *Californian Illustrated Magazine* 5, no. 2 (1894): 270–76.

"Sphinx Club Dines War Secretary: Mr. Taft Discusses the Moral Awakening of the United States." *Fourth Estate* (April 25, 1908).

Spinney, George F. "Newspaper Methods Yesterday and To-Day." *Pearson Magazine* 23, no. 5 (1910): 599–611.

"Spirit and Purpose of the Ideal Newspaper as Visualized by George Booth: President of *Detroit News*, in Address at University of Michigan, Makes Impressive Appraisal of Comparative Value of Material and Spiritual Factors in Newspaper Making—Sees Pendulum of the 'Clock of the World' Swinging with Resistless Force toward Brotherhood of Man." *Editor & Publisher* (February 2, 1918): 4–5, 28–29.

Stead, William T. "The Future of Journalism." *Contemporary Review* 50 (November 1886): 663–79.

———. "Government by Journalism." *Contemporary Review* 49 (May 1886): 653–74.

Steffens, Lincoln. *The Autobiography of Lincoln Steffens*. New York: Harcourt, Brace, 1931.

Stelzle, Charles. *Christianity's Storm Centre: A Study of the Modern City*. New York: Fleming H. Revell, 1907.

———. "How One Thousand Workingmen Spend Their Spare Time." *Outlook*, April 4, 1914, 762–66.

———. *The Workingman and Social Problems*. New York: Fleming H. Revel, 1903.

Stewart, Jane Agnes. *The Frances Willard Book*. Philadelphia: Current Syndicate, 1906.

Storey, Moorfield. "The Daily Press." *Atlantic Monthly*, January 1922, 41–44.

Strong, Josiah. *The Challenge of the City*. New York: Missionary Education Movement of the United States and Canada, 1911.

———. *Expansion under New World-Conditions*. New York: Baker and Taylor, 1900.

———. "The Increasing Oneness of the World." *Homiletic Review* 56, no. 6 (1908): 468.

———. "An Instructive Experience." In *Sagamore Sociological Conference*. Sagamore Beach, MA: Sagamore Sociological Conference, 1912.

———. *The Next Great Awakening*. New York: Baker and Taylor, 1902.

———. "Methods of Promoting Arbitration." *Advocate of Peace* 60 (October 1898): 212–13.

———. *The New Era; or, The Coming Kingdom*. New York: Baker and Taylor, 1893.

———. *Our Country: Its Possible Future and Its Present Crisis.* New York: Baker and Taylor, for the American Home Missionary Society, 1885.

———. *Our World: The New World-Life.* Garden City, NY: Doubleday, 1913.

———. *The Times and Young Men.* New York: Baker and Taylor, 1901.

———. *The Twentieth Century City.* New York: Baker and Taylor, 1898.

———. "Why the League for Social Service." *Social Service* 6, no. 3 (1902): 42–43.

Strong, William Ellsworth. "The Religious Press in America." In *Recent Christian Progress*, edited by Lewis Bayles Paton, 447–55. New York: Macmillan, 1909.

"The Sunday Question." *Christian Union*, September 10, 1879, 202.

"Sunday Religion." *Lutheran Observer* 71, no. 3718 (1903): 1006.

"Supplying of Current Daily Newspapers in Free Library Reading-Rooms." In *Papers and Proceedings of the Fourteenth General Meeting of the American Library Association*, 44–45. Boston: American Library Association, 1892.

Taber, Henry M. *Faith or Fact: Illustrating Conflicts between Credulity and Vitalized Thought; Superstition and Realism; Tradition and Verity; Dogma and Reason; Bigotry and Tolerance; Ecclesiastical Error and Manifest Truth; Theology and Rationalism; Miracle and Immutable Law; Pious Ignorance and Secular Intelligence; Hypocrisy and Sincerity; Theocracy and Democracy.* New York: Peter Eckler, 1897.

Tayler, Charles B. *Katherine.* London: Religious Tract Society, 1843.

Taylor, Frank. *The Newspaper Press as a Power in Both the Expression and Formation of Public Opinion.* Oxford: B. H. Blackwell, 1898.

Tenney, Edward Payson. *Contrasts in Social Progress.* Concord, NH: Rumford Press, 1910.

"That Newspaper Conference: Professor Ross Says It Was So Successful Another Will Be Held at Madison in 1913." *Editor & Publisher* (September 14, 1912): 12.

"Theology and Yellow Journalism: The Bane of the Headline." *Biblical World* 33 (June 1909): 363–66.

"'Thieves,' 'Liars' and So Forth." *Crisis* 4, no. 3 (1912): 121–22.

Thompson, Hugh Miller. *More Copy: A Second Series of Essays from an Editor's Drawer on Religion, Literature, and Life.* New York: Thomas Whittaker, 1897.

Thorpe, Merle Harrold. *The Coming Newspaper.* New York: Henry Holt, 1915.

Troeltsch, Ernst. *The Social Teaching of the Christian Churches.* Vol. 2. Translated by Olive Wyon. Louisville, KY: Westminster John Knox Press, 1992 [ca. 1912?].

Trollope, Anthony. *The Writings of Anthony Trollope.* Philadelphia: Gebbie, 1901.

"The Truth Will Prevail." *Editor & Publisher* (August 24, 1912): 8.

Tucker, George. "Progress of Population and Wealth in the United States in Fifty Years, as Exhibited by the Decennial Census Taken in That Period." In *The Merchants' Magazine and Commercial Review*. New York: Freeman Hunt, 1861.

———. *Progress of the United States in Population and Wealth in Fifty Years, as Exhibited by the Decennial Census*. Boston: Little, Brown, 1843.

Turner, W. B. "The American Newspaper." *Californian* 2, no. 9 (1880): 287–89.

Twain, Mark, and Charles Dudley Warner. *The Gilded Age: A Tale of Today*. Hartford, CT: American; Syracuse, NY: Watson, Gill, 1874.

"Two Views of the Sunday Newspaper." *Public Opinion* 20 (May 7, 1896): 595.

"The Unity of Christendom." *Christian Unio* (May 21, 1885): 7.

"University Training." *Editor & Publisher* (October 17, 1903): 4.

Van Buren, William. "The Press as an Educator." In *Proceedings of the Michigan Press Association*, by Michigan Press Association, 14–16. Nashville, MI: News Steam Print, 1885.

Vaughan, B. F. "Some Influences of the Secular Press." *Herald of Gospel Liberty* 2 (September 2, 1886): 551–52.

Vedder, Henry Clay. *Socialism and the Ethics of Jesus*. New York: Macmillan, 1912.

Vincent, George E. "The Press and the People." In *Proceedings of the National Newspaper Conference, July 29–August 1, 1912*, edited by National Newspaper Conference, 9–13. Madison: University of Wisconsin Press, 1912.

W. S. J. "Detroit Letter." *New York Evangelist*, February 3, 1898, 24.

"The Wail of the Has Been." *Journalist* (May 5, 1905): 244.

"Wants to Be Yellow: Arthur Brisbane Seeks the Top Round in Saffron Journalism." *Editor & Publisher* (December 9, 1911): 5.

Ward, Harry Frederick. *The Social Creed of the Churches*. New York: Abingdon Press, 1914.

Ward, Julius H. "The Future of Sunday Journalism." *Forum* 1 (1886): 389–98.

———. "Paper by Rev. Julius H. Ward." In *American Congress of Churches: Proceedings of the Hartford Meeting, 1885*, edited by Executive Committee of the American Congress of Churches, 107–14. Hartford, CT: Case, Lockwood & Brainard, 1885.

Warner, Charles Dudley. "Newspapers and the Public." *Forum* 9 (April 1890): 198–207.

———. *The Relation of Literature to Life*. New York: Harper and Brothers, 1897.

Washington, George. *Washington's Farewell Address*. New York: D. Appleton, 1861.

Wasson, James B. "The Editor as a Preacher." *Editor & Publisher* (December 23, 1911): 7.

Watterson, Henry. "The Newspapers of New York: Some Reminiscences of the City's Papers, Past and Present." *Fourth Estate* (September 9, 1916): 12.

"Watterson Dinner: Distinguished Editor Guest of the New York Press Club; Pleads for Clean Journalism—Declares That News, Like Victuals, Should Be Served Hot and Savory—Recounts Early Experiences and Tells of Difficulties in Finding Work—Old Virtues Best." *Editor & Publisher* (June 4, 1910): 4.

"The Week." *Zion's Herald*, August 30, 1877.

Weigle, E. D. "The Ministry and Current Social Problems." *Lutheran Quarterly* 24 (October 1894): 467–80.

Wells, Newell Woolsey. "A Christian Daily." *Homiletic Review* 14, no. 2 (1887): 110–15.

"What Is News? A Symposium from the Managing Editors of the Great American Newspapers." *Collier's*, May 13, 1911, 42–45.

White, Richard Grant. "The Morals and Manners of Journalism." *Galaxy* 8 (December 1869): 840–47.

White, William Allen. *The Old Order Changeth: A View of American Democracy*. Milwaukee: Young Churchman, 1917.

"Whitman Raps Newspapers: Resents Unfairness and Ignorance but Says True Information Heralds Reform." *Editor & Publisher* (March 11, 1916): 1218.

Wilcox, Delos F. "The American Newspaper: A Study in Social Psychology." *Annals of the American Academy of Political and Social Science* 16, no. 279 (1900): 59–62.

Wilde, Oscar. *De Profundis*. New York: G. P. Putnam's Sons, 1909.

Willard, Frances Elizabeth, Carolyn De Swarte Gifford, and Amy R. Slagell. *Let Something Good Be Said: The Speeches and Writings of Frances E. Willard*. Urbana: University of Illinois Press, 2007.

Willets, Gilson. "Pastor Sheldon's Editorial Experiences: How the *Christian Daily* Was Welcomed by the World and How It Looked—Practically Applying the Text: 'What Would Jesus Do?'" *Christian Herald and Signs of Our Times*, March 21, 1900, 230–31.

Williams, Charles R. "Speech of Charles R. Williams." In *Reunion of the New England Society of Indianapolis, Indiana, and Third Annual Banquet in Celebration of Forefather's Day*. Indianapolis: Carlon & Hollenbeck, 1894.

Williams, Walter, and Frank L. Martin. *The Practice of Journalism: A Treatise on Newspaper Making*. Columbia, MO: E. W. Stephens, 1911.

"William T. Stead: A Character Sketch." *Altruistic Review* 2, no. 4 (1894): 171–79.

Wilson, Woodrow. *The New Freedom: A Call for the Emancipation of the Generous Energies of a People*. Garden City, NY: Doubleday, Page, 1918.

Wise, Stephen S. "The Moral Power of the Press." *Homiletic Review* 60, no. 5 (1910): 408–12.

Wix, Samuel. "On the Sunday Press." *Christian Remembrancer; or, The Churchman's Biblical, Ecclesiastical & Literary Miscellany* 13, no. 9 (1831): 631–33.

Woods, Robert A. "The Social Awakening in London." *Scribner's Magazine* 11, no. 4 (1892): 401–24.

Woodson, Carter Godwin. *The Negro in Our History*. Washington, DC: Associated Publishers, 1922.

Yarros, V. S. *Our Revolution: Essays in Interpretation*. Boston: R. G. Badger, 1920.

———. "The Press and Public Opinion." *American Journal of Sociology* 5 (November 1899): 372–82.

"'Yellow Journalism' Defined." *Editor & Publisher* (January 20, 1917): 14.

Secondary Sources

Adams, Henry. *The Education of Henry Adams*. Boston: Houghton Mifflin, 1961.

Allan, Stuart. *News Culture*. Maidenhead, UK: McGraw-Hill/Open University Press, 2010.

Anderson, Benedict. *Imagined Communities: Reflections on the Origin and Spread of Nationalism*. London: Verso, 2006.

Andrews, J. Cutler. *The North Reports the Civil War*. Pittsburgh: University of Pittsburgh Press, 1955.

Andrews, Robert. *The Concise Columbia Dictionary of Quotations*. New York: Columbia University Press, 1989.

Allert, Craig D. *Revelation, Truth, Canon and Interpretation: Studies in Justin Martyr's Dialogue with Trypho*. Leiden: Brill, 2002.

Baldasty, Gerald J. *The Commercialization of News in the Nineteenth Century*. Madison: University of Wisconsin Press, 1992.

———. *E. W. Scripps and the Business of Newspapers*. Urbana: University of Illinois Press, 1999.

Barth, Alan. "The Cult of Loyalty." In *Contemporary Moral Issues*, edited by Harry K. Girvetz, 53–61. Belmont, CA: Wadsworth, 1963.

Bell, Emily. "The Rise of Mobile and Social News—and What It Means for Journalism." In *Digital News Report, 2015: Tracking the Future of News*, edited by Nic Newman, David A. L. Levy, and Rasmus Kleis Nielsen. Oxford: Reuters Institute for the Study of Journalism. https://reutersinstitute.politics.ox.ac.uk/sites/default/files/Reuters%20Institute%20Digital%20News%20Report%202015_Full%20Report.pdf.

Bellamy, Edward. *The Religion of Solidarity*. London: Concord Grove Press, 1984.

Berry, Stephen J. "Why Objectivity Still Matters." *Nieman Reports*, July 15, 2005. http://www.nieman.harvard.edu/reports/article/101090/Why-Objectivity-Still-Matters.aspx.

Berry, Wendell. *The Way of Ignorance, and Other Essays*. Emeryville, CA: Shoemaker & Hoard, 2005.

Birkhead, Douglas. "The Progressive Reform of Journalism: The Rise of Professionalism in the Press." In *Rhetoric and Reform in the Progressive Era*, edited by J. Michael Hogan, 113–44. East Lansing: Michigan State University Press, 2003.

Bleyer, Willard Grosvenor. *Main Currents in the History of American Journalism*. Boston: Houghton Mifflin, 1927.

Blumenthal, Sidney. "Journalism and Its Discontents." *Salon*, October 25, 2007. http://www.salon.com/2007/10/25/walter_lippmann/.

Boyer, Paul S. "In His Steps: A Reappraisal." *American Quarterly* 23, no. 1 (1971): 60–78.

———. *Urban Masses and Moral Order in America, 1820–1920*. Cambridge, MA: Harvard University Press, 1995.

Brackney, William H. *Baptists in North America: An Historical Perspective*. Malden, MA: Blackwell, 2006.

Brown, Candy Gunther. "Religious Periodicals and Their Textual Communities." In *The Industrial Book, 1840–1880*, edited by Scott E. Casper et al., 270–78. Vol. 3 of *A History of the Book in America*. Chapel Hill: Published in association with the American Antiquarian Society by the University of North Carolina Press, 2007.

Brown, Ira V. *Lyman Abbott, Christian Evolutionist: A Study in Religious Liberalism*. Cambridge, MA: Harvard University Press, 1953.

Buddenbaum, Judith M. "'Judge . . . What Their Acts Will Justify': The Religion Journalism of James Gordon Bennett." *Journalism History* 14, nos. 2–3 (1987): 54–67.

———. "The Media, Religion, and Public Opinion: Toward a Unified Theory of Cultural Influence." In *Religion and Popular Culture: Studies on the Interaction of Worldviews*, edited by Daniel Stout and Judith M. Buddenbaum, 19–38. Ames: Iowa State University Press, 2001.

———. "The Religious Roots of Sigma Delta Chi." In *Media and Religion in American History*, edited by W. David Sloan, 206–15. Northport, AL: Vision Press, 2000.

Burrell, Ian. "'There's No Longer This Church versus State': How *City AM* Is Tearing Down the Editorial/Commercial Divide." *Drum* (blog), June 2, 2016. http://www.thedrum.com/opinion/2016/06/02/theres-no-longer-church-versus-state-how-city-am-tearing-down-editorialcommercial.

Byrom, Thomas. *The Dhammapada: The Sayings of the Buddha*. New York: Vintage Books, 2012.

Calhoun, Charles W. *The Gilded Age: Essays on the Origins of Modern America*. Lanham, MD: Rowman and Littlefield, 2006.

Campbell, W. Joseph. *The Year That Defined American Journalism: 1897 and the Clash of Paradigms*. New York: Routledge, 2006.

Carey, James. "Afterword: The Culture in Question." In *James Carey: A Critical Reader*, edited by Eve Stryker Munson and Catherine A. Warren, 308–39. Minneapolis: University of Minnesota Press, 1997.

———. "Communications and Economics." In *James Carey: A Critical Reader*, edited by Eve Stryker Munson and Catherine A. Warren, 60–76. Minneapolis: University of Minnesota Press, 1997.

———. "The Communications Revolution." In *James Carey: A Critical Reader*, edited by Eve Stryker Munson and Catherine A. Warren, 137–38. Minneapolis: University of Minnesota Press, 1997.

———. "The Communications Revolution and the Professional Communicator." In *James Carey: A Critical Reader*, edited by Eve Stryker Munson and Catherine A. Warren, 128–43. Minneapolis: University of Minnesota Press, 1997.

Carey, Patrick W., and Joseph T. Lienhard. *Biographical Dictionary of Christian Theologians*. Westport, CT: Greenwood Press, 2000.

Chewning, Richard C., John W. Eby, and Shirley J. Roels. *Business through the Eyes of Faith*. San Francisco: Harper & Row, 1990.

Christians, Clifford G. "Fifty Years of Scholarship in Media Ethics." *Journal of Communication* 27, no. 4 (1977): 19–29.

Christians, Clifford G., John P. Ferré, and P. Mark Fackler. *Good News: Social Ethics and the Press*. New York: Oxford University Press, 1993.

Cocks, Joan. *The Oppositional Imagination: Feminism, Critique and Political Theory*. London: Routledge, 2012.

Collier, Patrick. *Modernism on Fleet Street*. Aldershot: Ashgate, 2006.

Commager, Henry Steele. *The American Mind: An Interpretation of American Thought and Character since the 1880s*. New Haven, CT: Yale University Press, 1952.

Cronin, Mary M. "Trade Press Roles in Promoting Journalistic Professionalism, 1884–1917." *Journal of Mass Media Ethics* 8, no. 4 (1993): 227–38.

Cronin, Mary M., and James B. McPherson. "Pronouncements and Denunciations: An Analysis of State Press Association Ethics Codes from the 1920s." *Journalism & Mass Communication Quarterly* 72 (Winter 1995): 890–901.

Croteau, David, William Hoynes, and Stefania Milan. *Media/Society: Industries, Images, and Audiences*. Thousand Oaks, CA: SAGE, 2012.

Curtis, Susan. *A Consuming Faith: The Social Gospel and Modern American Culture*. Columbia: University of Missouri Press, 2001.

Dahl, Gavin. "'Journalism of Neutrality Is an Illusion' and Inadequate to Democracy, Says Professor." *RawStory*, May 9, 2010. http://www.rawstory.com/2010/05/robert-jensen-interview-audio/.

Davies, Jessica. "The *Independent*'s Hiring Writers to Do Both Native Ads and Edit Content." *Digiday*, March 17, 2016. http://digiday.com/publishers/independent-building-native-ad-team-tapping-journalists/.

———. "Why Trinity Mirror Created Disgusting and 'Purposefully Disruptive' Branded Content for Skyl." *Digiday*, December 23, 2015. http://digiday.com/publishers/trinity-mirror-created-disgusting-purposefully-disruptive-branded-content-skyl/.

Dewey, Joanna. "Textuality in an Oral Culture: A Survey of the Pauline Traditions." In *Semeia 65: Orality and Textuality in Early Christian Literature*, edited by Joanna Dewey, 37–65. Atlanta: Scholars Press, 1995.

Dicken-Garcia, Hazel. *Journalistic Standards in Nineteenth-Century America*. Madison: University of Wisconsin Press, 1989.

Diggins, John Patrick. *Pragmatism: Modernism and the Crisis of Knowledge and Authority*. Chicago: University of Chicago Press, 1994.

Doctor, Ken. "Between the Lines of Today's Big Tribune Reshuffle." *PoliticoMedia*, March 2, 2016. http://www.capitalnewyork.com/article/media/2016/03/8592568/between-lines-todays-big-tribune-reshuffle.

Doll, Meagan. "7 Questions for Craig Silverman on Verification and Rumors." *Mediashift*. http://mediashift.org/2015/03/7-questions-for-craig-silverman-on-verification-and-rumors/.

Dorn, Jacob Henry. *Washington Gladden: Prophet of the Social Gospel*. Columbus: Ohio State University Press, 1967.

Dorrien, Gary J. *Idealism, Realism, and Modernity, 1900–1950*. Louisville, KY: Westminster John Knox Press, 2003.

———. *The New Abolition: W. E. B. Du Bois and the Black Social Gospel*. New Haven, CT: Yale University Press, 2015.

———. *Social Ethics in the Making: Interpreting an American Tradition*. Chichester, UK: Wiley-Blackwell, 2009.

———. *Soul in Society: The Making and Renewal of Social Christianity*. Minneapolis: Fortress Press, 1995.

Douglas, George H. *The Golden Age of the Newspaper*. Westport, CT: Greenwood Press, 1999.

Edmonds, Rick. "Tribune Publishing's New Management Is in Place—Now How Will They Make Money?" Poynter, March 2, 2016. http://www.poynter.org/2016/tribune-publishings-new-management-is-in-place-now-how-will-they-make-money/399029/.

Emery, Edwin. *The Press and America: An Interpretative History of the Mass Media*. Englewood Cliffs, NJ: Prentice Hall, 1992.

Evensen, Bruce J. "The Evangelical Origins of Muckraking." In *Media and Religion in American History*, edited by W. David Sloan, 186–205. Northport, AL: Vision Press, 2000.

———. "The Muckrakers as Evangelicals." In *The Muckrakers: Evangelical Crusaders*, edited by Robert Miraldi, 1–24. Westport, CT: Praeger, 2000.

Fawal, Richard. "Can Explanatory Journalism Cure the Internet?" Brookings, February 26, 2016. https://www.brookings.edu/blog/fixgov/2016/02/26/can-explanatory-journalism-cure-the-internet/.

Ferré, John P. "Protestant Press Relations in the United States, 1900–1930." *Church History* 62, no. 4 (1993): 514–27.

———. "Sunday Newspapers and the Decline of Protestant Authority in the United States." *American Journalism* 10 (Winter–Spring 1993): 7–23.

Finnegan, Richard J. "Social Responsibilities of the Newspaper." *The Annals of the American Academy of Political and Social Science* 219 (1942): 166–68.

Foner, Eric, and John A. Garraty, eds. *The Reader's Companion to American History.* Boston: Houghton Mifflin, 1991.

Fox, Richard Wightman. "The Culture of Liberal Protestant Progressivism, 1875–1925." *Journal of Interdisciplinary History* 23, no. 1 (1993): 639–60.

Friedman, Saul. "How the Truth May Be Told by the MSM." *Nieman Watchdog*, September 18, 2007. http://blog.niemanwatchdog.org/?p=152.

"FTC Issues Enforcement Policy Statement Addressing 'Native' Advertising and Deceptively Formatted Advertisements." Federal Trade Commission, December 22, 2015. https://www.ftc.gov/news-events/press-releases/2015/12/ftc-issues-enforcement-policy-statement-addressing-native.

Fuller, Wayne Edison. *Morality and the Mail in Nineteenth-Century America.* Urbana: University of Illinois Press, 2003.

Gabriele, Sandra, and Paul Moore. "The *Globe* on Saturday, the *World* on Sunday: Toronto Weekend Editions and the Influence of the American Sunday Paper, 1886–1895." *Canadian Journal of Communication* 34, no. 3 (2009): 337–58.

Gans, Herbert J. *Deciding What's News: A Study of "CBS Evening News," "NBC Nightly News," "Newsweek," and "Time."* Evanston, IL: Northwestern University Press, 2004.

Gerbner, George. "Violence in Television Drama: Trends and Symbolic Functions." In *Media Content and Control: Television and Social Behavior*, edited by George C. Comstock and Eli A. Rubinstein, 28–187. Washington, DC: Government Printing Office, 1972.

Giddens, Anthony. *The Consequences of Modernity.* Stanford, CA: Stanford University Press, 1990.

Gilkeson, John S., Jr. "The Rise and Decline of the 'Puritan Sunday' in Providence, Rhode Island, 1810–1926." *New England Quarterly* 59, no. 1 (1986): 75–91.

Girvetz, Harry K., ed. *Contemporary Moral Issues.* Belmont, CA: Wadsworth, 1963.

Glasser, Theodore L., and Stephanie Craft. "Public Journalism and the Prospects for Press Accountability." *Journal of Mass Media Ethics* 11, no. 3 (1996): 152–58.

Goodman, Peter S. "Beyond Left and Right: It's about Reality." *Huffington Post*, February 10, 2011. http://www.huffingtonpost.com/2011/02/10/beyond-left-and-right-its-about-reality_n_821582.html.

Goodwin, Doris Kearns. *The Bully Pulpit: Theodore Roosevelt, William Howard Taft, and the Golden Age of Journalism*. New York: Simon & Schuster, 2013.

Gorrell, Donald K. *The Age of Social Responsibility: The Social Gospel in the Progressive Era, 1900–1920*. Macon, GA: Mercer University Press, 1988.

Greenwald, Glenn. "Bill Keller's Self-Defense on 'Torture': The *New York Times* Editor Dismisses Debates over 'Torture' as 'Tendentious Political Correctness.'" *Salon*, July 3, 2010. http://www.salon.com/2010/07/03/keller_2/.

———. "Martha Raddatz and the Faux Objectivity of Journalists." *Guardian*, October 12, 2012. https://www.theguardian.com/commentisfree/2012/oct/12/raddatz-debate-objectivity.

———. "The Rise of Trump Shows the Danger and Sham of Compelled Journalistic Neutrality.'" *Intercept*, March 14, 2016. https://theintercept.com/2016/03/14/the-rise-of-trump-shows-the-danger-and-sham-of-compelled-journalistic-neutrality/.

Habermas, Jürgen. *The Structural Transformation of the Public Sphere: An Inquiry into a Category of Bourgeois Society*. Cambridge, MA: MIT Press, 1989.

Hall, Stuart. "Cultural Studies: Two Paradigms." *Media, Culture & Society* 2, no. 1 (1980): 57–72.

Hamington, Maurice. "Jane Addams." In *The Stanford Encyclopedia of Philosophy*, Fall 2014 ed. http://plato.stanford.edu/archives/fall2014/entries/addams-jane/.

Handy, Robert T., ed. *The Social Gospel in America, 1870–1920*. New York: Oxford University Press, 1966.

Hare, Kristen. "Today at the South Florida *Sun Sentinel*, a Switch to Digital Thinking." *Poynter*, October 14, 2014. http://www.poynter.org/2014/today-at-the-south-florida-sun-sentinel-a-switch-to-digital-thinking/273845/.

Harrington, Walt. "A Writer's Essay: Seeking the Extraordinary in the Ordinary." NiemanStoryboard, March 28, 1997. http://niemanstoryboard.org/stories/a-writers-essay-seeking-the-extraordinary-in-the-ordinary-2/.

Hatch, Nathan O. *The Democratization of American Christianity*. New Haven, CT: Yale University Press, 1989.

Hayes, Kevin J. *The Oxford Handbook of Early American Literature*. Oxford: Oxford University Press, 2008.

Hegel, Georg Wilhelm Friedrich. *Miscellaneous Writings of G. W. F. Hegel*. Edited by Jon Bartley Stewart. Evanston, IL: Northwestern University Press, 2001.

Herrick, James A. *The History and Theory of Rhetoric: An Introduction*. Boston: Allyn and Bacon, 2001.

Hoeveler, J. David, Jr. "The University and the Social Gospel: The Intellectual Origins of the 'Wisconsin Idea.'" *Wisconsin Magazine of History* 59, no. 4 (1976): 282–98.

Hofstadter, Richard. *The Age of Reform: From Bryan to F.D.R.* New York: Alfred A. Knopf, 1955.

Holzer, Harold. *Lincoln and the Power of the Press: The War for Public Opinion.* New York: Simon and Schuster, 2014.

Hopkins, Charles Howard. *The Rise of the Social Gospel Movement in American Protestantism, 1865–1915.* New Haven, CT: Yale University Press, 1940.

"House Republicans Pass Health Reform Repeal as Democrats Defend Law." *PBS NewsHour,* January 19, 2011. http://www.pbs.org/newshour/bb/politics-jan-june11-healthcare_01-19/.

Hudson, Frederic. *Journalism in the United States, from 1690–1872.* New York: Harper & Brothers, 1873.

Hughes, Helen MacGill. *News and the Human Interest Story.* New Brunswick, NJ: Transaction, 1981.

Hutchins, Robert M. *Report of the Commission on Freedom of the Press: A Free and Responsible Press.* Chicago: University of Chicago Press, 1947.

Jensen, Billie Barnes. "A Social Gospel Experiment in Newspaper Reform: Charles M. Sheldon and the *Topeka Daily Capital.*" *Church History* 33, no. 1 (1964): 74–83.

Jewett, Robert, and Ole Wangerin. *Mission and Menace: Four Centuries of American Religious Zeal.* Minneapolis: Fortress Press, 2008.

Johanningsmeier, Charles. *Fiction and the American Literary Marketplace: The Role of Newspaper Syndicates in America, 1860–1900.* Cambridge: Cambridge University Press, 2002.

Kant, Immanuel. "An Answer to the Question: What Is Enlightenment." In *What Is Enlightenment? Eighteenth-Century Answers and Twentieth-Century Questions,* edited and translated by James Schmidt, 58–64. Berkeley: University of California Press, 1996.

Kaplan, Justin. *Lincoln Steffens: A Biography.* New York: Simon and Schuster, 1974.

Kaplan, Richard. "The News about New Institutionalism: Journalism's Ethic of Objectivity and Its Political Origins." *Political Communication* 23, no. 2 (2006): 173–85.

Kent, Thomas. "'Build Your Own Ethics Code' for Digital Journalists." European Journalism Observatory, June 23, 2015. http://en.ejo.ch/ethics-quality/build-your-own-ethics-code-for-digital-journalists.

Kinneavy, James L. *A Theory of Discourse.* Englewood Cliffs, NJ: Prentice Hall, 1971.

Kinsley, Michael. "The Twilight of Objectivity." *Slate,* March 31, 2006. http://www.slate.com/id/2139042/.

Latta, Maurice C. "The Background for the Social Gospel in American Protestantism." *Church History* 5, no. 3 (1936): 256–70.

Lee, Alfred McClung. *The Daily Newspaper in America, 1690–1940.* New York: Macmillan, 1937.

Lee, James Melvin. *History of American Journalism*. Boston: Houghton Mifflin, 1917.

Leeuwe, Xavier van. "How Do We Mend the Unspoken, Harmful Division of Newsrooms and Business Units?" *Medium*, June 14, 2016. https://medium.com/@XvanL/how-do-we-mend-the-unspoken-harmful-division-of-newsrooms-and-business-units-48e045479998#.l40tav1iw.

Lehuu, Isabelle. *Carnival on the Page: Popular Print Media in Antebellum America*. Chapel Hill: University of North Carolina Press, 2000.

Lippmann, Walter. *Drift and Mastery: An Attempt to Diagnose the Current Unrest*. New York: Mitchell Kennerley, 1914.

———. *A Preface to Morals*. New Brunswick, NJ: Transaction, 1982.

———. *Public Opinion*. New York: Harcourt, Brace, 1922.

———. "Two Revolutions in the American Press." *Yale Review* 20, no. 3 (1931): 433–41.

Little, Miles, Christopher F. C. Jordens, and Emma-Jane Sayers. "Discourse Communities and the Discourse of Experience." *Health* 7, no. 1 (2003): 73–86.

Lowry, Rich. "Trump's Evil Empire: Trump Rode His Mutual Enmity with the Media to the White House." *National Review*, August 25, 2017. http://www.nationalreview.com/article/450808/donald-trump-media-republicans-hatred-leftist-media-trumps-all-else.

Mann, Thomas E. "Explanatory Journalism: A Tool in the War Against Polarization and Dysfunction." Brookings, February 29, 2016. http://www.brookings.edu/blogs/fixgov/posts/2016/02/29-explanatory-journalism-polarization-mann.

Marvin, Ginny. "Consumers Can't Tell the Difference between Sponsored Content and Editorial: In a New Study, Consumers Identified Native Advertisements as Articles a Large Percentage of the Time." *Marketing Land*, September 9, 2015. http://marketingland.com/consumers-cant-tell-the-difference-between-sponsored-content-and-editorial-142050.

Marzolf, Marion Tuttle. *Civilizing Voices: American Press Criticism, 1880–1950*. New York: Longman, 1991.

May, Henry F. *Protestant Churches and Industrial America*. New York: Harper & Row, 1949.

McChesney, Robert W. *Communication Revolution: Critical Junctures and the Future of Media*. New York: New Press, 2007.

———. "Freedom of the Press for Whom? The Question to Be Answered in Our Critical Juncture." *Hofstra Law Review* 35, no. 3 (2007): 1433–55.

McCloskey, Deirdre N. *Bourgeois Equality: How Ideas, Not Capital or Institutions, Enriched the World*. Chicago: University of Chicago Press, 2016.

McCloud, Scott. *Reinventing Comics: How Imagination and Technology Are Revolutionizing an Art Form*. New York: HarperCollins, 2000.

McCrossen, Alexis. *Holy Day, Holiday: The American Sunday.* Ithaca, NY: Cornell University Press, 2000.

McEachern, Claire Elizabeth. *The Poetics of English Nationhood, 1590–1612.* New York: Cambridge University Press, 1996.

McKee, John DeWitt. *William Allen White: Maverick on Main Street.* Westport, CT: Greenwood Press, 1975.

McLellan, Michele. "A 2016 Snapshot of the Local News Startup Business." Tow-Knight Center for Entrepreneurial Journalism, May 29, 2016. http://towknight.org/2016/05/micheles_list_2016_survey_results/.

Mencken, H. L. "Newspaper Morals." *Atlantic Monthly*, March 1914, 289–97.

Merrill, John C., and S. Jack Odell. *Philosophy and Journalism.* New York: Longman, 1983.

Michael, Ryan. "Journalistic Ethics, Objectivity, Existential Journalism, Standpoint Epistemology, and Public Journalism." *Journal of Mass Media Ethics* 16, no. 1 (2002): 12–13.

Miller, Perry. *The Life of the Mind in America: From the Revolution to the Civil War.* New York: Harcourt, Brace & World, 1965.

Mills, Rilla Dean. "Newspaper Ethics: A Qualitative Study." *Journalism Quarterly* 60, no. 4 (1983): 589–602.

Mindich, David Z. *Just the Facts: How "Objectivity" Came to Define American Journalism.* New York: New York University Press, 1998.

Mirando, Joseph. "Embracing Objectivity Early On: Journalism Textbooks of the 1800s." *Journal of Mass Media Ethics* 16, no. 1 (2001): 23–32.

Morgan, Howard W. *The Gilded Age.* Syracuse, NY: Syracuse University Press, 1968.

Morgan, J. Graham. "The Development of Sociology and the Social Gospel in America." *Sociological Analysis* 30, no. 1 (1969): 42–53.

Moses, Lucia. "The Case against Combining Publisher and Editor Roles." *Digiday*, March 4, 2016. http://digiday.com/publishers/case-combining-publisher-editor-roles/.

Mott, Frank Luther. *American Journalism: A History, 1690–1960.* New York: Macmillan, 1962.

———. *Golden Multitudes.* New York: Macmillan, 1947.

———. *A History of American Magazines, 1741–1930.* Cambridge, MA: Belknap Press of Harvard University Press, 1966.

Muller, Dorothea R. "The Social Philosophy of Josiah Strong: Social Christianity and American Progressivism." *Church History* 28, no. 2 (1959): 183–201.

Murtha, Jack, and Chava Gourarie. "Do Buzzfeed's Native Political Ads Cross a Line?" *Columbia Journalism Review* (October 20, 2015). http://www.cjr.org/analysis/a_major_player_in_the.php.

Newbigin, Lesslie. *Truth and Authority in Modernity.* Valley Forge, PA: Trinity Press International, 1996.

Nietzsche, Friedrich. *The Birth of Tragedy & The Genealogy of Morals*. Translated by Francis Golffing. New York: Anchor Books, 1956.

———. *On the Future of Our Educational Institutions: Homer and Classical Philology*. Translated by J. M. Kennedy and Friedrich Wilhelm Nietzsche. Edinburgh: T. N. Foulis, 1909.

Nixon, Justin Wroe. "The Status and Prospects of the Social Gospel." *Journal of Religion* 22, no. 4 (1942): 346–58.

Nord, David Paul. "Benevolent Books: Printing, Religion, and Reform." In *An Extensive Republic: Print, Culture, and Society in the New Nation, 1790–1840*, edited by Robert A. Gross and Mary Kelley, 221–46. Vol. 2 of *A History of the Book in America*. Chapel Hill: Published in association with the American Antiquarian Society by the University of North Carolina Press, 2010.

———. "The Evangelical Origins of Mass Media in America." In *Media and Religion in American History*, edited by W. David Sloan, 68–93. Northport, AL: Vision Press, 2000.

———. "Teleology and News: The Religious Roots of American Journalism, 1630–1730." *Journal of American History* 77, no. 1 (1990): 9–38.

Norman, Jim. "Americans' Confidence in Institutions Stays Low." Gallup, June 13, 2016. http://www.gallup.com/poll/192581/americans-confidence-institutions-stays-low.aspx?g_source=Politics&g_medium=newsfeed&g_campaign=tiles.

"NPR Clarifies Cokie Roberts' Role after Anti-Trump Column." NPR, March 14, 2016. http://www.npr.org/sections/thetwo-way/2016/03/14/470340825/npr-clarifies-cokie-roberts-role-after-anti-trump-column.

"The *NYT*: We Changed Reality Because Cheney Wanted Us To." *Atlantic*, July 1, 2010. http://www.theatlantic.com/daily-dish/archive/2010/07/the-nyt-we-changed-reality-because-cheney-wanted-us-to/185229/.

O'Brien, Frank Michael. *The Story of the "Sun": New York, 1833–1918*. New York: G. H. Doran, 1918.

O'Connor, Rory. "A for Activist: No Longer Journalism's Scarlet Letter." *AlterNet*, June 28, 2016. http://www.alternet.org/activism/activist-no-longer-journalisms-scarlet-letter.

Outing, Steve. "Climate Change: Get over Objectivity, Newspapers." *Editor & Publisher* (August 28, 2007). http://www.editorandpublisher.com/columns/climate-change-get-over-objectivity-newspapers/.

Overholser, Geneva. "The Inadequacy of Objectivity as a Touchstone." *Nieman Reports*, December 15, 2004. http://www.nieman.harvard.edu/reports/article/100725/The-Inadequacy-of-Objectivity-as-a-Touchstone.aspx.

Park, Robert E. "The City: Suggestions for Investigation of Human Behavior in the City Environment." *American Journal of Sociology* 20, no. 5 (1915): 577–612.

———. "The Natural History of the Newspaper." *Journal of Sociology* 24, no. 3 (1923): 273–89.

Parker, Elliott. "Fantasy Theme Analysis: 'In His Steps.'" Paper presented at the 2001 AEJMC Conference. http://list.msu.edu/cgi-bin/wa?A2=ind0109B&L=AEJMC&P=R19993&I=-3.

Polhemus, Robert M. *The Changing World of Anthony Trollope*. Berkeley: University of California Press, 1968.

Powell, Lyman P. *Mary Baker Eddy: A Life Size Portrait*. New York: Macmillan, 1930.

Pratte, Paul Alfred. *Gods within the Machine: A History of the American Society of Newspaper Editors, 1923–1993*. Westport, CT: Praeger, 1995.

Purcell, Edward A. *The Crisis of Democratic Theory: Scientific Naturalism & the Problem of Value*. Lexington: University Press of Kentucky, 1973.

Rader, Benjamin G. "Richard T. Ely: The Lay Spokesman for the Social Gospel." *Journal of American History* 53, no. 1 (1966): 61–74.

Raeburn, Paul. "The Journalist as Advocate: Is There Any Other Kind?" *Undark*, March 29, 2016. http://undark.org/article/the-journalist-as-advocate-is-there-any-other-kind/.

Raymond, Joad. *The Invention of the Newspaper: English Newsbooks, 1641–1649*. Oxford: Clarendon Press, 2005.

Riordan, Kellie. *Accuracy, Independence, and Impartiality: How Legacy Media and Digital Natives Approach Standards in the Digital Age*. Oxford: Reuters Institute for the Study of Journalism, 2014. http://reutersinstitute.politics.ox.ac.uk/our-research/accuracy-independence-and-impartiality.

Ripley, John W. "Another Look at the Rev. Mr. Charles M. Sheldon's Christian Daily Newspaper." *Kansas Historical Quarterly* 31, no. 1 (1965): 1–40.

Roberts, Robert R. "The Social Gospel and the Trust-Busters." *Church History* 25, no. 3 (1956): 239–57.

Roderick, Kevin. "Broad, Villaraigosa, Riordan Sign Protest Letter to *Tribune*." *LAObserved*, September 10, 2015. http://www.laobserved.com/archive/2015/09/broad_villaraigosa_riorda.php.

Rodgers, Ronald R. "'Journalism Is a Loose-Jointed Thing': A Content Analysis of *Editor & Publisher*'s Discussion of Journalistic Conduct Prior to the Canons of Journalism, 1901–1922." *Journal of Mass Media Ethics* 22, no. 1 (2007): 66–82.

———. "The Problems of Journalism: An Annotated Bibliography of Press Criticism in *Editor & Publisher*, 1901–1923." *Media History Monographs* 9, no. 2 (2007): 1–40.

Rose, George Maclean. *A Cyclopaedia of Canadian Biography: Being Chiefly Men of the Time; A Collection of Persons Distinguished in Professional and Political Life; Leaders in the Commerce and Industry of Canada, and Successful Pioneers*. Toronto: Rose, 1886.

Rosendale, Timothy. *Liturgy and Literature in the Making of Protestant England*. Cambridge: Cambridge University Press, 2007.

Sampson, George. *The Concise Cambridge History of English Literature*. Cambridge: Cambridge University Press, 1990.

Santayana, George. "Spirit in the Sanctuary." *American Scholar* 33, no. 1 (1963): 21–26.

Scherer, Michael. "In Defense of the Mainstream Media." *Time*, January 14, 2011. http://swampland.blogs.time.com/2011/01/14/in-defence-of-the-mainstream-media/.

Schiller, Dan. "An Historical Approach to Objectivity and Professionalism in American News Reporting." *Journal of Communication* 29, no. 4 (1979): 46–57.

———. *Objectivity and the News: The Public and the Rise of Commercial Journalism*. Philadelphia: University of Pennsylvania Press, 1981.

Schlesinger, Arthur M. *Viewpoints in American History*. New York: Macmillan, 1922.

Schmalzbauer, John Arnold. *People of Faith: Religious Conviction in American Journalism and Higher Education*. Ithaca, NY: Cornell University Press, 2003.

Schmauk, Theodore E. "The Sunday Newspaper." *Christian Advocate*, January 17, 1889, 35.

Schneirov, Matthew. *The Dream of a New Social Order: Popular Magazines in America, 1893–1914*. New York: Columbia University Press, 1994.

Schudson, Michael. *Discovering the News: A Social History of American Newspapers*. New York: Basic Books, 1978.

———. "The Objectivity Norm in American Journalism." *Journalism* 2, no. 2 (2001): 149–70.

Schudson, Michael, and Chris Anderson. "Objectivity, Professionalism and Truth Seeking in Journalism." In *The Handbook of Journalism Studies*, edited by Karin Wahl-Jorgensen and Thomas Hanitzsch, 88–101. New York: Routledge, 2009.

Schultz, Stanley K. "The Morality of Politics: The Muckrakers' Vision of Democracy." *Journal of American History* 52, no. 3 (1965): 527–47.

Seitz, Don Carlos. *The James Gordon Bennetts, Father and Son, Proprietors of the "New York Herald."* Indianapolis: Bobbs-Merrill, 1928.

Shafer, Jack. "From Tom Paine to Glenn Greenwald, We Need Partisan Journalism." Reuters, July 16, 2013. http://blogs.reuters.com/jackshafer/2013/07/16/from-tom-paine-to-glenn-greenwald-we-need-partisan-journalism/.

Sharpe, Dores Robinson. *Walter Rauschenbusch*. New York: Macmillan, 1942.

Shoemaker, Pamela. "Hard-Wired for News: Using Biological and Cultural Evolution to Explain the News." *Journal of Communication* 46, no. 3 (1996): 32–47.

Simmel, Georg. "Metropolis and Mental Life." In *The Blackwell City Reader*, edited by Gary Bridge and Sophie Watson, 11–19. Malden, MA: Blackwell, 2002.

Smith, Gary Scott. *The Search for Social Salvation: Social Christianity and America, 1880–1925*. Lanham, MD: Lexington Books, 2000.

Smith, Jeffery. "Sunday Newspapers and Lived Religion in Late Nineteenth-Century America." *Journal of Church and State* 48 (Winter 2006): 127–52.

Smith, Michael Ray. *The Jesus Newspaper: The Christian Experiment of 1900 and Its Lessons for Today*. Lanham, MD: University Press of America, 2002.

Sommerville, C. John. *The News Revolution in England: Cultural Dynamics of Daily Information*. New York: Oxford University Press, 1996.

Soukup, Paul A. *Christian Communication: A Bibliographical Survey*. New York: Greenwood Press, 1989.

Startt, James D., and W. David Sloan. *The History of American Journalism*. Westport, CT: Greenwood Press, 1994.

Stray, Jonathan. "Objectivity and the Decades-Long Shift from 'Just the Facts' to 'What Does It Mean?'" *Nieman Reports*, May 22, 2013. http://www.niemanlab.org/2013/05/objectivity-and-the-decades-long-shift-from-just-the-facts-to-what-does-it-mean/.

Streckfuss, Richard. "Objectivity in Journalism: A Search and a Reassessment." *Journalism Quarterly* 67, no. 4 (1990): 973–83.

Swift, Art. "Americans' Trust in Mass Media Sinks to New Low." Gallup, September 14, 2016. http://www.gallup.com/poll/195542/americans-trust-mass-media-sinks-new-low.aspx.

Swingle, L. J. *Romanticism and Anthony Trollope: A Study in the Continuities of Nineteenth-Century Literary Thought*. Ann Arbor: University of Michigan Press, 1990.

Thompson, John B. *Ideology and Modern Culture: Critical Social Theory in the Era of Mass Communication*. Cambridge: Polity, 1990.

———. *The Media and Modernity: A Social Theory of the Media*. Stanford, CA: Stanford University Press, 1995.

Tilly, Charles. *Big Structures, Large Processes, Huge Comparisons*. New York: Russell Sage Foundation, 1984.

Tocqueville, Alexis de. *Democracy in America*. Translated by Arthur Goldhammer. New York: Library of America, 2004.

Trachtenberg, Alan. *The Incorporation of America: Culture and Society in the Gilded Age*. New York: Hill and Wang, 1982.

"Tribune Publishing Co. Reports Fourth Quarter 2015 Results." Tribune Publishing Company, March 2, 2016. http://investor.tronc.com/phoenix.zhtml?c=254385&p=irol-newsArticle&id=2174108.

Tuchman, Barbara W. *A Distant Mirror: The Calamitous 14th Century*. New York: Alfred A. Knopf, 1978.

Tuchman, Gaye. "Introduction: The Symbolic Annihilation of Women by the Mass Media." In *Hearth and Home: Images of Women in the Mass Media*, edited by Gaye Tuchman, Arlene Kaplan Daniels, and James Walker Benet, 3–38. New York: Oxford University Press, 1978.

———. "Objectivity as Strategic Ritual: An Examination of Newsmen's Notions of Objectivity." *American Journal of Sociology* 77, no. 4 (1972): 660–79.

Underwood, Doug. *From Yahweh to Yahoo! The Religious Roots of the Secular Press*. Urbana: University of Illinois Press, 2002.

Visser 't Hooft, Willem A. *The Background of the Social Gospel in America*. St. Louis: Bethany Press, 1963. Originally published in Haarlem, Netherlands, in 1928.

von Ewald, Georg Henrich August. *Commentary on the Prophets of the Old Testament*. London: Williams and Norgate, 1875.

Ward, Stephen J. A. *The Invention of Journalism Ethics: The Path to Objectivity and Beyond*. Montreal: McGill-Queen's University Press, 2006.

———. "Why We Need a Radical New Framework for Media Ethics." *MediaShift*, August 6, 2015. http://mediashift.org/2015/08/why-we-need-a-radical-new-framework-for-media-ethics/.

Washington, Booker T. *My Larger Education: Being Chapters from My Experience*. Garden City, NY: Doubleday, Page, 1911.

White, Ronald C., and Charles Howard Hopkins. *The Social Gospel: Religion and Reform in Changing America*. Philadelphia: Temple University Press, 1976.

Williams, Raymond. *Communications*. Harmondsworth, Middlesex: Penguin Books, 1973.

Williams, W. H. A. *H. L. Mencken*. Boston: Twayne, 1977.

Zacher, Dale E. *The Scripps Newspapers Go to War, 1914–18*. Urbana: University of Illinois Press, 2008.

Index